Sam O. White, Alaskan

*Tales of a Legendary
Wildlife Agent and Bush Pilot*

by JIM REARDEN

PICTORIAL HISTORIES PUBLISHING COMPANY, INC.
Missoula, Montana

Library of Congress Control Number 2006938470

ISBN 978-1-57510-130-9

FIRST PRINTING January 2007

COVER ART Rusty Huerlin, "Trapper on Snowshoes," 15½×19½
TYPOGRAPHY & BOOK DESIGN Arrow Graphics

PRINTED BY Friesens Inc.
Altona, Manitoba, Canada

Published by Pictorial Histories Publishing Company, Inc.
713 South Third Street West, Missoula, Montana 59801
PHONE (406) 549-8488, FAX (406) 728-9280
E-MAIL: phpc@montana.com
WEBSITE: pictorialhistoriespublishing.com

Contents

ALSO BY JIM REARDEN

Forgotten Warriors
OF THE ALEUTIAN CAMPAIGN

Alaska's Wolf Man
THE 1915–55 WILDERNESS ADVENTURES OF FRANK GLASER

The Wolves of Alaska
A FACT-BASED SAGA

Castner's Cutthroats
SAGA OF THE ALASKA SCOUTS

Koga's Zero
THE FIGHTER THAT CHANGED WORLD WAR II

Travel Air NC9084
THE HISTORY OF A 75-YEAR-OLD WORKING AIRPLANE

Jim Rearden's Alaska
FIFTY YEARS OF FRONTIER ADVENTURE

Arctic Bush Pilot
FROM NAVY COMBAT TO FLYING ALASKA'S
NORTHERN WILDERNESS

Tales of Alaska's Big Bears

In the Shadow of Eagles
FROM BARNSTORMER TO ALASKA
BUSH PILOT, A FLYER'S STORY

Shadows on the Koyukuk
AN ALASKAN NATIVE'S LIFE ALONG THE RIVER

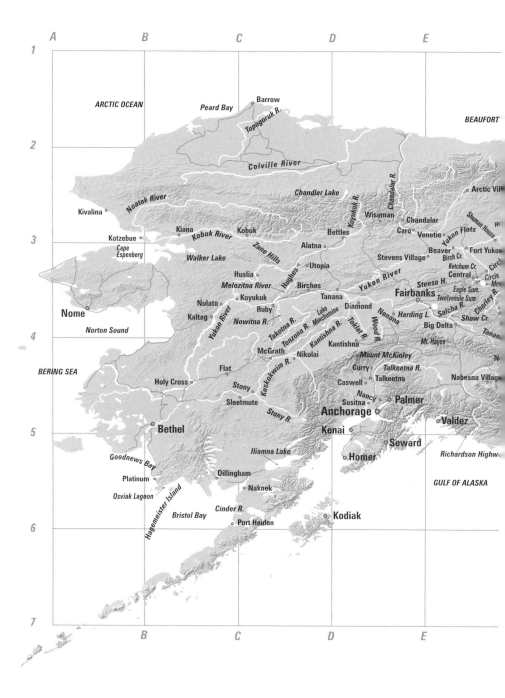

Sam O. White's Alaska

G   H   1

YUKON TERRITORY

2

R.

3

R.

4

Juneau ★

5

Sitka

Petersburg

Wrangell

Ketchikan

G

Foreword

SAM O. WHITE was bigger than life; he was a big man physically, big at heart, big-voiced, a big personality, and huge in generosity. My brother Merrill, my sister Jean, and I grew up on Kellum Street in Fairbanks directly across the street from Sam's home. Our families were close, and though not a blood relative, Sam was fully as close to us as a blood-related uncle to three kids could have been.

I can still hear his booming voice when I knocked at his door. "Come in Richard. How's it goin'? Pull up a chair. How about some ginger ale?" was the usual ritual. He loved ginger ale and always had it on hand, and never spared it when we arrived.

When we were comfortably settled, and after inquiring about our lives, a story would usually begin. As the reader will learn from this volume, he was a consummate story teller, with much descriptive detail. We sat at the edges of our chairs as he took us on his adventures to the far reaches of Alaska or of his early life in Maine. He seldom talked about his World War I experiences.

I'm one of the few living Alaskans who knew some of those who were part of Sam's early life in the Territory. I also worked with Sam in his later life, and followed his career as a bush pilot. I was greatly influenced by his countless stories of high adventure.

I was too young to remember much about his game warden adventures, but his flying adventures made a deep impression. Flying, of course, was always an important topic in our house because of my father's aviation career, and the careers of both Merrill and me. It seemed perfectly natural to us that Sam would be in the same business.

My father Noel and Sam White were the two men who influenced me most as a child and a young man, and I can safely say that was also true for brother and sister.

Nothing characterized Sam more than his high standards and moral principles. With his stories, he somehow instilled in us a deep sense of what was right, and what was wrong. He also impressed on us how important it was to do things safely; do it safely, and you could survive almost anything, he preached.

Richard Wien, October 2006.
Author

We three Wien kids were not the only ones who were influenced by Sam. Many other young people came under his wing and absorbed his philosophy.

Merrill remembers with awe an example of Sam's generosity. At the age of 17 he had just received his private pilot's license. At about the same time Sam arrived in Fairbanks with his brand new L5 Stinson. That airplane represented most of Sam's net worth.

"Merrill, go fly it," Sam offered. During lunch hour at school, after seeing Sam land, Merrill ran all the way from school to Weeks Field. He flew the plane around the pattern, and raced back to school before the bell rang.

Upon learning of the plans for this book, Merrill commented, "Sam's stories gave us a great insight on wildlife. Our hunting trips with him were inspirational. His ability to survive in the wilderness was so great that we never worried about him when, in deep winter, for weeks at a time he flew geodetic crews into the remotest parts of Alaska. We knew he could handle virtually any situation."

Sam's loyalty was unwavering for those he respected. The friendship and bonds between Sam, my Dad, and my dad's brother, Ralph Wien, was like something from a dramatic movie.

Sam survived two major accidents. After a mechanical failure which caused both skis to hang straight down, and with the engine wide open, his plane crashed on the runway at Circle City. He was badly injured. He was also severely burned at the village of Ruby when a pressure lantern exploded in his cabin and sprayed him with burning gasoline. Both times he asked for my dad, Noel, to come for him; no one else would do.

The daylight rescue flight to Circle City was an easy one. The flight from Fairbanks to Ruby was made in winter with the temperature forty below zero. Such flights are not made lightly, but Sam needed him and my father didn't hesitate.

When he landed at Weeks Field, both Merrill and I were so affected by the sight of Sam's burns, and later seeing him in the hospital, that we became physically sick. We worried about him as we would family.

I spent much time with Sam as he healed from both incidents. I never heard him complain or feel sorry for himself, despite his pain, especially from his burns.

As one of the earliest—and unquestionably the most dedicated—game wardens in the Interior, he enforced hunting and trapping regulations for the first time ever. Sam couldn't abide seeing game wasted. Prior to his arrival, hunting and trapping had been wide open, with no regard for seasons or bag limits.

Sam's philosophy was straightforward. "It's the law, and I will enforce it," he said. And he did so with an even hand, despite being reviled by many. As the reader will learn, Sam's high principles were one of the reasons for his resignation as a game warden.

As a bush pilot, Sam made friends everywhere he flew, providing superior service, and building strong relationships even with those he had earlier cracked down on for game law violations. He was kind and thoughtful, and understood the needs of bush residents, Native and white alike. No passenger who flew with Sam was ever injured.

Sam and his wife Mary were known for their great generosity. They had simple needs, and gave away items they thought were needed by others. I was the executor of Sam's estate, and he left this world with very few physical possessions. He didn't need them.

He took with him something far more valuable; the devotion, utmost respect, and admiration of a legion of friends who remember Sam for what he was—a giant of a man.

—RICHARD WIEN

Preface

FROM THE 1940s until about 1970, a tangled mass of moose and caribou antlers piled twelve feet high around the trunk of a dead tree at 902 Kellum Street in Fairbanks, Alaska, were part of history, a memorial, and a landmark. Tourists photographed them. Some of the bolder visitors rang the doorbell of the small green frame house.

To the woman who responded they asked; "Did your husband shoot all those animals?" "Why are all those horns piled there?" "Could I buy some of those?"

The man who lived in that house until 1976, and who piled those antlers, was a six-foot-two, 200-pounder with a booming voice. No Alaskan has ever had more loyal and devoted friends, friends who lived across the Territory and State from the Arctic Ocean south. A letter mailed in 1968 addressed simply, "Sam O. White, Alaska," was promptly delivered.

Samuel Otho White was born in Maine in 1891, where he became a lumberjack and hunting guide. He joined the Army to fight Germans in World War I. He arrived in Alaska in 1922 to help map the then-Territory.

His claim to fame in Alaska? For fourteen years (1927–41) he was a pioneering game warden who brought respect for game laws to a wild land where laws of any kind were minimal. He was also the first flying wildlife agent in the United States, and probably, the world. Then, for twenty-one years, he served Alaskans as a skilled bush pilot, when men of that calling deserved the title.

He knew Alaska as few men have, for, on foot, with dog teams, boats, and airplanes he roamed for thousands of miles across the length and breadth of this vast land.

Sam O. White collected these moose and caribou antlers over a period of years. Most were naturally shed, although several were from moose he killed. Around 1970, the dead tree in his yard around which they were piled rotted away. The antlers were moved to AlaskaLand in Fairbanks where they remained for a time. NOEL WIEN

The following, written mostly by Sam O. White, and edited by me, describe many of his adventures, and details the lives of some of the pioneering Alaskans he knew.

—JIM REARDEN

Introduction

"BE SURE TO LOOK UP Sam White when you get to Fairbanks," well-wishers urged.

It was June, 1950. I had just been awarded a Master's degree in Wildlife Conservation from the University of Maine, at Orono. In my pocket was a letter from Dean Duckering at the University of Alaska (now the University of Alaska Fairbanks), confirming I was to organize a new wildlife department, and teach wildlife management there. Word had spread on the Orono campus.

Sam O. White was famous in his home state of Maine. I later learned that for many years he had written about his Alaska adventures to relatives and friends in Maine. They had shared them with various Maine newspapers. Many in Maine were proud of Sam O. White's exploits in Alaska.

I looked him up that summer at Fairbanks. We talked about Maine, about his flying, a few words about his work as an early Alaska game warden. Our interests were similar, and we saw each other from time to time. In 1956 I moved to the Kenai Peninsula, and we occasionally corresponded. When I traveled to Fairbanks, we usually had a visit.

I was honored in the early 1960s when he asked if I could help him with some writing. When he was in his eighties, he told me he planned to leave his papers to the University of Alaska Fairbanks Rasmuson library.

In 1988, I left my position as Outdoors Editor at *Alaska Magazine* and turned to writing books. Included were biographies of long-time Alaskans—Koyukon Indian Sidney Huntington (*Shadows on the Koyukuk*), and bush pilots Rudy Billberg (*In the Shadow of Eagles*), and James L.(Andy) Anderson (*Arctic Bush Pilot*). I also wrote about sourdough Frank Glaser (*Alaska's Wolf Man*).

Strangely, Sam O. White was an intrinsic part of the lives of these four.

In May, 2005, I found Sam's papers at the UAF Rasmuson Library. Included were about fifty essays labeled "stories" by the library. Sam wrote most of these in the late 1950s while based at the Koyukuk River village of Hughes as a bush pilot for Wien Airlines. I have edited and included the best of these, and with a series of twelve articles he wrote for the *Alaska Sportsman* magazine (December, 1964 to November, 1965), they make up the bulk of this book.

Also in the Sam White collection at UAF, and which I have used, are Sam's 1927-41 daily game warden field diaries, transcriptions of several taped interviews, log books of the 1925 reconnaissance survey he made for the Coast and Geodetic Survey between Big Delta and Eagle, and miscellaneous papers.

After Sam's death, Harland White, Sam's youngest and only surviving son, and his wife, Julia, residents of Maine, assembled ten albums of photos, clippings, letters, and other of Sam's memorabilia. They presented them to the Dead River Area Historical Society (DRAHS) at Stratton, Maine. Stratton lies hard by Eustis, where Sam was born and lived as a boy and young man. Thus, local folk who have long revered the name Sam O. White, can enjoy the collection.

In October, 2005, my wife Audrey and I spent five days at Stratton in the Historical Society's museum where I made copy negatives of the photos in the collection, and Audrey copied about 250 clippings, letters, and other papers relating to Sam life.

Many of the photos herein were made in my darkroom from the copy negatives I made of the Sam O. White collection at DRAHS. Some of the photos were probably taken by Sam, many were not. I have credited DRAHS for these photos, since they now reside in their museum. Where known, I have included the photographer's name.

While in Maine, we interviewed Julia White. Her husband, Sam's son Harland, a decorated veteran of World War II, is under care at a veteran's hospital. From Julia, we learned facts about Sam not available elsewhere.

In May, 2006, at Fairbanks, Richard Wien, son of pioneer pilot Noel, shared with me his memories of Sam White. As he and his brother Merrill and sister Jean grew up, the Noel Wien family lived directly across the street from Sam and Mary White. Richard and Merrill both contributed valuable insights into Sam White's character and life. Richard allowed me to copy letters written by Sam to him, and to his father.

Thus I have used many sources to assemble what I have come to call "Sam's Book."

—JIM REARDEN
Sprucewood
Homer, Alaska

Acknowledgments

THIS BOOK WOULD NOT have been written without the help of many. Richard Wien started off by putting me in touch with Harland O. White, Sam O. White's son, and his wife Julia, in Maine. The Whites shared with me memories of Sam, and pointed me to the Dead River Area Historical Society (DRAHS) in Stratton, Maine, where they had donated ten albums plus many photos and items for a Sam O. White display.

At Stratton, Mary Henderson, President of DRAHS, graciously opened the museum, although it was closed for winter, so my wife Audrey and I could copy photos, and various of Sam's papers in the Sam O. White collection.

Work in the museum went smoothly because of the generous help of Bob and Sandy Schipper, members of DRAHS, who provided a camera tripod, lights, work tables, and food—much wonderful food—while we worked.

The Rudy Billberg family—Rudy and Bessie, son Roy, and daughter Cathy McKechnie—contributed letters written by Sam, as well as a collection of maps that had been owned by Sam White. Roy Billberg wrote me, recalling intimate memories of Sam as he grew up near him in Fairbanks.

Dr. Paul Eneboe critically read an early draft of the manuscript—all 165,000 words—and helped with many constructive ideas.

My daughter Nancy Kleine also read an early draft, and re-organized my placement of comas, verbs, and other parts of the language, and suggested many other improvements.

James G. (Jim) King, who knew Sam White well, sent me copies of Sam's writings he had been hoarding, plus many photos. He too read an early draft and made many constructive comments. He contributed details on the makeup and workings of the old

Alaska Game Commission, for which he worked early in his brilliant wildlife conservation career.

My longtime friend Sidney Huntington contributed his memories of Sam from the 1930s and into the 1950s.

Kelly Bostian, Managing Editor of the *Fairbanks Daily News-Miner*, granted me permission to use material about Sam that appeared in that newspaper.

Michael Carey permitted me to quote material from his writings that appeared in the *Anchorage Daily News*.

Finally, Richard Wien and his brother Merrill shared their memories of Sam, as well as many photos. Richard also reviewed an early draft of the manuscript, and, with help from Merrill, wrote the Foreword, which reveals much about the character of Sam O. White.

My wife, Audrey, helped and supported my work on this book every step of the way.

To all of these I offer my heartfelt thanks.

—JIM REARDEN

Book One

The Early Years

Memories of Eustis Ridge

Although Sam O. White lived in Alaska for 52 years, he never lost his Maine accent. He dropped consonants, didn't say "smart," but "smaht," "wondah," instead of "wonder," "ahmy," instead of "army."

EUSTIS, WHERE I WAS BORN November 26, 1891, is a community of about seventy-five souls in west central Maine, about twenty miles from the United States-Canada boundary. While the centuries rolled from the 1800s to the 1900s, I grew up on nearby Eustis Ridge at a hillside farm which my folks hewed out of virgin timber. I was one of nine children. A sister and a brother died during a whooping cough epidemic. Diphtheria wiped out an entire neighboring family.

We lived on a dead-end road five miles from Eustis in a three-room log house. We kids walked two and a half miles to a red-painted country school house. The wonder is that it was painted at all. It was a two-term school arrangement, with school in session during the summer. I didn't quite get through eighth grade.

I have long yearned to return to see Eustis again. I clearly remember the fishing and swimming holes, the lovely hardwood-evergreen forests, the rivers and lakes.

We lived partly from the farm, and partly from the surrounding wild land. We had little or no money. Everything was on a barter or exchange system. We had warm clothes, and plenty of wholesome food.

When I was about 10, I often ran the two and a half miles between my home and that of my grandfather.

One occasion stands out. One early morning, sheep in a pasture behind grandfather's barn bleated urgently, raising a great commotion. My

Uncle Allen, and my grandfather, Benjamin Durrell,
armed themselves and rushed to
the pasture. A huge black bear
was among the sheep, slashing
at the frightened animals.

Grandpop, in his early
seventies, caught sight of
the bear, raised his old black
powder .56/56 Spencer carbine, and touched it off. The
rifle roared, and the bear
folded like a wet rag. Grandpop had to wait for the smoke
to clear before he could see
the result of his shot.

I arrived and saw the big
old bear lying on saw horses
where it was being skinned.
My eyes must have been big,
for I have never forgotten the
sight, or the story that went
with it. When the skin came

*Ellen D. White, Sam White's
mother, with Sam's World War I
souvenirs. 1919.*
Sam O. White, courtesy of DRAHS

off the bear it was easy to see why it had folded. His left side was
caved in and the bullet had penetrated the boiler room and lodged
in the skin on the far side of its body.

The bear had killed and disabled six sheep, a big loss for a
small farmer in the days when the dollar was worth one hundred
valuable cents.

A few years later, when grandpop was about eighty years along,
my cousin Richie, still a kid, spotted a deer nibbling apples in the
orchard, and told grandpop. Grandpop fetched the Spencer, rested
it on the bars of the fence, and with a single shot, bowled the deer
over, pizzle end up. Venison, and meat from an occasional bear,
was important to us.

Once, between these incidents, when I was old enough to have a
gun (a .32 Special Winchester carbine) Richie, my cousin Guy, and
I were shooting at a target. Grandpop came out with the .56/56,
to show us how. We kids were always delighted when grandpop
shot his Spencer with us. On this day, the wind occasionally blew

his beard across his face so he couldn't see the gun sights; he had to keep wiping it away.

He put his lead plumb center. As the old Spencer roared, a cloud of smoke rolled out of it, and the roar reverberated from the surrounding hills. The old rifle used black powder-loaded copper rimfire ammunition that looked like fat, blown-up .22 cartridges.

Around Eustis Ridge most folk were like us—living from small farms and the land. We milked one or more cows year-round. We made cottage cheese as well as brick or cartwheel cheese, and, of course, butter, and other things from milk. Much of my mother's cooking used cream and milk, and the food was, of course, rich and sustaining.

My grandmother had a screened pantry and a well where she cooled the milk, after which the cream was skimmed. All food had to be covered, for swarms of house flies were about. At times their buzzing sounded like a sawmill.

Sheets of 8×16-inch flypaper were set around the house. It was covered with a molasses-like substance which was sweet enough to lure the flies, and sticky enough to hold them once they landed.

Occasionally we heard a rumpus and someone would run and open a door to let an inexperienced cat, wrapped in a square of fly paper, flee outside. It was usually gone for a day or two, but eventually turned up minus the fly paper and some fur. The same cat was rarely caught twice.

Some smart Yankee invented flypaper mounted on a cardboard roll. One hooked it to the ceiling and pulled out the paper and it hung down about two feet, and if anything, it was more effective than the sheets. It was also much easier on cats.

My cousin Guy and I commonly paused during our fishing or hunting expeditions to help our nearest neighbors, old Rutillus ("Till") Fuller and angelic Mrs. Fuller. We hauled in hay, plowed, or did whatever work he needed doing. Sometimes his old horse played out while plowing a small field, or hauling hay to his barn. Guy then hightailed it home to return perhaps with a hay rack, but always with fresh and strong horses to finish whatever job was involved. Sometimes our help lasted two or three days. To us, it was as much fun as hunting or fishing.

I'll never forget the pleasure on the faces of the Fullers when we gave them a few trout, a hunk of venison, or a brace of partridges.

Little Mrs. Fuller would put a wrinkled hand on our heads and say in her old cracked voice, "Blessed, blessed, blessed."

She was a grand old lady and my idea of a true angel. Once I did something I shouldn't have, and my mother didn't whale the daylight out of me as she should have. Instead she said, "You were so good to help the Fullers with gathering their potatoes."

We heated the house and cooked with firewood, which we cut in late fall, a year in advance of its use. We hauled it home in winter and sawed and split it towards spring, then tiered it up in a shed so as to be well-seasoned and dry for use.

Spring planting was a busy time, for it needed to be done over a short period. During the growing time we weeded, hoed, and killed bugs with Paris Green sprayed by hand. Then came haying, and after that, harvesting of crops.

In spring we tapped maple trees, and spent days boiling the clear sap. Forty gallons of sap made one gallon of sweet syrup. It brought seventy five-cents a gallon when we could sell it; mostly there was no market for it.

School continued even when seasonal activities were at their height. I didn't quite complete the eighth grade.

When I was a older, we acquired a Buckeye mowing machine for cutting hay. It was pulled by two horses. We also had a horse-drawn hay rake. However, about half of our acreage was too rough for machinery, and had to be worked by hand.

While the men and boys did virtually all the outside work, the women of the family sewed clothing, and repaired worn garments. They picked gallons of wild berries, made pickles, and put up a variety of preserved fruits, vegetables, and meat. They made soap each fall, and carded wool fresh from our sheep. I can still hear in my mind the mournful sound of the old spinning wheel in early winter as, for many days, it ran from daylight until dark.

I don't think the constant work hurt us. On the contrary, it developed our muscles and kept us out of mischief. We had our pleasures and our sorrows, of course, and to be sure, there were times when it seemed good to simply sit and rest. However, we had to keep moving if we were going to eat.

It was wonderful life.

2 The Maine Years

We used to eat sugar beets raw and cold, and we were raw and cold too. They staved off hunger, but were poor fodder for hungry cold me. There was another vegetable that grew in the fields we used to eat. Mangles we called them, but I disremember where we got the name.

—Sam's recollection of his time during World War I as a soldier in France.

[AUTHOR] Samuel Otho White was known as Otho White during his early years in Maine. He shed Otho as a first name, but retained the O. when he left Maine, and thereafter was known as Sam O. White. During his years in Alaska he rarely put his name on anything without including the O.

Young Otho roamed the forests surrounding Eustis Ridge, becoming a skilled marksman as he shot partridges, rabbits, deer, and other game—basic food for his family. His skill with a rifle benefited him for much of the rest of his life.

"From the time I was 14, I caught and shot five or six black bears every year. Each brought ten dollars—five dollars bounty, and five dollars for the hide. Lots of money in those days."

In 1910, 19-year-old Otho White, Registered Guide and trapper, set four bear traps, ". . . on the West Eustis township about five miles distant from Tim Pond."

When he returned, two bears were in traps. One of these, held by front foot toes, pulled loose and, ". . . tore at me like an express train," he said.

His rifle jammed. "I had thrown the lever, but couldn't close it. Finally re-closed it by striking the lever with my fist. Throwing the gun to my shoulder, I fired, and jumped sideways for my life just as the bear scooted by me, stone dead."

One of Sam's boyhood pals was Wayne Fletcher, who, as an adult, owned Kibby Kamp, a deep woods lodge near Eustis. Sam often wrote Fletcher describing his life in Alaska. Fletcher often read the letters to guests at the lodge, including 7-year-old Bob Schipper.

As an adult, Schipper, a world-traveled transport plane pilot/ navigator, retired in Stratton, Maine. He wondered if his boyhood hero Sam White still lived. In August, 1968, he wrote him, addressing the letter, "Sam O. White, Alaska."

It was promptly delivered, and Schipper and Sam entered into years of correspondence. Later, Schipper repeatedly visited Sam at Fairbanks.

Schipper joined the Dead River Area Historical Society (DRAHS) at Stratton, and helped with information about his friend Sam White when Harland and Julia White (Sam's son and daughter-in-law) presented ten albums of Sam's photos and historical records for display in the Society's Stratton museum.

Upon receiving Schipper's first letter, Sam replied, "A friend of Wayne Fletcher's is automatically a friend of mine. He and I always hit it off good. When I was about 15 and lovelorn, he recovered a letter I had written to a fair lass who in no way reciprocated my feelings. Worse, she posted it on the school's outhouse door for all to see. Fortunately, Wayne saw it and destroyed it."

Sam called himself a "7th grade dropout", for he didn't finish the eighth grade. Big and strong, at the age of 14 he started working winters in Maine logging camps. At first he was a swamper. Next he became a bucker, pulling one end of the two-man crosscut saws then used to fell trees and trim logs. He then became a tree feller and loader. In 1908 he left the woods with ninety-one dollars after three months work.

Sam as a scaler (estimating board feet of logs) in 1916, on the South Branch of the Dead River, near Eustis, Maine.
Sam O. White, courtesy of DRAHS

Sam White was a steersman for Lombard log haulers like this one (note steersman on front) during the winters of 1914, 1915, and 1916. For this dangerous job he was paid four dollars a day, big wages at the time.
DRAHS

In 1914, a woods boss asked Sam, then 23, if he was ready to steer a Lombard log hauler, a behemoth of a steam-powered machine that pulled a train of sleds loaded with logs. He leaped at the opportunity. The pay of four dollars a day was even better than that of the engineer, the fireman, or the conductor—the other crew members of a Lombard. It was big money.

Otho White first saw Lombards one afternoon in 1901 when he was 10. His teacher dismissed school to allow the children to watch two of these machines clatter by at four and a half miles an hour. Smoke, sparks, and steam filled the air. Their chugging and musical whistles resounded for miles; they were huge, noisy, powerful, and impressive.

Steersmen for Lombard steam log haulers were heroes to youngsters, much as many kids look upon astronauts today. Being a Lombard steersman was a doubtful honor. Not all who worked in the woods were willing to take the job. The catch? These giants of the woods didn't have brakes. Brakes wouldn't work because of the tremendous weight pulled by this puffing, spark-tossing machine. It commonly towed fifteen, twenty, or more green-log-filled sleds with a total weight of 300 to 500 tons. Braking on a hill could have caused the train to jackknife.

Steersmen sat on the front of the Lombard, above two huge steering skis, that were turned by a large, geared steering wheel wrestled by the steersman.

The steersman lived with the possibility of being crushed between an out-of-control Lombard and a tree, hence the elevated pay. The other three crew members could easily leap from the machine; the steersman couldn't.

Sam was a Lombard steersman in 1914, 1915, and into 1916, when he figured he might be pushing his luck, and took a job as a timber scaler.

He once commented, "I remember sweating when it was below zero, wrestling with that big wheel with tons of logs on sleds behind that iron monster, zooming downhill at twenty miles an hour, dodging trees, and doing my damndest to keep on the trail. I was scared many times. I'd look downhill and check out the curve—there always seemed to be a curve—and wish I were still a tree feller. I used to feel like the old Lombard was going to tip over when we sped down a Hay Hill and entered a curve."

Sam worked at his father's farm and sawmill between winter seasons at logging camps. Another of his early employments included an axe and shovel job for one dollar a day. At 16 he became a Maine hunting guide—a category reached by only the well-qualified.

He once wrote to Bob Schipper, "I'll tell you how to get bucks in September when they are fat and good eating, before they travel in the rut. Put on a pair of old coveralls and go into the cedar swamps where they bed down. Get down on your face and crawl slow and easy. A worm's eye view gets your eyes below the thickest brush, and I picked 'em off right in their beds.

"It takes patience and is hard on clothing. I used a twenty-inch barrel Model 99 Savage .303. It was thick like a crowbar with no taper or beauty. I always kept it pointing ahead for instant use. I don't remember anyone else using this method."

Sam White (arrow), before being sent to France during World War I. His cousin, Guy A. Durrell, is marked with an x. COURTESY OF JULIA WHITE

In 1915, Sam married Pearl Mills. They met while he was hunting and trapping near her home at Lac Megantic, Quebec. They had three sons, Burnham, Jesse, and Harland, in that order.

In late 1916, Sam went to work for the International Boundary Survey, a job he held until 1917. World War I loomed, and Sam was sucked into it.

He entered the Army February 27, 1918, serial #1673309, as a private wagoner (a leftover title from the Civil War, for a horse handler or wagon driver). In time his expert marksmanship earned him a place with Lyman's Rangers, made up of selected members from every state, Alaska, and Canada.

He reached the rank of sergeant, and was variously assigned as an artillery observer, a motorcycle dispatch rider, and a Browning Automatic Rifleman.

He was overseas from June 22, 1918 to March 11, 1919, and engaged the enemy at the St. Mihiel [France] defensive sector.

"For days on end, when we were at the front line and it was raining, with mud up to our waists, we never got out of it, day and night, weeks on end. We stood in the mud and crawled around in no man's land and never got dry for weeks.

Sam White (arrow), with other soldiers of the 111th Infantry, 28th Division. Major General Charles H. Muir, commanding. Resting at Chateau Thierry, while on their way to take part in the counter offensive, July 21, 1918. COURTESY OF JULIA WHITE

"The frontline food situation was terrible. We ate from a big milk can full of boiled rice. There were bullet holes in the can, and blood spattered on it; once there was a scalp inside. We had to eat the rice anyway. There was seldom anything else.

"Once we got warm bread. The soldier who was packing the bread was shot and fell on the bread, and the bread was warmed by his body. We found him that way. Sometimes the cooks used a big cleaver to cut cans of salmon down the middle, and handed half a can to each man. It was already frozen. I have never liked canned salmon since.

"I wasn't the loser for all this. I felt pretty good about it [doing my duty] and being there. It was a matter of hoping I'd survive to get back home."

He was honorably discharged July 11, 1919.

Sam had long been interested in Alaska. Jack Allman, from Fairbanks, and Donald Buckingham of Ketchikan, were also members of Lyman's Rangers. From them, Sam learned much about

Alaska. "When I went into the Army I weighed 200 pounds," he said in a 1968 interview. "When I came out I weighed 176. They really beat a fellow up in those days.

For Sam's 70th birthday celebration, long-time Maine friend Bill "Ikey" Robinson, remembered how he and another buddy were lying at night in a foxhole. German snipers lurked nearby. A motorcycle chugged near. They couldn't believe anyone would approach such a dangerous area on a machine. It was Sam. They dubbed him with mud to camouflage his white face, and kept him in the foxhole for the night.

Sam told Roy Billberg, son of Rudy Billberg, a fellow bush pilot and a Fairbanks neighbor, something of his experiences in WWI. "I've lived two lives: one of normal living, and another life of sheer terror," he said.

He told Roy he had fought in the trenches until the war ended [Nov. 11, 1918]. "When you're in a trench, and about to go over the top and charge the Germans," he said, "you're so afraid that you can hardly control yourself. You're shaking so bad you can hardly get your rifle ready. But once you're over the top and running toward the enemy, something else kicks in and you are not afraid any more. I saw men falling on both sides of me, but kept running. The concussion of artillery blew me first one way and then the other, but I'd land on my feet and keep running.

"It was often bayonet fighting, but I'd get super-human strength. I knew anything in front of me would topple."

Sam praised the Salvation Army. "They were always at the front where the action was," he recalled.

"Even when shells were exploding behind a hill, the Salvation Army lasses, in their tin washbasin helmets and gas masks, were often on the other side of that hill, carrying on business as usual.

In an August 4, 1962 letter to Noel Wien, Sam wrote, "*There were good American farm girls in that [Salvation Army] dugout, maybe from Maine and Minnesota, and they were putting out hot chocolate and doughnuts and wearing gas masks and hob-nailed hats. We had one half-hour respite, and the hot chocolate and doughnuts worked wonders. Probably it was the sight of those girls that inspired us most.*

"*Each man got two doughnuts. A tin can was on the plank that served as a counter. If a man happened to have change in his pocket, he dropped it in. If he didn't, nobody said yea or nay.*

"It was different with some other organizations. With them it was no money, no service, even for us dough-boys." Sam.

Sam O. White loved people, and he left hundreds of friends in his life's wake.

One day as he stood eating from his mess kit in a small town in France, a little French boy tugged at his sleeve and pointed to a house across the street. There, a smiling older lady beckoned from a window. He responded, and afterward he often visited with the family who lived there, to eat, and to get warm. He became attached to them, and after the war corresponded with them.

Pearl J. Mills White, Sam's first wife. 1949 photo.
SAM O. WHITE, COURTESY OF DRAHS

The correspondence ended abruptly with World War II and the German occupation of France.

Then, in 1944, the old lady wrote Sam from Reims [France]. A few snippets: "We cannot tell you how happy we were to see your dear and devoted compatriots [American soldiers]. Our happiness cannot be described, but it is comprehensible after so many years of slavery and privation.

"The beginning of the war was a great calamity for us in the tragedy of Dunkirk. My dear Pierre [the little French boy who had tugged at Sam's sleeve] was killed by a machine-gun.

"The Americans I see are many of them tall and strong, and they remind me of you. Also they tell me they are volunteers. They will mail my letter, and I hope and trust they will translate it.

"I hope you both are still in good health and happy and that your plane will take you over beautiful country. We still look at the pretty cards you have sent us with pleasure, and we can picture the snow and scenery and the little settlements."

After discharge from the Army, Sam worked the summer of 1920 for the International Boundary Survey, and then transferred to the Coast and Geodetic Survey.

"Having been in the Army gave me a leg up for the civil service examination I took for the Coast and Geodetic position. I got a five percent preference, and that is probably what put me over the top because I was woefully shy of education," he said.

Mapping Alaska

In 1922 the United States Coast and Geodetic Survey sent
me to Alaska. Much earlier I wanted to come here anyway,
but wanted to fight in the war first.
—SAM O. WHITE. FROM AN AUGUST, 1966, INTERVIEW.

IN APRIL, 1922, while working for the Coast and Geodetic Survey in Utah and Arizona, with the help of a veteran's preference I passed a civil service examination, thus qualifying me to be assigned to Alaska to do reconnaissance work for the Survey.

I arrived in Seward and rode the Alaska Railroad to Anchorage. My first real taste of the North came when the train stopped at Nellie Neal Lawing's roadhouse at Lawing, at the east end of Kenai Lake. Many a newcomer to Alaska first encountered Nellie when the Alaska Railroad train stopped at her museum-like roadhouse. She was a respected hunter, trapper, cook, dog musher, and pioneer. She was a frail little woman when I met her, but I sensed her driving urgency to get things done.

At her roadhouse were bigger bear skins that I had ever imagined, and moose racks like none I had seen in Maine. Nellie had a pelt or trophy mount of about every Alaskan game animal. She died at Seward in 1945 at the age of 80.

When we started our reconnaissance work I was speedily introduced to the problems of survey work unique to Alaska.

Few regions of Alaska had been properly mapped. About forty percent of the country had indifferent maps. The arctic coast was sketched, not mapped. If you relied on a map, you could be fifteen or twenty miles from where you thought you were; there was that much error on many of the existing maps.

Sam, with his dog Smokey, at Station Portage in 1923 when he was a reconnaissance man in Alaska for the U.S. Coast and Geodetic Survey. Bill Scaife was the engineer in charge. U.S. COAST AND GEODETIC SURVEY

We started work north of Anchorage, then a small, raw, village. My first job as a reconnaissance man was to find and blaze a packhorse trail about ten miles across Bullion Swamps[1] north of Anchorage.

I selected a route and blazed it with little difficulty, but a few days later, while leading a pack train across, we lost my trail by a

---

1. Probably adjacent to Bullion Mountain, which lies fourteen miles N.W. of Palmer in the Talkeetna Mountains. [AUTHOR]

beaver pond. The beaver had cut down both saplings I had blazed. It took some casting about to find the trail again.

In the meantime, one horse mired, and we nearly lost her and her pack. By the time we pulled her out, she had the longest neck in our entire horse string.

Midway through the season I had my first tangle with a grizzly bear. I was cruising trail for a move, and left camp about two and a half hours ahead of my pack train. Near the head of Peters Creek, about two-thirds the way to my destination, I rounded a large outcropping and found myself between a huge sow and her two yearling cubs, which were also pretty big. I instantly put on the brakes.

The sow was about 150 feet away and hadn't seen me. I cautiously started to step back around the outcropping. On about my second step she spotted me, emitted a blood-chilling roar, and bounded toward me.

I held on her left side between the neck and shoulder and fired. She went down in a heap. Struggling to get up, she rolled over on her back with all four feet waving in the air.

She soon regained her feet and made a shorter bound toward me. I fired a second shot in the same place and she went down again. This time she could only crawl in my direction, still roaring, and chopping her jaws. She sure had big teeth and a cavernous mouth. I finished her with a third shot.

I felt very depressed over that kill. She was a beautiful animal, a fine specimen of grizzly. It was a shame to have to destroy her. The cubs hung around for a time, and then left. They were old enough to care for themselves.

I climbed on the outcropping and waited for the pack train. Our horses were veterans--they nibbled grass close to the dead bear with seeming unconcern.

We saw many grizzlies over the next few days. None offered hostilities when we apprised them of our presence.

While in the vicinity of the Talkeetna River, our party ran low on food in late summer. A couple of our crew went to a cache we had established and discovered a wolverine had been there. Everything but one sack of flour had been heaved off the cache and was on the ground, destroyed as only a wolverine can destroy things.

However, that one sack of flour had lodged in the fork of a limb. The wolverine had worked on it, but aside from chewing the tough tarp, had done no damage. They retrieved the flour and we worked for the next two weeks on a menu of flour, meat from game we killed, and blueberries.

Wolverines were numerous in this vicinity and north to Broad Pass. Near the end of the season, in addition to reconnaissance work, I assisted in light keeping--meaning I helped to establish lights on high points. A following observing or survey party measured angles on them at night in preliminary map work.

I carefully placed an automatic light atop a mountain on a station we called "Montana." Powered by dry cell batteries, it was turned on and off by clockwork.

In camp that evening we received a signal light message from the observing party to the south. "Light out on Montana."

I beat it up the mountain in the dark with another set of batteries. Upon arrival, I heard a snarl, a scrabbling, and saw a shadow detach itself from the light stand. I missed a snap shot at it, and heard a growl as the wolverine left.

On the stand, made of stout spruce poles, and weighted with a half ton of rocks, Mr. Wolverine had chewed up the dry cell batteries. He had even apparently eaten some with great relish. These batteries were the type common in telephone installations in those years.

I tore out the wreckage, replaced batteries, and readjusted the light. I mounted guard until one a.m. when the observing party finished.

I climbed the mountain again next morning, checked the light, and set it on another station. My two companions returned to camp about two hours after I had left and found a horrible mess. All food was destroyed, including a hundred pounds of prime moose meat. One pair of shoepacks and an axe were missing.

We made a diligent search, and found nothing. A large wolverine had been there. We were mystified as to how, in two hours, he could accomplish all that destruction and still have time to make off with the shoepacks and axe.

We still had two weeks of work, and we did it on mucky salmon, caribou, ptarmigan, and frosted blueberries.

In September, on our way to the railroad, we came upon a well-stocked cache. We took beans, salt, oatmeal, sugar, and coffee, items we badly needed. We made a list, posted it on the cache, and signed our names.

Later, in Anchorage we called upon A. A. Shonbeck, owner of the cache. He refused payment.

LATE THE FOLLOWING April (1923) Bill Scaife, the engineer in charge, Oscar Risvold, my packer, and I arrived via the Alaska Railroad at Caswell to do reconnaissance for another summer of Coast and Geodetic Survey quadrangle work. It was about noon, and we were about fifty yards below the station house adjusting our backpacks and three dog packs for the hike ahead. The section foreman came to us.

"I've got the best cook in Alaska, but I don't dare invite you to eat," he said. "You guys just walk up near the front door and do some more adjusting."

We hustled, and were busily making the unnecessary adjustments when the door opened and a tirade of cussing was directed toward us.

"A fine bunch of cheechakos! Blankety-blank-blank. You know it's dinner time, and you don't know enough to come in and eat!"

It was the cook, a tall, slender, good-looking middle-age lady.

"You knotheads," she said. "Come in and eat."

We did just that. She was a real cook and a sourdough, having spent many years in Alaska. After we ate our fill, she insisted we take a loaf of her bread with us.

I saw more of this kindly and capable lady later at Fairbanks where she married a good friend of mine, and lived out her very useful life.

We left Caswell and headed east into the mountains. Creeks were high, and there was much snow and water. Our three dogs packed some of our food. We fed them on ground squirrels and marmots, which were numerous, succulent, and sustaining.

Bill constantly talked about roasted porcupine, and I tried to discourage him. We made camp one evening under some spruce trees and beside a singing creek. I was perturbed when the dogs became interested in something up a tree. When Bill was busy elsewhere, I looked, and sure enough, there was a porky.

I re-tied the dogs to a tree at some distance. But Bill soon spotted the porky and brought him down. He cooked and cooked that porky, but each time we tried to eat it, it was like chewing on a Kelly Springfield tire, which aren't noted for being tender.

Bill finally offered it to the dogs, who also disdained it. That was the last of the porky business.

From this camp, which was about forty miles from the railroad, we turned north and proceeded in a zig-zag fashion, selecting probable sites for stations. At times we slept on spruce boughs atop ten feet of snow. On other nights we had bare ground.

The creeks ran southwest, which required many crossings. We waded the smaller ones and built a fire and dried out on the north shore. It was spring, and most of the creeks ran full. It sometimes required hours to find a suitable tree to cut down for a bridge to span the water. All the creeks were turbulent and swift; if we had fallen in, survival would have been unlikely.

Just out of the mountains, we came to a large stream. Scouting, on a bank where the stream narrowed we found a tall spruce about thirty inches at the stump. It needed to be undercut accurately, and to leave a thick scarf to hold it to the stump so when it hit it wouldn't bound and drop over the bank.

One had to watch it fall; if it showed a tendency to crowd up or downstream from the center of desired impact, one had to be quick to cut the corner that would draw it up or down the proper amount.

I got the tree undercut, and had started on the back scarf. But I was so pooched out I had to rest. Bill always insisted that I did too much of the work, when usually he'd end up doing two-thirds of it. He insisted on finishing the tree. I stressed the importance of keeping a strong scarf on the stump and watching the tree fall, and to give instant attention to the appropriate corner.

He attacked the tree with vigor. It fell, missing the mark on the opposite bank by two feet, bounced at the butt, and leaped a full three feet. The current then seized it and snapped it in the middle like a match. Our hours of work evaporated.

Bill was very disappointed. I assured him that while I was becoming an expert with an axe, he was becoming an expert with logarithms, and it was altogether possible I would have missed too.

After a rest and a pot of tea, we set off again, and about two-and-a-half miles downstream found where the stream split into two channels, the big one on our side. There we dropped a big cottonwood tree to the gravel bar island in the center, walked across it, and waded the smaller channel to the far shore.

We were beat. About thirty feet from the creek was an eight-foot bank, topped by a spruce-covered bench. We tied the dogs under one tree, and made camp under another about fifteen feet from the bank.

It snowed four inches that night. About two a.m. the dogs started an awful tumult. I sat up and peered, but could see nothing. The bristled-up dogs were looking toward the creek. I looked for five minutes. Finally the dogs quieted, and I went back to sleep.

Early next morning I built a fire while Bill went to the creek for water. When he reached the bank he looked in astonishment and came tearing back for his rifle. I grabbed mine and followed.

Right under the bank in the fresh snow was the grand daddy of all fresh bear tracks. I followed them upstream and downstream. At no time did the bear swerve right or left or change his step cadence. When the dogs set up their clamor, he was no more than fifty feet from them, and he was even closer to us. We concluded he had important business, and had no intention of being diverted.

Our vitality waned as we rationed grub. We couldn't take any big game, since we could use no more than twenty-five pounds of meat before it spoiled. We stretched what food we had with squirrels, ptarmigan and other small game.

We packed a small reserve of sugar on one of the dogs, saving it as a last luxury. We crossed the next creek on a log, and the knothead pup with the sugar decided to swim. There went our sugar. I guess it sweetened the stream.

A few days later we hit the railroad at Talkeetna, and entrained for Anchorage.

By late August, the observing party which followed in our trail, was in the barren high hills at the head of the Chunilna River. I had trails selected and the stations ready for the next two quadrangles, and since we were closing down work September 1, I cruised and marked a trail for the observing party to follow all the way to Curry and the railroad.

Oscar, Bill, and I arrived there August 25 and were put up in the big old comfortable log roadhouse that Nellie Neal (Lawing was her married name, acquired later), who I had met in 1922, had operated during railroad construction.

Next morning we awoke to a snowstorm, with six to eight inches on the ground. I realized snow would cover many of my trail markers, for much of it was above timberline where the markers were rock cairns. I took off alone to intercept the observing party.

Snow fell steadily, and although I had good snowshoes, I kept bogging down. Next morning it was still snowing. I made it over the top of a bare ridge, and bogged down. I could go no farther. I cached what foodstuff I had with me under some rocks, and returned to Curry for help.

Oscar, Bill, and I left early the following morning, each packing extra snowshoes for the observing party. We arrived at timberline late that evening and built a spruce bough wickiup under a spruce tree whose wide branches came close to the ground.

Early next morning we started up a barren ridge. We wore black mosquito nets to prevent snow blindness. By then there was thirty-seven inches of snow. It was still falling.

We reached the area where I had cached the foodstuff in the rocks, but I had difficulty locating it. Suddenly, I saw dark figures against the snow.

"Look. Caribou," I exclaimed.

"No," one of them argued, "them are whistlers."

I sent my dog Smokey to see what they were. They were mice, working on the food I had left. This illusion is commonly caused by fog or snow against a flat white background. The mice had used about a fourth of my supplies, but we gathered up the remainder and headed up the ridge, taking turns breaking trail.

It was then that the blizzard really hit. We still had four or five miles to go up the ridge; we then had to turn south and where there was a steep cliff, drop off the ridge with only one possible trail down. Visibility went to practically nothing. I had to use a compass to make sure of direction. The blizzard was so intense it drove snow through every opening in our clothing where it melted, causing considerable discomfort.

We had to make it to timber or perish. At length we came to the cliff where we were to turn south, but I couldn't find the trail down. We were in grave danger, and couldn't waste time searching. We needed to find shelter.

I hated myself for it, but it was the only solution I could think of. I worked my way to what looked like the edge of the cliff and pushed my dog Smokey into the void, half expecting never to see him again.

We then huddled under a rock to wait. In about twenty minutes he returned along the edge of the cliff, wagging his tail, pleased to see us.

His tracks were obliterated in a matter of seconds by the blizzard, but I urged him ahead and he led us down the trail to the head of timber, and we found we were on the right creek.

Here we found a large spruce tree with branches touching the ground, and the lower several feet interlaced with wild hay. We cut space under the branches where there was no snow, and where wind couldn't penetrate. There we spread our sleeping robes, built a large fire to the lee, and hung wet clothes to dry.

We divided the night into two-hour watches to keep the fire going and to see that clothes didn't burn. Though the fire was in the lee, at times when the wind hit, flames stretched horizontally along the ground.

In the morning as we prepared our almost non-existent breakfast, a large flock of ptarmigan landed near. Bill took the .22 rifle and got close enough to shoot, but he was so tired that he settled down in the snow to steady his aim. At that instant every last bird took to the air, and two-thirds of our breakfast disappeared down the creek.

We couldn't waste time mourning, but packed up and made our way down the main creek. Almost at once we came upon the trail of the struggling observing party, and fired a shot. An answering shot came, and we soon joined them.

Their grub situation was little better than ours, but they did have some caribou meat which we cooked. As soon as the aroma rose from the cooking, one of the horses joined us at the fire. "He eats caribou steaks," the packer explained.

Sure enough, he ate several steaks with us.

All of the horses were in bad shape. I was filled with pity whenever I looked at them. Eight horses had disappeared when the blizzard hit the party in the hills. Five more were to drop before we got back to the railroad.

It was obvious the trail I had earlier prepared for this party to reach Curry could not now be used. I had to find another trail down the creek, through hip-deep snow. It took five days for us to make it back to the railroad track five miles below Curry, at great hardship for both man and beast.

Where we had to cross a large and swift stream, as he swam, my faithful dog Smokey was swept under a drift pile. Oscar leaped into the pile, lay flat, and fished around underneath until he came up with the almost drowned Smokey. We stopped and dried the big dog with a blanket and a fire. After he had led us down the cliff to safety, he was considered an important member of the party.

Shortly, we left that creek and made a beeline over a low ridge to the railroad. There we lost the last of the five horses that died after we had joined the party. He sank to the ground and could not get up.

I stumbled ahead, found the railroad tracks, and made it into Curry. One of the railroad men loaded several bales of hay onto a hand car, and I ran this back to where the horses were to reach the tracks. Fortunately those five miles were downgrade, as I was so pooched out that my arms and legs bent like rubber hoses.

When I arrived we had to give way as about fifteen frantic horses fell to and beat the bales apart with their hooves so they could dive in.

When we got back to Curry, the railroad management again put us up in Nellie Neal's old roadhouse, which had two good stoves and plenty of coal. The food and warmth were most welcome.

One night Bill Scaife had more supplies than he needed.

The building had a balloon ceiling common in those days. It consisted of a layer of thin drill stretched across rafters to pretty up the interior. This ceiling, in place for many years, bulged ominously in places. The biggest bulge was near the stove and above the cot Bill had selected.

"Bill," I said as I banked the fire for the night, "What do you suppose makes that ceiling bulge? I'll just poke at it and see."

Bill, who was in his sleeping bag, looked at the ceiling.

"Leave it alone!" he yelled.

Too late. I had nudged it with the coal shovel.

The ceiling split and the crash that followed was like a farmer dumping a load of rocks. A huge pile of dried doughnuts, hotcakes, cookies, and other baked goodies buried Bill's cot. He struggled to get out from under the mess, all the while roaring like a wounded bear. The gang joined in the chorus, mightily enjoying the incident.

I should have saved some of that pastry. It would make valuable keepsakes today, as this was Nellie Neal's dining room where she fed construction crews of the Alaska Railroad around 1916.

Squirrels, appreciating the quality of her cooking, had cached a huge supply of it in the balloon ceiling.

My First Alaska Winters

Very few people I know have led a more exciting life than Sam O. White.
—James ("Andy") Anderson, one-time bush pilot at
Bettles, Alaska, letter to author, February, 2006.

PERLEY, MY YOUNGER BROTHER, was a member of the Coast and
Geodetic Survey party I was recon man for in the summer of 1922.
After he and I completed our 1922 summer's work, we decided to
spend the coming winter in Alaska.

But what to do? We were experienced lumberjacks and farm workers, and I had the rudimentary training needed to work at surveying
for the Coast and Geodetic Survey. However, none of these skills
were in immediate demand. I made a trip to Fairbanks in November
and found no openings there for which we qualified.

Although we were never full-time trappers, as boys we had
both done a bit of trapping in Maine, and, except for wolves and
wolverine, for about the same kind of animals as are in Alaska.

An uncle had taught me woods craft. He was a poacher, but he
had his principles; he wouldn't shoot a doe with a fawn at any time of
year, nor would he set beaver traps closer than fifty feet from a beaver
house. That was about his limit of hunting and trapping ethics.

Despite our inexperience, Perley and I decided to become
trappers for the winter. This was a common profession in Alaska
then, and, for some, it was quite profitable. Fur prices were good,
and fur was in demand.

Where to trap? We talked with old-timers who knew the
country. "Best place for you is probably along the Anchorage-
McGrath trail," one sourdough recommended.[1]

---

1. This is known today as the Iditarod trail, famed for the annual Iditarod dog team
race from Anchorage to Nome.

So we gathered a dog team of mostly nondescript animals, some of which looked like dogs, others which looked like something else. Some were given to us by old-timers who wanted to help—or get rid of marginal dogs. One of these dogs, named Kempt, given to us by the Flickenstein Brothers of Wasilla, was the key to the team. He was big and black, a good worker and a leader of sorts. He didn't much care where he worked in the team so long as he could have at least one good fight a day, preferably with a strange dog team. In a pinch, a fight with one, or all, of his team mates satisfied.

I think he preferred to work in the wheel position (next to the sled). That way if he suspected any dog up ahead wasn't doing his share, Kempt would nail him. Eventually, none of the dogs dared slack off for fear of the big jaws behind.

We outfitted in Anchorage and shipped dogs and all to Nancy via the Alaska Railroad. At Nancy, we met residents Billy Austin and his wife. When we told them what we were up to, they helped us no end. We even stayed overnight as their guests, enjoying the wonderful meals of Mrs. Austin. They refused pay; important to us, as we were not flush.

From Nancy, we mushed down the trail about half way to Susitna Station where we camped and relayed our supplies on to Susitna Station.

At the time roadhouses were found every twenty or thirty miles on major trails across Alaska. They were sometimes crude, but after a long day of mushing dogs or traveling on snowshoes, they provided warmth, food, and safety. Travelers could remain overnight, get meals, have a place to tie dogs, and commonly buy dried salmon to feed dog teams.

We went to the Susitna Station roadhouse, run by a Mrs. Johnson and Bill Dennison. Here again we ran into pioneers who wanted to help. We left, feeling both were good friends.

After a day or two of outfitting and gathering information, we started the long trek from Susitna Station to a creek which name I do not remember, but which was about half way between Skwentna Crossing and Mountain Climber on the Anchorage-McGrath trail.

It turned cold and the snow was deep, but there was some travel on the trail, so we didn't have to break trail. We pitched a tent and went to relaying again. After considerable struggle, we arrived at Skwentna Crossing and the roadhouse there run by old-timers Mac MacElroy and Jack Rimmer.

I'm sure they immediately sized us up as rank cheechakos (newcomers). Above the door to their roadhouse a sign read, "Lunch $1.50. Meal $2.50. Gorge $4.00." Mac McElroy was a professional cook, and a good one. In addition to running the roadhouse, they trapped, but they did not trap beaver. In fact, no one in the country trapped beaver in those days. Instead, the animals were shot after breakup. Trappers thought it impossible to trap beaver through the ice. "Too much snow and ice to contend with," we were told.

"Beaver is all we're interested in trapping," we told the pair. We had learned how to trap beaver through the ice in Maine.

They told us we could use their traplines if we only sought beaver. We readily agreed. Jack Rimmer even made me an ice chisel with which to cut holes in the ice.

We then left Skwentna Crossing for the creek with no name, relaying our outfit. We found a level spot a quarter mile below the trail at the fork of two creeks, with good timber, clear pure water, and lots of dry wood. I still get thirsty when I think of that lovely pool of water.

We tromped the snow down, threw water on it to freeze it solid, built a cabin wall four logs high, pitched our tent on it, banked it with snow, put a foot of finely chopped spruce boughs on the floor, installed our wood stove, and moved in. It was a snug and orderly home.

We built a thirty-foot-long and five-foot-wide bridge across the beautiful four-feet-deep pool there. To accomplish this we used three big cottonwood trees for stringers, some corduroy work, and on top of that, spruce boughs and snow. We figured it would hold a couple of tons, and were proud of our engineering. Even the dogs seemed to get a kick out of crossing it.

Water beneath the bridge remained open for about seventy-five feet downstream, and a hundred feet upstream. A few beaver lived in and around this pool. We decided to let them be—it was fun to see them. A mistake.

We spent a day cutting firewood. Over the next two days we located live beaver houses, and set fourteen traps. We weren't planning to make a big catch; we wanted to make just enough to get through the winter without getting financially behind.

For the next three days we cut more firewood, and built a cache. Jack Rimmer arrived with a team of big, well-trained and beautiful dogs. "Catch any beaver yet?" he asked. He still didn't believe it possible to catch beaver while waterways were frozen.

"We're just now going to check traps we set four days ago," we told him.

He wanted us to show him how we set beaver traps under the ice, so we invited him to accompany us. It is a simple system. Bait sticks are nailed to a pole, and a trap is fastened near the bait. The pole is then thrust through a hole cut in the ice of a beaver pond. We found six beaver in our fourteen traps. Rimmer's eyes were big as we hauled number six from the water.

We pointed out that we didn't set traps closer than fifty feet from a beaver lodge, which insured that we didn't catch kits.

Dog feed was no problem—the team happily ate beaver meat and waxed fat and glossy, even though we worked them hard.

Jack Rimmer and Mac McElroy, using our methods, caught twice the number of beaver we did that winter—their first-ever winter catch of beaver.

On stormy days we did camp work and cut more firewood, which was easy—dry wood was available in abundance within 200 feet of our tent. Early-on we cut enough to last the winter.

We made several trips to Skwentna Crossing and discovered we were now non-paying guests at the roadhouse—Rimmer and MacElheny were that pleased at learning from us how we trapped beaver.

One day while crossing on the ice of the Skwentna River, Perley was ahead on snowshoes, breaking trail. I drove the dog team off the bank and noticed what appeared to be lumps of snow on a log sticking from the bank. As I passed, I wondered, "Why is that snow in lumps?"

I looked back and realized that the "lumps" were fifteen or twenty ptarmigan taking a siesta. The dogs and I had passed within twenty-five feet of them, and even the dogs had not noticed them. I was still about thirty feet away, and I whistled to Perley who was seventy-five yards ahead, pointing to the log. He understood at once, and moved closer and started shooting. Perley was a crack shot, and I saw the heads of six of those birds shatter as they dropped from the log.

Six was enough, and he stopped shooting. I had to walk toward the rest of the birds to make them fly.

That day we found one of our traps holding two beaver toes, an upsetting sight. The trap was on a platform built on a dry pole, over an open pond of beautiful clear water. Beneath it the water was twelve feet deep.

I threw my coat over my head, peeked into the water, and made out a large beaver lying on the bottom.

We fastened a trap to the end of a pole, and with it reached into the water, snapped the trap on one of the beaver's feet, and brought it to the surface. It had a big prime pelt. The animal was missing two toes.

During that winter we saw many moose, and had to be careful to avoid their concentrations. They were cranky, and a dog team is a tempting target. Snow was at least seven feet deep on the level, tough going even for the long-legged moose. We always went way around them. They seemed to have plenty of feed. Their problem was wolves, but they had places tromped down here and there where they could put up a good fight.

Along the trail toward McGrath was Mountain Climber roadhouse run by a German national named August Scharfe. He also trapped, basing himself at his roadhouse. Residents of the region called him The Lying Dutchman—World War I hadn't made Germans popular in the U.S. He dropped by our camp for lunch now and then.

He insisted we should use smoke bombs dropped into their lodges to get beaver. We told him we didn't believe in their use. One day while we were gone he passed through and left about fifteen smoke bombs on our table.

"Now what in Tophet will we do with them?" Perley asked.

"We'll destroy them before we have company and get a bad reputation," I told him.

Accordingly, we built a big fire and tossed the bombs into it. Not the best idea. The valley filled with smoke and it stuck for two days. Even on the third day, with the smoke gone, we could smell traces of the bombs.

"It wouldn't surprise me if they saw that smoke from Anchorage," Perley wryly suggested.

About a week before we broke camp I was driving the dog team back to camp with three beaver carcasses for skinning. The temperature was below zero. As we came to the bridge, as usual, the dogs put on a burst of speed. As they passed the bridge center, I heard an ominous crack, and the bridge collapsed.

Suddenly, the sled and I were in the water. Some of the dogs had reached the far bank, but other dogs were in the water with me.

I let out a whoop, and Perley came running. I swam to the bank, crawled out, and headed for camp. My clothes immediately started to freeze.

Perley pulled the dogs and sled out of the drink while I got into dry clothes, wondering what had happened.

Unknown to us, beaver living in the pool had been gnawing on the bridge's cottonwood stringers, gradually weakening it. They were near camp and, instead of trapping them, we had made pets of them. We remembered seeing wood chips on the bottom, but spruce boughs and snow hung across the stringers, and we didn't see that they were being undermined.

Perley and I left the Skwentna in April with a load of sixty-six beaver skins. All were "large" or "blanket" (trade categories for beaver pelts). With more traps we could have easily doubled our catch. However, we were satisfied.

We sold them to Louie Schulman in Anchorage for a tidy sum that was far more than we expected.

During the summer of 1923 we again worked for the U.S. Geodetic Survey in Alaska.

That fall Perley felt the home ties pulling, and returned to Maine. In Anchorage, I acquired a fancy dog team. Then came an emergency call from Susitna Station Roadhouse. Our good friend Mrs. Johnson was very ill. Could I help by using my dog team to get her to Nancy, where she could get better care?

From Anchorage I shipped my dogs via the Alaska Railroad to Nancy, and raced with them to Susitna Station. I wrapped Mrs. Johnson in sleeping bags and blankets, loaded her into the sled, and took her to Nancy. There was little snow, and the trail was rough. The poor woman must have suffered agonies on that bumpy ride, but I didn't hear a word of complaint.

At Nancy the good neighbors turned out to help her. Sadly, Mrs. Johnson died shortly.

I drove the dogs to Talkeetna, where I put in most of the winter. It was a sleepy little town, but it was on the railroad, which provided a little local action. I rented a cabin and hauled firewood from across the Susitna river. I soon met Scottie MacKenzie, an old chap wintering there. He proposed that I move from my rented cabin into his. He would wash the dishes and saw firewood; I would cook and haul the wood. It seemed like a fine idea, and I accepted.

Scottie spent most of his evenings at the roadhouse run by a Mr. Neuman, a very fine old man. They played pan (panguingue—a card game popular in Alaska), and I guess poker, but the pots were mostly groceries. Scottie came home with a sack full of first class edibles nearly every night.

The games weren't taken very seriously; if a player got the worst of it, Scottie and the others dropped sacks of groceries off at his cabin. The idea was to make sure that everybody was eating.

Those were golden days. If one wanted ptarmigan for a feed, it was only necessary to go to the bank of the Susitna River with a .22 rifle, and a few well-aimed shots produced the goods.

From Talkeetna I moved on to Fairbanks to put down roots. It seemed to me that friendly Fairbanks was the place to be.

The population in the Territory in the early 1920s was about 55,000. By 1930 it was 59,000. It was easy to keep track of people, even though they might live at considerable distance.

I knew when Jack Rimmer died a few years later on his trapline. Mac MacElroy cooked at various mining camps for many years after that winter. I used to visit with him from time to time.

A few years after our winter of beaver trapping, Bill Dennison drowned in the Skwentna River when his boat swamped. A man and his sister who were with him managed to get ashore. The man pulled his sister across a floating log and pushed it to the beach. He lit a fire, and made a bed of spruce boughs. Having accomplished this, he lay down and died. The sister walked to McDougal, a small camp near where the boat swamped.

August Scharfe, who ran the Mountain Climber Roadhouse, was a loner, not very popular, but outside of the smoke bombs, we found he was not a bad sort. A few winters after we left, he disappeared from his trapline. Although a search was made, no trace of him was found. Everything was shipshape at his home cabin. Any one of many things could have happened to him—a fall through a hole in the ice, a broken leg and freezing to death, a heart attack, caught in an avalanche.

Life in bush Alaska could be precarious, it seemed especially so in the early days when there were many lone trappers.

Fairbanks became home. Even as this is written, forty plus years later, I don't know of a better place to live.

The Good Life: Fairbanks in the Mid-1920s

Sam's house was filled with and surrounded by water during the 1967 Fairbanks flood. For days he sat at his highest window, which was open, surveying his unintentional lakefront property and passing boats. He posted a crude sign below the window: "August 14, 1967, Fairbanks, Alaska. 48 inches of water and still a damned good place to live."

—FROM A LETTER TO THE AUTHOR FROM CAROL PHILLIPS, WHO SPENT A WEEK ACROSS KELLUM STREET FROM SAM'S HOUSE DURING THE FLOOD.

I MOVED TO FAIRBANKS in the fall of 1924. I thought it was for keeps. For $150 I bought a comfortable cabin on a dandy lot on Barnette Street. I lived there for a year or two and sold it for the same sum. I then bought a comparable lot behind the old school house. It had a picket fence around it, a cache, and a livable cabin. That school house later burned down one night when it was 50 below zero.

The town had a distinct life style, and many interesting citizens. During winter, traffic consisted of horses and dog teams. Big dog teams occasionally arrived in town from along the Yukon River, and occasionally from the Kuskokwim, Koyukuk, and Tanana valleys. These were mostly freighting teams, and no teams of today compare. They were well trained and could pull big loads all day long.

Dog fights were common, sometime occurring between two teams, occasionally three. When a fight started with its howls and roars, every loose dog in town, regardless of how distant, came pell mell to get into the fight. The big, tough, and loose town dogs, of which there were plenty, were no match for the big sled dogs of the river towns. Usually after one sharp-toothed slash from a

Sam, at Fairbanks in 1925, using his motorcycle to pull a sled.
Sam O. White, courtesy of DRAHS

Yukon sled dog, if it wasn't too late, the townie fled. They had great courage on arrival at the fight, but it quickly evaporated when they lost a chunk of hide.

Dog teams preferred to travel on the board sidewalks instead of the streets. One theory was that it put them closer to the sides and corners of buildings, and to telephone poles. The base of every downtown light or telephone pole in winter accumulated a big yellow glacier cone as far up as the biggest dogs could reach.

Household water was delivered by horse-drawn rigs. One well-known water man with a team of large horses used a big tank wagon in the summer. In winter he had a tank sled with a built-in Yukon stove to keep the drain valves and water from freezing.

There was no drainage system in the red light district on Fourth Street, and the girls threw waste water out on the board sidewalks, where, of course, it froze. One day when it was about sixty below zero, and ice fog limited visibility to less than the width of the street, while walking up Cushman street I heard a roar of rage coming from Fourth Street.

I hustled over there and found Deputy Marshal Jack Buckley and another guy trying to help a water man to his feet. He had been delivering two five-gallon tins of water to one of the girls when he stepped on the ice formed from tossed-out waste water. His feet went out from under him and his head hit the ice first, knocking him out. And, of course, he spilled the water in the two tins.

He came to shortly to find himself lying on his back, frozen down. Try as he could, he couldn't break loose. He became angry and started to roar.

I arrived, and the three of us managed to lift him to his feet, but in so doing we ripped him loose from the frozen-down back of his leather coat. This in no way alleviated his anger, and it appeared he might try to clean up on the three of us if we didn't get out of his way.

He finally calmed and went his way, still grumbling.

I had a dog team, and three or four ten-gallon friction-top milk cans with which I usually hauled my own water from Rabbit Island, where Theo Van Bibber boarded dogs and kept his own dogs.

Van Bibber was an old-time market hunter when game meat was all that was available in Fairbanks and vicinity. Completion of the Alaska Railroad in 1923 ended most market hunting; refrigerated meat could then be brought in by sea and rail.

Powerfully built, Van Bibber stood six foot two. He had a foghorn voice; you could hear him whisper from a block away. He always had a large team of big well-trained dogs. He fed them well, and worked them hard. He was also a great gardener, and in summer he gave away many fresh vegetables. Mrs. Van Bibber made the best home-made sauerkraut in the world—for many years she annually put up a small keg for me.

The water at Van Bibber's place on Rabbit Island was very good. A hand-operated pump was inside the well house, and all were welcome to help themselves.

My route home from Rabbit Island went through town, and along the way I was often invited into a one cabin or another for a doughnut or a piece of pie. To be polite I'd usually offer my host a few gallons of the fine Rabbit Island water. I seldom arrived home with a full load.

One day as I passed a cabin surrounded by a picket fence and an open gate, the door opened and a housewife busily swept out odds and ends. A big yellow cat stood beside her. My dogs spotted the cat. At that point I lost control. With excited yips the entire team sprinted through the gate and up the steps. Fortunately, the sled jammed in the gateway. Nevertheless, five or six of my dogs managed to get into the house.

The cat, dog-wise like most cats in Fairbanks, disappeared. With her broom, the lady started whacking the yelping and barking invaders. The broom broke off, leaving her with the wood handle, with which she continued to lay about. I was soon among the excited dogs with my own persuader, and they were soon subdued. I dragged them out of the cabin to the sidewalk, where I hitched them firmly to a power pole.

I went back to survey the damage. It looked considerable, and I visualized spending a good part of the next few years paying the tab. However, the good lady got another broom and went to work. She straightened the tipped-over chairs, and rearranged the rugs—then poured me a cup of coffee and cut me a slice of apple pie.

Not to be outdone, I went to my sled and surveyed my water supply. When the sled had jammed in the gateway it had tipped, and much of the water had leaked away. I gave the lady what water I had left and went back for another load. I made it home this time without encountering any cats.

Damages? One household broom.

A year or so later I bought a motorcycle and pulled my sled around town with it, thus avoiding the many untoward things that can go awry with a dog team.

ONE NOVEMBER a little Jewish chap showed up in town at about the time the thermometers squeaked down to forty and fifty below. He was slight and short, and wore an overcoat that was many sizes too large for him. It covered his feet and brushed the ground or snow as he walked. He was odd-enough-appearing in the overcoat, but to top it off he wore a Boston bean-pot hat (a derby) and a pair of oversize shoepacks someone had given him.

He hung around the tavern run by Billy Root, and the Horse-shoe Cigar Store run by Harry Phillips. One day at the cigar store I overheard him ask a long-time Fairbanksan to loan him a rifle.

"Just for tomorrow. I want to go out and shoot a moose," the little man explained.

Others in the store grinned and rolled their eyes. Moose weren't common near town, and the little man didn't appear to be a hunter. Nevertheless the fellow loaned him a rifle.

Next morning the "walking overcoat" got as far as the foot of the hill where the new cemetery is located. There he shot a cow and a calf moose. They dropped right in the road.

This was just prior to formation of the Alaska Game Commission, when some semblance of game laws arrived. At the time the Territory's game laws were sketchy. I could never find a book or pamphlet of the game laws. No hunting or trapping license was required.

One local Territorial game warden clerked in a hat store. He occasionally made a trip afield when funds were available. Another had not left town to spend any of his allotment. He was informed that the $750 he had must be spent before the year ended and the deadline was approaching. He went to a cabin outside town and spent the money on simulated boat trips and per diem. He seemed grateful that he had been tipped off to the deadline.

After killing the moose, the "walking overcoat" hired a man with a team of horses and a wagon to haul them into town where he sold them for $100. That was a lot of money then, even in Fairbanks.

The cold was getting to the little man, and he used his hundred dollars for transportation out of Alaska to Stateside. That was the last Fairbanks ever saw of him.

SPEAKING OF MONEY, at the time in Alaska's Interior the smallest piece of acceptable change was a two bit piece (twenty five cents). If you put two dimes and a nickel on a counter, or any other combination for twenty five cents, it wasn't accepted; it had to be a single two bit piece.

If you were buying a small item that cost less than two bits, sometimes the merchant gave it to you, saying he would add the amount to your next purchase.

I remember buying a jar of mentholatum at the Mackintosh and Kubon Drugstore. The manufacturer had labeled it to sell for seventy five cents.

"How much?" I asked. "It's seventy-five cents the world over, but one-dollar-and-a-half here," I was told.

The merchant then laughed heartily and added, "It's the freight, you know."

A PAIR OF identical twins of Scandinavian descent lived in Fairbanks. Their oldest and best friends claimed they couldn't tell them apart. They looked alike, and dressed alike. I have forgotten their names, but they were popularly known to everyone as "Coat and Vest." Some claimed they were so identical that from day to day they got their own identity mixed up; they didn't know themselves apart.

They were a slight, well-liked pair, each tipping the scales at about 140 pounds. They worked in the mines in various creeks that surround Fairbanks.

They always came to town to celebrate July 4th, at which time they would get slightly tanked up. On one July 4th, one of them went to the Model Cafe for breakfast. After eating he sneaked out without paying. Shortly, his brother arrived and sat up to the same counter to order breakfast.

"You just had your breakfast and ran out without paying," the waiter accused.

"No," Coat said. "I haven't been in here today, and I've had no breakfast."

An argument developed, during which Vest arrived and announced to the discomfited waiter that he wanted to pay for the breakfast he had eaten.

Next, Coat hired a taxi and cruised around town and ran up a sizable tab. He stepped into a blind pig (prohibition era bar)for a drink, and disappeared, leaving the taxi driver holding the sack. Shortly, Vest showed up and the driver collared him for the bill.

"I haven't ridden in your taxi, and I don't owe you a thing," Vest claimed. The argument built, and just before it came to blows, Coat showed up to pay his bill to the confused cabbie.

These two spent the entire fourth playing such tricks on different citizens of Fairbanks.

There was another character of Scandinavian descent who also worked on the creeks, and who had a unique way of celebrating the fourth. He was a well-liked and good man who never caused any trouble.

On each 4th of July, he engaged a taxi for the day. He then sat in solitary splendor in the middle of the rear seat, eyes glazed and fixed straight ahead as the taxi cruised around and around town. He carried his likker with him, and remained in a dazed but happy condition during his long ride.

I USED TO VISIT a spry little 80-year-old man who lived in an old log cabin on Wendell Avenue. He had a fine cook stove and a good supply of firewood. I cannot remember his name.

I had a very poor cook stove in my cabin, and asked if I could use his stove to make a supply of beans and doughnuts for the trail. We called it chuck in those days. He would furnish half the food material, the fuel, and the cook stove. I was to do the cooking and freezing.

He agreed, and I went to work. First I cooked a large quantity of the famous bayo beans, which are no longer available. They were the favorite of Alaska's sourdoughs. The trick in cooking them was to boil them with ham hocks until they were almost done. Then, in the last few minutes, the beans were cooked dry.

We took the nearly cooked beans to an unheated building in which no one was living and spread them atop a large table, where the individual beans froze solid.

We poured the frozen beans into ten-pound flour sacks and tied the sacks. When moved they rattled like buckshot. The frozen ham hocks were sacked separately.

When on the trail, one dipped enough beans for a meal, added water and a ham hock, and brought the combination to a boil.

All the next day I made doughnuts, which we also froze and bagged.

We split the results equally, and we were both happy.

This little old friend left Fairbanks the following summer when I was out in the hills, leaving no forwarding address. I never saw him again, nor could I locate him. I understand he went to finish his days with relatives in the states.

ONE WINTER I left Fairbanks with my dog team to work at nearby Goldstream. I left two fat mountain sheep in my cache, of which I'd used a small part of one.

I boarded at Whitehorse Smith's restaurant at Fox, and fared very well. His cook was Miss Geddes, an elderly spinster, who saw to it personally that everyone had plenty of good food to eat.

Old-time humor often had an odd twist, as in the case of Whitehorse Smith's name. He was a nice old man. We called him Whitehorse because he *didn't have* a white horse. The crick was filled with Smiths, and most of them seemed to have white horses. But this Smith didn't have a white horse. His horse was another color. So everyone called him "Whitehorse."

One day Chief Deputy Marshal Jack Buckley and Deputy Ben Thompson arrived at Fox via dog team. They were heading for a creek near Olnes where a prospector had become a mental case. He was also suffering from weakness and malnutrition.

A friend had found him at the bottom of his thirty-five-foot shaft, too weak to climb the ladder. The friend had managed to get him to his cabin, and had then hightailed it to town to report to the Marshal.

Late that evening they brought the man to Fox and to Whitehorse Smith's restaurant, where they remained for the night. Kindly Miss Geddes cooked the most delicate and delicious things for the poor man, and at first allowed him a little food only every hour or so.

When he left for Fairbanks with the Marshals next morning, he had regained some strength, and his mentality had improved on everything except one subject.

As the party prepared to leave, he urgently tried to convince everyone there that all he had to do was get a grubstake so he could go back to his mine shaft and remove three more feet of earth from the bottom of the hole. That done, there would be millions lying there waiting for his gold pan. He was well along in years, and I never saw him again.

WHITEHORSE SMITH'S restaurant was crude, compared with present-day eating places. The food was plentiful and good, and there was a homespun aspect about the place. Miss Geddes presided over the kitchen and lunch counter with a grace that left nothing to be desired.

A number of us had bunks in another building, and Whitehorse himself slept just off the dining room on a couch with plenty of bedding. As one walked into this "bedroom", which was a big room containing a wide variety of junk, from steam hoists to gold pans and shovels, the floor shimmied and creaked ominously.

Leaning against the wall over each end of his bed were four-to-eight-foot-long mammoth tusks that had been uncovered in frozen ground by mining. Their butts rested on the rickety floor. These tusks weighed hundreds of pounds and formed an arch over his bed. If they had fallen they'd have driven his bed through the floor.

SEVERAL OLD-TIMERS lived at Fox that winter, working for the Fairbanks Exploration Company. They decided to throw a weekend party in one of their cabins. Since I had a mountain sheep and a half in my Fairbanks cache I told them I'd retrieve the half sheep for the party.

Come Saturday I hooked up my dog team and drove to town and my cabin. I had just lit a lamp, and had a fire started, when a knock came on my door. At my bidding a little, old, stooped white-haired man came in. He had an impressive handlebar mustache, also snow white.

He said, "Pardner I got sort of fed up on moose meat, so I went into your cache and took a few sheep chops, a roast, and some stew meat.

He added, "I had lots of good fat moose meat, so I left you some good T bones and a few roasts."

Indeed he had. For the few pounds of sheep he had taken, he left me double the amount of moose meat, and in choice cuts beside.

I assured him that although I was a cheechako (newcomer), I knew the customs of the country, and what he had done was ok with me, and that I appreciated having the moose meat.

I returned to Fox with what was left of the half sheep and the moose meat, and on the next weekend we had our party and it was a swell affair that I still like to remember.

AT THE TIME there were few permanent buildings in Fairbanks, Even on Cushman, the main drag, and on Front (First) there were many vacant and dilapidated buildings. I remember a vacant building near the Model Cafe on First Street with windows out and a door hanging by one hinge. A few bums slept there in summer. All sidewalks, where there were any, were board. The boards shrank in the sun, leaving cracks wide enough to trap the high heels of such ladies who elected to walk in them.

On Cushman Street, from the corner by the bridge to the jewelry store on Second, was a vacant lot which was considerably lower than the sidewalk. A skookum railing had been built to guard anyone from a tumble into the vacant lot.

On summer days eight or ten men sat on this railing, waiting for a lady or ladies to get a high heel caught. This was an opportunity for the chivalrous to leap to help extract the lady—and of course with the potential of being able to get a hand on an ankle—or better.

One day I saw six or eight men sitting on the rail. As they had done for months, they were whittling grooves in the railing with pocket knives. Two women came tripping along, and sure enough, one caught her heel in the walk.

The men all surged as one to get off the rail to go to her aid, but the whittling had taken its toll, and the railing broke. Every man tumbled into the vacant lot, bottoms up and heels flying.

The two women laughed until they were near hysterics. Other spectators, including me, also roared.

MINING (MOSTLY FOR GOLD), trapping, and commercial fishing (mainly for salmon) were then the economic engines of the Territory. Fairbanks, of course, was the center of much gold mining. Nearby Goldstream Creek was well named. Sluice boxes were everywhere there. Trestles that supported water flumes crisscrossed that stream like jackstraws. I remember walking up the creek and seeing crisscrossed flumes, ten, twenty, and more feet off the ground.

During winter when the ground was frozen, miners removed what they called "dumps"—gold-rich material—from their claims. In the spring when the world thawed, they'd bring water via the flumes from different creeks to wash their dumps to extract the gold in sluice boxes.

To make their claims pay, they had to find rich gold pockets. A seepage pond lay between the junction of Goldstream and Engineer Creek. The nearer miners got to it from all directions, the bigger the nuggets. When a miner got too close, water flooded his claim. It was too big an operation for small miners to drain the pond.

A woman owned several claims near there. She had a log cabin with a cupola on the roof in which she sat and watched the men working her claim. She had field glasses and .30–30 carbine handy, and kept an eye on her men.

Eventually the Fairbanks Exploration Company moved in with a dredge. First they sluiced off the thirty-five or forty feet of overburden, or muck, then they ran the dredge through. The oldtime miners who had fought that seepage pond would like to have known how much gold was under it. The F.E. Company could have told them, but they never released that information.

Sheep Hunt

I have turned sissy. I have quit hunting. Oh sure, I go to the moose
pasture, but I do not hunt. When a thieving black bear cornered me
in the shack, instead of shooting him I dumped a pot of hot tea on his
unsuspecting head, pot and all. Man did he light out. He bellered like
a bull, and when he hit the woods he ran smack into a birch tree
and let out an agonizing bawl. I saw him no more."
—SAM O. WHITE. LETTER TO THE REV. PATTERSON KELLER, MARCH 16, 1966.

IN THE FALL OF 1924 I lived at Fairbanks in a two-room cabin on
Barnette Street. It seemed appropriate to take a trip to the Wood
River mountain sheep country to collect my winter's meat. Moose
and caribou were out, as the mating season had passed for them,
leaving their meat unpalatable. Mating season for sheep is later,
and their meat is good until about the first of November.

I owned five big well-trained sled dogs. English-born Sourdough Todd Harrington, who had done much prospecting and
some mining, also had a well-trained team of five dogs. He too
needed winter's meat, and we cast our lot together.

One sharp morning we took off from Fairbanks with our two
dog teams on the Wood River trail, and after a couple of days of
diligent travel, arrived at the Cottonwood Cabin on the bank of
Wood River. This river, which flows northwest from high in the
Alaska Range, drains into the Tanana River.

Here we remained overnight, and next day we drove our teams
up the frozen Wood River. Todd knew the country, and he pre-
dicted overflows on the river ice. He was correct, and it took us
two days to reach the Sheep Creek cabin, which is roughly sixty
straight-line miles from Fairbanks. This was a well-built cabin on

the bank of Sheep Creek, a tributary to Wood River, and adjacent to sheep country.

We parked our sleds and moved in. Todd was familiar with the country, and described it to me, warning me to watch for snow slides.

Next morning Todd elected to follow up Sheep Creek, and since I was unfamiliar with the area, he suggested I follow the base of the mountains on the northeast side. This sounded good to me, for I would be in position to glass the hills for sheep all along. We were to meet on top of the mountain six to seven miles farther on, and return to camp together.

I got to the rendezvous point first and soon saw Todd approaching. He was about half a mile away as I sat waiting. The mountainside to the north was sheer for 800 or 1,000 feet, and drifting snow had extended the crest away from, and level with, the ridge crest. It overhung the cliff by about 200 feet. To my horror, Todd nonchalantly walked out on this overhang, following the edge of the hard-drifted snow.

I didn't dare attempt to warn him, as, at that distance I couldn't communicate the message I needed to convey. If I tried to warn him, I feared he might stop to try to understand, and thereby spend more time on the snow bank. All I could do was sit with my heart in my mouth and watch.

He finally walked off the overhang and reached the shoulder of the mountain. As he neared, he realized something was bothering me, and quickened his pace, and looked at me inquiringly.

I pointed at the overhang. It looked wicked from our position. Todd looked for a long moment and said, "My God, did I walk out over that?"

We headed back to camp, hoping to come across rams we had seen earlier, but they were gone. We separated, and each of us picked up a few ptarmigan for the pot.

Next morning we again split up, and decided not to rendezvous. I hadn't walked far when I spotted a band of seven big, fat rams. I climbed above them, and on all fours, came out on a pile of rocks within 100 yards of my quarry. I took two of the biggest and fattest, dropping them so quickly that they were down before the others fled.

I dressed them and lay them on a rock to cool and drain. I wanted to see the country a little farther on, and it was early, so I continued hiking.

I was soon opposite the huge overhang Todd had walked over the previous day. Below it was a deep, V-shaped, ravine that ran down to timber. I had crossed it the previous day, so decided to do so again. It was about half full of snow, with a solid crust that had held me nicely; in fact, I had to walk heavily on heels to keep from sliding.

Confidently, I headed across this 200-foot-wide ravine. I was about a mile and half above timber, and about two miles from the cliff and the huge overhang.

I got about half way across when I became aware of a downward movement, and a soft swishing sound came from beneath the snow and at my feet. It was an avalanche. I quickly leaped for the far bank, but didn't reach it. All creation erupted beneath me. I whizzed down the mountain at great speed. Suddenly, I was on my back, and it seemed as if I were lying on a big cake of revolving snow. Another big cake of overhanging snow slid over me, blotting the sky.

Next I sensed a violent jar and shock, and found myself in a pile of rocks speeding headfirst into alder brush, which was licking the daylights out of me.

I hung on to an alder for dear life. A torrent of snow rushed past with the speed of a free fall. Hurricane force wind battered me, and created a blizzard of snow. I heard boulders grinding against boulders, and big thumps as boulders struck boulders. Sometimes the snow flood crested six feet above me; sometimes it was at my feet.

At last it subsided. It had continued for perhaps two to three minutes.

I looked around and realized I was still in a most precarious situation. I had been whisked a good half mile down that ravine in a twinkling. Luckily, I had been cast onto a rock pile, a position I attained through no effort of my own. It was God's will. The only reason the blast of wind hadn't blown me out of there was because I had clung to the alders.

I peered toward the head of the ravine at the overhanging snow bank and saw that a comparatively small fraction of it had fallen. It had filled the ravine to overflowing.

As I watched, another huge piece of overhang broke off and hurtled into the head of the ravine. From my position, it looked like slow motion. I quickly ducked into the alders and embraced them tightly.

Immediately a great rushing sound came, and the next instant the valley crested again with snow, six feet over my head, and the blast of wind was even greater than before. It was all I could do to cling to the alders.

When the wind subsided, I stood. I glanced below me into the timber and the sight wasn't reassuring. Enough snow was piled up to bury much of Fairbanks. It was filled with black streaks of dirt, trees, broken branches, and rocks—a distressing sight.

I had about all I could take. I started thinking of returning to camp. But I was on the wrong side of the ravine. I had to cross its full width to reach camp.

Again, I surveyed the overhang, and my observations weren't comforting. Less than half of the overhanging snow had dropped.

I watched for a long time and considered going around the bottom of the slide. However, I didn't feel up to this long hike.

I finally got my courage up and was about to step off into the gully, when another big chunk fell off the overhang. Again, I dived for the rock pile, and once more clung to the life-saving alders.

A thought came. "I think I'm probably a brave man, but this isn't the kind of death I've had in mind."

Then came the same thunderous roar, the hurricane force wind, and the lashing back and forth of the alders. Branches flew off the frozen alders.

Another thought came. "Each time this happens I see something different."

Again the wind subsided and snow stopped moving. That surge had crested even higher than the previous ones, and a windrow of snow was shoved into my rock pile.

I looked long and searchingly at the overhang. Much still hung there, seemingly poised to drop. I waited and waited, and no more came.

There had been plenty of time for me to have recrossed the ravine, but of course there was no way of knowing until it was too late.

I finally decided to take a chance. I swiftly moved across the gully and up the far side, pretending there was no danger. I had reached the point where it didn't seem to matter.

I climbed out of the gully and headed towards camp without a backward look. I had gone perhaps half a mile when I heard a familiar sullen roar behind me. Another chunk of the overhang had fallen. I didn't even glance back, but kept hiking toward camp.

Todd was there, stirring a kettle of ptarmigan stew. Without looking up, he commented, "Did you hear the snow slides? It's a bad day for slides, so I came back to camp."

Then he looked up. My moleskin parka was in rags, and I was bruised all over and lame. "My God, are you hurt?" he asked.

I was unhurt; only bruised and scared stiff. Todd, being English, brewed me a pot of tea and it was done correctly. Never in all my life have I had a cup or a dozen cups of tea that tasted so good.

Todd insisted that I get some sleep. Afterward he served me a bowl of delicious, hot ptarmigan stew.

The day was still young, although it seemed to me an age had passed since breakfast. Todd hiked into the hills and soon had his two rams. I managed to retrieve the two I had killed. We left our sheep meat in the cabin's cache where it was safe and went up river to visit with our Fairbanks friend, Theo Van Bibber. We enjoyed his stories of earlier days for a couple days.

Then it became cold, and we mushed back to the Sheep Creek cabin where we spent one night. Next morning we started down Wood River with our loads of meat. It continued to grow colder, and we ran into frequent overflows on the river ice, forcing us to detour and lose time.

We came to what had been a stand of spruce timber, but during the previous summer a forest fire had destroyed many acres. Todd remembered a nearby cabin he had seen several times. "Wait here. I'll see if I can find it," he said.

Our dogs were all in, and it was now 45 below. Todd disappeared into the burned area, and a half hour later I heard a whoop and steered the dogs to where Todd waited at a small cabin. The door and window were gone, but we had canvas enough to cover them. We set up our Yukon stove and soon the cabin was cozy.

We thawed some "buckshot" beans, (bayo beans) of which we had a full bag.

We reached Cottonwood cabin next day, and it continued to grow colder, and we were still beset with overflows and many weary and time-consuming detours. Next morning, when we left Cottonwood cabin, the temperature was 55 below. We then reached the small cabin occupied by Charlie "Moose" Johnson. Although it was crowded, he welcomed us and served up moose stew and bannock.

Next morning Charlie lifted his head from his pillow and peered toward the cabin door. "You boys aren't going anywhere today. It's 60 below," he said.

I wondered how he could tell the temperature from his bunk. He later showed me where he had driven a long spike through the cabin wall so that it protruded some distance inside. He had calibrated it with his outside thermometer by filing a notch with every five degrees of frost that appeared on it. He could see the notches from his bunk.

We stayed with Charlie that day. By the next morning it had warmed to 35 below. After the deep cold it seemed warm. As we traveled along the sled trail on the Tanana Flats I both smelled and saw smoke and, as we rested the dogs, I asked Todd about it.

"Several-feet-thick layers of peat are commonly found under tundra swamps. Once they catch fire, they can smolder for years. A peat fire has been burning here for twenty years. Sometimes it breaks out and big sections of swamp falls into it. If we come to one near the trail, keep moving. Don't let the dogs stop. The fire could be burning under the trail."

We soon came to a place about 300 feet off the trail where a section about 200 feet square had fallen in. It was fascinating, and I stopped the dogs and climbed up on the sled for a better look. Steam and smoke were rising from the ground, and snow was melted from a large area. Beneath the smoke and steam I caught glimpses of live embers glowing from the hole.

I heard a shout behind me. Todd had caught up. "Get to hell out of there," he warned.

I did, and later when we stopped for a pot of tea, he scolded me mildly, although I could see he was seething. "Never stop near one of those places. I've known cabins to disappear in them."

He said that cabin occupants could feel the ground getting warm and they knew to move out before the ground caved in. Trapper and prospector cabins mostly have hard-packed ground, not wood floors.

Near Clear Creek Buttes, as we came to a straight stretch of trail, we saw a contraption moving toward us. A man was pulling it. Smoke was rising from it. I stopped and looked, but couldn't figure it out.

Todd stopped his team near mine and explained, "That's Old George Nelson. He traps here, and lives on Clear Creek. His sled is twenty-two inches wide with canvas stretched over it like a covered wagon. He has a tiny wood-burning stove in it, with his sleeping bag. When he hits the trail, he has his camp right with him. He'll go out for several days with it and camp whenever he gets tired. Or, he'll stop and snooze whenever he feels like it. He has no dogs."

We came to Old George and he insisted we have a hot cup of coffee. George sat inside his covered sled and reached out and poured for us as we sat on the edge of my sled.

I couldn't help but think, "What a country this is, with people like Van Bibber, the Johnsons, and the Nelsons. Who could resist its call?"

We reached Fairbanks that night. The hunt was ended and we had our winter's meat.

Todd Harrington was a wonderful chap with whom to hunt.

In his Fairbanks cabin he lived the life of a sourdough. The cabin had no floor—just packed earth. You couldn't see much of it, for he had row after row of magazines stacked, so the floor space was reduced to trails that ran from the door to the bed, to the table, to the stove.

His light was a single candle on the table and stuck in a milk can.

One evening I called on Todd and found he had a single electric clear-glass light bulb hanging from the center of the cabin. He was proud of it and told me, "Now I can sit anywhere in the cabin and read. I can also see to cook."

A few weeks later I again visited him. The light bulb was gone. He was back to the single candle. Before I could ask, he explained, "My light bill last month was ten dollars. I can't afford that. Besides, if I kept the light bulb I was going to have to clean up. The candle doesn't show the dust and dirt."

Todd died a few years later, and Fairbanks lost a kind and honest citizen.

7

Canoeing the Salcha

*In my day and age, one was not considered a canoeman unless he could
snub a canoe on a canoe pole, with a load, either down or upstream.
I did this one time at McKinley Park for old-time guide Dan Kennedy
and won his respect. I am told they do it yet in Maine. In Alaska
I have never seen anyone with a canoe do more than a little
half-hearted poling upstream in mild water.*
—SAM O. WHITE. LETTER TO AUTHOR JULY 8, 1975.

IN THE FALL OF 1924, the U.S. Coast and Geodetic Survey sold
all of its horses in Fairbanks and pulled out of the Interior. They
arranged for me to stay in Alaska so that during summer, 1925,
I could carry out a reconnaissance survey from Fairbanks to the
Yukon River village of Eagle.

To determine if a route up the Salcha River valley was feasible
for the recon survey, in June, 1925 I made a canoe trip up the Salcha, which enters the Tanana River roughly forty miles southeast
of Fairbanks.

One of the advantages of this route was the Alaska Road Commission winter trail that ran up the Salcha valley from Munson
to Salchacket. For many miles this trail followed a fairly straight
course, and was suitable for packhorses in summer.

The eighteen-foot guide model canoe I used to ascend the Salcha was made by the Old Town canoe factory in Maine. I grew up
with Old Town canoes in Maine, and felt at home in this one.[1]

---

1. Sam had the unusual technique of using a extra-long paddle and standing when
paddling a canoe. Several photos show him in canoes wearing knee-length leather boots,
popular with outdoorsmen at the time. He didn't plan to do any swimming or wading
while canoeing.

The canoe and I, with my outfit, which included Fox my ninety-pound malemute and companion for the trip, were trucked over the Richardson Highway to the Indian village of Salcha at the junction of the Salcha and the Tanana Rivers.

Fox was a super intelligent dog. I bought him and his four brothers in Anchorage in 1922. He had no bad habits. Fox was a trained leader, and he knew how to boss a team. His life's goal was to please me. He would never run in front of me, unless he had permission, regardless what game showed up.

He quickly learned proper behavior for traveling in a canoe, and I didn't have to worry about him upsetting it. I was offered $300 for him several times, but refused it. I don't think he would have worked for anyone else. Sadly, he died from an illness when he was still young.

The Salcha is a beautiful river with clear water. Although the lower reaches of the Salcha are fairly swift, it is not rough water, as there are no rocks. There are plenty of riffles over gravel bars, however. Upstream travel was about fifty-fifty between poling and paddling. Progress was by no means fast.

This being a spring trip, there was a good head of water. The only cabins along the river were a few belonging to trappers and prospectors. There was virtually no travel on the river at that time of year. Except for Fox, I found myself alone in remote and rugged wilderness.

Moose and bear abounded, and I saw many of both as I slowly traveled upstream. Fox also saw them, often before I did, but he never attempted to leap from the canoe to chase.

I eventually arrived at the Splits, roughly fifty miles as the raven flies from the mouth, and twice that in river miles. It is so-called because here the river forks into two about equal channels, and each drains a separate valley. I took the South Fork. Travel became progressively slower and was nearly all poling with swift water and plenty of rocky riffles. Flowering plants were blooming, and I was close to the both banks. Their scent filled the air, and it was very pretty.

I fired two shots on the trip. The first was at a large black bear. He had cornered a cow moose on a gravel bar and had killed one of her two calves. The dead calf lay on the bar, with big gashes on its flanks and teeth marks on its neck. He had the cow cornered against a bank, trying to kill the other calf.

I took a dim view of this. I was in the current and it was difficult to shoot accurately. I grabbed my .30–06 Winchester model 54 carbine and fired hastily, without really aiming—firing without getting the butt to my shoulder.

I doubt the bear realized what his trouble was, for when I shot he was in close contact with the cow. My bullet hit, and he reacted as if the blow came from the cow, for he danced away from her, probably thinking he'd press his advantage again.

Then, suddenly, he seemed to realize he was in big trouble. He let out a bawl and collapsed. The 180-grain bronze tip had passed through his lungs.

The cow stared at the downed bear, appearing to be dumbfounded. She immediately herded her surviving calf into the woods. As she left, I saw gashes on her rump where she had been raked by the bear's claws.

Fox remained in the background until the moose disappeared. I then gave him permission to worry the dead bear. He dashed in and nipped its rear, and leaped back a few times. He then decided the bear was dead, and, growling fiercely, pounced on it, and chewed its ears. After that he ignored the bear.

The bear was thin, since he was not long out of the den. There was evidence the cow had scored a few hits on him. I skinned a bloody shoulder, and found where one or more of her hoofs had struck, leaving a bloodshot area and much bruised flesh.

The dead calf was ripped by a big swipe on one flank, but the fatal wound appeared to be a bite into the neck. Teeth marks appeared on both sides on top of the neck.

The bear's stomach seemed to be nearly full. I opened it and found five partly-digested hooves of moose calves, and what appeared to be the ends of two partly-digested calf moose noses.

I had read all about the so-called balance of nature, and I thoroughly believed in it. That is, until mankind came along with gunpowder and repeating rifles. Then, it seemed to me, the balance of nature got a little out of whack.

If the bear hadn't been trying to kill that calf, I wouldn't have molested him. My sympathy was with the old cow. She was putting up a good defense, but she obviously needed help.

From the Splits upstream I saw increasingly large bears—all grizzlies. I was in no danger from them, as my progress was slow, and the grating of my iron-shod pole on rocks warned of my approach.

One or two stood their ground until I approached fairly near. In the end they curled their lips to show their fangs, then walked with dignity into the woods. In no way did they exhibit alarm at such a puny creature as I.

I finally arrived as far up the Salcha as I wanted to go. I cached the canoe and stored my little outfit high in a tree, then prepared to scale a nearby high peak. It turned into a three-day trip.

As I ascended the slope at the base of the high, snow-clad, peak, just above me I saw a band of about fifty Dall sheep ewes and lambs. Each had eyes riveted on me. They were alert, but didn't seem to be alarmed. My upward route passed nearby. They trotted off about a hundred yards, seemingly more curious than afraid.

As I climbed higher, I saw a huge, beautiful, grizzly bear digging rocks and turning them over as he searched for parky (ground) squirrels. It seemed to me the energy he expended in no way could be compensated by eating an occasional squirrel. I didn't worry too much about it, leaving it to the bear's judgment. I didn't approach too close to him, as he was a bruiser. Although he must have seen me, he gave no evidence of it, but methodically continued to bound from boulder to boulder, turning them with a front paw, and now and then making a jaws-open dive toward a squirrel.

About one that afternoon I was tired, what with canoeing early in the day, and the climbing. I found a place in the sunshine with a vertical rock at my back and got in a pleasant hour of sleep. I was awakened by Fox poking me with his nose. His hackles were up, but I saw nothing threatening. I never did see what had alarmed him, but I knew well enough that it had to be a bear, as their tracks were all about.

I climbed higher and at last reached the summit, where I had about two hours work in turning angles and observing distant peaks.

Having completed the work, I started down the mountain. It was rocky, and I had to be careful with each step. The peculiar part of the descent was the absence of sheep and bears; I saw none. However, I did see a band of about 1,500 caribou.

My canoe and outfit cached in the tree were untouched. I cooked, and Fox and I had a good feed. Fox, who was long, lean, rangy, and very quick, wasn't really hungry, as he had caught and eaten a number of squirrels on the way down the mountain.

I then caught some sleep, although it was occasionally interrupted by the abundant mosquitoes.

Launching the canoe for the trip downstream was a pleasure; I could ride for a change. The section above the Splits was fairly slow-going. I had to snub on the pole frequently, and drop from one pole hold to another. But after the Splits it was easier going and much faster. There I could let the canoe run on the paddle, and only snub occasionally to drop over a riffle, or around sweepers—trees or branches that had fallen from the banks.

About fifteen miles north of the Richardson Highway I came to a place where the river narrowed from about seventy yards to about thirty feet. Here a powerful current swept around a curve which was lined by huge piles of drift. This channel was clear when I passed upriver earlier, and I didn't think it would be obstructed; I assumed the current was swift enough to keep it clear.

I was mistaken. A cottonwood tree had swung across the river, completely obstructing the channel. It rested about two feet above the water, each end in a tangled pile of drift. I was traveling fast when I swept around the bend, and I could no more stop than I could fly. The bow of the canoe bumped under, and the log caught me in the midriff, lifted me bodily, and dropped me into the swift Salcha.

Strangely, the water didn't feel cold. I was whisked under a drift pile, and I sensed the fading of light. I clawed and swam frantically. For a moment my face dragged on the gravel bottom. Then light reappeared and I swam to the surface. I was behind a drift pile, about fifty feet from shore, in a mild backwater eddy.

I swam to the drift pile. Fox was on it and gleefully ran to me. I was glad to see him; I was feeling pretty lonely.

The canoe was jammed against the drift pile, held there by the powerful current. It was twisted nearly ninety degrees from bow to stern, and the stern was open to the current. Since cedar is resilient, I hoped it wasn't too damaged. But how was I going to break it out of the deadly grip of the current?

I found a long pole to use as a lever. Next, I pulled the bow rope from under the drift pile and tied it to a top log. That way, if it got away from me it wouldn't go cruising by itself downriver.

A half-used can of peanut butter was wedged in the narrow part of the bow—the only food I salvaged. I had tied my surveying instruments in, and they were still there.

I slipped the pole under the stern to lift it above the current. This took several heaves to break the current's grip, but when it broke loose, the current rushed to my aid and washed the stern onto the drift pile, where the canoe teetered in disastrous equilibrium.

I made a loop and a brace in the bow line and slipped it over Fox's head and onto his shoulders, and ordered, "Mush, Fox, mush!"

He threw his ninety pounds into the loop, which resembled a rough Siwash harness. I pulled at the same time. Our combined strength was just enough to yank the canoe out of the water and onto the drift pile.

After dumping the water, I found a few cracked, but not broken, ribs. The canvas wasn't even torn. Relieved of pressure, the canoe had straightened itself and was ready for use.

My iron-shod poling pole was gone. As I looked for a substitute I saw my paddle floating in the eddy behind the drift pile. I retrieved it with a drift pole I had found. Then I saw a dull metallic gleam under the back edge of the drift pile. It was my rifle.

I took off most of my soaked clothing and plunged into the water and under the drift pile, groping for the rifle, but came up with nothing. I climbed out, and again located the metallic gleam. It appeared to have moved. I plunged again, and this time my hand closed on the barrel. I was thankful for that as I climbed back on the drift pile.

I now had one-half can of peanut butter, one paddle, one canoe, my rifle which held five cartridges, a substitute poling pole, surveying instruments, and the wet clothing on my back. I found my hat lodged against the drift pile.

Fox and I climbed into the canoe and continued on. A warm sun dried my clothing. That evening and downstream a ways, I went ashore on a long sandbar with the river on one side, and a slough on the other. Grizzly bear tracks were all over the bar.

I carried matches in a watertight safe in my pocket. For extra drying and evening warmth I built a fire and ate a little peanut butter. I was weary, and both Fox and I stretched out on the warm sand and had a good sleep.

Hours later I awoke with Fox nudging me. His hackles were up. He was rumbling and staring down the sandbar. The sun was low, although the long daylight hours of spring were upon us.

I grabbed my carbine and spotted our visitor, a huge brindle-colored grizzly which stood on hind legs about 150 feet away, staring at Fox and me.

Slowly, I got to my knees. Then, carefully, to my feet. Fox continued to growl. We both stood facing the bear for what seemed like ten minutes. The big bruiser slowly dropped to all fours, turned his back on us, and with great dignity ambled down the bar. When he reached a fringe of willows, he bounded into them and disappeared.

The sun was still warm. I estimated it was two a. m. (my watch had stopped when I went into the water), and I wasn't satisfied with my rest. I rekindled the fire and stretched out for another snooze.

A couple hours later, I awoke with a raging hunger. I heard water splash in the nearby slough and peeked to see several ducks, about 100 feet distant. I rested on one knee and was just pulling a bead on a duck's neck, when I noticed two ducks converging. I held fire until they lined up, and squeezed off a shot. It worked. Two birds floated, dead. The others frantically leaped into flight.

Although Fox had never been trained to retrieve, at my command he plunged into the water and in two trips brought the birds ashore.

I built up the fire, and in a short time I had broiled duck. They were without salt, but tasted good anyway. Fox refused it. An old sourdough later told me that, unless very hungry, most dogs won't eat duck meat. I'm not convinced, but that was the case with Fox that day.

On my hat I had two fish hooks suitable for grayling. In my pocket I had a short piece of fishing line. With a willow pole, I tried using some of the duck meat for bait, but the grayling weren't interested.

I then tied tiny duck feathers to a hook, using a raveling from my shirt. Within half an hour I had plenty of grayling, and Fox had his fill of raw fish.

We arrived at the junction of the Salcha and the Tanana late next day. I hiked the short distance to the Alaska Road Commission camp, where the cook fed me roast beef, vegetables, and soup, topped off with all the apple pie I wanted.

After an overnight rest at the Road Commission camp, Fox and I, in the canoe, headed down the Tanana for Fairbanks. During our absence the road from Salcha to Fairbanks had turned to mud.

We arrived by canoe at Fairbanks a day and a half later, with surveying instruments, my rifle with four cartridges, and two fish hooks, one tied with duck feathers.

Reconnaissance, Shaw Creek to Eagle

The great contrast between then and now, was the amount of game.
It was just loaded. Moose, caribou, mountain sheep—everything.
Now we see very little of that, except in the most remote places.
—Sam O. White's comments on wildlife he saw on his 1925 Shaw Creek
to Eagle reconnaissance to interviewer Neville Jacobs, June 21, 1974.

In 1925, Sam O. White made a reconnaissance survey for the U.S.
Coast and Geodetic Survey through the wilderness from Shaw
Creek, which crosses the Richardson Highway seventy-five miles
southeast of Fairbanks, to Eagle, a village on the bank of the Yukon
River, a straight line distance of about 200 miles. [AUTHOR]

Sam and his partner on the survey, six-foot, powerful Dan McK-
enzie, walked. Six packhorses carried their food, tent, tarps, sleeping
bags, clothing, axe, shovel, rifles, and surveying instruments. Sam's
ninety-pound Malemute, Fox, was included in the party.

"Dan McKenzie could be content as long as he was in the
wilderness. He knew his horses and he was very capable. We just
had a ball all summer long," Sam said in a 1974 interview.

In Sam's log books (field diaries) of this reconnaissance he
mentions eighteen stations he established on various mountains.[1]
The two men also made thirty-two camps along the way, usually
spending two days, but up to four days, at each. Commonly, Sam
climbed peaks to establish two survey stations from each camp.

Among the Sam O. White maps sent to me by Roy Billberg
and his sister, Cathy McKechnie, is a cloth-backed one showing

---

1. Named by Sam: Shaw, Goodpaster, split, Ellen, bleak, desolate, Wilson (in honor of the
president), wolf, comet, attean, somerset, Gordon, hokum, king, lick, table, liberty, bush.

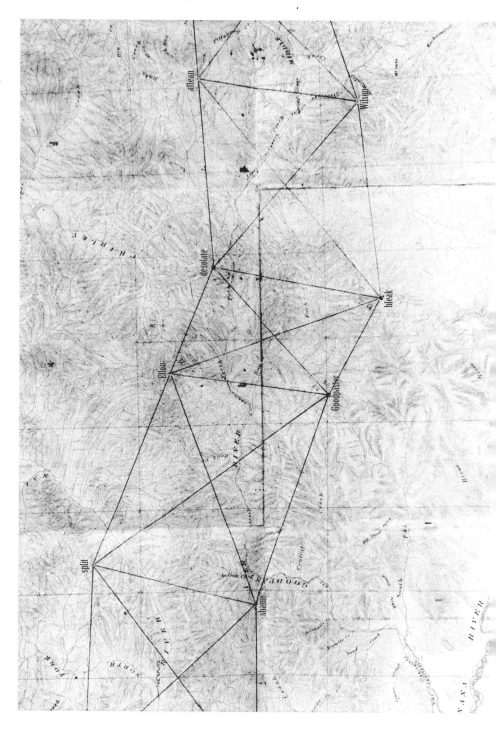

twelve of the triangulation stations Sam mentioned in these diaries. It's probably a copy, made during the 1925 reconnaissance.

The following, in Sam's words, which I have taken largely from his 1974 interview with Neville Jacobs, detail his experiences on this reconnaissance. His log book entries from the trip are in italics.

[SAM] I STARTED preparations for the reconnaissance on July 1, 1925. I planned it to run into the head of the Salcha River, up the Goodpaster River, and down the Fortymile River valleys. This would extend the surveying scheme already in existence, and connect it to the 141st Meridian on the U.S. Canada boundary at Eagle.

The work began by locating a base line at Fairbanks. West Base was selected near the Alaska Railroad tracks west of the city of Fairbanks, about one fourth mile from the Alaska College and School of Mines [now the University of Alaska Fairbanks]. East Base was located near the old Astronomical Station, about one fourth mile west of Fairbanks.

From Shaw Creek, which crosses the Valdez Trail [later named the Richardson Highway] seventy-five miles southeast of Fairbanks, I followed the line from one mountain range to another. It was a quadrangle affair, worked by triangulation.

This job was preparation for making accurate maps of Alaska—upgrading with more precision the crude maps then in existence. With then-current topographic maps, it wasn't uncommon to put two of them together, only to find a river missed connecting by as much as eight or ten miles. Distance measurements for the old maps were often made by pacing off on foot, and, sometimes, by estimating.

We established camps, and from them climbed nearby peaks to establish stations at prominent above-timberline landmarks. Each station, from twelve to about twenty five miles apart, had to be visible from the other stations.

I had a plane table, a magnetic compass, and a telescope. I first established the stations on various peaks. I took bearings from each station and plotted them on paper. It was rather crude, but my

FACING PAGE: *Part of a map prepared by Sam during his 1925 reconnaissance survey from Shaw Creek to Eagle. Sam established eighteen named triangulation stations and measured the angles to the others to form this map (eight stations appear on this segment).* SAM O. WHITE, COURTESY OF CATHY MCKECHNIE

reconnaissance didn't require any more accuracy. The observing party to eventually follow with big, precise instruments, would measure things right down to a hair. We roughed out the route and established stations from which they could work.

Dan McKenzie, my packer, arrived from Seattle with five horses. Another horse was acquired in Alaska. With the six horses, he left Fairbanks on July 6, assisted by Harold Woodward, a temporary extra hand. I remained to arrange shipment of a canoe to Eagle and other details, and followed later by truck.

I arrived at McCarty (near Shaw Creek) on July 11, and found the outfit in camp and everything in fine condition, with the horses getting used to their packs and the swarms of flies that followed them.

Mosquitoes were fierce on much of the trip, and we built smudges to discourage them. The horses soon learned to stand in the smoke.

We started on the flats between the Goodpaster River and Shaw Creek, and, where possible, swung onto the ridges where traveling was much easier.

On July 12, Woodward and I cruised a trail to Quartz Lake. On the 13th we cut and blazed it back to the Richardson Highway.

On July 14 we packed up at 4 p.m. and thus by night travel somewhat avoided murderous swarms of flies and pushflies [Sam called mosquitoes "pushflies"] and the discomfort of the hot sun. At 7 p.m. we said goodbye to Harold Woodward and turned our backs on the highway and other signs of civilization. Harold was the last person we were to see until we arrived at Dome Creek, near the U.S.-Canada boundary eight weeks later.

After leaving the flats and taking to the timber, the inexperienced horses, bothered by swarms of mosquitoes, often left the trails we had cut, and bolted through the timber. The tarps and saddle bags, as well as leather straps, which had seemed to be in good condition, were much deteriorated from previous seasons' use. Each day, after putting in from five to seven hours on the trail, found us repairing bags, straps, and tarps. Thus, between July 14 and July 22, we worked from eighteen to twenty hours each day

On July 22, we arrived and made Camp Eight at the head of Indian Creek, a headwater of the Goodpaster River, roughly sixty straight-line miles from the Valdez Trail. The horses were badly in need of rest.

I left Dan in camp with the outfit, and made a siwash trip to the Salcha River with Fox for company, a handfull of grub, no bed, no extra clothing, and only such instruments as were needed to occupy [establish a station] the mountain peak in question. I traveled nights, slept by day in the sun, and supplemented my food supply with berries and grouse. My last meal on this trip was one tablespoon of powdered milk.

Salmon were running in the Salcha, and I came upon several grizzly bears busily catching them. I needed to cross the river. To avoid these bears I went upstream another bend. I came to a riffle that promised an easy crossing, and there, about 100 yards away were three more fishing grizzlies. Probably, no matter how far I went upstream there would be grizzlies, so I waded across between two groups of bears. I had to help Fox. He wasn't long-legged enough to reach bottom, and I didn't want him to wash downstream into the bears.

We reached the other side safely, but Fox was alarmed at the bears. As we moved through the timber, he walked sideways, watching behind. He kept bumping my shins, warning me about the bears. I'm sure there were bears in the woods, but we missed them.

July 24. Left fire site at 2:30 a.m. and headed for Split station. Hard going. Climbed up side of Mt. thru heavy dangerous slide rock. Arrived at peak at 7 a.m. Slept in sun until 9 a.m. then did observing and left peak, found berry patch and ate, then traveled to river. Saw caribou. Ate last of grub. Posted fire sign. Slept some, then started for camp eight and traveled until 3 p.m. on 25th. Too tired and hungry to go farther. Built fire.

July 25. Slept by fire from 3:30 a.m. until 9 a.m., then found berry patch and ate, then left for camp eight. Somewhat rested but hungry. Arrived at camp eight at about 11 a.m. All in. A H—— of a trip. Traveled day and night on little grub and no bed through rough country.

Next, we went up the Goodpaster River. I gave Dan a landmark to go by, but the "landmark" turned out to be a bear taking it easy. We didn't discover it was a bear instead of a rock until the animal changed his position a couple of times.

July 30th. Left Camp 10 in rain and proceeded upriver. Found caribou horns tangled in telegraph wire. Shot caribou (sorry—poor meat; animal skinny) cut across niggerhead[2] flats. Hard going. Arrived at Johnson Bros. cabin ½ mile below the Forks [Eisenmenger fork and Goodpaster fork] *tired and wet. First cabin on trip.*

---

2. Tight bunches of grass growing close together, with deep crevices between. When walking on them, one tries to balance on top, with the chance of your foot sliding into a foot-deep crevice between bunches.

July 31st. I took siwash outfit and headed for station Goodpaster. Got to peak in rain. Line to Shaw [station] *in doubt. Discarded this point from scheme and returned to camp at midnight plum worn to a frazzle. Selected peak 5070 to be Goodpaster* [station].

Aug 2nd. Climbed Ellen (5600 ft.) [station] *and between showers got first one station and at last all of them. Mountain covered with slide rock but caribou trail made climbing easy. Saw one sheep or goat track.*

On August 11, I came to six sheep where they were bedded on the mountainside. I shot a ram out of the bunch. At the time any ram was legal. A big old ewe jumped up when I shot and ran right up to me and pushed her nose against my leg. The wind was blowing quite hard, and she apparently wanted to get a whiff of me. After bumping me she looked at me in apparent bewilderment, and ran back to where she had been bedded and stood looking at me.

The others then got up one by one. Fox stood beside me. I think the dog is what decided the sheep to leave, for he looked like a wolf. They ran off a little way and stood around, acting a bit confused.

Coming down from station I saw four sheep two miles away running in my direction. They stopped and looked back, then ran again. I hid in the rocks and the sheep passed about fifteen feet away, going slowly, jaws hanging down and tongues out and blowing hard. I lay in rocks two hours covering their trail but no wolves came along. The four sheep were feeding on the mountainside, so I went to where my sheep was cached in rocks, and packed him to camp.

We had plenty of chuck to feed us. On the entire survey we killed four caribou. They were mostly thin, but the meat was welcome. As active as we were, we needed a lot of food. Our staple breakfast was hotcakes and bacon. With caribou and sheep meat, we often tossed young leaves and the pods of pea vine into the pot. We also used fireweed, and wild onions. For flavor, we often put a leaf of skunk cabbage into our food. It kind of takes the place of garlic, but is pretty stout; you don't want to put too much in.

With the sheep meat, and some of the caribou, where there was gravel we'd dig a hole, build a fire in it and get some coals. We'd wrap a hunk of meat or some fish (we caught grayling and whitefish both) tightly in wet grass. We'd then plaster the grass all over with mud, lay it on the coals, put more coals on top, and bury it overnight. That produced as fine a roast as you can cook in a modern stove.

We had needed meat. When we had eaten a big feed of the food we had with us, it didn't really satisfy. There was a big increase in our energy when we added the caribou and sheep meat to our diet.

Aug 13th. Broke Camp 18 and proceeded over the summit. Left the Goodpaster river at about 12 o'clock noon where it was no more than a foot wide by one or two inches deep. Passed over the hump and at 12:30 p.m. was on Joseph Creek[3] waters and headed for the Fortymile River. Saw a caribou and found two sets of horns entangled in the old telegraph wire. Saw old cabin at about 2:30 p.m. and bunch of traps hanging in tree. Raining hard, we were soaking wet. Camped at 5:30 p.m. on bank of Joseph Creek. Roasted saddle of sheep and ate the works. Raining hard. Mosquitoes bad.

Aug 14th. Broke Camp 19 and traveled down Joe Creek [Joseph Creek]. Saw two caribou killed by wolves. Arrived at Joe Village [Joseph Village] at 4:30 p.m. Found five or six graves on the hill. The wolves had dug into these and we found a shoulder blade, which I identified as human. After leaving the village, which was only three tumble-down cabins, and a four-posted cache, I saw a coal black animal on a flat to our right. It was a wolf, and in a short time two more showed up. A little later a fourth wolf showed; this one was also coal black. They were about 700 yards away.

We sized them up with the telescope, then I took a shot at the nearest. Shot struck in water under him and they all beat it. I took a second shot but the distance was too great for a moving object. It seemed rather strange that two of the wolves should be black and two gray. They were very large. We then cut across the flats and followed up a creek. While pitching camp I saw three black bears on the hillside N.E. of the old telegraph post.

Three of the log cabins and a cache were still standing at the abandoned Joseph Village on Joseph Creek. We found five or six Model 73 .44 caliber Winchesters in a cache. The cache had a good roof, and the guns were all in fair condition, certainly they were shootable. There was no ammunition.

We rolled them in canvas, tied them with ropes, and left them so they'd be there if anybody ever wanted them.

---

3. Joseph Creek, a headwater of the Fortymile River, is now classed as a wild and scenic river.

A burial ground for the Indians of that village was on a little hill on a point of land between Joseph Creek and the Fortymile River. Human bones were scattered about, dug up probably by wolves and bears. We also found parts of two human skeletons in a cabin that had almost tumbled down.

Later, we were camped at the head of Vanilla Creek, close to timberline where a few dry poles of dead spruces stood. It was a nice place to camp, with cool breezes. It was an ideal summer day, calm and clear. As we sat in front of the tent after dinner, we heard an awful rumpus downstream. Grunts, roars, crashes, and thumps. Neither of us had ever heard anything like it. We thought it might be two grizzlies fighting, or two bull moose. We were too new in the country to know what it was.

We worked a couple more days from that camp, then packed up to move. Traveling downstream, we watched for the origin of the rumpus. We couldn't have missed it blind-folded and with a cane. On the bank of the creek was an area 300 feet long and 100 feet wide completely torn up and pulverized. Jack spruce were broken off and reduced to kindling. At the lower end of this devastated area lay an immense rack of moose antlers, the skull, and several joints of the neck bone, all picked clean. With the moss torn up, the exposed frozen earth had thawed, and it was mostly a big mud hole.

In about the middle of this mess was a wolf's tail sticking out of the mud.

A wolf pack had killed a huge bull moose there.

"I'm going to pull a wolf out of that mud," I told Dan, as I grabbed the wolf tail. All I got was the tail. The wolf was gone.

A four-inch chunk of wolf hide hung from a knot on a nearby dead spruce. On the upper side of the area, we found a big standing dry spruce with a smooch of blood twelve feet from the ground, along with a banner of wolf hide two inches wide and six inches long, hanging on a knot, waving in the breeze.

How many wolves were involved I could not say, but it must have been a terrific battle. From appearances, we figured the moose had killed at least two of the wolves. The uninjured wolves had probably eaten their injured or dead brothers, as wolves do.

The moose bones, still fresh, had been cleaned of meat. The wolves hadn't cracked any for the marrow. Wolves' jaws are powerful—they can easily crack the largest moose bone.

It had been a huge bull, and he was in his best fighting trim of the year. He had obviously struggled long and hard, but there had been too many wolves for him.

We saw wolves almost every day of our trip, including packs of fifteen or twenty. We also saw caribou by the thousands all through the country from Shaw Creek to Columbia Creek, near the end of our survey. Moose were also common.

Both black and grizzly bears were fairly common. We especially noticed much grizzly sign, and saw more grizzly bears, in the Fortymile River country. We never left our camps unguarded for more than one or two hours without caching our supplies out of bears' reach. An unguarded camp in this region was sure to be robbed. In some instances bears walked past our camp at close range, and always made a half circle to assure themselves that the camp was guarded before they continued about their business.

We found two game licks [mineralized soil eaten by wildlife] at Columbia Creek. We camped just below the lower lick where we found a soda water [mineralized, and charged with carbon dioxide] spring. It tasted brackish to me. The horses stuck their noses down to it, but refused to drink.

Moose, though, loved it, and came to drink. They crossed the creek, which was nice clear, cold water, and dashed to the lick. They didn't waste time, because wolves often hid nearby, waiting for an unwary visitor. The moose were nervous when in the lick. They were thirsty when they arrived, with sides caved in, which we could easily see. They drank that soda water and their sides filled out. One drink is all they'd take, for they didn't want to stay around long. They got pumped full of water, their sides bulged, and they dropped their heads and walked all around to see if wolves were near. They burped loudly after drinking the charged water. Really loud. It was unexpected and very funny.

They would then leave as fast as they had arrived.

I found a second lick one day when I left Dan in camp taking care of the horses. I had hiked nine miles to the head of Columbia Creek and established a station there, naming it "Lick."

Off on the right was a creek with a long straight stretch. On each side were spruce trees bigger than anything we'd seen all the way from Shaw Creek. Evidently the ground was warmer; perhaps it didn't freeze. Amidst the big timber was an open patch, which proved to be another soda spring.

The spring bubbled through an opening on top of a twenty-feet-high cone that looked like volcanic ash. It was about 100 feet through the base. Moose walked to the top of the cone, and almost had to stand on their heads to drink from it.

In this position they were vulnerable to wolves. They drank as fast as they could, and as much as they could, then hurriedly backed out and hight-tailed it away from there.

Trails made by moose radiated all directions from the lick, like spokes in a wheel. Some were two feet deep. The nearer to the spring, the deeper the trail.

We learned later that a nearby mining outfit at O'Brien Creek got their moose meat at that lick. They sent a hunter, waited two and a half hours, then sent a man with a packhorse to bring out the meat. If he didn't have a moose when the packhorse arrived, they sent another hunter next time.

I returned to this lick, climbed about twenty-five feet up in a tree, found a comfortable seat, and watched moose behavior.

Moose had undermined nearby trees by eating the mineralized muck or mud at their bases. They pawed into it to eat. Wind had blown a lot of these trees over. Spruce trees have no tap root; their roots spread all directions parallel to the ground. With the mud around their roots eaten and trampled, high wind easily pushed them over.

Eight or ten moose came while I watched. Cows climbed the cone and poked their heads down to drink, then quickly left. A bull arrived. He didn't drink, but ate mineral out of the ground around the base of trees.

He was nervous, and frequently lifted his head to stare at nearby brush and timber. He ate, then peered at the same place again. After while he left, and, like the cows, he didn't waste time. In fact, he ran, looking back.

He hadn't much more than left when two big wolves walked into the open from the brush the bull had been watching. They were close to me, and appeared to be absolutely stuffed, probably with moose. I shot both. They smelled awful. A twenty dollar bounty was paid for wolves at the time, but I wasn't interested and left them there.

Horse feed at this time was getting pinched by frost in a few places, but Dan found a good swale of green grass half a mile beyond a thicket near camp. He put the horses there, with hobbles and bells on a couple of them.

The next morning he went out to check on them. Instead of walking around the thicket, he started through it. He'd gone about a hundred feet when he parted branches and found himself looking into a wolf's face.

He shot it, and in an instant the air was full of wolves—behind him, in front of him, and, he claimed, sailing through the air over his head. Dan emptied his rifle, then reloaded as fast as he could. He was badly spooked, and ran out of the thicket.

The wolves raced across the creek, and were still in range. He fired a few more shots at them. All missed. Dan had a good rifle, but he was a poor marksman.

He headed back to camp, never mind the horses.

When I reached camp that afternoon he was still in a high state of excitement.

"I killed two, and wounded others," he said.

"We'll go find those two in the morning and and you can collect the bounty," I suggested.

"I'm not going into that thicket again," he declared.

I couldn't have persuaded him to go into that thicket again for a hundred bounties. That explosion of wolves, some almost within arm's length, had really scared him.

Next morning I found the two dead wolves in the thicket, and a clear trail where a crippled wolf had left. I followed the trail but soon lost it.

I dragged the dead wolves out to a delighted Dan. He skinned them, and later collected the bounties.

Aug. 15th. I left Camp 20 and climbed Peak 5400, selected a point for station, and named it "Wilson" in honor of President Wilson. Saw two fresh-killed caribou [by wolves], *but saw no game. Arrived back at camp at 5 p.m. While eating (about 6:30 p.m.) a black bear walked past camp just across the creek.*

Aug. 22nd. Awoke in morning to find it snowing hard. Snowed all day. Broke camp in p.m. and traveled down Manila Creek. Saw old cabins. Saw two moose that had been killed by wolves. Saw one large bull moose. Pitched camp in dark. Left mark on tree.

We put new shoes on the horses while en route. Five of the animals caused no trouble, but one kicked or tried to bite if he had a chance.

When he needed shoes on three feet, to throw him we took him to a nice soft meadow and hobbled all four feet, then ran ropes in between and cinched them up. At the last minute he wised up and bucked and jumped. He got out of the soft area and fell under a bunch of crisscrossed, fallen logs.

"What now, Dan?" I asked.

"We'll shoe him right there," he decided. We then tied the horse to the logs so he couldn't injure us. A serious injury to one of us would have ended our survey.

That horse groaned and cried all the while we worked on his feet. Tears actually ran from his eyes. I was sorry for him, but then remembered the times he had tried to bite and kick me, and decided it was his own fault.

Sept. 2nd. Overcast. Champion Creek flooded. Horses on north side. Took ¾ day to get them across. Moved at 3 p.m. from Camp 28 to Camp 29. Picked camp site in dark. Slept on sidehill rolled in a tarp.

We found a nice surprise at Liberty Fork, where I'd arranged for John Powers of Eagle to cache some horse feed for me. He had also cached a jar of honey, a dozen lemons, and a couple dozen eggs. We went for them in a big way.

Sept. 4th. Clear, cool. Moved from Camp 30 at station "Gordon" to Camp 31 at forks of O'Brien and Dome Creek. Fine going until near O'Brien Creek where trail got rocky and very steep. Sorrel horse very poor and wobbly. Arrived at Forks and found cabin and saw a gold miner, the first person we had seen in eight weeks. He cooked up a fine supper. His partner came in later. Had a fine visit.

We carried the reconnaissance triangulation on through to Eagle, arriving there September 22. Eagle had about twenty residents, and we auctioned the six horses there at prices ranging from seventy-five cents to seventy-five dollars. A couple were bought for dog food. That included the kicker and biter.

An old miner bought one of the horses and took it to his mine. In later years I got to Eagle a few times, and whenever I saw that miner, that horse was with him. They became real pals; the horse followed him around like a dog.

It was a relief to get off the trail and dispose of the horses. Now we were to travel down the Yukon to Circle, and from there walk home to Fairbanks.

Eagle to Fairbanks by Canoe and Trail

Sam was known by some as "Roarin' Sam," because of his deep strong voice, which became especially loud when he was angry. He also had a loud, infectious laugh.

—LETTER TO AUTHOR FROM ROY BILLBERG, NOVEMBER, 2005.

EAGLE, OUR GOAL on the recon from Shaw Creek, is one of the prettiest town sites on the Yukon River. Here the Yukon turns north for a ways, and there are nearby hills on the south bank. Mission Mountain rises over Eagle, and is a beautiful sight on sunny days.

The Northern Commercial Company, known all over Alaska as the N.C. Company, had a trading post at Eagle. A Mr. Harridan was the N.C. Agent. On the counter sat a heavy tin pan holding $32,000 worth of gold nuggets. Mr. Harridan invited me to lift the pan that I might see how heavy it was. I put my hands under the sides of the pan and lifted. The bottom of the pan didn't leave the counter. Sides of the pan bent in and would not have stood the strain of lifting it from the counter.

In the Alaska of those years, gold was commonly left in such containers as informally as sacks of flour and bales of dried fish (sled dog food). It was quite safe.

On the bright morning of September 29, we left Eagle in the canoe I had arranged to be shipped to Eagle. It was a bit frosty, but it warmed as the sun rose. Dan wielded the bow paddle. Fox rode in the middle, while I paddled in the stern. We were bound for Circle.

Mrs. John Powers, of Eagle, a kindly person, gave us a couple of loaves of excellent bread, a great treat. We had lived on hotcakes and bannock for bread all summer. John Powers, her husband, freighted from Eagle to Chicken, with stops at Franklin, Steel Creek, Jack Wade, and other places. Freight arrived summers via sternwheeler steamers, and, with pack horses Powers hauled it to mines at various destinations in the Fortymile country.

Since we wanted to see the Yukon, and not knowing if other opportunities would arise, to look over things of interest we stopped and frequently went ashore. These were mostly natural objects, as the hand of man had not as yet done much to change the banks of the Yukon.

One place changed by man was Heinie Miller's wood yard. Heinie had built himself some skookum buildings from logs, and he furnished firewood for the steamboats that plied the river. As I write this [Author: probably in the late 1950s] the buildings are still standing, but of course Heinie has gone to his reward.

As we went ashore at Heinie's, Fox bristled and looked menacing. This meant a bear, or bears, were close. A large black bear was in the nearby brush, and we soon put the run on him, much to Fox's disgust. He'd have preferred that we kill it.

Fox never barked, in fact I don't think he could bark. When pleased he would produce a deep, low rumble; when warning of bears, another deep rumble. I don't claim he was a wolf dog, although he was the color of a wolf, and had the general lines of a wolf, except that he was deep-chested.

After having a good look at the wood yard we paddled on. That night we camped in a pretty setting of spruce. We wanted meat, and tons of it was all around us, but we could not bring ourselves to kill one of those hulking caribou or moose. Instead, we settled for a few berry-fed, delicious, spruce hens.

We stopped at Nation River, had a look around, and met a few old timers. Once, as we traveled down river, we had to beach the canoe and watch a caribou herd swim across the Yukon. It wouldn't have done to paddle the canoe into that hundred yards wide, jam-packed, swimming herd. They streamed across the river for fifteen or twenty minutes—a wonderful sight.

Next day we went ashore for lunch and to limber up after sitting and paddling half a day. I walked behind the riverbank timber and there sat a steam tractor. It was a bull wheel job, about the size of a D6 caterpillar, and, with fire in the boiler and a head of steam, it looked as if it was ready to go. Barney Hansen, an old-timer at Eagle, recently told me it is still there

This brought memories of the old Lombard Steam Log Hauler I worked on and around as a young man in Maine.

Next day we arrived at a trappers' cabin in a beautiful grove of tall straight, spruce trees. There was no underbrush, and it resembled a cultivated park. The cabin was set about 150 feet back from the bank of the Yukon. On a pole between two trees hung six fat caribou carcasses. On another pole hung a couple of moose, also sleek and fat.

The cabin was newly and expertly built, and would have made a wonderful picture. Of the two old-timers who occupied it, for many years thereafter I was to know one, Shorty Schneider. The other man was a bit older, and he never talked. He sat on his bunk and smoked his pipe and said nothing except when spoken to. His answers were usually "yes" or "no."

"My partner doesn't talk, but I talk enough for both of us," Shorty remarked. This was true. Good-natured Shorty was a fine entertainer.

They invited us in and furnished each of us with a dried caribou skin with which to sleep on their floor. For supper, they fed us from a kettle of good moose stew.

The next morning we had a fine breakfast of hotcakes and moose liver. They had an abundance of wild berries, on which we also feasted.

We were greeted by snow that morning, and spent a miserable day paddling, for it snowed all day. It was still falling when we arrived at Circle around 4 p.m.

At Circle City we put up at the Tanana Roadhouse run by Mr. and Mrs. Joseph Romaker. Mrs. Romaker was a wonderful cook; her food seemed especially fine after the food we had cooked for ourselves those many weeks. In a nearby shed, the Romakers had two to three tons of moose and caribou meat for the roadhouse winter supply.

Mrs. Romaker was the target of a crude frontier prank in 1922 that brought laughter to many across the Territory.

A party of Royal Canadian Mounted Police traveled through Circle City, headed for Herschel Island in the Canadian Arctic to carry out the execution of two Eskimos who had been convicted of murder. On their way, when they stayed at the Tanana Road-house in Circle, Mrs. Romaker chided them for going to so much trouble to execute two "poor Eskimos."

The sergeant in charge promised to bring her a souvenir on their return. As they returned through Fort Yukon, the mounty picked up a pair of rubber gloves at the hospital and stuffed them with moss, then froze them. At Circle he handed Mrs. Romaker the package. She opened it and nearly fainted before discovering they were frozen gloves, and not a pair of hands.

We stored our canoe with the N.C. Company at Circle, which was run by veteran trader Oliver Anderson. He was exceedingly kind and helpful. I had been in Alaska for only three years, and I was deeply impressed by the way people fell to to help us.

The Steese Highway from Fairbanks to Circle didn't exist. The first forty-five miles from Fairbanks to Cassiar Creek had been brushed out; the remainder was a well-used trail, with roadhouses about a day's travel apart.

We weren't alone in planning to walk to Fairbanks. At Circle, a man and a woman, both of questionable character, wanted to attach themselves to us. I believe he was a pimp. They had been at Dawson, Yukon Territory, far up the Yukon River, and the police had told them to get out. They had then come downriver on a steamer. They were not in good physical shape for that long walk. To make it worse, four inches of snow was on the ground, and it was growing cold. They were afraid to tackle the trip alone.

A third person, a 70-year-old retired banker named Moffit, also asked to join us. He was a sportsman from Outside who had been hunting. He was a pleasant companion who took the hike in stride.

The 165 miles to Fairbanks was just a good stretch of the legs for Dan and me, for we had been walking all summer. On this walk we didn't have to worry about horses, or finding a trail. We reluctantly agreed that the three could accompany us, knowing they would hold us up. We couldn't say no.

We left Circle October 3. Our first overnight stop was at the Ferry roadhouse near Birch Creek, about twelve miles from Circle. It was run by a big, good-natured Scandinavian whose name I do not remember. He was not the best cook in the world, but he kept us alive. His coffee was a terror. What he lacked in the food department was made up for in helpfulness.

Next day, we had not gone far and had just passed Jumpoff

Roadhouse, eighteen miles from Circle, when, in the snow we saw a freshly broken trail made by a large band of wolves. It was three feet wide and beaten down solid. The scent of wolves was heavy in the air. It alarmed the man and woman from Dawson, but Mr. Moffit became excited, and had his rifle ready.

We frequently saw caribou from this point on until just beyond Twelvemile Summit. The wolves, of course, were living on caribou.

That poor woman had an awful time. It was all she could do to keep up a slow walking pace. We all carried packs, and we took some of her things in our packs. Dan and I had sold or stored most everything at Eagle, and we weren't packing any grub. We had lunch sandwiches made up at roadhouses as we left them, and, of course, we ate morning and night at roadhouses.

We stayed overnight at the Central Roadhouse and Trading Post, run by Riley Erickson and Old Man Staid. I was to see these two many times in ensuing years.

Next, we stayed overnight at Miller House, and after that, there was a gap of about forty miles to the Coal Mine—a two day walk over Eagle Summit.

On the south side of Eagle Summit we encountered engineer Donald McDonald. He had been locating engineer for the Alaska Railroad, which was completed in 1923. He was now working for the Alaska Road Commission, locating the route for what would be the Steese Highway.

He was also largely responsible for much of the locating for the Alaska Highway (first called the "Alcan") during World War II. I had known him at Anchorage, and we renewed our friendship and had a nice visit.

Berry Camp, on the south side of Eagle Summit, was shut down for the winter. However caretaker Jack McCloy welcomed Dan and me, telling us to help ourselves. "I have to go up on the ridge and dress two caribou I just killed," he explained.

We hadn't mentioned to him the other three in our party, who had lagged behind. Jack held a big butcher knife, and he was covered with caribou blood. He opened the door to leave just as the woman reached it. She stared wide-eyed at the bloody man with the huge knife, let out a wail, and collapsed.

Dan and I rushed to her assistance. Jack fled through the back door.

About then Moffit and the other man arrived and were struck dumb to see Dan and me trying to bring the woman to life. After a bit her eyes fluttered and she came to, only to pass out again. Soon she came to again, and we hurriedly explained that all was well, and that Jack McCloy was really a friend, and harmless.

We all rested, had a pot of tea and lunch, made sandwiches to take with us, and took off on the next stage of the journey. That night we stayed at a small unoccupied log cabin. It was an uncomfortable night for our companions, but Dan and I, being used to it, slept soundly under a tree. This gave the others more room in the cabin.

Next day we slogged up Twelvemile Creek. It was tough going, and in some places we had to wade in the creek. About 3 o'clock I told the party I'd leave them and hurry up to the Twelvemile Roadhouse to let the man there know we were coming so he could prepare a meal. We had heard that an old man was staying there.

When near Twelvemile Summit I saw some mountain sheep, and many caribou.

I knocked at the door of the roadhouse. It was jerked open, and a wild-looking old man stuck his face into mine and aggressively declared, "I can't see if you are a white man or what. I am blind. I am sick. I am broke. I don't have any firewood."

I learned his name was Steve Radey, and I did my best to soothe him, then told him four others were coming down the creek and that we all had money to pay for meals and a night's stay. I told him Dan and I would cut him a good supply of firewood.

That pacified him and he went into the kitchen and started making things fly. I returned down the creek and explained to the others the situation. "By all means pacify the old man. He's kind of unstable. Don't cross him," I urged. Dan and I then rushed back to the roadhouse where we cut Steve a supply of wood.

The others eventually stumbled in. Steve rushed to them and gave them the same story he had handed me. The two from Dawson pacified him, but Mr. Moffit commented, "Well, Mister, you are in a hell of a fix."

For a minute it looked as if Steve would go berserk, but Dan and I calmed him. He felt that Moffit wasn't sufficiently sympathetic, and had doubts about allowing Moffit into the house, but after a time he relented, and things were patched up.

Dan and I helped Steve in the kitchen, but the others collapsed. The woman was exhausted.

We got the table heaped high with chuck. Once Steve got under way he turned out to be quite a cook. He had excellent bread he had baked, and there was a big hunk of meat on a platter in the center of the table. There was also a stew that looked excellent. There was boiled rice, apple sauce, and beans.

I had seen some sour caribou meat hanging from a pole behind the roadhouse, and I knew it was the source of the stew, and the centerpiece of meat on the platter.

I warned the others not to eat any meat. I told Steve I wasn't much of a meat eater and filled up on rice, bread, apple sauce, and some beans. The others followed suit until Moffit cut off a piece of meat, ate it, and declared it was delicious. The others then pitched into the meat, despite my black looks and shaking head. Even Dan, who should have known better, and to the great pleasure of Steve, sliced himself a big chunk.

We shoved off early next morning, after paying Steve, and in addition, making up a generous kitty for him, which pleased him mightily. We assured him we had never been treated better, and left him in high spirits. The poor man had cataracts on both eyes, and shouldn't have been alone.

We had started up Twelvemile summit when the first of the gang became sick. Inside an hour, every single one was sick. They could travel about 100 yards with some difficulty, then make a stop beside the trail behind the nearest bush. The great trouble, especially for the woman, was the absence of bushes on the summit.

None of them were up to carrying their packs, which I relayed up the mountain and down the other side. We had planned to make it to Faith Creek Roadhouse that night, but instead, had to settle for the first trees we came to at the head of Faith Creek. We were lucky to make it that far. All four of my companions were as weak as a rag, and I was all in from having to relay all their packs.

The poor woman, already the weakest and poorest traveler, was in pure misery.

I made up a spruce bough bed for them where all could enjoy their misery. I then crossed the creek and made my camp under a tree. Next morning I shot a few ptarmigan and a couple of spruce hens, then cooked them for their breakfast. None was

Sam in his Maine-built 18-foot Old Town canoe, with Fox, his 90-pound malemute. He was on the Yukon River bound for Circle from Eagle, after his Shaw-Creek-to-Eagle reconnaissance. Sam stood when he paddled a canoe, using an extra-long paddle. Photo taken in September, 1925.
U.S. Coast and Geodetic Survey.

very enthusiastic about eating. All were weak and in no condition to travel.

"I'll hike ahead to the Faith Creek Roadhouse and get some medicine. You take your time coming down Faith Creek. I'll be back as soon as I can and meet you," I promised.

At the roadhouse I got some lunches, a full can of black pepper, and some sugar, and rushed back to meet them. I heated a kettle of hot water and sugar, and gave each a cup full with half a teaspoon of black pepper. They complained, coughed, and sneezed, but managed to get it down. I got a second dose into them half an hour later. That did it. They were cured. In an hour their eyes were fiery red and burning, a result of the pepper. They worried, but I assured them they would be ok. Although it seems drastic, I didn't think it was dangerous. It does overcome diarrhea.

We all arrived at the Faith Creek Roadhouse late that evening. The kindly proprietor had a good meal ready. He had even made a pan of biscuits as soon as he had heard my warning shot that we would arrive soon. He had gone to some lengths to fix a bunk with privacy for the woman.

The owner had blueberries that he put up in five gallon kegs, as we used to put them up in Maine. We called them "pickled blueberries." They are packed with a layer of blueberries, and then a layer of sugar, all the way to the top. He had dug holes to permafrost and had set his kegs on the frozen ground, and buried them.

"You going to pick any more?" I asked him.

"Yes. The berries haven't frozen yet," he answered.

"Put me up a keg," I requested, and paid him for it right then. He was to deliver it when freeze-up came. In early November he drove to Fairbanks with his dog team and delivered to my door my keg of blueberries. They were delicious, and lasted me and my friends all winter.

We slept in next morning. The woman and man from Dawson were still shaky, so I added their packs to mine for the day so we could travel.

That night we had to sleep in the bush again, and it was pretty frosty. Dan and I made spruce bough beds for everyone and kept fires going most of the night.

We arrived at the Cassiar Roadhouse the following day. It was run by a very pretty young woman wearing civilized store clothes. She had an attractive and well-mannered daughter of about six or seven.

Her uncle, who had owned the roadhouse, had died, leaving it to her. Her husband had died. Bravely, she left her home in Washington state to take the place over, and was running it by herself. The dollar and a half a meal we each paid was her first income.

Mr. Moffit pitched in to help her in the kitchen. Dan and I cut her a good pile of firewood. She was an interesting and agreeable lady, and I kind of kept track of her. She married soon after to a nice young fellow. They had two children. Then, in about four years, she died of cancer. A few years later her husband died, also of cancer. I lost track of the three children.

From there we trudged on into Fairbanks. A wagon road from Chatanika made walking easy for the last miles. It was good to get home.

That winter I had to go back to Washington, D.C., to put in several weeks trying to bring my field notes of our Shaw Creek to Eagle recon so they were understandable, the sort of work I do not relish.

I took a furlough home to Maine for the rest of the winter.

It was good to be with relatives and friends again, but otherwise Maine seemed different. Everything looked small.

My next assignments were in Minnesota and Iowa, and then to New Orleans for the winter where we worked in the Barataria Bay and Grand Isle area. By then it was painfully apparent that the Coast and Geodetic Survey would not be returning me to Alaska for many years. But luck was with me, and I was to be north again in a matter of months, working in another profession.

Sam O. White, Alaskan

I never did aspire to big money, which always seemed to require that a man had to go after it in ways that I could not countenance. I wanted to live a certain life, and I lived it pretty near to schedule and to the hilt.
—SAM O. WHITE, WRITTEN IN THE LATE 1950S.

[AUTHOR] SAM'S FUTURE IN Alaska was settled in March, 1927, while working in Louisiana with the Coast and Geodetic Survey. He received a wire from the Alaska Game Commission offering him a job as game warden. The salary offer of $2800 was more than he was receiving from the Survey.

Once back in Alaska, he became an Alaskan for life. He never wavered in his devotion to the Territory and the State. After a year and a half as a game warden at Fort Yukon, for the remainder of his life his home was at Fairbanks. He repeatedly wrote, and orally proclaimed, that Alaska was the finest place in the world to live.

Sam's arrival in Alaska in 1922 had changed his life. As a boy, he had dreamed about Alaska. His first taste of Alaska settled his future; the life style, the frontier spirit, the challenges, suited him. Alaska was everything he had dreamed, and he determined to make it his home. His early life in Maine—farming, logging, and guiding—was the perfect preparation for life in Alaska.

"In 1925 I made notes of game populations from Shaw Creek to Eagle. The Alaska Game Commission had just been formed. They had few maps of the Interior, so on my way to Washington D. C. that fall I stopped at Juneau and turned my notes and some maps over to them. I had the maps marked where there was horse feed, camping areas, and trails," Sam told an interviewer in 1968.

It is probable that he applied for a position with the Game Commission during that Juneau visit.

His survey jobs had required him to be away from his wife Pearl and three young sons for months at a time. He had met Pearl while hunting and trapping in Quebec, near her home at Lac Megantic, a few miles across the border from Maine. Pearl, it seems, was very close to her family.

He sent money for Pearl and their three sons, Burnham, Jesse, and Harland, to join him in Alaska. Pearl's family was horrified. They refused to allow her to move to that far off land of ice, snow, igloos, and God knows what else.

Harland O. White, Sam's youngest son, in Italy, during World War II. He was wounded in action in Italy.
SAM WHITE, COURTESY DRAHS

Sam and Pearl divorced. She remained in Maine and married Charles Edwin (Ed) White, one of Sam's brothers. Ed's wife had died, leaving him with six sons. Sam continued to send money to support his three sons.

Sam never wrote about, or spoke, to Alaskan friends about his brother marrying his ex-wife. It must have been a vexation to him.

Sam once told Roy Billberg, "When I left Maine, I left under kind of a cloud." Another time he wryly expanded. "My girl in Maine told me, 'Sam, I love you so much, I'll follow you anywhere you go. No place is too far.' So I told her I'm going to Alaska. And she said, 'That's too far.'"

That sounds suspiciously like one of Sam's exaggerations, but it may well have been true.

As the years went by Sam keenly felt the loss of his sons, if not his first wife. Burnham, the oldest, and Jesse, the middle son, never became close to Sam. When they were adults, he invited

Harland was a Maine state trooper after WWII. He became a sergeant, then a lieutenant, and retired after twenty-two years of distinguished service.

Sam O. White, courtesy DRAHS

Mary and Sam, with Sam's son Harland and his wife Julia, at Fairbanks during one of Harland's eight visits to Sam and Mary at Fairbanks.

Sam O. White, courtesy DRAHS

them to visit him in Alaska, but neither ever did. Burnham was an auto mechanic and Jesse was a blue collar factory worker. Both have passed on.

Harland the youngest (nicknamed "Tic") became close to Sam. He, and often his wife Julia (Julia Janet), visited Sam at Fairbanks eight times. Their first visit was in August, 1960, when Sam was stationed as a bush pilot for Wien Airlines at the Koyukuk River village of Hughes.

On August 17, 1960, Sam wrote to Noel Wien: *Dear Noel:* "*Tic and Jan arrive on Pan Am at 10 a.m. August 26. They leave September 9. I want every minute I can get with them. It is the first visit of near relatives I have had in my 38 years in Alaska.*"

Harland, Sam's youngest, is, like Sam, tall and slim. He has more than a passing resemblance to his father. His career was similar to Sam's. Both served in the Army and fought Germans in world wars, and both worked in law enforcement.

Harland enlisted in the Army at age 17, and during World War II spent three years overseas. He was briefly stationed in Africa, but most of his overseas duty was in Italy, where he was wounded in front line action.

He was discharged in 1945. Shortly, he became a State Trooper in Maine, and was soon promoted to Sergeant, then to Lieutenant.

Sam's three sons (l. to r.) Burnham, Harland, and Jesse White, in 1982. In 2006 only Harland survived. SAM O. WHITE. COURTESY DRAHS

He retired after twenty-two years of distinguished service with the Maine troopers.

For the next ten years, until full retirement, he worked as a bank courier, making deliveries from the Portland area.

Harland and Julia live in southern Maine.

Book Two

GAME WARDEN/WILDLIFE AGENT

Fort Yukon Game Warden

*Wolves began to howl nearby and on all sides. The dogs were terrified.
I brought them in close and built a brush fence around them and my
tent. Caribou by the hundred thousands were all over the place, but
those wolves were much more interested in my dogs*

—SAM, DESCRIBING A FEBRUARY, 1928, CAMP HE HAD ON THE CHANDALAR RIVER.

[SAM] MY LIFE ABRUPTLY changed with a March 1927 telegram
from the Alaska Game Commission offering me a position as a
game warden. My life-long dream was coming true. I could now
plan my future in the Territory. I had been gone from Alaska about
a year. I could hardly wait get to Juneau to learn what was expected
of me, and where I was to be stationed. At the time I was hired
there were eighty-four people on the Commission's payroll.

[AUTHOR] The Alaska Game Commission was created in January, 1925, by an act of Congress. Initially the Bureau of Biological
Survey in the Department of Agriculture was charged with imple-
menting the act. In 1940 the Biological Survey was transferred to
the Department of Interior as the U.S. Fish and Wildlife Service.
The Game Commission was made up of the Executive Officer,
and four Alaskans, one appointed from each judicial division. It
recommended rules, regulations, and policies for the management
of big game, small game, land fur-bearing animals, and sport fish.
Its recommendations were almost always accepted in Washington,
by the secretary of agriculture until 1940, and after that by the
secretary of the interior. The rules and regulations were federal
law, published in the Federal Register.

Appointments of Alaskans to the Commission were made
through Washington. Appointees had to have been residents for
at least five years.

The first regulations were printed in May, 1925. They closed the season in summer for most furbearers, with no open season anywhere for marten and beaver. Cow and calf moose were protected. Possession and use of poison was banned.

There was a provision for making needed changes, and there were many of these in the early years. The public and the wardens suggested changes for the Commission to consider. Over the years Sam O. White contributed some of these suggestions.

Sam with motorcycle, at Big Delta, Alaska, fall, 1927. SAM O. WHITE. COURTESY DRAHS

During the life of the Commission, 1925–1960, fifteen men served as commissioners. They included traders, a logger, a dentist, a physician, and hunting guides. Earl Ohmer, a seafood processor and mink farmer of Petersburg served for thirty years. Andrew Simons, then Alaska's most famous guide, of Lake View (near Seward) served for twenty-eight years.

Control of fish and game was assumed by the State of Alaska's Department of Fish and Game on January 1, 1960.

In the Game Commission's later years, the Executive Officer was also the Regional Director of the U.S. Fish and Wildlife Service. Those who served as Executive Officers during Sam's time with the Commission were Ernest P. Walker (1925–1928), Hugh W. Terhune (1929–1935), and Frank Dufresne (1936–1943).

Sam, at the age of 36, arrived in Alaska in 1927 for the second time. He was broke, as the following diary entries reveal. To learn the ropes as a warden, he worked in Southeastern Alaska for four months.

Italics in the following are selected entries from Sam's official daily diaries. They illustrate some of his experiences from the

A meeting of the Alaska Game Commission. From left, Dan Ralston, U.S. Fish and Wildlife Service; Clarence Rhode, FWS and Executive Officer. Commissioners are; either Harry Brown of Kobuk, or Garnet Martin, of Nome; Andy Simons, Lake View; Forbes Baker, Fairbanks; and Earl Ohmer, Petersburg. U.S. Fish and Wildlife Service

Alaska Game Commission Wardens, in 1937 (title changed to Wildlife Agent in June, 1938). Those identifiable; far left,1. Pete McMullen, next unknown, 2. Harold Galwas, 3. Wayne House, 4. Sam O. White, 5. Clarence Rhode, 6. Frank Glaser, 7. Carlos Carson, 8. Jack Benson. Behind Benson unknown. 9. Gren Collins, 10. Jack O'Connor. Warden with pipe is probably Ray Woolford. U.S. Fish and Wildlife Service

Alaska Game Commission wildlife agents conferring in the Fairbanks office in 1939. From left, Sam O. White (standing), Jack Benson, Pete McMullen, Frank Dufresne (Executive Officer), Clarence Rhode, Jack O'Connor, Gren Collins (standing), and Frank Glaser, animal control specialist. U.S. Fish and Wildlife Service

time he arrived in Ketchikan through August, 1928. Missing are entries on cooking dog food—of which there are many—cutting firewood, repairing harness and dog sleds, and other humdrum, everyday chores.

March 14, 1927. Arrived in Ketchikan on the SS Northwestern. *Transferred to the* [Game Commission] *motorship* Seal *and sailed to Wrangell in the afternoon.*

March 22, 1927. Wired T.M. Hutt for loan of $20. Hope she comes.

March 26, 1927. At Wrangell. Money arrived.

May 3, 1927. In Juneau office. Completed drawing up plans for a clinker built poling boat.[1]

---

1. The Sam O. White display at the Dead River Area Historical Society's museum at Stratton includes a set of mechanical drawing instruments that belonged to Sam. He drew plans for buildings as well as boats.

July 12. Leave Juneau aboard SS Alaska *bound for Seward.*
July 17, 1927. Arrive Anchorage, Sunday.

[Sam] I arrived at Fairbanks July 19, 1927 where Frank Dufresne[2] was agent-in-charge for the Game Commission. I was to be stationed at Fort Yukon, but my first assignment was to guide a predatory animal control expert to the wolf-infested upper Tanana River, and the Ladue river area near the Canadian border.

The predator expert and I left Fairbanks in early July and joined John Hajdukovich, a trader on the upper Tanana (who served as a Game Commissioner 1939–42), on his scow-type river boat which was loaded with about two tons of supplies for his posts at Tanana Crossing and Tetlin.

The silt-filled, braided, shallow and swift Tanana River is a bad piece of river. John had a Native crewman stationed at the bow with a long hooked pole. When the going got tough and the engine couldn't make headway, the poleman hooked into a crevice in a bluff or rock, and the one-man pull would break the deadlock. It took expert timing between the poleman and the boat operator.

We spent August in Tetlin while the predator expert taught the Natives how to trap wolves in summer without harming other valuable fur bearers.

Natives were busily bringing in meat, which the women cut into thin strips and dried for the winter. A mammoth caribou migration arrived while we were there, and the woods were alive with the animals from Big Delta to Nabesna.

In September we made a two-week trip north along the border into the Ladue River valley. Here, too, were caribou in great numbers, along with many moose. They filled the valleys and covered the hills. Wolves were everywhere. They seemed to concentrate their depredations on caribou, which were easier to find and pull down than moose.

In attacking caribou, wolves commonly eat them alive. They catch one, grab a few mouthfuls of meat, hair, and hide, and bolt it down. The caribou runs on, spewing blood. The wolves overtake it and the process is repeated. I once saw three wolves down a caribou five times, the fifth being the last.

---

2. After twenty-three years with the Commission, and his stint as Executive Officer, Dufresne became an Associate Editor for *Field & Stream* magazine. He wrote three books on Alaska's wildlife and numerous magazine articles.

I've also seen live moose with large holes eaten out of their hams by wolves. They usually live from one to three days. Often the wolves don't come back to finish them. Ravens complete the job.

Some folk claim that wolves kill only the sick and injured. It is possible they concentrate on these because of the ease of killing. But six wolves can kill the biggest bull moose at his fightingest best. I once saw that happen on a bar in the Toklat River. I circled my plane and watched for an hour, but the fight lasted longer than that because it was underway when I arrived. When it was over, an acre of the bar was torn up. I have a conviction that four wolves, or maybe three, could do it. But, back to 1927.

We remained on the upper Tanana until late September. At Fairbanks I outfitted, and in November, with a fifteen-dog team, I left for my new station at Fort Yukon.

November 9, 1927. Worked all last evening at roping up sled. Dufresne helps me hitch up dogs and drive them to train. Leave Fairbanks 8:30 a.m. Arrive Chatanika 2:30 p.m. [A narrow-gauge railroad then ran the roughly twenty miles from Fairbanks to Chatanika. Sam took advantage of this for the start of his journey.]

November 11, 1927. Clear. 20 degrees below. Leave Belle Creek Roadhouse without dogs. Snowshoed to Beaton's cabin. Called at cabin of E.H. Brown and Julius Stuver at Chatanika bridge. Found them skinning a fox. Brown admits catching fox in a trap. Admits that he knew it was out of season. Has no license. Is resident citizen. Seized fox skin and go to Beaton's cabin and call Dufresne [telephoned]. *He will handle case for me as I want to proceed to Fort Yukon.*

Brown promises to report to Dufresne promptly on arrival in Fairbanks on November 26, and not later than November 30. Brown and Stuver do not try to avoid questions, but answer willingly and without hesitation.

In p.m. seized guns from Hector Beaton [an alien without a permit] *and sent a .250 Savage and a .30 Winchester to town to Dufresne by Brown. Savage belongs to Frank Stander, adjudged demented. Leave .22 at Belle Creek Roadhouse for owner Ed Peterson.*

Brown duly reported, handed Frank Dufresne the evidence and rifles, and admitted his guilt. Talk about the honor system. But there was a spirit like this all through the Interior in those days.

One evening early on my journey to Fort Yukon, I was beat from driving my dogs all day, and stopped at a roadhouse. The proprietor was very drunk and quite hostile, but said I could stay if I furnished my own sleeping bag and did my own cooking. I agreed to this and went to care for my dogs.

On my return, the owner was in a towering rage. He accused me of stealing his bottle of hootch [prohibition was in effect]. I knew it could not be far away, so I pacified him by offering to help him find it.

We started in the most likely place, in the bunk, under the bunk and behind the bunk. Then we branched out and I spotted it where he had dropped it. It was bobbing in the slop bucket.

He promptly offered me a drink, which I more promptly declined.

I didn't get much rest that night, what with putting out a fire he started with a candle, and being accused of trying to burn down the joint. Morning came at last, and with much relief I took off.

Sunday, November 13, 1927. Clear at 20 below zero. Leave Cassiar Roadhouse at 1:30 p.m. Travel up Chatanika River. Strike several overflows. Had to climb steep bank to get out of water. Then snub sled back down steep bank to get onto ice. Find several traps baited, but not set. Dogs very tired and I have to walk most of the way. Arrived at Faith Creek Roadhouse about 7:30 p.m.

November 15, 1927. 12 degrees below, clear. Traveled by dog team 20 miles. Leave Twelve-mile Roadhouse at 8 a.m. Arrive Miller House at 5:30 p.m. Issue one resident trapper license en route, and take two applications. Climbed Eagle Summit. Very steep on north side. Sled tips over and rolls down snowbank. Dogs all tangled up. Turned dogs loose. Looked bad. Slipped. Hanging on edge of snowbank and dogs all over mountainside. Sled slipped to foot of mountain one mile. Dogs come back, and I hitch up and proceed to Miller House. Wear out two dog chains snubbing [brak-ing, with chains wrapped on runners] sled down mountainside.

My trip wasn't made any easier by my strange and willful lead dog. For the first week or so, he and I didn't see eye to eye, so to speak. He was a good worker and knew the commands, but executed them only when he happened to agree with them. Sometimes he thought up some pretty wild ideas all on his own.

Running down off the north side of Eagle Summit we came upon an abandoned cabin which had started to glacier in from a nearby creek. The door was frozen shut, but a half-window was open on our side.

The window caught my lead dog's attention. He made a dash for it and jumped right through the opening into the cabin. The other dogs gleefully followed, and within moments they were all inside with the nose of the sled wedged tightly into the opening.

There was no prying the sled loose, nor the frozen door open. Finally, with my axe I worked on the stove pipe hole in the frozen sod roof until I had chopped an opening big enough to get through. Then I untangled the dogs, and boosted them out of the stove pipe hole one at a time by the dim light of a candle

It was long after dark by the time I got done, but I couldn't stay in the cabin because an overflow might bust loose during the night and trap me. So I hitched up the dogs and went down to the first timber where I siwashed for the night.

I arrived in Circle City a few days later and stopped at the Tanana Roadhouse, run by Mr. and Mrs. Joe Romaker. I had been there in 1925, and it was nice to see these friendly folks again. The next morning it was sixty below zero. I holed up for the cold spell, which lasted a week.

The roadhouse was an old rambling two-story structure, with sleeping quarters upstairs. Its floors and stairway were warped, and two cables attached to vertical timbers on either side of the house ran across its ceiling to hold its bulging walls in place. My room had a sagging, unlevel, floor which squeaked and groaned every move I made. But it was a comfortable room and roadhouse.

Mrs. Romaker was a frail but energetic little old lady. She kept busy in the kitchen, and the moose stews, roasts and steaks, together with home-baked bread and pies of wild blueberries and cranberries, were out of this world for flavor.

Joe was a big easy-going chap, always telling stories of the early days. He kept busy lugging wood and stuffing it into three different stoves, one of which was a 100-gallon drum. He'd stoke the stoves, sit, and tell me a story, and it would be time to stoke stoves again. All in all, it was a very pleasant week.

November 24. [At Circle] 45 below. Work all day on sled. Reinforced by winding with rawhide. Cut off handlebars and placed bow over back of sled. This makes it much stronger and easier to handle. Exercise dogs. Thanksgiving dinner at Northern Commercial Company with wireless boys.

November 27. 45 below. Davis of Circle delinquent on trapper's report. Uses poison on Birch River, and has used poison for many years. Is an outlaw on other scores. Rather bad man. One man reports he was cautioned about putting hand inside wolf skin owned by Davis as there was danger of poisoning.

Davis also wanted for bootlegging. Prominent citizen here has $180 of personal money up for conviction of Davis on bootleg stuff, as Davis' liquor gets into hands of Natives.

[AUTHOR] Sam made no further comment on Davis in his diary.

The confidant says certain people in Fort Yukon are very much concerned over arrival of game warden. Does not mention names. Something to work on.

Note: Circle to first cabin, 22 miles. First cabin to second cabin, 13 miles. Second cabin to third cabin, 16 miles. Third cabin to Fort Yukon, 20 miles.

November 29, 1927. Tuesday. 45 below. At Circle. Exercise dogs on traplines south of town.

December 3. 30 below at mid day. Leave Circle at 7:45 a.m. Tough going all day through niggerhead flats. Tipped over 50 times. Dogs do well, but are all in. Arrive 22-mile cabin at 4 p.m. plumb worn out. Cut wood and prepare for next day.

December 7, 1927. 50 below. Leave 17-mile cabin at 10:20 a.m. Arrive Native cabins (Indian settlement) 12 miles above Fort Yukon at 12 noon. Call on and have talk with Natives who have little caribou meat and little fish. Everything ok [legal]. *Good going on* [Yukon] *River.*

Met the Circle-Fort Yukon mail carrier Curtis "Curly" Wells on trail at 1:30 p.m. Arrive Fort Yukon at 3 p.m. Cold as hell. Spent p.m. until 6 o'clock in going about town with Bill Butler, Deputy Marshal. Call on Commissioner and others. See Jack Donald, J. C. Carroll, Harold Horton.

I arrived in Fort Yukon at the beginning of winter 1927, the first resident federal Fish and Wildlife Agent for the area. This struck many of the old timers as rather funny. The need of regulatory laws for game and fur wasn't apparent to them.

Fort Yukon residents were more or less hostile to game conservation. Until I arrived, everything had been wide open; bag limits for moose and caribou, although on the books, were ignored, as were closed seasons. Same with furbearers.

It was mostly an Indian village, about the biggest Native village in the Interior. Natives were lukewarm to the conservation of wildlife. The white old-timers were hostile at first. The local

Fort Yukon in 1927. Sam O. White, courtesy DRAHS

Commissioner, who acted as judge in legal matters, was also quite hostile.

The town was divided into two factions; the old-timers and the mission. The mission was generally hostile toward game law enforcement, but after I had been there for three or four months, they warmed up a bit.

The next several years produced an abundance of fur, and I doubt that my presence the first year had little affect on the rise or fall of furbearers. Same with moose and caribou, both of which were plentiful.

It was a beginning that had to be made. The situation over the next many years was going to change. Most locals thought the free and easy way of using fur and game would last forever.

Fort Yukon was a great fur center in those years, when fur was King in Alaska. It was the great collecting point for fur in all Alaska. Nearly all the fur from the upper Porcupine River came down through Fort Yukon, as did the huge catch of muskrats on the Old Crow Flats (in Yukon Territory). The Yukon Flats themselves yielded great quantities of fur, and the back country to the north, as well as to the south as far as Beaver Creek, Birch Creek, and Preacher Creek, contributed.

This was truly frontier country then. The airplane had not yet changed lives, and all mail arrived and left by river steamboat or by dog team. Great dog sled loads of fur went out of Fort Yukon during winter and spring. They were bulky, and in some ways, resembled loads of hay under canvas.

There was adventure tied up in each bundle of fur, of which nothing will ever be known. Trappers disappeared, and there were other tragedies. The old-timers of this period were frontiersmen of the first magnitude. They were hearty, rugged chaps who worked hard, and when it came to play, the same.

However, there was little leeway for play in the lives of these trappers. Play time was during the all-too-short summer. Most came downriver from their traplines in early June, and had to return back up the northern rivers in late July with boat loads of supplies and equipment so as to get to their operating grounds before freeze-up.

Trappers south of the Yukon had a little more leeway, but they too were usually gone in early August. Of course there were many who trapped on the Yukon Flats who usually came in to Fort Yukon during Christmas holidays. A few combined summer fishing with their winter trapping. They sold fish [salmon] for dog food, and fed their own dogs with them.

The dog population on the Yukon was immense. Nearly everyone, including the Indians, had a team of from seven to eighteen dogs.

George Davies and Bert Stewart ran the picturesque two-story-log, Fort Yukon Hotel. It was a paying concern. During the fur boom of those years, it grossed an average of $250 a day.

The Fort Yukon Hotel in 1927, owned and operated by Bert Stewart and George Davies. SAM O. WHITE, COURTESY DRAHS

In addition to renting rooms, good and substantial meals were served. While I bached it, I ate there twice a day at $1.50 a meal. Meat was always moose or caribou, or fish from surrounding rivers and lakes. At the time, high cost prohibited bringing in domestic meats.

December 10, 1927. 10 below. Very warm. About town. Put out bids for dog food and equipment. Northern Commercial Company won. Got 1,000 pounds [dried] fish [dog salmon], 50 pounds tallow, one tent, one stove, 20 gals. gasoline, one gallon of Zerolene, delivered to cabin. Take in picture show in evening.

Hear that Native came in and asked fur dealer Carroll if he would buy marten. Carroll refused to buy. Later Native comes back with money. Suspect he sold to certain dealer in town [marten season was closed].

In December I made a short patrol to Rampart House on the border to contact the Royal Canadian Mounted Police. On the way I overtook a Native family which had stopped to make tea. They had a month-old baby well wrapped in fur, and since it was 48 below, I was interested in seeing how they kept the baby warm.

They had cut a bunch of crotched willows and stacked them about two feet high close to the fire. They laid the baby on top, and the heat from the fire worked its way up through the branches.

That evening, I reached a shelter cabin just after dark, cut plenty of wood, and was ready to settle in when this Native family and another arrived. There was barely room for all of us to stretch out on the cabin floor. Dinner and breakfast came out of my grub box and strained it a bit.

As I entered the Ramparts at Howling Dog Rock,[3] I heard a dull rumbling and the familiar clickety-click of caribou[4] moving. Around a bend of the Porcupine River came a solid front of caribou. The dogs went wild. I had to tip the sled and anchor it to a pile of ice to hold them. Many thousands of caribou kept coming.

When the leaders drew near, they sheared towards the south bank, and passed within fifty feet of me. I climbed on an ice hummock and looked over a sea of brown furry backs.

---

3. During Hudson Bay Co.'s time on the Porcupine River, dogs used in pulling freight barges upstream couldn't haul loaded boats past a vertical cliff here. While the boats were being pulled up by men with ropes, the dogs had to scramble up the steep back slope of the rock and down again to join the party, or they remained behind and howled. Thus the name.

4. Caribou's lower legs click with each step. The sound can be heard even when the animals are on sand or other soft surface. It may benefit caribou as a means of keeping track of one another.

The Alaska Game Commission building at Fort Yukon, 1928.
SAM O. WHITE, COURTESY DRAHS

On the shore opposite me was open water of the Porcupine River, with a big whirlpool. I'd been warned about it by trapper W. C. Curtis. Before the caribou showed up I had heard its gurgling and sucking sound. As the herd sheared away, many of the animals were crowded off the ice into the whirlpool. I watched them go around and around until they reached the vortex, where they disappeared beneath the ice.

The dogs had caused the herd to turn. If I had loosed them, they would have run sled and all into the caribou, and that would have been disastrous.

It was 62 below when I arrived at Rampart House, just across the Canadian border. Two Native dogs there froze to death that night and were promptly chopped up and fed to their team mates.

Rampart House sits on the side of a hill atop the steep banks of the Porcupine River. Winds sweep through here, and it is very cold. I remained two days, conferring with the RCMP.

Dan Cadzow operated a trading post at Rampart House. He was a powerful character who annually took in about a quarter of a million dollars worth of fur. A lot of the fur was exchanged for groceries and clothing.

The local Native women made much of their clothing themselves, and they were a well-dressed bunch. They were also well fed as far as a meat diet went. That's about all they were used to, with a little flour and beans.

Cadzow's volume of trade goods was not large. Silver dollars was the smallest change at his trading post; six cream crackers, such as came in barrels, $1; four candles, $1; and so forth. Under these conditions, my grub box didn't get half filled.

Dan had a two-story frame house with hardwood floors, the only frame house north of the Yukon. Rachel, his Native wife, was a very fine old lady, respected by everyone.

Dan often made trips stateside, accompanied by Rachel. Sometimes he chartered a special train while touring the country. He acquired a new boat every year, and didn't take pains to preserve the old ones during break-up.

The old frame house is abandoned now. Last time I was there it sat forlornly empty, its white paint and green trim peeling. Rachel lived there alone for several years after Dan died.

January 10, 1928. Talked to Natives about wolves and coyotes. One Native said that when he was in the Chandalar he saw one part of the river completely packed where a wolf pack had passed. Said he counted 52 tracks. Saw a beaten track beside the river. Said he saw evidence of 200 wolves. White trappers come in later and tell the same story, only they estimated 250 wolves.

January 12, 1928. Leave Fort Yukon at 8:30 a.m. Travel down river until 12 a.m. I arrive at Schurett's cabin at 3:30 p.m. Dogs all in. Stop and feed and rest until 7:30 p.m. Resume journey and travel until 12 midnight and arrive at mail carrier tent. Damned near dead. Issue one resident license.

January 13, 1928. Leave mail carrier tent at 8 a.m. Arrive White Eye Roadhouse at 7:30 p.m. 28 miles. Dogs all in.

Later in January, I left Fort Yukon to make a patrol via Beaver to Caro and Big Squaw and return via the Chandalar and the Native village, then known as Chandalar Village, now called Venetie. I followed the mail trail from Fort Yukon to Beaver, and a trail of sorts from Beaver to Big Squaw. I left most of my outfit in a shelter cabin at Orenzic Crossing, and followed a trapper's trail up the Orenzic.

The trapline belonged to Joe Roberts, a Portuguese national. He had roughly $7,000 in fur, which was a heap of money then. He also had a new and very well built cabin. He could sit on his bunk and eat off the table, and also attend to the cooking on the stove. He had about seventy-five pounds of sausage made from moose meat and moose casings, which was expertly spiced and delicious. He was also eating lynx meat, but did not urge me to partake.

January 25, 1928. Leave Joe Roberts' upper cabin 8:30 a.m. and pick up two lynx and one mink [from Roberts' traps]. *Take these to his home cabin and hang in cache where he has eight other lynx, two mink, one red fox and one wolverine not yet skinned. Then proceed to Orenzic Crossing at Alaska Road Commission relief cabin at 3:30 p.m.*

At a shelter cabin on the way from Caro to Big Squaw I found an elderly Eskimo couple and a seven or eight-year-old child, all stark naked. It was 50 below outside, but the cabin was hot and stuffy. Ventilators were stuffed tight, and a three to four-inch layer of caribou hair covered the floor. They professed not to speak or understand English.

I unstuffed ventilators, got out my grub, and cooked my meal, making a liberal allowance so as to have some left over for them. When I finished eating, the man came to the table (he had put on a pair of caribou-skin pants) and said quite distinctly, "Baby (the child) got no milk. Me got no bread."

I gathered my dishes, and put the left-over food in a gas can and gave it to them. The old lady removed a man-sized chew of tobacco from her mouth and laid it on the table. They ate the leftovers like animals. They had been living on straight caribou and rabbit, along with an occasional ptarmigan they could snare. I was glad to get out of that mess.

At Squaw Creek mining camp I found Carlson and Amero, two older men, working hard sinking holes and hauling spruce logs three miles uphill with a dog team. I stayed two or three nights, and since it warmed up, I started the return trip with a long run by moonlight.

I stopped at the shelter cabin to give the elderly couple a can of coffee, some sugar, and what cornmeal I could spare. They received the gifts stoically, and if they appreciated it, they did a good job of concealing it. I had never seen people so destitute, and I was depressed over them for days.

On February 5, from Caro I left the trail and took off down the Chandalar River, a stream of many channels and wide gravel bars. Snow was deep, and travel was difficult. The dogs got ornery. When we came to a cross channel where ice was in sight with no snow on it, my leader made for the ice and I couldn't stop or turn him.

Within moments, the sled and dogs broke through. Standing in water up to my knees, I cut the tow line with my axe. The dogs took off on caribou trails into the woods, and I let them go.

The Alaska Game Commission dog team driven by Sam White in the Circle country, March 1928. Sam O. White, courtesy DRAHS

I fished everything out of the water but one bale of dried fish [dog food] that went under the ice. Everything but my bedding got soaked. I rushed up on the bank, got a big fire going, and changed into dry clothes. After that I retrieved the dogs from where they were tangled around some trees.

By then it was dark. A half mile downstream I pitched the tent, set up the Yukon stove and cooked a meal of sorts, with plenty of hot tea.

To top off the day of troubles, nearby wolves began to howl. They were close and all around us. The dogs became terrified. I brought them in and built a brush fence around them and my tent. Caribou were all over by the hundreds of thousands, but the wolves were more interested in my dogs. It seems they love dog meat.

I didn't get to bed at all that night because of the wolves. Come early morning we again set out. The dogs were slow and mean, and a fight started, which I broke up quickly and firmly. We floundered through deep snow until about noon when I spotted what appeared to be a freshly-broken trail ahead. I urged the dogs toward it, but they cowered and refused to move a few hundred feet short.

I grabbed my .30–30 carbine and went to the trail. It had been recently made by wolves, and was about four feet wide and packed solid. I saw wolves flitting about in the woods on the east bank, but they were too far for my .30–30.

About then the dogs took fright and rushed to me. I then became the leader and got them away from there, where they settled down.

Chandalar Village in 1928. It is now known as Venetie.
Sam O. White, courtesy DRAHS

I camped that night on a point with gravel bars all around except for a small neck of timber which I fenced off with brush. I slept, and to heck with the wolves. They howled everywhere, but wouldn't cross the open gravel bars, or the brush fence.

Next morning the dogs were ready to cooperate for once, and we left in a hurry. We arrived at Chandalar Native village [Venetie] in the late afternoon.

February 8, 1928. At Chandalar Village. Give talk to Natives on laws, as they want to know. Say first game warden ever visit them. Population 50. Buildings 16. Want school here. Put sled in cabin and repair and plane edge of skis down one half inch on each side as gravel bars badly splintered them. Dogs badly needed rest. Many wolf signs. Have to protect dogs with brush fence each night on rivers. Dogs do not rest while on river because of encounters with wolves.

Wednesday, March 6, 1928. [At Fort Yukon] *Making dog moccasins, bags for chuck* [food], *and working on filing cases. Exercise dogs. Airplane arrives from Circle and departs for Fairbanks.* [This is the first mention of an airplane in Sam's field diaries].

March 14, 1928. Leave Fort Yukon at 1 p.m. Pitch camp at 5 p.m. Dogs soft. Jenny Roberts and the chief of the Chandalar Native village tell me they have one bad actor in their camp. Wastes meat. Threatens

Husky dog teams of nomadic Eskimos on the Coleen River, 1928.
These nomads eventually settled in Anaktuvuk Pass in the arctic
Brooks Range. SAM O. WHITE, COURTESY DRAHS

to shoot warden. Bad outlaw. They ask me to curb this sport. I tell
them to get evidence and I will pinch him.

On another trip in March I was threading my way up a mountain stream with the same dog team. I came to an ice jam with
a fair-sized body of water backed up behind it. Remembering
the old-timers' warnings of "gushers," I carefully made my way
around it.

Back on the creek, I urged the dogs along when I realized they
were very nervous. I then became aware of a sullen roar ahead.
It grew louder by the second. A small willow island was close. I
headed the dogs for it, and got prompt and enthusiastic coopera-
tion. Just then a wall of tumbling ice blocks came around the bend.
Water spouted ten feet high from that moving wall.

We reached the willow island just as the flood hit the upper
end of it. Ice piled up at the head of the island, and both channels
of the river were seething cauldrons. Water rose to my knees, and
covered some of the sled, but almost immediately it started dropping as the torrent swept on. In five minutes the water was off the
island, and in twenty minutes the small channel was dry.

We crossed over and I pitched camp and spent the rest of the day and that night drying the gear. I was shaken by the experience. It proved again that it pays to listen to the old sourdoughs.

March 15, 1928. Arrive at Native settlement 35 miles from Fort Yukon. Heavy storm. No sign of trail. Almost impossible to make dogs face the gale. Find two lynx snared. Evidently belong to Johnny Ross, who I met yesterday. Will lay over tomorrow if bad weather.

March 16, 1928. Friday. Heavy gale. 20 degrees below. Leave Stephen's place at 10:30 a.m. Blinding gale. Can hardly see. No trail on lakes and flats. Arrive F. E. Foster's cabin at 4 p.m. Dogs all in. Can get dog food here. Green salmon [frozen, not dried]. *Foster has passed word and sent out letters that all trappers take up their traps. Good to have someone help. Frostbit my cheeks on big lake in heavy gale.*

March 18, 1928. Sunday. Leave F. E. Foster's cabin at 10:30. Arrive Shuman House at 4:30 p.m. Arrive at Joe Ward's cabin at 5:45. No trail in places. River trail not visible. Meet Big Steve on trail at 1:40 p.m. with mail. Rampart to Fort Yukon trail from here to Shuman House. Better trail. Whoopee!

March 20, 1928, Tuesday. Leave Chief J. Herbert cabin. 30 below. Heavy wind. Pass the two Native teams at 9 a.m. Cannot pass point. Try three times. Wind sweeps dogs off their feet on the bare ice.

Work out into middle of river and after a time got past point. Arrive Chief John Herbert main cabin at 2:30 p.m., 38 below. Wind

Shuman House on the Porcupine River, 1928. Sam O. White, courtesy DRAHS

The 22-Mile shelter cabin on the Circle-Fort Yukon trail in 1928. The freight sled belonged to mail-carrier Curly Wells.
SAM O. WHITE, COURTESY DRAHS

just tearing down river. Natives arrive at 4:30 p.m. Will have to lay over tomorrow until wind goes down and warmer. No trail. Snow piled high in places. Ice swept bare in other places.

March 21, 1928. From Burnt Point to Howling Dog. See band of caribou on portage. Wind blowing a gale. [traveled] *Ten miles on river, 8 miles on portage. Break one ski on big hill at Howling Dog. Stop at cabin with W. C. Curtis.*

March 23, 1928. From Howling Dog to Old Rampart. Inspect Charlie Strom's fur dealer's report.

On one of my last patrols with that team before the spring break-up, I made a run up Birch Creek and headed the dogs up a high bank to pick up the trail to Circle City. As the sled progressed upward, it moved slower and slower. Finally, when the dogs disappeared over the top, it came to a dead stop.

I snapped the tow line, yelled dog team language, and heaved on the gee pole. Nothing happened. Finally, figuring the tow line had fouled, I climbed the bank. There lay fifteen dogs, all stretched out in the sun, sound asleep. That convinced me there had to be a better means of transportation than a dog team.[5]

---

5. This is one of the stories Sam often told to explain why he decided to start flying.

A cabin Swallow at Fort Yukon, 1928. From left Jack Donald, Mary Burgess (later Mrs. Sam White), Sam White, and Fred Schroeder.
SAM O. WHITE, COURTESY DRAHS

April 6 & 7, 1928 [At Fort Yukon]. Met with U.S. Commissioner to seal Canadian fur. Go to all Native cabins and caches and tell them any fresh-killed moose must be accompanied by the head, and positively no killing of cows and calves. Some of them got pretty hot about this, but I tell them no fooling, that I mean business. In p.m. sealed all of game meat in hotel cold storage.

April 8, 1928. Leave 17-mile cabin at 8 a.m. Arrive Halfway Cabin at noon. Make tea. This cabin used by Natives. Very dirty. No wood. Leave Halfway Cabin at 1:30 p.m. after resting dogs. Arrive at cabin 22 miles from Circle at 5 p.m. [traveled] 30 miles this day. Met Curly Wells U.S. mail carrier at this cabin.

April 9, 1928. Leave 22-mile Cabin at 9 a.m. after big dog fight with mail carrier's team. Arrive Circle at 3 p.m. Visit Commissioner and Marshal. Go through Native village with Marshal and warn all about cow moose.

April 20, 1928. Talked with Johnson at house of Marshal McLain. Johnson says he did not use poison, but knows who did, where he got it. Says one of the drug stores in Fairbanks sold the poison in $5 vials and that he saw it in the possession of a person whose name he will give me later. When the time comes, he will tell me all he knows.

May 5, 1928. About town. Made box for nails, clean up yard, etc., ice does not go out of Tanana (pealuk) [bad luck] *for me. No ice pool money. Down to Native town and talk with John Slocum in afternoon. Cook dog food.*

May 12, 1928. Make desk out of lumber from boat crates. Made office chairs from same material.

May 18, 1928 Out to aviation field. Helped get it in shape for aviators to land on. About town in p.m. see four caribou swim lake back of hospital. Cooking dog food.

May 24, 1928. On waterfront until midnight watching boats come in from Porcupine and Black Rivers.

June 13, 1928. Up Porcupine River all day. Fine going. Take swim in slough.

August 11, 1928. Tell Natives to wait until September first to kill moose.

[AUTHOR] Sam didn't record the date in his federal diary, but in late August, 1928, he and his new bride, the former Mary Burgess, a nurse at the Fort Yukon hospital, left Fort Yukon by steamer, arrived at Nenana and spent a night there, then took the train to Fairbanks.

During the remainder of his fourteen years as a game warden, Sam was stationed at Fairbanks.

Fort Yukon Old-timers

*The old-timers of this period were frontiersmen of the first magnitude,
hearty rugged chaps who worked and played hard.*
—SAM O. WHITE

THE FUR BUSINESS was booming when I arrived at Fort Yukon in
1927. Trappers based in Fort Yukon worked in both Alaska and
Canada, trapping mink, otter, weasel, wolverine wolf, and lynx,
plus muskrats by the hundreds of thousands. At the time, for every
dollar, you had a hundred cents which went a long way. Fur was a
high-priced item. A trapper could get $65 for a lynx. Some of the
trappers I knew at Fort Yukon caught fifty to sixty lynx during
a trapping season.

Most of the muskrats that came through Fort Yukon were from
the Old Crow Flats in Canada. It was tremendous rat country. The
trappers there lived pretty tough. I was once there on the eighth of
May when it was 30 degrees below, and I landed a wheel plane on
the ice. There are hardly any trees there. It's mostly marsh land,
and the river roams very crookedly.

Many of the trappers on the Old Crow Flats had no tents—just
a tarp. They rolled up in it in the worst of weather, or they'd use
it for shelter, moving it from one side to the other, whichever way
the wind blew.

Many of the trappers were truly well-to-do in terms of money.
Some invested in stocks in Canada (Canadian-Pacific Railroad
was popular) and the U.S. Most of them had bank accounts in
Canada.

GEORGE DAVIES AND BERT STEWART owned the Fort Yukon
Roadhouse. Before moving to Fort Yukon, at a village on the

Kuskokwim River they had accumulated a large consignment of contraband fur. Being aliens, they were pinched for an outlet to move the stuff. Airplane transportation had just started, and a local pilot volunteered to help them peddle their illegal furs. He then hauled all their furs to Fairbanks.

He went south with their fur, and they never saw him again.

This supposedly happened in 1926, a year before I was employed by the Alaska Game Commission. I heard of this deal from several sources. The clincher for me was when Bert Stewart himself told me about it; he was willing to come clean in order to get the erring pilot punished.

There was no vestige of evidence, and I had only Bert's word. I could take no action.

HARRY HORTON was a successful fur trader at Fort Yukon. During his first winter there he trapped. The next winter, he set up a trading post and a prominent local Native's daughter moved in with him as house keeper. This arrangement prevailed for several years, but it was a thorn in the side of the local missionaries. They brought court action against him for cohabitation, or some such charge, and the case was set over for the District Court in Fairbanks.

This was before the days of airplane transportation in Alaska. For the trial, a caravan of dog teams set out from Fort Yukon to Fairbanks, some taking government witnesses, and some taking witnesses for the defendant. I heard that the trial cost in the neighborhood of $80,000. The verdict favored the Hortons.

Having shown the government that they did not have to get married, on the return trip to Fort Yukon they married, and lived quite happily together for many years.

In the early 1930s Horton was feeling his age. He had amassed a sizable fortune, supposedly a quarter of a million dollars. He wanted to return to his former home in New York state. He gave his wife their house in Fort Yukon, settled a reasonable income on her, and went back to Albany New York to end his days.

At its heyday, Horton's store was a gathering place for the big-time poker players of Fort Yukon. I heard that a $1,200 kitty was not unusual there on almost any poker night.

WHEN I FIRST KNEW J.C. "DAD" MOORE in 1927 he was getting along in years, but he was moderately active. He owned a motorboat on the Yukon, and often chartered it. He was a kindly old gentleman, and quite a contrast with the usual frontiersmen of that community.

In the summer of 1928 he made a trip to the states to visit his daughter. While Outside he bought a Chevrolet sedan. After using the car in the states, he decided that since a road was being built from Fairbanks to Circle (the Steese Highway) he would ship his car to Circle City, and keep it there to run to Fairbanks now and then when the road was completed. He could run his boat from Fort Yukon to Circle, drive to Fairbanks, and return the same route.

He shipped the car to Alaska over the railroad to Whitehorse, Yukon Territory, and instructed the purser on a steamboat to haul it down the Yukon river to unload it at Circle.

The purser or steamboat crew got his instructions mixed up. Instead of unloading it at Circle, they bypassed Circle and brought it to Fort Yukon.

At the time there were no motor vehicles in Fort Yukon other than motorboats and a tractor, consequently there were no roads. But Dad had the boat crew unload the car there anyway, deciding to make the best of it. He could ship it upstream to Circle later if warranted.

While he was aboard the steamer settling with the purser, the sedan, ashore, filled with Natives, who upon Dad's arrival demanded a ride. He agreed, and half-serious said, "That'll be one muskrat skin for each person."

They all came through, as it was the custom among Natives at Fort Yukon to carry a few muskrat pelts around with them, using them for cash.

Dad drove them to the Hudson Bay burial ground, then back to the mission, then back to the steamer landing. When he got there, another gang of Natives was waiting for a ride. All that could crowd into the sedan did so—and all paid one muskrat skin.

That day and the next day Dad got pretty well worn out hauling Natives around Fort Yukon. He hired George Moriarity, the local barber, to run an eight hour shift with the car. George's wife then took an eight hour shift. Then Dad took another eight hour shift.

The car could run about a mile and a half in a round trip from the mission to the Hudson Bay cemetery and through the Native village. For a time, the car was so busy that Dad could hardly get time to grease it and gas up.

This developed into a taxi business. Native families, who lived practically next door to Carney's moving picture hall and soft drink counter, called for the taxi to pick them up. They took the prescribed trip to the Native village, to the mission and to the cemetery and return. They then watched the movie, ate ice cream and drank pop. When the movie ended, they sent a messenger for the taxi, and repeated the round trip, only to return to their home close by the movie emporium.

I was very fond of Dad Moore, and spent many pleasant hours visiting with him in his cabin.

WALDO C. CURTIS was a trapper on the Porcupine River at Howling Dog. He was a New Englander from New Hampshire, with a mischievous disposition. He was always jobbing someone. He was a good trapper, and made good money which he invested wisely. He also had plenty of money in the bank. Nevertheless, he persisted in living tough.

When trapping muskrats on the Old Crow Flats, he cooked ten rats at a time by inserting them in a five gallon gasoline can, heads down, and tails lopped over the side. He cooked them for one hour, then reversed them and cooked for another hour. He added one cup of flour and stirred.

That made one week's food for him.

I first met him when I arrived at his cabin at Howling Dog. It was perched on the bank of the Porcupine River, with a wonderful view across the river.

It was in February, 45 degrees below zero, and late in the afternoon. I stayed overnight. Next morning it had warmed to 30 below with the darndest howling blizzard the North can kick up. I doubt if a man and a dog team could have survived an hour in it.

The storm lasted three days, during which I remained holed up with Curtis. One day I was lying on a bunk and glanced at a hole in the ceiling logs, obviously made by a shotgun. It looked as if someone had been fooling with a shotgun, and it had accidentally fired.

"Curtis, how did that charge of shot get in your ceiling?" I asked.

"Oh, hell," he said, "that's where I shot a damned game warden last summer."

I was in Circle one April en route to Fort Yukon, where an old-timer, bowed with years and hardship, wanted to give away his seven-dog team. He was kind-hearted and didn't want them killed.

I took one, a big, stocky animal that looked very capable. He was covered with long hair right to the end of his nose. The hair was about eight inches long. It parted in the middle of his back, and, like a load of hay, neatly hung down both sides.

He was a great worker who was always digging in, and needed no encouragement. Unfortunately, he was also a great fighter with a quick temper, especially if he decided some other dog in the team wasn't doing his share.

On my three-day journey to Fort Yukon from Circle, he temporarily crippled two of my regular dogs. I soon discovered his secret weapon. He had a head and jaws like a grizzly bear, which looked innocent because it was covered with hair. Also, he had so much hair that other dogs couldn't easily bite him; all they got was a mouthful of hair.

When I arrived at Fort Yukon I ran into Waldo Curtis.

"Where did you get that dog?" he asked. "Is he a good worker?" I answered, "I paid $35 for him in Circle. He's a young dog and a good worker."

Curtis said, "I'll give you $35 for him. My three dogs are so old I need a young one to help them haul wood. I want the harness and chain with him."

"Ok," says I, and Curtis took the dog home.

Two days later I saw Curtis. "Confound your damned hide, I should have known better. You're from New England too," he blurted.

"What's wrong, Curtis?" I asked, pretending innocence.

"Wrong! Yesterday I had three dogs. Today I have one."

"What happened," I asked, beginning to feel guilty.

"That damned dog I bought from you ate my old dogs up on the first trip to the woods," he said. Then he laughed.

If anything changed, from then on it seemed Curtis looked on me with more respect. We still remained fast friends. I sent a check for half of the $35 to the old fellow in Circle who had given me the dog. I never told Curtis the dog had been given to me; it seemed wise not to.

Later, when I was flying into Fort Yukon for Wien Airlines with mail, freight, and passengers, Curtis told me he was expecting a case of whiskey, and thought it would be on my next trip. "Put it in a bag, and pack it around through the woods to behind my cache at the cabin. I'll meet you there," he requested.

This I did. When I arrived with the goods, Curtis was there, but so was Mrs. Curtis. She gave me a withering look that made me cringe, then flounced into the cabin and loudly slammed the door. She didn't approve of booze.

Curtis said, "It appears to be the last time you can come to see me while Mrs. Curtis is here."

"On the contrary," I said. I'll have lunch with you on my next trip."

He grinned at me and snorted.

On my next flight to Fort Yukon I had a quart Mason jar chock full of strawberries, and a pint of real cream. With these visible in my arms so they couldn't be missed, I brazenly knocked on the Curtis door.

Mrs. Curtis jerked the door open and gave me a devastating look. Then she spotted the strawberries. Her mouth opened, but for a few moments nothing came out. Then she said, "Come in."

I happily entered, Curtis sat in the far end of the cabin, looking surprised. I handed the strawberries and cream to Mrs. Curtis. She asked, "Can you stay for lunch?"

I assured her I could, and would be delighted.

She brought out a rather battered table from another room, and put some of the loveliest linen on it that I had seen in many a year. She then set the table correctly, and prettily, and we had a lunch the likes of which I had never seen in Alaska. We had a delightful time.

From that time on I took a great liking to Mrs. Curtis. I admired a lady who could set such a charming table in a trapper's cabin, and who so easily overlooked my earlier transgression.

As for Waldo, he commented, "I've seen everything now."

JOE WARD trapped just below Burnt Paw on the Porcupine River at "Joe Ward's Camp."[1] He was English, and had very pleasant mannerisms.

---

1. *Dictionary of Alaska Place Names*, Geological Survey Professional Paper 567, lists Joe Ward Camp (*village*, pop. 5), on right bank of Porcupine River, 15 mi. N of Chalkyitsik, Yukon Flats, as well as the nearby Joe Ward Slough.

Joe didn't always keep dogs. When he did have them, he didn't always use them on his traplines. His trapline cabins were spaced one-half-day of snowshoeing distance apart. If the going was good he could make the second cabin easily. If the going was tough, and he was delayed, he could make the half day cabin.

He kept blankets and grub at each cabin, placed there in the summer. During the summer, he also cut a good supply of wood for each cabin. Thus, in winter he had no work to do, no dogs to care for, and he could concentrate on trapping.

He always caught $6,000 worth of fur. Once he reached this goal, he pulled his traps, even though the season ran for another two weeks or even a month. As a result, his traplines produced well year after year.

Joe was a practical conservationist without declaring himself to be one. He invested his money wisely, and was well-to-do. He lived simply and independently. He had a cool and level head, and much common sense. He was much respected along the Yukon and Porcupine Rivers.

HARRY MARTIN trapped on the Porcupine River about twenty miles below Howling Dog. One of his cabins was six miles from the Curtis Cabin at Howling Dog. He was a loner; he wanted no company, and he called on no one. He usually had six dogs and six small toboggans which, when loaded with gear, he hitched individually to each dog. His caravan of toboggan-pulling dogs with Harry at their head must have been some sight.

His cabin was built into a hill, so that he had to build one end only; the hill made the far end. It was crude beyond words. Two dogs lived in the cabin with him with kennels under his bunk.

The place was always filthy. When the various trappers on the Porcupine came downriver after breakup, they got together for the trip to Fort Yukon, camping nights on river bars for the several day trip. Not Harry. He pitched his lone camp across the river from the others.

In Fort Yukon he built a "dog house" cabin far above town and stayed there while in town, which was never long. He outfitted as fast as he could and took off up the Porcupine again.

Harry got married on one of his trips to Fort Yukon. No one seemed to know quite how it happened, but it did. It didn't last long, however.

During winter a few years after the marriage broke up, Harry was found dead in his cabin. One of his dogs defended the cabin and the body so vigorously that it had to be shot before the body could be removed for burial.

HARRY HEALEY was smallish, but as hard as nails. Southbound, I once stopped at a trail cabin on the Porcupine River between Old Rampart and Rampart House. It was cold. The cabin had a good stove, and I fired it up for lunch. A frozen and animal-chewed caribou hind quarter lay on the floor of the cabin.

There was also a two-pound lard pail in a corner, likewise on the floor. It was full of a greenish mold. I heaved both items out so I wouldn't have to look at them while eating lunch. As I started to eat, Harry Healey showed up with his long string of big dogs. He tied his sled to a tree to anchor the team, and came in.

"Harry, you're just in time. I have enough lunch for both of us," I said.

"No. I cook mine own lunch," he responded. Then he looked all over the cabin, under the bunk, under the stove, and table.

"What are you looking for?" I asked.

"Where is mine sourdough, and where is mine caribou meat?" he asked, kind of exasperated.

I had heaved his treasures into a snowbank behind the cabin. I told him so, and he retrieved them. He then thawed pieces of chipped green sourdough and chopped chips off the caribou leg and fried them on the stove. They must have tasted better than they looked or smelled because he ate with great relish, while I had to avert my gaze.

Harry disappeared one winter. It was generally believed he broke through the ice on the Yukon, or some other river.

BILL O'BRIAN trapped on the Black River. Although he had trapped there for years, he still lived in a tent. He was rough and tough, and lived hard. He had a team of nine large malemutes.

In the dead of winter when it was very cold, he broke his leg. He managed to crawl into his tent and get into his sleeping bag. He couldn't cut firewood, and he had none ahead.

He shot the dogs he could see from the tent, and then himself. Two of his dogs escaped his shooting.

He was not missed for some time. When friends checked on

him, they were horrified to find him dead, and that the two dogs which escaped his rifle had devoured part of Bill.

Later I saw the Berglund girls driving those two dogs in their team. They had named them Coffin No. 1, and Coffin No. 2.

JOHN ROBERTS was a loner at first, but he later married Mrs. Berglund, widow of John Berglund. The now Mrs. Roberts was the mother of the three Berglund sisters, all of whom were as capable as any man on a trapline, and in living in the woods.

Mr. and Mrs. Roberts trapped on the Black River, and had a couple of substantial caches and cabins there.

At one time while, patrolling with an aircraft, I was at their place with Royal Canadian Mounted Police Constable Walter Bayne. The Roberts fed us for a week and refused to take pay.

We slept in a tent two of the girls had pitched for us across the creek from their cabin. The girls also brought us ice for water, swamp hay for our beds, and wood for our stove. When we returned to the Roberts place in the afternoons, the girls helped us take care of the airplane.

The two sisters ran a long trapline, and were catching a good amount of fur.

By then John Roberts was up in years, and had obvious tremors. He could no longer get out on the trapline. Mrs. Roberts kept one year's supply of staples on hand at all times. She had preserved great quantities of wild berries, and we lived like kings while there, for she was an excellent cook.

[AUTHOR] Evelyn Berglund Shore's book *Born on Snowshoes* (Heritage Press, 1954), was reprinted in 1993. The Berglund women were also written up in Ernie Pyle's *Home Country, 1935.*

TONY ROSE, a Portuguese national, trapped the Yukon Flats, and prospected the Chandalar and the Orenzik Rivers (Hadweenzie River). He was a fine man, always exuding sunshine and good cheer. He talked a lot, and was always cheerful.

He owned a Springfield rifle, and showed it to me with pride. He was a dead shot with it.

One winter day I was flying the mail down the Yukon River to Beaver when I spotted a wolf on the river in front of Tony's cabin. I went after it with the Fairchild 71, and got him out of the middle of the river and headed towards Tony, who stood on the river bank. He was watching what he thought was a show put on for his benefit.

The wolf ran up the bank within 100 feet of Tony, and he never saw it. Nor had he taken his rifle to the river bank.

Unknown to me in the few years that had passed when I had seen Tony infrequently, his eyes had failed, and he could see nothing at a distance.

The next time I saw him he said, in his usual cheerful way, "Sam, that was a good show you put on for me that day."

He didn't know the wolf had been there.

FRED DeMARS was an independent and successful trader at Circle City where I first met him in 1925. He was vague about his place of birth, but we gathered he was from the New Orleans vicinity of Louisiana.

Everything was neat, clean, and orderly at his Circle City trading post. If a careless customer left muddy tracks on the floor, Fred immediately mopped it up.

Later, when he had moved to Fort Yukon and set up a larger trading post, and I was flying for Wien Airline with mail, passengers, and freight, it was my custom when landing in winter to immediately draw oil from the plane's tank and take it to the nearest trading post when I remained overnight.

When taking it to Fred's I had to see to it that there was no oil on the outside of the can, and that it was set on a burlap sack or a piece of cardboard carton. Everything in his trading post was as neat as a pin. His living quarters, connected to the store with a doorway, was also kept neat and clean.

A well known story along the Yukon about Fred fits with his demeanor. Before outboard motors arrived, boats were rowed down the Yukon. Many fur buyers, carrying large sums in money belts, traveled the Yukon in the early days.

A fur buyer asked Fred to row him from Fort Yukon down the Yukon River to Tanana. A price was agreed on, and they started out, with stops at fish camps, cabins, and villages along the river. The buyer carried a large sum, and had to break out his money belt while buying furs, revealing the cash to Fred.

Fred decided to have a little fun at the expense of the buyer. Fred was a wicked-looking individual, with arched eyebrows and piercing eyes. So, during the day, while rowing, Fred occasionally stopped and stared at the buyer. This he did several times during the day, and after fixing the man with his stare, he would look around as if he was searching for a hiding place for something.

That night by the campfire on the bank Fred followed with more staring.

Next morning, the buyer, bleary-eyed from lack of sleep, threw his money belt across the fire. "Take it all. Only don't kill me. I have to sleep. I can't stay awake any longer."

Fred laughed at him and tossed the money belt back.

One summer, years after Fred had established his Fort Yukon trading post, I visited Waldo Curtis at Fort Yukon. The previous evening Fred had gone to a birthday party and consumed much liquor.

The day after the party, around 1 p.m., Curtis remarked, "I haven't seen Fred since last night. After the party last night he stopped here for a topper-offer. He looked pretty tough. Maybe we'd better go check on him."

Fred's trading post was locked. The door to the living quarters was also locked, and there was no answer to our calls or knocking. The windows were curtained so we couldn't see in. There was, however, a small high window in the gable end.

I found a couple of boxes to stand on and peered through that window. I was jolted to see Fred, in his longjohns, lying dead on his bed.

Curtis hailed a passing Indian and asked him to summon the U.S. deputy Marshal and the U.S. Commissioner. He then turned to me and said, "And you and I, my friend, better get the hell out of here or the Marshal will want to put us to work."

We were not called to testify, as there were plenty of other witnesses. After all, we had not been inside the building.

When Fred's assets were inventoried, among them was a $1,000 bond, and two or three $1,000 bills. And at the Northern Commercial store he had several more bonds, plus currency totalling close to $10,000, a lot of money at the time.

NAPOLEON VERVILLE, a Canadian, spent four years in the Canadian Army in World War I. He was a hard case who drank heavily, and loved a fight. He made several trips into Interior Alaska, traveling as far as Nome. He created trouble everywhere he went.

He once posed as a Deputy U.S. Marshal, and searched several caches. At Koyukuk Station he got into a fight with a trader, and but for the help of a couple friends, it might have been tough for the trader.

It seemed as if Nap, as he was called, didn't seem to care much how a fight came out. He took his share of shellackings and seemed to enjoy them.

Throughout the above I had no contact with Nap, but he became involved in several game law violations in Alaska. When I got around to actively looking for him, he had gone to Old Crow, in the Yukon. I thought it best to talk with the detachment of Old Crow Royal Canadian Mounted Police.

I went to Fort Yukon (I was then stationed in Fairbanks) and learned that Nap was there, and so was a Constable and another from the RCMP detachment at Old Crow. Napoleon was on good behavior, since the Constable was in town. I learned then that he had a well-developed respect for constituted authority.

I discussed Nap with the RCMP and they informed me that they were his guardians, and that he was a World War I hero. He received a pension check from the Canadian War Department, which was sent directly to the RCMP. They asked what I had on him, and if I had enough to jail him. I showed them my evidence, which was ample to jail him for a considerable spell.

The RCMP promised that, in a few days, if I didn't jail him, they'd take him back to Old Crow, and they'd see to it that he gave us the very minimum of trouble thereafter.

This was ok with me. They also said if he returned to Fort Yukon and got into trouble, they'd appreciate it if I'd fly him in the Game Commission aircraft to Old Crow for them. This I also agreed to.

They told me he had a most amazing war record, and had been severely wounded several times, but had always bounced back for further service. He was rawhide tough.

After our conference, we rounded Nap up and the Constable explained to him the deal we had made. Whenever he was in Fort Yukon, he was to do as I ordered.

Nap agreed to this. He obviously had great respect for the RCMP.

Months later, Nap went on a big drunk in Fort Yukon and froze his feet. He was in the hospital there, but he got up at night to sneak into town.

One afternoon I met him in town. Toes of his moccasins were

red with blood, yet he walked without limping. I marched him back to the hospital and ordered him to do whatever the nurses instructed him to do, and to mind them implicitly. Nap remembered what the Constable had told him, and whenever I gave him an order, he always responded with "Yes sir, Mr. White."

I told the nurses that if he got out of line they were to tell me. Since Nap knew that the orders came from the RCMP, he was a good patient for the next few days.

I then flew him to Old Crow and returned him to RCMP supervision. We had no further trouble with Napoleon.

There is more to the story of Napoleon Verville.

It took place in 1932 when the infamous "Mad Trapper of Rat River" was on his rampage through Canada with the RCMP hot on his heels. This story has been written repeatedly in various magazines, and, I believe, in a book. Movies, with the usual Hollywood fanciful stories, have been based on the event.

Verville was with the police after the Mad Trapper had wounded a policeman. It was Verville who made dynamite bombs, and heaved them onto the Mad Trapper's cabin stronghold. The police had returned to drive the outlaw out of his cabin and capture or kill him.

Making the bombs and delivering them to the roof and the door of the cabin was right down Verville's alley. He knew how to do this. First he had to sneak through the snow, using all available cover, and he did it well. A piece of the roof caved in from the blast, and the door was shattered. Still, the Mad Trapper met every advance with rifle fire, and the officers had to call off the assault to take a wounded policeman to Aklavik.

When they returned, the Mad Trapper had headed for the mountains. He laid a clever ambush, and killed Spike Millen, one of the RCMP. From there it was difficult to trail him in the mountains, since the wind had blown snow and his tracks away in many places. Temperatures ranged from minus 45 to minus 65.

At this stage the police brought in an aircraft, and soon located the fugitive's trail on the Bell River, or near Eagle Creek, not too far from Lapeer House.

They cornered him in the middle of the river, and a police party coming up the river with a dog team met him mid-river. There was no time for anyone to make the shore, so they opened hostilities right there. It was difficult to make effective rifle shots on the broad white surface. Either Jim or Frank Jackson (I forget which) crawled through the snow to the bank and got behind a tree where he could look down and see the fugitive.

The Mad Trapper whanged a couple of shots into the tree. Jackson couldn't return fire, for he was out of ammunition. He called the shots for the police and for others who were shooting, and they began to connect. After he had been hit a few times the Mad Trapper expired.

His fingerprints were sent to police offices around the world. None could identify him. In Aklavik he had given the name Albert Johnson.

I was told that a set of false teeth that did not fit him was in his effects, but I don't remember the source of that story. I also forget which of the two Jackson brothers told me the story of the chase, including Napoleon's part in it. Whichever it was, he was loud in the praise of Napoleon Verville's part. "Nap was made for that kind of work," he told me.

[AUTHOR] Sam once discussed Albert Johnson, "The Mad Trapper of Rat River," with Roy Billberg. In a February, 2006, letter to me Roy wrote what he remembered of Sam's story: "For a time in the winter of 1932, it looked as if Johnson might escape into Alaska. A Mounty flew to Alaska to brief lawmen. A special hand-picked group of Alaskan lawmen was formed to carry on the hunt if Johnson reached Alaska. Sam was to be one of the party, slated to do the flying."

Mary Burgess White

Sam is painfully popular. He's very kind and thoughtful about people.
He likes people underfoot. I don't always.
— MARY WHITE

[AUTHOR] IN LATE AUGUST, 1928, when Sam White arrived to become the agent-in-charge at Fairbanks for the Alaska Game Commission, he was accompanied by his pretty bride, Mary Burgess White. They had been married at Fort Yukon that summer, before Sam's transfer to Fairbanks. Sam was 37, Mary was nearly 40.

Mary White was 85 on January 22, 1973, when, for the University of Alaska Fairbanks Oral History Program, she was interviewed at the White home in Fairbanks by woman journalist Mike Dalton and Doris Southall, a nurse.

Speaking with a New England accent, she described volunteering to be a missionary nurse in 1927. She was sent to the one-doctor and two-nurse Hudson Stuck Memorial Hospital at Fort Yukon.

The hospital could accommodate about twenty-four patients. There were a few rooms for adults, plus a children's ward. Most of the children had tuberculosis.

"Poor little things," she remembered. "I used to take the little ones up in my arms and sing, and dance with them, during evening vespers, before I put them down for the night. They were babies, and awful sick. Most of them died. There was so much tuberculosis.

"When the big paddle-wheel steamers arrived during summer we'd see smoke down the river and someone in town would yell, 'Boat coming, boat coming.' The children who were up and around ran down to the river to see it come in.

Mary Burgess White. Photo date unknown. SAM O. WHITE, COURTESY DRAHS

"We'd dress the children up in red jackets, and they'd sit up, and the tourists wandered around the hospital, gazed, and asked unnecessary questions, and, finally, left. The children all spoke English, and visited with the tourists.

"It wasn't all pleasure. I remember one pesky tourist boy who was about eight years old. He pointed and asked, 'What's the matter with that one? What's the matter with that one?' I had an awful time with him.

"It took some time for the children to calm down after the tourists left.

"In addition to nursing, when there was no one else available, I also used to conduct the church service, which I'd been trained to do," she said.

They were an unlikely couple; big, booming-voiced, hearty, well-traveled, worldly, people-loving Sam, and the quiet, rather shy, devout, unworldly nurse.

"Sam likes people underfoot. I don't always. People make me kind of nervous if there are too many," she said.

Mary Burgess, born in September, 1888, in Millbrook, New York, was the daughter of the Reverend Thomas Burgess, a priest in the Episcopal church. Her grandfather had been a bishop in the church. Her mother died when she was 2 years old giving birth to her brother. She was reared by aunts in a home with servants, where she was waited on as a child and as a young woman.

"People had servants in those days. They were paid something like four dollars a month. We had a Polish girl, and an Irish family doing our things. That's long ago. As a result, I didn't know how to cook, and had never washed clothes until I married Sam."

She entered nursing school when she was 20 years old, but dropped out. "I guess I wasn't given enough responsibility when I was younger," she explained.

She then took two years of Deaconess and business training (mission training) at the Episcopal Deaconess School in Philadelphia. After that she did church work, mostly near her home

She was accepted for nurse training again when she was in her 30s. She attended a three-year missionary nurse training program at Rhode Island Hospital, in Providence, graduating in 1926.

Nursing came naturally to Mary. "I loved children. My doctor brother in Providence had four children. I used to live with them and care for the children. I had an advantage over the other nurses in training in that I had lived in a doctor's house, and I knew some of the medical terms," she said.

At the time of her interview, although her brother was retired, three of her nephews were doctors. In addition, two grand nieces were doctors, one of whom, Dr. Joan Burgess,[1] was in Anchorage. All were named Burgess.

At Fort Yukon, Mary became acquainted with Sam, the tall, friendly game warden. She frequently saw him ". . . go zipping by the hospital, standing on his sled behind his dog team. And, oh, he looked so romantic," she remembered. A realist, she also commented on his

Mr. and Mrs. Sam O. White, probably in 1929 or 1930.
Sam O. White, courtesy DRAHS

courtship; "There wasn't much competition."

Mary had been at the Hudson Stuck hospital less than a year when she and Sam married. "We were married by a woman U.S. Commissioner. I didn't dare tell my family that we weren't married in a church before an Episcopalian minister."

This disparate couple settled in Fairbanks and remained together until Mary died in October, 1974, at 87.

"We lived in eight different places before we moved to Kellum Street. We lived in one house in what is now AlaskaLand. In one of our houses, on Wendall Avenue, we couldn't shut the front door, so we piled tin cans on a chair in front of the door so if anyone came in they'd make a noise.

"In that house I'd put a tub on a chair in the living room, carry all the water into the living room, and do the washing. The kitchen was a little bit of a thing, hardly big enough to hold a tub on a chair.

---

1. Dr. Joan Burgess practiced medicine in Alaska for more than thirty years. She died in Anchorage June 29, 2006, at 72.

Mary B. White and one of the houses in Fairbanks where she and Sam resided. They lived in eight houses before settling at 902 Kellum Street.
Sam O. White, courtesy DRAHS

"In one house the kitchen was the only place to take a bath. Several times I'd be bathing and, without knocking, the kitchen door opened, and a man called, 'Only the laundry man.'

"I didn't want the laundry man at that particular time.

"In our house at 1500 First Avenue the only way you could get to the bathroom was to walk next to the foot of our bed. At times it was a bit embarrassing for me if we had a male guest.

"We lived all over town in those eight places, and finally bought this place. There was nothing but brush surrounding us when we moved here, and no road. There was no electricity, no running water, no sewer line, no ninth street. The road to this house was built while we were here.

"The house was originally two rooms. Sam added to it. Across the street was a field where the water man turned his horses loose to graze [in the early years, Fairbanks' household water was delivered by horse-drawn wagon or sled].

"This house is nicely arranged. If men callers come to see Sam, they can talk in privacy, and I have my own area. I can come and go to the bathroom and take a bath without any bother.

"We don't like TV. Sam
wouldn't have it in the
house," Mary said. "We've
had people loan us a TV and
we haven't even turned it on.
We have two radios, but we
don't turn them on either. We
do get newspapers."
"Do you fly often with
Sam?" the interviewer asked.
"No. I wouldn't go in
the plane for anything. I'm
not much good as a pilot's
wife, because I don't like to
fly," she answered. "About
as close as I got was when
Sam had his hangar at Weeks
Field. I used to take the cat
and go with him and sit and
crochet while he worked on
his airplane."
Mary was deeply involved
with her church. "I taught

*Sam and Mary White at 902 Kellum
Street, Fairbanks, probably in the
1940s.* Sam O. White, courtesy DRAHS

Sunday school in Fairbanks for years. I have only one talent. I can
tell stories to children. I used to tell them Bible stories. I haven't
done this for years now—too old," she said, rather sadly.

"I used to help with the Episcopal church bazaar with embroidery.
But nobody wants embroidery any more. When I was young there
were camisoles and tiny, fine, embroidery like I used to do.

For a time she worked as an office nurse for various doctors,
including the elder Dr. Romig, the well-known pioneering Alaska
doctor. In 1950, Sam's hands were badly burned in a cabin fire.
He went Outside (the south 48) for treatment, and returned and
stayed at St. Joseph's hospital. "I went to St. Joseph's to help him
every day for about a month. He could do nothing for himself,"
she remembered.

"Is Sam a church goer?" Mary was asked.

"No. He never goes. He belongs, theoretically. When anybody
comes and tries to give him literature, or tell him about another
church, he always says, "We're Episcopalians.""

"I tell him, 'You never go.'"

She added, "He was brought up on a farm and didn't have much chance at church. His mother was a grand old woman. I guess there was no church anywhere near the farm. He's a good man though. He's very kind and thoughtful. He's done an awful lot of kind things for people," Mary commented.

Though they were markedly different, "They respected one another," their daughter-in-law Julia White assured me (THE AUTHOR) in an interview. "When Harland (Sam's son) and I visited, quite often in the evenings Mary would tire, excuse herself, and go to bed, while Sam was just warming up to an evening of visiting," Julia said.

Mary told the interviewers, "I didn't mind being alone while Sam was off flying and earning us a living. He was often gone for weeks at a time."

Actually, Sam was often gone flying for months at a time, as when he had the mail contract to fly from Ruby, and when, for seven years, he flew from the Koyukuk River village of Hughes for Wien Airlines.

Mary never accompanied him to bush stations. She remained in Fairbanks, patiently awaiting his return. As they both aged, and Sam retired from flying, Mary was happy to have him home.

"Sam does all the cooking now. He likes to cook. He wouldn't do it if he didn't like it. I do all the dishes. It's hard for me sometimes, but I've got to do something," Mary said.

Sam and Mary never had children, but they housed many a young person over the years. Among them, John Sackett, son of trader Jack Sackett, of Huslia village. He lived with the Whites for several years while going to school in Fairbanks. There were others, for the White home was often a haven for kids from the bush, or Fairbanks kids that needed a home.

14
Learning to Fly

I couldn't stand to see game wasted. When I had to depend on a dog team, so much of my assigned area went without patrols I felt I was more or less a figurehead officer. I didn't like the idea of going around looking wise—that's the hardest thing in the world for me to do. There was a job to be done, and I was conscientious about it—I wanted to stop the waste, the illegal killing. To do it, I had to get out there where the action was.
—SAM O. WHITE

DURING MY FIRST YEAR and a half as a game warden for the Alaska Game Commission, I was married to nurse Mary Burgess, I was transferred from Fort Yukon to Fairbanks, and I took the first step towards getting a divorce from my dog team.

I was troubled having to depend on a team of free-thinking dogs for transportation. A dog team is an inefficient mode of travel. It was kind of silly in a way. Most of my time was taken up taking care of the dogs, feeding them, exercising them, training them, instead of the important and constructive activity of enforcing game laws.

A good part of my annual expense allotment, usually around $2500, supposedly for travel, went down their throats. For earlier years, of course, it was about the only possible method of winter travel in the Interior, other than shanks mare. But now, there was an alternative—the airplane.

When I saw what an airplane could do, I realized that the only way the Game Commission was going to get anywhere enforcing wildlife laws in Alaska was by taking to the air.

I didn't know how to fly, but since others could fly, I figured I could learn to do it too. It turned out that I figured right. I had a little mechanical knowledge, but that was about all.

I didn't get any help from the Game Commission. Just the opposite. "Our most successful agents travel on snowshoes," Frank Dufresne informed me when I told him I planned to learn to fly.

I got into the air in 1929, only because I paid all the costs with my own money, including buying an airplane for $3500.

I ordered Golden Eagle Chief, NC569K, an open-cockpit, parasol-type monoplane, from Golden Eagle Aircraft Corporation of Inglewood, California. It was powered with a ninety-horsepower, seven-cylinder radial LeBlond 7-D motor. It was supposed to cruise at 108 miles per hour, and had front and rear single-person open cockpits. It arrived at Fairbanks in a crate on September 5, 1929.

It was test hopped for two hours on September 7, and on September 9 Noel Wien flew the plane for twenty minutes; Ralph Wien also flew it for twenty minutes; Sig Wien flew it for thirty minutes, and Linus (unidentified) flew it for twenty minutes.

Though it sounded promising, that was the only promising thing about it.

After it flew for a few hours, the engine was damaged, probably from the unsuitable wood propeller. The airplane was grounded

Noel Wien (left), in 1925, with one of the Hisso-powered Standard biplanes with which he started flying commercially from Fairbanks in 1924. Passenger unidentified. NOEL WIEN, COURTESY RICHARD WIEN

Noel Wien in the cockpit of the 1921 Fokker F. III airplane which he flew on the first commercial flight from Fairbanks to Nome. The airplane had no brakes, accommodated five passengers.
NOEL WIEN, COURTESY RICHARD WIEN

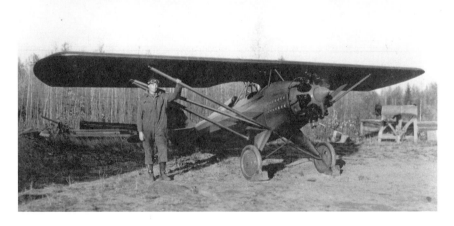

Sam with his first airplane, a Bone Golden Eagle. It proved a poor choice for Alaska, and he sold it after flying it about thirty hours. He did, however, learn to fly with it, and with it made his first solo flight.
NOEL WIEN, COURTESY DRAHS

for about a year, the engine repaired, and it was fitted with a new steel propeller.

I met pioneering pilot Noel Wien in the fall of 1924 at Nenana, and even then had hopes of getting him to teach me to fly. Noel was Alaska's first bush pilot. Over the years he made uncountable mercy flights, whisking the injured and sick to medical help. In 1924 he made the first flight from Anchorage to Fairbanks. He was the first to fly to the Kantishna and Kuskokwim country, the first to fly from North America (Alaska) to Asia (Siberia). He was an international celebrity. He was also quiet and modest.

Noel was usually too busy to instruct me, so, shortly, he turned me over to Ralph, his very capable brother. In 1928, in my spare time, whenever I could scrape together the $35 per hour needed for instruction, I took flying lessons from Ralph Wien. I soloed in my Golden Eagle Tuesday evening, August 5, 1930, after sixteen hours of duel instruction, mostly with Ralph. It seemed as if half of the population of Fairbanks was at the ball-field airport to witness the event.

After I soloed, I bought a drum of gas each month, which was all I could afford on my $2800 annual salary. On nice days, I flew mornings and evenings until the drum was gone, then waited until my next salary check arrived so I could buy another to continue flying.

Sadly, shortly after he had soloed me, on October 12, 1930, Ralph was killed at Kotzebue. Noel Wien then completed my flying instructions.

There wasn't much choice of airplanes in those days. I flew the Golden Eagle for thirty hours and sold it for $500, and was lucky to be alive. It fell out from under me two or three times. I quit fooling with it when it became apparent that it was not made for Alaska. It couldn't carry a decent payload. I sold it to Harold Gillam, who was earning a reputation as a skilled pilot. He wanted it for some chaps at Copper Center.

I then ordered a new, open cockpit, Kinner-powered PT (primary trainer) Swallow biplane (NC422N) from Gillam. When it arrived in September, 1931, Noel Wien and I went to Valdez to take possession. At the time there were only twenty-two airplanes in Alaska. On the flight back to Fairbanks we were pleased to find the plane evidently would do everything I required of it.

It was a training plane but it could be modified so it would do the work I wanted, although its flight range was limited to two-

Sam and Mary White, about 1930. Airplane make is unidentified.
PIONEERS' MUSEUM, FAIRBANKS

and-a-half-hours. I could fly from Fairbanks to Fort Yukon, but I
had to gas up before returning. It took me one hour and fifty-five
minutes to fly the 135 miles from Fairbanks to Tanana on a calm
day. In 1931, eighty miles an hour, or more than a mile a minute,
sounded awfully fast.

The Swallow turned out to be a pretty good airplane for me because I could land it short and take off short. It handled well on snow—I could drive it around like an automobile.

I hardly ever had anyone with me, so whatever had to be done with the airplane on the ground, I had to be able to do alone, and the Swallow was fine that way.

I had many adventures with the old Swallow, for I was still learning how to fly. One March day I broke an oil line flying to Kantishna. I picked a little swamp to land in, and made it fine. It was just the width of the airplane and about 300 feet long.

I repaired the oil line, and had enough spare oil so I could fly. It was late in the day, so I pulled the plane into the brush and camped for the night, hoping that in the morning the wind would come from the right direction for a take off.

When I landed, the plane left deep ski tracks in the snow. That night it turned warm, and became foggy. About midnight it came off cold, there was a hailstorm, and the wind blew.

I couldn't see how I was ever going to get out of there. When I started the engine I had to tie the tail down because the wind was blowing so hard. One end of a rope was tied to a tree, the other end was tied inside the cockpit. With the engine running, I climbed in, revved her up, and cut the rope. I headed down my tracks. To

Sam's Swallow biplane in the Kantishna country in 1931, with contraband seized from an illegal trapper. Courtesty Jim King

my amazement, the hail in my ski tracks performed almost like ball bearings. Once my skis were in those tracks I quickly picked up speed and easily lifted off.

As is common with most new fliers, during my first hours in the air, I expected the motor to quit at any moment. After many hours went by and this did not happen, I built confidence. It was then, of course, that the motor quit.

It was March, and Art Hines, another pilot, and I, were cruising at the head of the Salcha River, looking for Frank Pollock, who was missing with his plane in that vicinity. There was a small glacier below us, and plainly visible from aloft were two small hummocks, wide enough apart to let the ski-mounted landing gear through, but appearing high enough to endanger both lower wings. I had to land short of these hummocks to keep from smacking into a rock wall.

The abrupt silence of an aircraft engine while flying is a memorable event. Quick and good decisions must be made. We went in between the hummocks without touching. Instead of a stiff jolt and a rending crash, there was a soft thump and we kept going. When we stopped, the crankshaft that turned the propeller was inches from the rock wall.

At first we could find nothing wrong. Then we drained the carburetor and got a pint of water. So, that was it, and we were ready to go again.

A difference of opinion developed over which way to take off. I solved it by saying, "I brought her in; you take her out."

The take off was more harrowing than the landing, as there were high peaks and narrow valleys all around us. But Art had steady nerves, and we made it. Ten minutes later we spotted Frank Pollock, but since he was okay and ready to take off, we didn't land. He got to town before we did, for we cruised around and visited a couple of trappers on the Chena River.

From that dead stick landing I gained confidence, and firmed up the following philosophy: "No matter where the motor quits, there is always one place smoother than the rest. Pick it out and head for it."

That applied for wheels and skis, so I had to find one for floats. After a few years of flying planes on floats, I came up with this: "Pick out the wettest place you can find and head for it."

Both seemed to work for me, with a good measure of luck thrown in.

In my early days of flying in Alaska, based on available maps, almost no location in the Territory was in the right place. If, based on the map, one flew from Fairbanks to Beaver, the village on the Yukon River, you could find yourself fifteen to twenty-five miles out of place when you hit the north bank of the Yukon.

Not only that, the north bank of the Yukon itself was not where the maps said it was.

Most of the old bush ships were magnetized, and their compasses would not hold a heading. Therefore, it was seldom that a compass could be used to advantage. With imperfect maps and useless compasses, for pilots not familiar with Alaska's geography, getting lost was common.

As a result, we developed a system of flying drainages, and using the compass only when we had one that worked. This didn't mean that we followed rivers and creeks. Instead, for every place we wanted to go, we cut drainages at certain angles that corresponded with the place we want to reach. We worked on a trial and error basis until we had been over a route a few times, had straightened the kinks, and organized our landmarks.

Then we could go to wherever we wanted as straight as a string. To accomplish this we had to fix in our minds not only major drainages, but also the smaller drainages right down to the smallest creeks.

After we had flown a number of routes and memorized the angles and the landmarks, we had a map of Alaska pretty much in our heads.

For example, an old-time bush flight from Fairbanks to Kotzebue works out as follows: Cross the Yukon River at a certain angle after leaving Fairbanks. If you cross at the correct angle, you next come to the forks of the Tozi (Tozitna) River, which is behind a row of hills, an offshoot of the Ray Mountains.

Cross that river at the right place and you next come to the headwaters of the Melozi (Melozitna) River. You then pass over the hills, and next cross Indian River. After that is the Koyukuk River, which you cross about two miles below Hughes. Then you cross Hog (Hogatza) River, fly over the flats and through a small pass. You then come to the head of the Pick River, follow it, and fly down the south limit of the Kobuk River, which you cross at Kiana. You then fly over the hills to Kobuk Lake (Hotham Inlet) and into Kotzebue.

Once you have these drainages fixed in your mind, and get landmarks lined up, you have it made; with decent visibility, you cannot go wrong.

When I started flying game patrols, I was disappointed because I could not spot as much as I had hoped from the air. However, this changed rapidly for the better as I gained experience. Within a year, it was amazing what I could discern from aloft. I could identify moose, caribou, lynx, and wolf tracks in the snow. On good days, if I flew low enough, I could even see squirrel tracks. Snowshoe hare, ptarmigan, and other small game tracks are also easily identified. Of course a man's snowshoe trail, and a dog team's passage are clear.

I flew my own airplane for six or seven years to do my job as a Wildlife Agent, costing me, personally, around $15,000, because the Game Commission refused to reimburse me. That was the main reason I eventually had to sell my Swallow in 1937. Flying and keeping an airplane was expensive, and I couldn't afford to continue to subsidize the Game Commission. Money didn't come quickly and easily in those days. I didn't fly patrols for about a year.

I got the Game Commission airborne, against their will. They hadn't the slightest idea that planes would be of any value to them. I made game counts from the air—they hadn't realized it could be done, and I couldn't convince them. They regarded me as being a nut about airplanes. Which, of course, I was.

When I first flew around the country with my own plane I created much havoc among trappers, fur buyers, and especially aliens who weren't properly licensed. Many aliens lived on the creeks, in the Yukon River valley and elsewhere—people the Game Commission had never heard about. Most didn't have licenses. Some government officials surreptitiously helped these illegals dispose of their furs, making a little profit for themselves.

Since an alien special license cost $100, a lot of these men trapped without benefit of license, or had falsely taken out resident trapper's licenses, which were only two dollars. They didn't get much sympathy from me, for they were often hostile to the United States government. After about a year of my aircraft patrols, something of a rush on citizenship papers developed. The air patrol also helped to bring pre-season and post-season trapping under control.

My being able to fly patrols kept game violations down, because people knew I could show up unannounced, any time, and any place, especially in winter. I got some unheard of results with airplane patrols. At the time some who lived in the woods committed atrocities on the game. They didn't know how to defend themselves from my eyes in the sky, because I could be on top of them so fast. My patrols, for the first time, gave some protection to the game and fur. Fur, of course, was one of the life-bloods of Alaska in those days.

Years after I flew those early patrols with the Swallow over the Interior, some Indians told me, "Before we got to be friends, Sam, we used to shoot at your airplane."

I wondered where those holes in the fabric came from; now I know. Good thing I didn't know this at the time. I'd have probably put a steel plate under my seat.

Frank Dufresne, as Executive Director, had the first and best chance to buy airplanes for the Game Commission. I had about broken my neck to convince him that we had to use airplanes, but it fell on deaf ears. In 1936, $30,000 became available for new transportation equipment. I was still using my own plane, and having difficulty being reimbursed for the gas I burned. I campaigned hard to have the money used to buy three new Stinson Juniors, available then for $7,500 each.

Dufresne spent the money for four Seattle-built "scout boats," that were sent to Fort Yukon, Marshal, McGrath, and Dillingham.

The boats were lemons. They were slow, and even with the engine running full blast they plowed water. They were also deep draft, a fatal flaw for river running in Alaska. They were always running up on gravel bars. I never got in any of them. If I had, I'd probably have been so mad I'd have quit right then.

The four boats were surplussed the following year.

After I sold my plane in 1937, I quit flying on my job for a time, and after that I occasionally chartered [leased] planes. At first I personally contracted for the leases, a power I had in general. Juneau didn't like it, but I got it done before they knew about it. I used the planes and got good results. In fact, I always got good results while patrolling with a plane.

One spring I saw where I could precipitate an awkward situation for the brass in Juneau.

By boat, it took me two-and-a-half months to seal the beaver pelts from Fairbanks to Kaltag. The seal certified that the beaver had been taken legally; unsealed pelts could not be exported. With a plane, I could do the sealing in a week, and get in a second trip to pick up late arrivals. At the same time I could cover the Koyukuk River and even lap over into another warden's district and provide him with transportation to seal more beaver.

By my second year of flying to seal beaver skins, things really began to open up as I gained experience in doing my old job a new way.

But the brass in Juneau decided I had spent too much money buying gas for the airplane. I didn't have much money left in my budget at that time of year, so one spring I told them I'd do it their way, knowing full well what it would precipitate.

I told them I needed an outboard motor. They sent me three, all used to the point of worthlessness. At that time of year, fur buyers Charlie Goldstein and Muskrat Johnny Schwegler traveled by airplane and bought fur big time.

With my outboard-powered boat, I started from Fairbanks, planning to go as far as Holy Cross to seal the beaver, and then up to Koyukuk. I expected to be gone all summer.

Charlie and Muskrat Johnny flew down the Yukon three times to buy beaver that season, but they couldn't buy them because I hadn't been there to seal them. You can imagine how they felt. I certainly knew. That's the reason I did it that way.

When I reached to Tanana I was on the third motor. Two had quit, and were not repairable. The third was falling apart. I couldn't go any farther. I didn't seal a single beaver skin on that trip. I caught an airplane and returned to Fairbanks.

Johnny and Charlie went to the Game Commission office in Juneau and raised particular hell. "You send a man out with broken-down outboard motors to do a job that should have been done by airplane. We were traveling by airplane, and everybody else there travels by airplane," they said. "You idiots are living in the past."

That was what precipitated the Game Commission's buying, in 1938, for my use, a two-place Monocoupe, their first airplane. It was a hot little thing, but it was okay. They wanted to buy me a Cub. They could have bought two Cubs for the price of the Monocoupe, but I wouldn't go for a Cub.

The Monocoupe, which had a closed cabin, a big improvement from the open cockpit airplane Swallow, was a high-wing monoplane with a ninety-horsepower Lambert engine. It was a pretty good engine, and it was a wonderful airplane for two-place.

The Lambert Monocoupe purchased in 1939 by the Alaska Game Commission for Sam's use. This two-place airplane, ". . . was a hot little thing, but it was okay," Sam wrote. Sam White, courtesy DRAHS

It was built strong and well. The Cubs were fragile and not too reliable.

Airplane numbers were building in Alaska. In 1937 there were 101. By 1939 the number had leaped to 175.

I went everywhere with the Monocoupe like I did the Swallow. I quickly learned that I had to stay with the Monocoupe controls full time, including on the ground, until I had come to a full stop.

At a meeting in Anchorage, Dufresne asked for ideas from each of the agents that might help the Commission. He saved me to the last, and I thought he was going to pass me up. When he called on me, I proposed that the Commission select two or three agents who were capable and wanted to fly, and train them at Game Commission expense. Then buy airplanes for them, just like they bought dog teams and boats.

"It wouldn't cost any more in the end, and the results would be much better," I said.

With the exception of two young fellows who wanted to fly, and who immediately applauded, there was a stunned silence for about two minutes.

"Well, that was a dilly," Dufresne said. He was dog crazy and wanted to stick with dog teams. I was glad to get rid of the dogs as fast as I could.

When a warden with a dog team left town, half a dozen people tipped others off that the game warden had just left Fairbanks, and by which trail.

When I flew with an airplane, no one knew where I was going, and I could drop in on anyone by surprise anywhere within a couple of hundred miles of Fairbanks. That made a lot of people wary, and I'm sure it cut down on the killing.

In 1940, the Game Commission finally bought two Fairchild 24 airplanes. Agent Ray Renshaw and I went to the factory in Hagerstown, Maryland, to fly them back to Alaska. Ray's (NC28539) had a Ranger engine; mine (NC2840) was powered by a Warner engine. They had just started to build mine when we arrived. This pleased me because there were some things I wanted on it that would be easier to include as they built, rather than adding on later.

I outlined what I wanted to a superintendent. He said, "I'll tell you mister, you will never get this stuff put on from this factory because we have a tough inspector right here in the factory. He won't let you get away with anything."

"All right," I said. "Where is this inspector?"

He was out, so I wrote down what I wanted, and sketched them out. The super showed my drawings to the inspector, who said, "Go ahead and put the stuff on for him. I've never been to Alaska, and don't know what an airplane there should have on it."

When I returned to the factory, they were almost taking their hats off to me. Their inspector was pretty reasonable after all. I got everything I wanted.

One of the changes I requested was a simple Parker valve on the bottom of the oil tank so I could easily and quickly drain oil in the winter. If you put a valve on the end of a drain tube, as on many planes, the oil in the drain tube can freeze in cold weather. With the valve near the tank, it stays thawed, and you can drain oil immediately.

With an airplane, as with a dog team, I often found myself weathered in for days on end at out-of-the-way places. One of those was Alatna. I got hung up there a number of times with an airplane when temperatures ranged 50 below or colder.

January 21, 1932. Leave Tanana 11:30 a.m. hop for Alatna.

Clear and bright 25 degrees below. Heavy ground fog north of Ray Mountains. See many caribou tracks. Get nearly to Koyukuk, but turned back at Kanuti River account of ground fog. Land at Tanana at 2:45 p.m. Tie ship down to ice.

January 23, 1932. At Tanana. Heavy snow squalls on Ray Mountains. Will await good weather to avoid getting into a jackpot.

January 25, 1932. Early a.m. clear all around, but 40 below. May try for Alatna after sun comes up. (Later) Leave Tanana at 40 degrees below at 1 p.m. arrive Alatna at 3 p.m. 48 below on landing on Alatna bar. 10 below most of the way over. Freeze face while landing.

January 26, 1932. At Alatna. 50 below.

January 28, 1932. 58 below at Alatna. Go through Sam Dubin's fur. Seize two unprime mink. Frank Sheridan. Have to return to Tanana on account of oil [probably for airplane].

February 1, 1932. At Alatna. Deep snow.

February 3, 1932. At Alatna. Romped over runway with snowshoes. Still snowing. Cleared ice off lower wing and tail surface.

February 4, 1932. At Alatna. Spend all day rubbing ice off wings.

February 5, 1932. At Alatna. 35 below. Warm up motor, attempt take off at 10:30. Break through snowshoed runway and bogged down. Dig out and try again. Gave up at 11:10. Unable to get off, and oil cools off in tank. Right wing drags in snow. P.M. shovel out ship, and brace up skis on skids. Work on runway until 5 p.m. with snowshoes for tomorrow takeoff. 40 below at 6 p.m. Getting colder.

February 6, 1932. At Alatna. 55 below. Too cold to attempt to take off. Heavy ground fog.

February 7, 1932. 60 degrees below. Try to get away anyhow. Warm up and take off at 1 p.m. Arrive Tanana 2:30 p.m. See caribou and Native hunters camped on lake in Old Man country. Circle, and all come out and wave. 0 in air at 3,000 feet. Cross Ray Mountains at 4,000. High wind.

February 9, 1932. Steam up. Ready for hop to Fairbanks. 40 below at Tanana, 30 below at Fairbanks. Leave Tanana 1 p.m. arrive Fairbanks 2:30 p.m. Coldest flight yet. 20 degrees below at 3,000 feet all the way to Fairbanks.

[AUTHOR] Sam made the above-described flights with his open cockpit Swallow. The only way it was possible for him to fly when ground temperatures were so low was due to a temperature inversion; in winter when ground temperatures are 40 degrees below or colder, it is commonly much warmer at several thousand feet, as his diary entries indicate.

On February 9, Sam wrote "steam up," in his daily diary, meaning getting the plane engine warm with a plumber's pot. The term was probably a quirky holdover from his years as a steersman in Maine for the steam-powered Lombard log hauler. This was the first use of "steam up" noted in his diaries, but he used it frequently afterward.

[SAM] It was my habit when going to Alatna to take to the long-time missionary ladies a couple of quarts of fresh milk and a pint of fresh cream. When the two long-timers were relieved by two younger women for a year's vacation, I did the same for the newcomers.

An elderly Native woman, said to be in her nineties, lived across the river from the mission. She certainly looked that age. They called her Sitsu, which means "old woman." Sitsu never crossed the river when there was an aircraft in the vicinity. Whichever side she was caught on, there she stayed, until it left.

One day an airplane landed and caught her in the middle of the river. She burrowed into the snow and remained there until her relatives retrieved her.

Once when I arrived at the mission with milk and cream fresh from Bentley's dairy at Fairbanks, Sitsu was there. The inexperienced substitute missionaries thought it would be a wonderful treat to give her a taste of the cream. I tried to tell them it would be a waste, but the girls filled a water glass half full of the precious fluid and handed it to Sitsu. Not one to do things by halves when it came to handouts, she took a great big mouthful.

A look of absolute consternation spread over her wrinkled visage, and she exploded in one big blurp. Cream and saliva flew everywhere. Some went into the container, and some into what was left in the glass. That pint of cream was shot from about anyone's point of view. That was the last time I brought milk or cream until the two veterans returned from their vacation.

Once when I flew to Alatna, I went to the mission for lunch. The missionary women commonly shooed the locals out when they had a visitor for lunch. But on this occasion an old Indian who had never before seen an airplane, sat and stared at me. Finally, he was nicely asked to go and return after lunch. He got up, took a last long look at me and said, "Must be just like God."

He couldn't have known how far wrong he was.

There were, of course, flights when things went wrong. In November, 1935, I spent several days at Wiseman where a few old timers still dug small amounts of gold.

Sunday, November 10, 1935. Early a.m. warm up. Load up and leave for Fairbanks at 2:05 p.m. At 2:10 forced down eight miles below Wiseman by motor failure. Tie down ship and walk up to Pete Haslim's cabin.

I had some hand mail from the Wiseman residents, and one old-timer had entrusted a fairly good-sized gold poke to me to take to a bank. This was a common practice in those days.

One moment the motor was roaring nicely and the next it was dead. That brought me to life fast. The plane was on skis. Back a mile or two I had spotted a cabin on the bank of the Koyukuk River. Silently, except for singing wing wires, I glided for the river, squeezed over the trees, and landed in about two feet of snow on a very short bar. The bar was so small I skidded off, crossed an ice-covered channel, ran up a bank onto another bar, and stopped. For a parking place I couldn't have done better with a tractor.

It was about thirty below zero. With snowshoes, I walked back to the cabin. The door was opened by Pete Haslim, an old friend, who was putting in the winter there. Pete was well along in years and had one bum leg. He was living pretty much on rabbits, and his only light was a candle. His ten-by-twelve-foot log cabin, though tiny, was a good one, freshly built, in a beautiful setting of spruce trees.

In one corner was a battered Yukon stove with several holes burned in the top. These were covered by flattened tin cans that were not fastened down. Consequently, when the stove was jarred, the cans slid off the holes, and the draft made the wood burn too fast. This called for constant readjusting of cans over the holes.

Pete's bunk was across the back of the cabin, and he had only two blankets, but I had brought a couple with me from the plane, and slept well.

Next morning for breakfast we cleaned up all of Pete's grub—two hotcakes apiece and some bayo beans. Since I had food in the plane, I retrieved it, and gave it to Pete. I also retrieved my sleeping bag and the poke of gold. For thirty dollars, I arranged for Pete to put a cord of dry wood at the airplane. On snowshoes, I then headed for eight-mile distant Wiseman.

I made Wiseman okay, but I sure felt that lump of gold on my back. I tried all kinds of ways to pad it on my packboard, but it didn't help.

November 14, 1935. Leave Wiseman with [pilot] *Frank Pollock at about 12 noon. Arrive Fairbanks 4 p.m.*

I missed the Armistice Day party the American Legion threw on the eleventh, which was the reason for my failed attempt for Fairbanks on November 10.

I ordered another motor, and gathered items I needed to install it.

December 17, 1935. Leave Fairbanks for Wiseman via Pollock Service at 9:45 a.m. Arrive Wiseman 11:30 a.m. Walk down to Marion Creek preparing to stake landing area for plane bringing engine and equipment.

Early on December 18 I staked out a landing area near my downed plane. Herm Joslyn, one of Alaska's famed bush pilots, later a Pan American Airways pilot, landed there with the new engine. Ted Hoffman, a master mechanic, had volunteered to hang the engine on my ship, and Johnny Paul, a weather bureau man, was along to help.

We pitched a tent over the nose of the airplane, set up a new airtight heater, and moved into one end. I lit a Coleman lantern for the mechanics, and started burning the cord of wood Pete had piled near, while Ted and John plied their tools.

By midnight they had the old engine removed. We then crawled into our sleeping bags on mattresses of spruce tips, and slept well while nearby wolves howled.

The boys got the new motor hung next day.

December 20, 1935. Test new motor. Ok. Break camp and fly to Pete's cabin. Camp there overnight. Flying time and test one hour 45 minutes.

Pete had gone into Wiseman, so the boys set up the new stove which we had used in the tent, while I walked back to the scene of the landing to pick up a few things we couldn't take in the ship.

When I got back to the cabin I found a frenzy of cleaning underway. When they had fired up the new stove, the cabin became heated like never before, producing unpleasant odors. Our Coleman gas lantern threw a much better light than had Pete's candle, disclosing the source of the odors.

Rabbit entrails, heads, and skins had been tromped into the spruce-tip floor covering. Blood stains covered the table, which the boys planed off with my sharpest axe after scrubbing wouldn't do the job.

With everything slicked up, we had a good meal and slept comfortably, as the airtight heater held fire all night. It was the boys' first experience in a trail cabin.

Next day, we left the heater in the cabin for Pete and put our leftover grub in his cache, and flew to Wiseman, where we stayed at Martin Slisco's roadhouse.

Martin decided to throw a dance for us—a simple matter handled on short notice. He stepped out of doors and rang the roadhouse bell. Everyone came running, and the dance was underway in minutes. The only two unmarried Native girls were very popular, and never left the floor until the dance ended.

After the dance, Martin invited the three of us into his living quarters and served us lunch. While we were eating, we talked mining and gold.

"I'll show you a nugget," Martin said, reaching to the wall behind him, and out from the moss chinking between logs he plucked a huge gold nugget. It was very heavy and worth more than $700, and that at the old gold price.

He handed it around so that each of us could inspect it, then stuck it back between the logs. It came from Hammond River.

Next day Ted and John hitched a plane ride back to Fairbanks. I flew to Bettles and Alatna, and started for Fairbanks again, expecting to fly right through. It turned out otherwise.

At Jim River I flew over a heavy layer of ground fog. The Yukon River was socked in too, and there was a heavy overcast toward Fairbanks.

I decided to look for a hole and found one at the mouth of the Dall River where there

Martin Slisco in 1931, roadhouse owner at Wiseman.
Sam White, courtesy DRAHS

was a cabin, and dived down through. From there I flew to Stevens Village six miles upriver. Fog was so dense over the village I couldn't see to line up with anything. I flew back to the Dall and the cabin. The hole was closing, but I got down okay. Ten minutes later there was nothing but solid fog.

As I got the cabin ship-shape, a couple of Native men arrived. One was Barney Grant, who was murdered several years later. They had shot a lynx which they skinned on the only table, of all places. They then cooked lynx meat for their dinner.

Next morning they cooked and ate their breakfast, still with bloody hands from the night before. As for me, I wasn't hungry just then. In addition, I was covered with ten million lynx fleas. They chewed hell out of me for about six hours and were gone. The famous cooties [body lice] of the American Expeditionary Forces in Europe during World War I never chewed me up any worse than those fleas. I would, however, prefer the fleas, as they do not live long on a human host, while the cooties continue living and chewing forever.

The fog was as thick as ever the next day, so I walked six miles to Stevens Village and stayed the night with trader Dave Drolette. He was glad to have company. He had a moose stew simmering that was a humdinger, and we feasted while I listened to stories of his early days of prospecting and trading.

Dave was one of the good, honest fur traders on the Yukon. That night he told me that the large pike of the Yukon flats swallowed full-grown ducks and muskrats. At the time I may have doubted him a little, but a few years later I verified it. I saw a full-grown muskrat taken out of the stomach of a pike a Native had caught in a net.

Wind blew the fog away next day, and while Dave urged me to stay, I was restless and had things to do. I walked back to Dall Creek, fired up the Swallow, and finally made it back to Fairbanks.

When I told my wife about the fleas, I had to submit to a delousing campaign. Being a registered nurse, she would not accept my story that they had all dropped dead as soon as they bit me.

Forced landings because of weather or mechanical failure were fairly common in those days, and I wish I could blame my first real crack-up on such problems. But alas, that was not the case. The problem was traceable to cockpit trouble—lack of experience, and doing the right thing a split second too late, which made it the wrong thing to do then.

I was on a beaver sealing trip down the Yukon River in June, 1935, flying a chartered four-place Stinson Junior, 1934 model.

There was then on the Yukon an Episcopal bishop by the name of John Bentley. He was well known throughout Alaska and much loved by all. He often traveled the rivers in a poling boat with an outboard motor. As I made my way up and down the rivers, I often saw him chugging along. I always descended and buzzed him a "hello."

This particular June morning, Bishop Bentley left Nulato for Kaltag in his boat. An hour later I left Nulato, Kaltag-bound also, and soon spotted the good bishop on the river. I gave him a friendly buzz and continued on my way.

When I reached Kaltag I took a hard look at the river bar used for a landing field. It was not a good one for the purpose, and there had been a few minor aircraft mishaps there. But the weather was fine and the machinery up front was clicking along, so, with caution, it looked okay.

Somehow I stubbed my toe. The ship went over on its back in a rending crash, and slid twice its length in a big cloud of dust. I crawled out unhurt physically, but my ego was shot. Villagers ganged around me, and when I assured them I was all right, happiness spread over their faces.

A white trapper, no means a sissy, said, "Sam, you scamp, you scared the daylights out of me. I'm sure glad you're not hurt."

Just then Bishop Bentley beached his boat on the bar and came running. "Well, well," he said, after looking the plane and me over, "I've caught up with you at last!"

That gave us all a good laugh.

I got a barge from Nulato, dismantled the aircraft, loaded it aboard, and took it back to Nulato where it was placed on an upriver boat to Fairbanks where, in good time, it was rebuilt.

As a final irony, in the April, 1944 *Alaska Sportsman*, Frank Dufresne bragged, "The Alaska Game Commission may claim justly that it is the first body of its kind to employ airplanes in wildlife protection. Having started in 1929 with one small biplane [AUTHOR: Sam's first airplane, the Golden Eagle, was a monoplane], the Game Commission fleet has now grown to five excellent airplanes. During the past year they flew more than 120,000 miles in game surveys and law enforcement."

15
Kantishna Patrol

*When I first arrived in Alaska some old sourdoughs put me wise how
to wade a short stretch of water when the temperature is at the bottom
of the thermometer. You dip your feet quickly in the water and yank
them out, and allow the water to freeze while dashing snow on it.
With a thin coating of ice on the outside of snow boots or mukluks,
one can wade a few quick jumps and stay dry. Upon emerging
from the water, you sop up drips quickly with loose snow.
I've used the method on a few occasions, and it works.*
—SAM O. WHITE

IN FEBRUARY, 1930, Jack O'Connor, another Game Commission
warden and I made a patrol from Nenana into the Kantishna country with a nine dog team. We'd heard rumors of one or more trappers using poison instead of traps to take furbearers. Neighboring
trappers were angry, and wanted this illegal practice stopped. To
our knowledge, no wildlife agents had ever been in the area.

It was very cold, and the rivers were badly glaciated, with
numerous overflows. Jack was a good man on the trail. He knew
every dodge and twist of the dangers, and how to avoid them. He
had arrived in Alaska in his early teens, had worked as a miner, then
had held several government positions, including chief of police
and fire chief of Fairbanks. Shortly after our Kantishna patrol, the
Game Commission assigned him to Holy Cross, on the Yukon
River. In the fall of 1931 he was assigned to Anchorage where he
remained for some years.

O'Connor was a barrel-chested five-foot-seven, 170 pounds
of sinew and muscle, with slightly bowed legs. He walked as if he
were on snowshoes even when he wasn't. In later years he became

Alaska Game Commission warden Jack O'Connor who accompanied Sam on the February, 1930, Kantishna patrol. "Jack was a good man on the trail," Sam said.
Sam White, courtesy DRAHS

Wildlife Supervisor for the Game Commission, stationed in Juneau.

Our rented dog team, four from one owner, five from another, took some time to get accustomed to one another. It was operational, and that's about all.

We left Nenana early in the morning of February 24. The temperature was 50 degrees below. Late that day we arrived at the Seventeen-mile Roadhouse, a long log building of two rooms, with a long dining table. Double bunks were built around the sides of the two rooms. Deep cold drains your energy, and we were tired from the day's travel. We tied the dogs to the crude dog houses near the roadhouse, saw they had enough dry grass bedding, and fed and watered them.

The roadhouse was run by Joe and Maria Oats. Maria was a good cook. The main course was moose stew, well laced with vegetables, which then was commonly and legally served at bush roadhouses. She also made a cake for us and the several other travelers who stayed there that night. She used a shallow tin for the cake that just fit the oven, and she even frosted it. No town bakery could have done better, and after the servings of stew, the cake rapidly disappeared.

Bill Burke, one of Alaska's most famous dog team mail carriers, was one of the guests. He was a lean and broad six-footer, and I think he was made of cast iron. He came into the roadhouse after a long day on the trail with an armful of dog moccasins, which he hung near the heating stove, next to everyone's drying socks. He didn't seem to be tired, although he had driven twenty-five or so dogs all day. His mail was piled on a big, tarp-covered, heavily-loaded basket sled with two double-ender trailer sleds hooked behind. Bill rode on the gee pole ouija board between the dogs and the basket sled.

The ouija board was a five-foot-long board, turned up like a ski in front. A tow-line from it snapped into the first tow-line ring behind the wheel dogs (the rearmost), thus the ouija board slid along between the sled and the dog team.

As the driver stood on the board, he guided the sled with the gee pole—a pole, lashed to the sled, that projected forward. It provided leverage for him to push or pull to head the sled where it needed to go. It was the only way the great weight of a freight sled, and the considerable power of the dogs, could be controlled

In tough places, where dogs slowed because of a rough or steep trail, the driver jumped off the ouija board to remove his weight. He could trot beside the sled for a ways, and then jump back onto the board when the dogs picked up their natural speed, which is a bit faster than a man wants to walk.

The tow line, to which the dogs are hitched, can be as hard as steel cable when the dogs are pulling, and a driver must be careful it doesn't catch across his ankles. There is much dancing on and off the ouija board when the towline crosses the board, as in a bend of the trail. Often, moose hide, hair up, was tacked to the top of the board to insure good footing.

On smaller teams, from seven to eighteen dogs, instead of a ouija board, short skis were used by many drivers. With running dogs ahead, a heavy sled behind, and a tow line snapping back forth between one's ankles, you had to be nimble, especially on down grades.

On smaller teams, from three to seven dogs, snowshoes were commonly used on the gee pole. Despite TV and Hollywood pictures, dog team drivers on the average trail, with a loaded sled, do little riding on the handle bars at the back of the sled. They're up front on the gee pole working like hell to keep the sled on the trail. Racing dog teams with an empty or lightly loaded sled are another matter.

The next morning was clear and cold, and Jack and I shoved off for Diamond, where we spent the night with L. C. Ohlson, an old-time prospector and trader.

We arrived late the next day at Knight's Roadhouse on the Toklat River. Henry Knight, the proprietor, always raised a big vegetable garden, and had a root cellar full of cabbages, rutabagas, carrots, potatoes, and other vegetables. He kept a fifteen-gallon boiler on his big stove, and served wayfarers large bowls of dark brown vegetable soup of a most satisfying and delicious flavor. The soup boiler perpetually simmered on the rear of a large two-oven wood range. Knight often threw carrots, cabbage, and other vegetables into the mix, but all I ever saw him take out of it was the dark brown liquid soup.

Next morning we headed up the Toklat River. On top of our load, and lightly hooked under the rope binding the covering tarp, we carried items we wanted to be readily available—bags of dry socks, extra snow boots, felt inner soles, matches, gloves, towels, and the like. Another sack held slivers of spruce, pieces of birch bark, and more matches.

Toklat River is bad for glaciering and overflows during deep cold. Our progress was slow and tedious. We had to go around some overflows, but others had frozen enough so we could skirt the edges.

Sam at camp in the Kantishna country, February, 1930.
SAM O. WHITE, COURTESY DRAHS

Jack went ahead most of the time, testing the trail and checking for overflows that had taken place after the last dog team had passed.

We finally came to a tributary creek where two trappers we wanted to check operated. This creek was a solid glacier for several miles, and, in some places the ice was fifteen to twenty feet deep. In places it overflowed on one side or the other—or even in the middle.

The glaciered area ran from bank to bank, or to the hills on either side of the creek. It was half a mile wide in some places.

We found the trappers, spent a night with them, and found everything legal. Next day we went back to the Toklat and continued downstream. It was 50 degrees below. As we crossed at the edge of an overflow I was on the gee pole, and O'Connor was ahead testing. Suddenly, the sled and I broke through.

Cutting a corner, the dogs had edged out too far on the overflow ice, and there the ice was too thin to support me and the sled. The dogs didn't break through. As I stood in the water, I turned the dogs towards shore and they yanked the sled out of the water. I stopped them there.

Jack grabbed the axe and two sacks on top of the load, and never missed a step as he ran to shore. I followed, kicking my feet and legs in the deep snow to absorb as much of the water as possible. The loose snow absorbed water, and insulated my wet feet from the cold. While I kicked, I moved rapidly toward the fire-to-be. By the time I reached shore, Jack had a few spruce bows down for me to stand and sit on. And, almost instantly, he had the first flicker of flame burning on birch bark and spruce splinters. He cut dry branches from the bottom of a spruce and piled them on the building flame. As I pulled my first socks off, he held out a towel and dry socks.

Within seconds both of my feet were dry and clad in dry socks. Jack handed me a pair of knee-high, dry, snow boots—a canvas and moosehide combination of Native-made moccasin that are light and well suited for cold.

Thanks to our preparation, and Jack's fast and positive work, my feet were again dressed without being nipped by the 50 below temperature. I was impressed with Jack. He didn't fumble once. He started the fire with one match.

On March 1, we found the poisoner we were after. Of all the violators of game laws, a poisoner was the most despised by his

Sam, on winter patrol in the Kantishna country, February, 1930. Note axe handle in pack. Sam never went afield without an axe, a primary survival tool. SAM WHITE, COURTESY DRAHS

neighbors. In the wild and woolly early years of the 20th century some trappers used poison as a lazy way to trap. They put out a pile of bait, with strychnine inserted in small gut-fat chunks scattered around it, and the furbearers—and anything else that eats these fat chunks—dies.

Jack and I arrived at the poisoner's cabin around noon and found two vials of strychnine in a box under a bed. The man arrived home at one o'clock. We searched his cache, and confiscated his furs. Jack placed the man under arrest at 2 p.m.

We took him to Nenana. On the way, he worked every angle he could, trying to influence us to relent. When this didn't work, he resorted to threats, alleging influence in Fairbanks, as well as Washington, D.C. If we valued our jobs, we'd better listen to him. He recited names for our benefit and some of them were impressive.

We proceeded, and he had to pay a fine, with jail time. The lady U.S. Commissioner at Nenana warned him not ever to appear in her court again on a poisoning charge.

A sad note is connected to our Kantishna patrol. On one of the creeks we visited, we met trapper Sam Fedderson. Another trapper, on the same creek, often hallucinated that "someone" (meaning his nearest neighbor, Sam Fedderson) was "gassing" their creek, trying to kill him. No one ever figured out what he meant by "gassing."

I liked Fedderson. He had long tried to become a U.S. citizen, but somehow his entry papers were never in order, and he had been unable to take the final step. Finally he got things in order, and with a little help from a few of his friends, including me, he became a U.S. citizen. He was exceedingly proud of this, and I occasionally saw him in Nenana and each time he thanked me repeatedly for giving him a lift.

The last time I saw Sam was in Nenana a couple of years after he had obtained citizenship. He was headed back to the creek for his winter of trapping. He was still exceptionally proud of his citizenship, and was living up to the code of a good citizen.

That winter, word filtered into Fairbanks that Fedderson had been shot and killed. A U.S. Marshal's party traveled to the creek and found his body. They returned with his hallucinating neighbor. The man claimed that Fedderson had gassed the creek again, so he took his rifle, went to Fedderson's cabin, ordered him outside into the 40 below zero temperature, not even allowing him time to put on mittens, hat, or coat, and marched him half a mile down the creek, and shot him dead.

The man was judged insane and committed to a mental institution.

I was at Knight's Roadhouse some time afterward, and Knight told me this nut had stood out in front of the roadhouse and fired all his ammunition into the air. He came into the roadhouse claiming he had just sunk the entire British Navy.

Decent and respected Sam Fedderson deserved a better fate.

One of my last patrols by dog team was into the back country about 130 miles from Fairbanks where five trappers were reportedly feeding moose meat to their dogs on a very large scale. I called on all five with the same results—all were feeding moose to their dogs.

At one empty trapper's cabin I found parts of twenty-one moose, most of them cows and calves, and I don't imagine I found all the heads, either, in the deep snow.

The man was out at one of his trail cabins, so I took off after him. I was on skis at the gee pole, between the dogs and the sled, when I came into sight of the trapper's trail cabin across a creek. The trapper's dogs began to bark, and he came out, grabbed a .30–06 that leaned against the cabin wall, pumped five cartridges out into the snow, and went back into the cabin, shutting the door behind him.

I seldom went armed when on patrol. Over the years I've had a few situations where gunplay could have occurred. Once a Scandinavian was standing behind a cabin door. When I kicked the door open, he was standing there with a .30-06 rifle in my gut with the safety off. He was shaking. I stood quietly and stared him down. He threw the rifle on the bunk. I checked, and there was a cartridge in the barrel, ready to fire. He got three months.

In this case, by cranking the shells into the snow, the trapper had clearly told me he didn't plan to use a rifle on me. As usual, I was unarmed. I left my dogs and sled where they were, made my way to the cabin, and knocked on the door. The reception I got was the one I least expected.

"Come in," he called. I went in. On the floor lay a fresh-killed calf moose.

"Where's the cow?" I asked, and he said, "Out back of the cabin."

A couple of days later we were all headed for the nearest U.S. Commissioner, Mrs. Hyde, who happened to be a very competent and conscientious elderly lady. Five dog teams were ahead of us, each owner in the same brand of trouble. There seemed to be no ill will [against me] in the bunch. We all stopped at the same roadhouses and brewed tea for lunches in one big kettle. Arriving at the seat of justice, the court action was taken care of in one long day.

I happened to be in the local pool hall that night, and everyone there was talking about the five guys who went to jail that day. One, named Nolan, said, "I'd like to know what that old hen would do to me if she ever got me up there."

That brought a laugh from everyone.

A year later, I caught Nolan in a violation, and took him to Mrs. Hyde's court. She read the warrant to him and asked, "How do you plead?"

"Oh, I done it. I guess I deserve the maximum," he admitted.

She took off her glasses and said, "Now you are going to find out what this old hen is going to do to you!"

I just about fell through the floor. Nolan thought I had told her, but I hadn't. Someone else had spilled the beans.

Roadhouses and Sled Dog Trails

When I first saw the Fairbanks-McGrath trail, there was so much dog team traffic over it that it was as solid as a house floor. When the depression hit, traffic declined, although everyone was still eating.
—Sam O. White

IN 1922, WHEN I first arrived in Alaska, horses and sled dogs were the kings of land transportation. Trails suitable for these animals spider-webbed the country. Roadhouses, spaced roughly a day's travel apart along these trails, offered overnight accommodations for travelers and their animals. A few modern versions of the old roadhouses are still found in their historic locations along the Steese and Richardson Highways.

I traveled mostly by dog team, and some by horse, and became familiar with many of the early roadhouses. The Nenana to McGrath trail had many colorful roadhouses that I remember—some fondly, others not so fondly.

After the Seventeen-Mile Roadhouse, the Diamond Roadhouse, and Knights Roadhouse, already mentioned, came Roosevelt on the Kabuki River. It wasn't run as a roadhouse in my day, but travelers could stay overnight there. It was occupied by a pair of fox farmers. When you entered, a fox was likely to run out from under your bunk, and it had sort of the odor of a fox den.

The next roadhouse that could claim livable accommodations, was the Kamisgaard Roadhouse at the end of Lake Minchumina, originally operated by a man of that name. The last time I was there it was operated by an old sourdough named Fritz Tittle. He was a friendly, agreeable host, and ran a good roadhouse. He was a good cook, and, of course, moose or caribou, as in other roadhouses of the time, was always on the menu.

One feature I vividly recall about this roadhouse were the moosehide bunks. They were laced hair side up, with rawhide, on a pole framework. It was a double-decker layout, one bunk above another. There were no blankets or other bedding; it was the custom then to carry your own sleeping bag.

No cold could come up through those bunks, but there was a fly in the ointment. If those bunks had been poured out of concrete, they couldn't have been any harder. On the ground or in the snow or ice, you can usually chip, shovel, or gouge a curved place for one's back, but on those moosehide bunks there wasn't a thing you could do but roll and twist from one position to another all night long. I tried a different bunk every night, but they were all the same.

Kamisgaard's Roadhouse closed in the early 1930s. Reginald White built a roadhouse half a mile away. Fishing was good in Lake Minchumina, and there were several fur farms around the lake that depended on the lake fish for feed. Every fur farmer and dog team owner had staked out a favorite fishing spot. When Reginald White arrived, the best spots were taken.

However, after a time, he found a fishing spot that did nicely. This was after he tried a couple of others that somehow attracted bullets from a hidden marksman; they dropped near his boat and he got the message.

White remained at Lake Minchumina for several years, then one winter he took his boat and movable property over the portage into the Kuskokwim drainage. The next summer he boated it all downriver to Stony River, where he established another roadhouse and trading post. I put in several comfortable nights with him at that location on my various trips up and down the river.

Another trapper lived at the north end of the lake. He asked no odds of any man, or even the government. I liked and respected him because he was so self sufficient. He had no use for me, since I was a "government man."

It may sound as if there was a crowd living around Lake Minchumina in those years. It wasn't crowded—the lake is an odd-shaped ten by thirteen miles, and lies sixty-six miles from Mount Denali (sometimes called McKinley). The mountain dominates the view to the southeast from this big, beautiful, clear-water lake.

Another local character who for many years lived alone on the shore of Minchumina Lake was Hjalmar (Slim) Carlson, a tall, slim, Swede. He was always in trouble with the game laws. He raised a big garden, and kept up to eighteen dogs, which he fed with fish he caught with a gillnet from the lake. I once walked in on him, surprising him as I had on previous walk-ins. I asked to see his license. He couldn't find it.

"Slim, you've been warned several times to have one. This time you're in trouble," I told him.

"Give me time. I'll find it," Slim promised, in his strong Swedish accents.

The nearest licensing agent, at Diamond, was eighteen miles away. I knew Slim would rush to buy his license as soon as I left.

Hjalmar (Slim) Carlson, in 1955, setting a wolf trap near Lake Minchumina, where he lived alone for nearly half a century. Though, ". . . always in trouble with the game laws, Slim basically was a decent man," according to Sam. AUTHOR

My job was to fly to Diamond to see if he actually had bought a license. I didn't particularly care whether he beat me. I took plenty of time, warmed the airplane, and took off, headed for Diamond, while Slim took off with his eighteen-dog team.

Half way, oil pressure dropped on the Swallow. I had a broken oil line. I quickly landed and shut her down. Oil streaked the snow on my landing run, and it was still dripping.

I scooped up all the oil-soaked snow I could, heated it over my plumber's pot, separated the water, and poured the oil back into the engine after repairing the broken copper tubing oil line.

I arrived at Diamond before the day was out, but, after buying his license, Slim had left. My mission was accomplished.

Slim was really a good guy, and he was always glad to see me. It was a good excuse for him to cook up a good feed. We would sit and eat and have pleasant conversation.

He was a poker player, apparently not a good one. While playing he would get drunk. He caught $6,000 to $7,000 worth of fur every year. In spring, after selling his fur, he commonly planned to go to Sweden to see his folks. I saw him in Nenana several times when he was liquored up, and he told me what was going to happen when he got to the old country. He would walk up to the gate and open it. His folks would see him and they wouldn't recognize him. Tears ran down his cheeks each time he told me this story.

He left Nenana with $5,000 to $6,000, plenty to get to Sweden and return, and do something for the old folks too. In Anchorage he got into poker games. He'd have to wire Fowler, [his fur buyer?] in Nenana to send him money enough to return to Nenana. Anchorage was as far as he got on two or three attempts.

One winter he cut his left thumb off while splitting firewood. He tried to sew it back on, holding the severed thumb in his mouth as he plied needle and thread, but it didn't work. He told me that because of the pain, for twelve days he never slept. Then he got terribly tired and the pain started easing, allowing him to sleep. He went to sleep in daylight, and woke up in daylight. He didn't know how many days had passed.

He pickled the thumb, and delighted in showing it to some-times-horrified visitors. Poor old Slim, always in trouble with the game laws, was basically a decent man.

Years later I was at Minchumina one winter day, flying a bush plane for Wien Airlines, my game warden days behind me. A local rugged individualist was helping me put logs under the skis, covers on the wings, tie down ropes under the tail and wings. In short, he was working his head off helping me put the plane to bed for the night.

We had no conversation. A Civil Aeronautics employee standing near noticed this, and gathered we didn't know each other, so he introduced us. The trapper replied, "I got no god damned use for an s.o.b. game warden."

The fact that I was no longer a game warden made no difference to him. In his eyes, I was always a game warden.

The CAA man looked confused, and couldn't seem to figure the situation out. With the trapper standing near, I explained, "Jim and I have been bad friends for many years."

No more was said, but Jim and I continued to work together harmoniously to prepare the plane for the morrow. The CAA man never did figure it out.

A man named Ohlson ran the Lone Star Roadhouse between Minchumina and McGrath. He had been a dog team driver, trapper, and prospector until old age caught up with him. He then settled down to winters in his roadhouse on the Fairbanks-McGrath trail, where he cooked and cared for overnight travelers .

His supplies arrived in the spring to be put on the only boat that would take them to Lake Minchumina. They then remained at Minchumina until October when a dog team could freight them to Lone Star over the trail.

Hotcakes, coffee, bacon and two eggs (if you were man enough to take 'em before they took you) was $2.50. There was also moose and caribou stew, which was always good. At $2.50 per meal this was not at all out of line when considering the distance and transportation involved in getting the supplies there.

It was at Lone Star Roadhouse that I learned why old-timers didn't like fresh eggs. They were used to cold-storage eggs, which might be as much as a year old, and which picked up a unique, strong, flavor. I could taste Lone Star eggs all day long. With them, you sure got your money's worth.

On one occasion I was at Lone Star for nearly a week. When I returned to Fairbanks I went to the Model Cafe and ordered two fried eggs. They were, of course, fresh, but they were so flat I couldn't taste them. However it didn't take me long to get used to fresh eggs again.

With the coming of airplanes, which hauled mail, freight, and passengers, death throes of the old trails were not prolonged; traffic on them soon disappeared, ending the days of far flung roadhouses. A big white sign with black letters I once saw at a remote roadhouse told the story. It read, "AVIATOR'S TRADE NOT SOLICITED HERE."

It didn't help. The airplanes won.

17

A Beaver Sealing Trip

*I have a big tree of moose horns in my yard. People stop from all
over and take pictures of them. I had to chain them down because
people steal them. I picked them up in the middle 1930s.
I only shot three of them. Lots of them were killed by wolves.
I brought them in from all over the interior of Alaska.*
—SAM O. WHITE

[AUTHOR] BEAVER WAS AMONG the most important animals in
the early fur trade of Alaska. Rifles became available to Alaska's
Natives in the late 1800s, and spring beaver hunting became an
annual activity. By 1910 Alaska's beaver were nearly wiped out,
not only by Native hunters, by others as well.

Between 1910 and 1923 the killing of beaver was prohibited,
and the animals recovered. The season was reopened, and shooting continued.

Half of the beaver that were shot sank. A careful and experienced hunter went prepared with a spear and a throwing weight
with hooks attached to a light rope for retrieving the animals.

Beaver again became scarce, and the season was again closed in
some parts of the Territory. Finally, shooting was prohibited, forcing trappers to catch beaver with traps or snares set beneath winter
ice. Each trapper was limited to a specific number per season.

A new conservation approach in the 1930s required that, before
it could be exported, each beaver pelt had to have a locked metal seal
placed on it by a wildlife agent. This was intended to enforce the
individual bag limit, and to eliminate shooting.[1] It also provided the

---

1. Beaver that had been shot were easily identified–a blood stain appeared on the skin
around a bullet hole.

Alaska Game Commission with a reliable figure on the number of beaver harvested. Fur buyers were required to report the number of furs of each species they bought, and the count of sealed beaver was a check against that figure.

Sealing beaver, as the wildlife agents referred to this duty, required them to make spring-time visits to remote villages and other areas where trappers congregated, to physically place seals on beaver skins.

Sam O. White's use of an airplane to travel to bush areas to seal beaver was a new and revolutionary approach. He could now complete the annual job in weeks; previously, wildlife agents spent months to seal beaver skins, traveling by boats on various rivers to reach villages, fur buyers, and trappers.

Beaver sealing ended with state management of wildlife (1960) at which time the annual limit was up to forty in some areas. Beaver are now abundant in suitable habitat throughout the state.

The following, written by Sam, details his experiences on one of his pioneering beaver sealing trips with an airplane.

[SAM] FROM FAIRBANKS, I flew my Swallow biplane N6422N on one of my early beaver sealing trips down the Yukon River. I was still inexperienced as a pilot, but I had as fool-proof an aircraft as it was possible to get in those days.

I found Wildlife Agent Eugene Tibbs at Nulato with his boat. We decided to combine our efforts. Many beaver pelts at Flat and McGrath needed to be sealed, and there were quite a few places to hit along the Koyukuk River.

Gene left his boat at Nulato and climbed into the front cockpit, and I the rear, and we flew the short distance to Koyukuk Station, sealed beaver there, and headed for Holy Cross. Here we sealed a few pelts that had shown up since Tibbs had come upriver with the boat.

We gassed up and headed for Flat. This was a hop over wet country. The winding Innoko was beneath us, and its timbered shores showed dark and green. We saw many moose feeding in the marshes along this route.

We passed over Reindeer Flats, a big area of swamps, lakes, and marshes. As I peered down I couldn't help but think what I would do if forced to land there, as we were far from being within

Sam's hangar at Weeks Field, with his PT Swallow.
Sam O. White, courtesy DRAHS

gliding distance of solid ground. I could visualize the swarms of mosquitoes that would assail us.

We reached Flat, my first trip there. I took a good look at the airport. At about a thousand feet above the runway I was in a turn, which turned out to be a skidding turn. My attention was centered on the runway, not on my flying.

A gust of air came down with a swoosh over the top wing and into the cockpits. I saw a blur as something zipped past my head, and I suddenly realized the airplane was at the beginning of a stall.

I neutralized the controls and the ship righted itself, and the nose went down enough to pick up the required speed for good control. We had lost a few hundred feet of altitude. Lesson learned. We had survived.

The blur that zipped past my head had been Gene's prized new hat. Our eyes stung, and there was grit in our teeth from the dust that had erupted from the floorboards as we had neared the stall.

The runway looked good, so I squared away and went in for a landing. I was a little rattled from the near stall, and I landed long. I put her down anyway, and we went whizzing down the runway at about thirty-five miles an hour. The end of the runway was close. In those days airplanes didn't have brakes. As luck would have it, there was a road at the end of the runway, so I used some rudder and finished the landing by running up the road a short way. No harm done.

My luck was holding. Gene never knew how close we came to disaster.

Some residents of Flat met us. Airplanes were rare visitors; when one showed up in a village, residents who could, usually turned out to meet it.

We quickly sealed the beaver at Flat, and went over to Tootsie's Tavern for lunch. Tootsie, a large personable black woman, served us an A-number-one meal.

After sealing all the beaver we could reach with an aircraft, we returned to Nulato and Gene's boat. I left him there, and flew to Ruby and then Tanana.

At Tanana the smoke was so thick from forest fires that visibility was almost nil. I sat down there and waited for evening, hoping as the day cooled, smoke might thin, and I could sneak on to Fairbanks.

The fire was burning all around Minto Flats and back of Manley Hot Springs. I climbed to 11,000 feet, but couldn't climb over the smoke. I dropped to 1,500 feet, and it looked encouraging. However, I hadn't gone far when I saw fire brands with smoking tails passing near and over the plane's wings. That did it.

I did a quick turn back to Tanana. When I arrived, what appeared to be the town's entire population was fighting a fire next to the runway.

I was in a fix. I had to land, but the runway was effectively closed. I followed the Yukon a short distance, and despite high water, found a bar that I hoped would be ok. It was rough, but I managed a safe landing on my big doughnut tires.

I sat out the night under a mosquito net, which I always carried. I sure needed it that night. The hum of mosquitoes was like a sawmill at peak capacity.

Next morning I flew back to the field at Tanana. The fire there was out. I was happy to go to Ghee's restaurant for breakfast. Ghee, the genial Chinese owner, poured me a cup of coffee that would have floated a steel wedge.

"Ghee, this coffee is pretty strong," I complained.

"Yess," he giggled, "him boil all night," He continued to cook my hotcakes and fry me eggs and bacon. He was unimpressed by my complaint.

I had no kick coming. I was much more comfortable in his restaurant than I had been out on the river bar listening to a million buzz saws thirsting for my blood.

There were then two eating establishments in Tanana. Hardworking old Joe Anicich operated the Tower House. He had arrived on the Yukon in 1898, and had made some money. I don't know if he had banked any, but I do know he kept a little strong box that bulged with Gold Certificates in a niche in the basement.

Joe always gave me the front room upstairs, and it had a good view of the Yukon. Tanana was in the dumps at the time, with very little travel and little of anything going on.

I always stayed at the Tower House, but I tried to split my eating between the two places. Neither was noted for its cuisine. A food inspector would likely have dropped dead at either place.

I sometimes tried to sneak out of the Tower House early in the morning, but Joe would usually nail me at the foot of the stairs with a hearty, "Good morning Sam. Breakfast is all ready." I would then, of course, eat with Joe. Joe and I were mostly the only occupants.

Joe had a scraggly 32-year-old parrot in a cage. He kept a newspaper at the bottom of the cage for sanitary reasons, and removed it once a week whether it needed it or not.

Joe sat this bird's cage on a stool between his chair and mine, so that the bottom of the cage was about even with the top of the table. As our meal progressed, Joe occasionally whacked off a piece of food with the table knife with which he was eating. Polly grabbed the food off the knife with a gnarled and none-too-clean claw. With the same knife, Joe would then whack himself off a piece of butter, or cut his hotcakes, or whatever.

Things were no better at Ghee's place, but they were different, making it possible to have a change of menu, so to speak.

Ghee's restaurant consisted of two low-roofed log cabins hauled together and placed end-to-end. Ghee had cut a wide door out of the two adjoining ends, so in effect, they formed one room with a slight partition. The ceilings were low, and were well hung with cobwebs.

His stove was a veteran of considerable size for such a small operation. Fortunately, the table where guests sat was near the end toward the river and street, which gave a feeling of security.

The combining of two cabins, and in some cases even three, was a fairly common custom. We called them "shotgun houses," on the theory that you could stand in the front door and fire a shotgun out the back door without hitting anything.

Sam, in the 1930s.
SAM O. WHITE, COURTESY DRAHS

Ghee kept his water, collected from the Yukon River, in a couple of cans on the floor and against a wall. A few ragged-looking cats hung around his place. They drank from both cans. To fill the coffee pot or soup kettle, Ghee dipped water out of them indiscriminately.

I was at Ghee's once with an FBI agent I was flying around looking for someone. A day or two of sixty-five below weather had trapped us at Tanana. "I'm thirsty. Isn't there any drinking water around?" he asked.

"Sure. Plenty. See those cans on the floor. They're full of water."

He frowned. "Ugh. The cats drink out of them."

Me. "That proves it's drinking water."

In the end, after suffering for some time, with a cup he dipped water from one of the cans and drank it.

I complimented him on his adaptability.

Ghee was a cheerful soul, and I was very fond of him. Joe was also a good man, and I counted him as a friend.

Joe had a white horse reputed to be thirty-five years old. In the summer, with this horse and a wagon, he used to haul my gasoline to the airport. In winter, Joe kept him in a cabin heated with a big wood stove. There was much hay and chaff, and I feared the horse would knock the stove over and set the place afire.

I mentioned this to Joe one day. "Don't worry. Old Mike is a wise old horse. He knows better than that," he said.

So, Old Mike lived dangerously. He never knocked the stove over, and he died a natural death.

Harry Nakagawa, a Japanese, also lived in Tanana. Everyone called him "Harry the Jap." There was a frozen silence between Harry and Ghee. They didn't see each other, but looked through and beyond whenever they came together. The Japs had invaded China, and reports of their atrocities had reached even bush Alaska.

Harry was elderly, but he was a worker, and very thrifty. Annually, he had a sizable vegetable garden. If it takes a green thumb to raise a successful garden, every finger and toe on Harry's hands and feet was green.

I never stopped in Tanana during the summer when his garden was blooming without getting a carton of delicious garden truck. Sometimes I could pay him, but mostly he objected to being paid.

During World War II, he was taken to an internment camp somewhere in the western United States. When he returned, he was unpopular with a few local residents who had leftover feelings about Pearl Harbor and all that.

Shortly after the war I was visiting with a resident of Tanana, unaware that Harry had returned. I heard someone walk by behind me. I turned, saw his back, and recognized Harry. I hurried after him, called, and shook hands. He was awfully pleased. It was a pleasure to see him expand. Harry was never a danger to the United States. He had been many years on the Yukon, and I liked him.

"Harry, how did they treat you down there?" I asked.

"Good. We had good houses to stay in, and good food and plenty of it. But the hours dragged, since there wasn't much work we could do. Also, there was a lot of waste."

Beside his large garden, every summer Harry always had three fishwheels working in the Yukon. They really piled up the salmon. He was as good a fisherman as he was a gardener.

Harry kept this up until he was past 70. He didn't get rich, for he generously gave much away.

The forest fires that stalled me in Tanana on that beaver sealing trip burned out with the help of some rain. Fire control then consisted of an official estimating the acreage burned after a fire was out. There were no funds to fight fires.

I left Tanana early one moist morning and was in Fairbanks one hour and forty-five minutes later, standard time for the 135- mile flight Tanana-Fairbanks with NC422N.

Ghee, Harry, and Joe have passed on to their rewards. Tanana doesn't seem the same any more. I sure miss the old days.

Village Traders I Have Known

Sam called mosquitoes "push flies." Food was "chuck." He used "motor" when referring to the engine (the latter day term) of an airplane. An airplane was a "ship." He became "pooched out," when he meant tired. He often resorted to the Maine idioms of "right smart" or "right quick," when conveying the idea of a sudden move.
— AUTHOR

THE TRADERS AT VARIOUS villages along the Yukon and Koyukuk Rivers were a colorful bunch. I became acquainted with many of them during my years as a Wildlife Agent when I visited their posts and reviewed fur buying records they were required to keep. Most were honest in their dealings with Natives and whites alike. They were in business to make money, of course, and some of them did very well indeed. Some were very paternalistic toward the Natives, and would forego profits to help those who needed it.

CARL BOHN of Ruby was one of the better traders. He was scrupulously honest. His trading post was one of a kind; nothing like it will ever be seen again.

During the days when steamboats were the primary means of transport in summer, and dog teams in winter, these traders had to get their year's goods on the last boat in the fall. This was not only a huge investment, it was also a mountain of goods.

When a steamer pushing loaded barges arrived at a village, the unloading frenzy could last well into the night. Some of the goods were taken directly from the barges into warehouses by steam winches. In villages where this wasn't possible, goods were piled in great mounds on the riverbanks, and covered with canvas.

Bohn's trading post was constructed of both log and frame, with ample space on the ground floor. The front part included groceries; hardware, outdoor clothing, and blankets were in the left rear.

A rickety stairway led to the loft, which consisted of three partial rooms that were unfinished, except for crude partitions. In two of these were staple groceries, traps, clothing, and what all, dumped on the floor hit-or-miss.

During the trapping season, the third room was always full of furs of great value, and dried or smoked baled salmon, used for dog food.

There were also two warehouses that were loaded to the eaves after the last boat had left. To prevent freezing, in one of these, the precious eggs and cases of milk were kept upstairs. Along toward spring the eggs got a little loud, as they weren't real fresh on arrival, having spent at least a month en route.

In the center of the first floor of the trading post was a round table. When it wasn't in use for a card game, it held current outstanding bills that lay like so much hay pitched into a feed stand. When the table was to be used for a card game, the bills were swept into cartons and set aside. No order was observed.

When someone asked for his bill, Carl would go to his book and look it up. He would then pause in deep thought, and fish around in one of the cartons. Or, if the bills were on the table, he'd paw around the pile. He usually came up with the desired bill in an astonishingly short time.

In the late 1930s Carl felt age slipping up on him and he hired help. It was handled in a typical Alaskan way. He tapped his old friend Sig Wigg of Ruby, an old and famous dog team driver who had hauled the U.S. mail for many winters. Sig and his wife Mame, a famous cook, ran the local roadhouse, but there was very little business at the time.

Sig worked for Carl for seven years without drawing a cent in pay. At the end of seven years, when Carl sold the trading post, he paid Sig off in a lump sum of $14,000. Sig at once paid a lump sum for his Social Security bill of seven years. Johnny Isordie was another who worked at a mine for many years without drawing any salary, and was paid off in this manner when his job ended.

I was in Ruby in the late 1940s when the first Social Security agent came down the Yukon. Sig and Johnny were old enough to qualify for Social Security payments, and they applied for the benefits. To their dismay, they lacked eligibility, since they had received credit for only one quarter.

I don't know how this came out in the end, but I do know that residents along the Yukon at this time had a low opinion of the Social Security outfit.

TOM DeVANE, another trader at Ruby, also had a large trading post. It was on the same street as Carl Bohn's. Tom's place was also built of logs, and he had quite a few innovations.

He had a sheet metal meat house in which he stored domestic meats, with a generator to run the refrigeration and furnish lights for his trading post during winter. He didn't need the lights in summer; in fall and winter he didn't need the freezer.

Spring water was piped under pressure to Ruby, reaching most of the lower part of town. The pipes lay mostly on the surface, since the ground is permafrost (permanently frozen). When thawed it is silt and muck.

DeVane had this water piped to his freezer house, where perforated pipes ran along the roof beside the electric freezer. The spray during periods of sunshine helped keep the meat house at a freezing temperature.

Tom DeVane eventually sold out to the Northern Commercial Company, which had stores or trading post all over Alaska and Yukon Territory. Their prices were on the high side, but they carried nothing but the best of goods, and stood squarely behind them.

The NORTHERN COMMERCIAL COMPANY was a good outfit. In 1924 I was in Nenana and needed expense money. I went to the N.C. Co. store there, where Milt Fleishman was the agent. I had never met Fleishman, but he cashed a check for me that was written on an Anchorage bank. That established my credit with the Northern Commercial Company. My account with them has endured to this day (February, 1966).

Once you had established your credit at one of their stores, you could draw goods at any of their stores. I found, if I was far from home, their stores would even advance money and the transaction would be transferred to my account at Fairbanks.

DOMINIC VERNETTI, an Italian at least by parentage, and a very aggressive businessman, had a trading post near the mouth of the Koyukuk River, at Koyukuk Station on the Yukon River. "Born in Michigan," he told a government official; to friends he admitted to having been born in Sicily.

Dominic was well-liked by all. He had a most unusual and pleasing personality. That, coupled with aggressiveness in business, may seem a bit strange to one who never knew him. He liked company and was very hospitable. He was a first class cook, and made wonderful bread as well as spaghetti. He worked hard, and was always busy.

I sat at his table many times feasting with Dominic on imported cheese and nipping on imported wine, of which he always had a good supply.

Dominic's wife, Ella, was a very attractive and energetic Native chief's daughter. She could run the trading post as efficiently as did Dominic. She too was an excellent cook; anyone stopping at Koyukuk Station was sure to be well fed. Ella could run a boat and drive a dog team with the best of them.

AT NULATO, "POP" RUSSELL was an honest, hard-working old chap with a big picturesque trading post near the downstream end of town. He knew the trading business from A to Z. He was kind hearted, and was very good to the Indians. On many occasions when through death and disaster some Indian waif was left without parents, Pop took the waif in and lavished great care on him or her.

Pop admired early day pilots, especially Pan American Airways pilots, and Noel Wien. He talked about them constantly, and their feats grew and grew in Pop's stories, until you would have thought they were supermen, not bush pilots.

He could bake the most lovely apple pies. Since that is a great favorite with me, I used to especially enjoy my stays with Pop at Nulato. He always made his pies in a deep dish, and the only way he knew how to cut a pie was in four pieces.

Pop also had a tag-end dental outfit, consisting mostly of forceps. He did all the tooth-pulling for the villagers of Nulato. Many needing teeth pulled also came from Koyukuk, Kaltag, and Ruby. He kept a large jar on a shelf in the kitchen for all to see of the most unusual "snags" that he had pulled. One look was enough to satisfy the stoutest stomach, but Pop loved to show them off and one could seldom get away with a quick glance. He made you really look at his prizes, and he expected you to make some appropriate remark.

Moreover, on your next visit more than likely Pop had made an addition his collection, and he insisted you view that too.

In the middle 1930s Pop built a frame addition to his log trading post. It was a two-story affair, with rooms on the second floor. It was primarily a roadhouse, with good beds and bedding. The rooms had large windows that provided good lighting.

I was staying there overnight one spring, headed downriver, and waiting for better weather. There were twenty-four hours of daylight, and at two a. m., with the sun shining brightly, I was awakened by screams and yells fit to raise the dead.

I leaped out of bed and peered out to see an Indian man with a long pole, fending off two Indian women who were armed with axes, one of which was double-bitted. My first impression was to run out and break up the fight. My next impulse beat that one all to pieces. I decided to let them chop and slash. I knew that in such drunken brawls it was likely if I interceded, all three would turn on me, and that one man alone would have little chance against two axes and a long spruce pole. So I sat by the window and watched.

If I had been betting, I would have bet on the women. Every now and then one dashed in and made a wild swing with an axe. Each time the man caught the axe on the end of the pole, and the slivers flew.

This went on for some time until all contestants were getting worn out, with no blood showing. But the man's pole was growing shorter. The woman with the double-bit axe made a wild swing, the man parried the blow, slivers flew, and the woman followed the blow and fell face-first onto the ground on top of her axe.

I thought this was the end of her. But the other woman stood over her and swung her axe wildly, and again the slivers flew. I was a nervous wreck, and couldn't see any ending to this but murder.

Just then a young Indian man stepped from behind a cabin about fifty feet away and loudly yelled, "Hey." He was staggering drunk, but he held up a bottle and with a long finger pointed at it.

The fight broke up right there. The man with the pole, without a glance at the woman with the axe, dropped what was left of his pole, and headed for the bottle. The woman still standing with an axe, dropped it and followed the man. The women on the ground sprang to her feet and they all ran after the man with the bottle, who by this time had disappeared into the cabin.

All such drunken brawls don't turn out so fortunately. In my role as a bush pilot I had to haul many such participants to a hospital or other medical aid. Too, there were some deaths from such brawls. Some were passed over as accidents, but an active bush pilot usually has a pretty good idea of what is going on in the country he serves.

I recall one brawl when one Indian was badly cut up. However, he survived. His opponent was his trapping partner. They lived and trapped in a remote and rugged country. One would suppose that such a fight would end the trapping partnership. But no, the next winter they were back together in the same old haunts and the same cabin, apparently happy, with no hard feelings.

I once complained to a conscientious welfare worker who seemed to be aware of the problem of Native drinking.

"It's their money. We give it to them for subsistence, but if they prefer to buy whisky with it, that's their business, not ours," I was told.

Wow! I had to adjust my thinking at this new and unexpected angle. I remember a brawl that included about twenty Indian women fighting in a cabin. A man went in to break it up. He was drunk, or he would have known better. Within moments he exited the cabin rather violently through a shattered window. He had broken ribs and many bruises.

So much for that.

JOHN SOMMERS was another well known trader at Nulato. He knew furs, and kept a good line of merchandise. He was a dog team mail carrier in his younger years. His wife was a Native woman who, while John drove huge dog teams over the long, cold and windswept trails, was also working, with the objective their Nulato trading post.

The Sommers raised a family of friendly boys and very attractive girls. They have all scattered to the far corners of Alaska and the other states to take their place in society.

Over the years I was in and out of Nulato many times, and I

had many meals with John and Mrs. Sommers and the family. Their hospitality was tops, and it is one of my fondest memories.

Their son Johnny was the apple of old John's eye. He wanted Johnny to carry on with the trading post, but Johnny was restless. The trading post wasn't for him. John did succeed in establishing him in a branch post at Kaltag, but Johnny's mind was elsewhere, and the post failed.

One day John invited me into his living quarters over the Nulato post to ask my opinion. He said the only thing that Johnny was interested in was flying. Should he help him get started as a pilot?

I was flattered that he would want my opinion. We discussed Johnny and flying, and I asked John many questions, which he answered at length. In the end, I told him I thought it would be the right thing to do to launch Johnny on a flying career.

This was done. It was not to be successful. Johnny was too restless and a bit too wild. A couple years later he crashed his airplane and died near the mouth of the Yuki River. The wreckage wasn't found for a couple of years. It was spotted by a helicopter pilot who happened to hover above a patch of timber and saw the wrecked plane directly beneath him.

Old John was disconsolate over the loss of his favorite son. I talked with him many times after Johnny disappeared and he never lost hope that he would eventually show up alive. It became an obsession with him. He didn't live very long after Johnny's disappearance.

Freddy Sommers wound up with the trading post. He is friendly, honest, kind, and very well liked.

TRADER SAM DUBIN, of Alatna, on the Koyukuk River, not only had a trading post, he owned the *Teddy H.*, a steamboat that hauled freight on the Koyukuk River, including inventory for his post.

Sam had a soft heart and did a lot of good. Once while I was there an Indian came into the post and wanted supplies on credit. He was already on Sam's books for a large amount, much of it in arrears.

"You already owe me a big bill, and it keeps getting bigger instead of smaller," Sam told him. "I want my money."

*Sam (left), Mrs. Sam Dubin, Miss Boyce, and trader Sam Dubin, at
Alatna, 1931.* Sam O. White, courtesy DRAHS

That sort of squelched the Indian, but he made one more plea.
"Sam, I got babies and wife and no moose meat and no milk. Babies
are hungry and it's too cold to hunt."

But Sam was adamant. "You bring some fur and pay your bill
and then I'll give you groceries."

The Indian dejectedly left the post. Sam began pacing, chewing his cigar. It was easy see he was agitated. Finally, he whirled
around to the Native clerk who worked in the post for him and
blurted, "Frank, you put him up a box of grub quick. I'll tell you
what to put in it. He has starving babies to feed. We can't let them
go hungry."

So, Sam had a box of grub worth around fifty dollars packed
and delivered to the Indian's cabin. He told me, "I won't put it
on the books. He can never pay for it anyway."

How many boxes of this kind he put up no one can even guess
but I know it certainly happened on more than one occasion.

A peek into Sam's warehouse at Alatna was an education. From
the rafters hung lynx, fox, marten, mink, wolverine, ermine and other
valuable furs aggregating many thousands of dollars. There was sacks
of flour and sugar, sacks of coffee and tea, lard and butter, slabs of

bacon, and a row of beans in hundred-pound bags. From the rafters hung a row of seal pokes filled with seal oil. This is a product of the coastal Eskimo culture—seals seldom venture far from salt water. Even at sixty-five degrees below zero those pokes smelled to high heaven, and even at that low temperature the contents remained fluid and pliable.

A seal poke is made by removing the animal's skin and closing all of the holes so it won't leak fluid, then hanging it in the wind to dry. The fat from seal carcasses is cut into strips and stuffed into the poke. When full, the mouth of the skin is sewed shut with sinew.

The filled skin is then hung in the sun until the fat is tried into seal oil. It can then be stored. Fresh seal oil is virtually tasteless, and has no odor. As it ages it develops a unique pungency.

At one time I was sure that Sam's trading post had Alaska's big ice pool [guessing the breakup time of ice in the Tanana River) won for me. He had, for sale, a dozen alarm clocks lined up on a shelf, none running, and each indicating a different time. I recorded the times and guessed at the a.m. or p.m. That spring I bought twelve ice pool tickets, one for each of the times indicated on those clocks. I didn't see how I could lose, but I did. One of my tickets got into the week the ice went out, and that's about as close as I ever came.

Two wonderful missionary ladies served the church at Alatna. To them, the ice pool was gambling, and gambling was the devil's work. I always bought a couple of ice pool tickets in their names, and after the tickets had been deposited beyond recovery, I told them their numbers. They scolded me mildly, and then, I learned later, they started to worry about what they would do with the money if they won.

The Wild Man of Nation River

The woods were full of aliens who were trapping without a
license, which cost $100. It took me about two and a half years
to bring them under control.
—SAM O. WHITE

DURING THE EARLY 1930s, trappers and others repeatedly reported a wild man on the Nation River, a large river that pours into the north side of the Yukon about thirty-five miles as the raven flies downstream from Eagle. The man had supposedly been active several years earlier along the Yukon River. Wherever he showed up, ammunition and food went missing.

Jim Taylor's home cabin was on the Yukon, near the mouth of the Nation. He had a long trapline up the Nation, with several caches of supplies and equipment. He repeatedly claimed losses from the so-called wild man.

In those days the Nation was terrific grizzly bear country. Consequently, Jim's caches were high and rugged, plenty grizzly proof. But year after year, things disappeared.

No one lived on the Nation above its junction with the Yukon, either on the Canadian or Alaska side.

I thoroughly inquired into the situation, and there was good cause to believe that some unidentified person was making assaults on caches. Taylor asked me to fly there and from the plane look for tracks and any possible habitation.

I talked this over with Art Hines, a pilot with a Swallow biplane similar to mine, and a partner in Service Airlines of Fairbanks. He became interested, and agreed to fly there with me to investigate. That way there would be two aircraft involved in case of trouble.

Sam's PT Swallow on the Nation River during the search for the "Wild Man." Sam has covered the cockpits to keep snow out, and has wrapped the engine with what appears to be an insulated cover.
Sam O. White, courtesy James King

Thus on March 13, 1933, a beautiful, clear day, we took off from Fairbanks headed for the Nation River and Jim Taylor's cabin. Art flew directly to the Nation, but I detoured to Circle Hot Springs to attend to some business.

While at the Hot Springs I nearly lost my airplane, which had sat for some time cooling as I attended to my business. I returned to the plane and started the engine, and stood beside it to climb into my flying suit. As I struggled with the awkward clothing, the Swallow's motor gradually revved faster and faster. On skis, it began to creep.

Fortunately for me, friends Ed Brown and Hank Brown had come to see me off. I was effectively hobbled, half in and half out of my flying suit. As the motor's speed increased, Ed grabbed a wing tip in an attempt to hold the plane. Hank, in front of the plane, leaped aside as the whirling prop neared him. The tail lifted, and with Ed holding the wing, it swung toward Hank. Hank threw himself flat to allow the tail to swing over him. He then scrambled to look for a better opening.

Ed jammed his wing tip onto the ground and held it there while the plane circled. Hank grabbed it elsewhere. Both hung on like the Irishman and his wildcat; it was more dangerous to let go.

Meanwhile, I shucked my flying suit and got onto the back side of the lower wing Ed was holding. That put me inside the arc the aircraft was traveling. I worked my way to the cockpit and the throttle by hanging onto the flying wires (rigging between wings of a biplane). I really yanked on the throttle when I reached it. That put the brute under control.

The three of us were pretty well steamed up. While we panted, we managed to laugh. It was funny, yet it wasn't really.

If it hadn't been for those two I would surely have lost my airplane. I thanked them handsomely, and soon left for the Nation.

Both men had cabins on various creeks, and there was always plenty of grub and equipment in their caches. Ed Brown had three cabins and caches on the Charlie River, which, in the winter of 1943 saved the life of Air Force Lieutenant Leon Crane, the sole survivor of a B-24 Liberator bomber crash in the vicinity.

When I arrived over the Nation, Jim Taylor and Art Hines were upriver somewhere. A patch of ice near the cabin looked a little rough, but not too bad to a still inexperienced pilot. It was rougher than it looked, and when I landed, I broke a center section wire, which left the fuselage sort of wobbly in the cage.

I found some lynx snares at Taylor's cabin, put them in place, and twisted them for tension with a spike, then secured the spike. I couldn't have done better if I had been at the Swallow factory at Wichita.

It was so good a repair that I didn't replace the snares until an inspector from Stateside saw them and had a fit. One would have thought I had jeopardized the health and life of every woman and child in the Territory. For some reason he didn't ground me. He sure ranted.

Art and Jim didn't have a wild man with them, nor had they seen any signs of him. We all went up to Jim's cabin, which was built in a beautiful setting on a bank overlooking the Yukon.

The cabin had two large rooms. In the far corner of one room sat a large cook stove. Beside the stove was a hinged door in the wall, with a wood box full of wood under the door. On the outside of the wall was a wood chute full of wood. When one opened the door, the wood automatically rolled into the box.

Next to the partition separating the two rooms was what looked like a trapdoor in the floor. It was the top of a dumb waiter, with two shelves. On the partition was a crank with a cable arrangement that raised the waiter from the basement by turns of the crank. The waiter rose out of the basement, and food on the shelves was nice and cool.

The floor of both rooms was covered with a good grade of linoleum. The eating table sat near the front wall by a window overlooking the Yukon River, a pleasant place to sit and eat.

In the second room, Jim had cots with plenty of blankets and comforters, pillows, pillow cases, and sheets, all snow white.

When Jim put a stick of wood into the stove, with a brush and dust pan he swept up slivers and bark, and also put them into the stove.

When a meal was eaten, dishes were whisked off the table, put into the sink, and washed immediately. The dumb waiter was cranked up again and the perishables were placed on it and cranked into the cool basement.

Shortly before Art Hines and I arrived, a group of perhaps twenty Native men, women and children, and only the good Lord knew how many dogs, had moved from Eagle and were camped about half a mile upriver.

Moose were everywhere. Snow was deep and the animals had moved onto the Yukon River and its islands in great numbers. There were also many wolves. I kept track of the moose killed by the Natives by flying around the islands and the camp. When I figured they had plenty of meat per person, I told them to quit killing moose, and to go after a caribou.

I wasn't sure how effective my words were, but the next morning these people were all on the river with their dog teams, headed back toward Eagle. Taylor got a bang out of this; the previous night he had told me they would not pay any attention to me.

In the meantime, Art and I made frequent flights up and down the Nation. I made a couple of trips to Eagle for gasoline. At the head of the Nation and somewhat north of there were thousands and thousands of caribou, and many wolves.

Once we saw wolves killing a caribou—a cruel sight. Someone once said, "Nature in the raw is seldom mild." An understatement.

March 15, 1932. Searched Nation and Charlie River for wild man. No results. Believe this must be the man Canadian police killed.[1] See many moose and wolves during search.

---

1. The infamous Albert Johnson, the "mad trapper of rat river."

We decided the wild man had either died, or had shifted his hunting grounds into Canada. We found no sign of him, so we called off the search. We flew to Eagle, where we replenished our fuel. Art headed for Fairbanks.

An Eagle citizen wanted a ride in my Swallow. "Sure," I agreed. "Pile in."

He stepped on the lower wing and saw the lynx snares and recognized them for what they were.

"Did something break there?" he asked.

"Yes. But don't worry. Those snares are plenty skookum."

He was suddenly pressed for time, and had to postpone his flight. This was ok by me, and we changed the subject to the salmon run on the Yukon.

A Steese Highway Patrol

A canoe should be loaded weight-forward for downstream travel and weight aft for upstream travel. —SAM O. WHITE

ALTHOUGH IN THE 1930s the airplane was a tremendous help in patrolling the wide reaches of Interior Alaska for the Game Commission, it wasn't the answer in all cases. Many jobs called for use of riverboat, canoe, dog team, shanks mare, or, as roads began to reach out from Fairbanks, the Game Commission's old pickup truck.

In the fall of 1935, on a trip into the Birch Creek country, I found the right combination was truck and canoe, starting with the truck as a decoy.

The Steese Highway touches close to Birch Creek and its tributaries as it winds from Fairbanks north to Circle City on the Yukon River. At one of these points lived a registered guide who had been keeping about fifty dogs for pay, and allegedly was feeding them illegally with caribou meat. If true, I wanted to lift his license, feeling he was incapable of being an honest guide. I had checked him several times by driving over the highway, but found no evidence of wrongdoing.

I decided I'd take a trip down Birch Creek from the junction of Twelvemile Creek and Eagle Creek near the highway, check the game population en route, and see if I could catch this guy from behind. I had an assistant accompany me to where I launched the canoe and took off down Birch Creek. He then drove my truck back to Fairbanks, making sure it was seen at many places along the highway.

I paddled and poled downstream, camping the first night at Harrison Creek, and the second at an unknown trapper's log cabin

Sam, running Birch Creek with his 18-foot Old Town canoe. Note length of the iron-tipped snubbing pole Sam used. Anyone who can pole and paddle a canoe wearing knee-length leather boots must have a lot of confidence in his ability with a canoe. SAM O. WHITE, COURTESY DRAHS

which was new and built by someone who really knew how. He had named the cabin, "The Great Unknown."

The weather was good and the country beautiful. Game was abundant and the moose and caribou mating season was in full swing.

I reached Buckley Bar where, on foot, I made a swing up to Windy Springs where mountain sheep come to lick the minerals.

Below Buckley Bar the Birch is swift and rocky until it flows out of the foothills. With my iron-shod pole, I had to snub the canoe all the way down, and the going was slow and tedious. I made the flats by late evening and camped on a large gravel bar. About twenty feet from the water's edge, a large spruce tree had lodged against the bar. Its roots held the bole of the tree about five feet off the bar, and behind the roots and under the bole was a groove about a foot deep made by a swirl in the water. On the roots hung dry grass and small roots which I gathered and laid as a mattress in the groove. With my sleeping bag on top, no luxury hotel ever provided a better bed.

Around midnight I heard a large animal run down the bank and splash into the creek. I dimly made out a huge moose, who seemed to be in a hurry. He hit the water, came out on the bar, stepped over the spruce sweeper about twenty feet from my bed, and was gone.

I was just turning this over in my mind when another huge shape loomed on the bank. It was a grizzly bear pursuing the moose. He hit the bar a bit lower than the moose had, and took off on a fast lope on the moose's trail. I lay awake for about half an hour, and finally decided neither was coming back.

I awoke again about five thirty. It was a beautiful morning. A spiral of smoke about the width of a pencil slowly rose from my evening fire, with not a breath of breeze to disturb it. I was so comfortable, I just lay back and snoozed.

About an hour later, still snug in my sack, down the bar about 400 yards I saw a small pair of moose antlers. They were moving slowly in my direction. As they came closer, I saw it was a "mulligan" bull [a young bull, with small antlers], and the mating season was passing him by. He strolled until he arrived opposite my camp and stopped just eighty feet away. There he assumed a relaxed position, and seemed to be taking a nap. His head drooped and the eye toward me closed.

He looked to be in real good condition, so I decided to take him before he awoke. Still in my sleeping bag, I shot at the butt of the ear. He collapsed and never twitched. I had rope, axes, saws, knives, and a six-foot square of canvas, so I did a real fancy butchering job. I hung the meat on a tripod to drain and cool. I spent much of that day caring for the meat, and remained there another night.

[AUTHOR'S NOTE: One of the unwritten benefits of working as a wildlife agent for the Game Commission was being able to take game while in the field, provided it didn't interfere with law enforcement duties. No one drew overtime pay, but agents needed to work nights and weekends during open seasons. Wages were low, and getting meat for winter was important to most agents.]

There was a heavy frost that night, and I kept the fire burning, hoping the big bear would not return. Luck was with me—he didn't.

I was on my way again early next morning with the moose meat aboard and a minimum of freeboard for the canoe. The current was swift, but there was plenty of water and no more rocks. I had the whole moose, from ears to knees, including the nose which I always saved for Grandma Callahan, a much beloved old Native woman in Fairbanks. I left the hide and entrails on the bar with the head and feet.

Two days later I beached my canoe less than a mile above where the Steese Highway crosses Birch Creek. It was close to the bridge where the guide was allegedly feeding dogs caribou meat. I again hung my moose meat on a tripod, and readied my lightened canoe for a dash to the bridge at dog feeding time.

About 3 p.m. I dropped down to just above the last bend and waited. An hour later I heard the general rumpus of feeding time—barks, howls, and general uproar—so I got into the canoe and shoved off.

The man was so engrossed in feeding the dogs that I was standing on the beach before he saw me. He had just thrown a hunk of meat to a dog, and had turned to pick up another, when he spotted me. The look that came over his face was something to see. He sat on a box and allowed as how he had been caught red-handed, which was literally true; as his hands were covered with gore.

Under the bridge, and screened by brush, hung twenty-two caribou. Parts of other caribou were scattered about. The case was terminated next day before a U.S. Commissioner in Circle City with a jail sentence and fine. The man also lost his guide's license.

I retrieved my moose meat and camp gear from the river, and Johnny Palm, the mail carrier, who had started the Fairbanks-Circle mail route with dogs, then graduated to horses, and now was driving it with a modern truck, hauled my meat to town for free.

Speaking of Johnny, here's a little story about him and his bosom pal Riley Erickson.

Riley and Old Man Staid ran the Central Roadhouse and Trading Post. Riley handled the store and post office; Old Man Staid cooked and took care of the roadhouse. Johnny Palm, of course was in and out of the roadhouse while carrying the Fairbanks-Circle mail.

When duck stamps [migratory waterfowl stamps] were first issued, 2,500 of them were sent to the Central Post Office, and Riley didn't knew what to do with them. About the same time, he started feeding several flocks of spruce grouse which hung around the roadhouse, and dusted in the nearby road. They became as tame as domestic hens.

The grouse season opened, and Johnny had his shotgun with him on the next mail run. He could scarcely believe hunting spruce grouse could be so easy. What he didn't know was the grouse he so easily potted were Riley's tame ones.

Riley was so angry he threatened to turn his friend in to me. But since Johnny had the proper license, and had done the deed all nice and legal, this wouldn't do. Then Riley thought of the duck stamps in his post office drawers. He then forced his bosom buddy Johnny Palm to buy a duck stamp for shooting his grouse.

Then there was Old Man Staid, the cook, a fine old gentleman. I was in Central one summer when a couple of young ladies from Fairbanks, who happened to be our neighbors, were on a walking tour and had stopped at the roadhouse for the noonday meal. From the table we had a clear view of the stove in the kitchen. There was Old Man Staid, cooking caribou steaks and at the same time vigorously combing his beard with the steak fork. And up on the stove's warming shelf sat a pan of rising dough, covered by a towel, on top of which lay a pussy cat with the dough bulging out around him.

I assured the girls Mr. Staid's cooking was excellent, but they were trying hard not to see another side of him.

Duck hunting presented a bit of a problem around Fairbanks in those days. It was the general theory that by the time hunting season opened in September, all the ducks and geese had already gone south. In the 1920s and extending into the 1930s on a diminishing scale, it was customary for many residents around Fairbanks to indulge in illegal shooting when ducks and geese returned in April and May.

In a way, this was understandable. Winters were long and rough, and in those days meat markets weren't stocked as they are now. During winters you could be certain that two cold spells, one in December and one in January, would hit the sixty-five- degree-below mark and stay there a while. When you looked at your thermometer and saw the red column resting at minus sixty-five in the morning, the same at noon, and the same at three p.m., and the same twenty-four hours around for several days, you begin to think the darned thing was stuck. It was small wonder that everyone wanted to get out and do something different when the warm weather and long daylight hours returned.

Fairbanks was a small town then. Big clearings and fields that now surround the town didn't exist. Ducks sat in puddles all over town; geese lit on the ball park. Shotguns often boomed within the city, and an occasional charge of shot was heard rattling on sheet iron roofs. A few people objected, but they were in the minority.

It was, of course, my duty to try to enforce the no spring hunting of waterfowl part of the International Migratory Bird Treaty. But it was absolutely impossible to take a shooter into court and get a conviction. The only thing I could do was to resort to harassment near town by grabbing a few shotguns and try to crowd the shooting farther into the country, trusting to time and changing events to some day put enforcement on a firmer basis.

Most of the seized shotguns were held for a month or two, and where releases were not obtained, were later returned to their owners. Frequently the owners were not the hunters from whom the guns were seized.

Anyway, for about two weeks every spring I didn't get much sleep. Teenagers, too, after being pretty much cooped up all winter had to get out and kick up their heels. Many of them had jalopies, and I took after them in the official pickup. I sometimes ran them into a blind road and gave them a good frisking.

One day I overhauled a bunch of these young chaps and shook them down without finding any dead waterfowl. I was walking back to my pickup when one of them yelled after me, "Hey, Sam, you didn't look in the tool box!"

Of course this story made the rounds, and brought many laughs.

Lots of jokes are tied onto game agents, and I fell heir to my share. One bright May morning about two a.m. I was tooling my truck along the old Valdez Trail, now called the Richardson Highway, when I saw an elderly man ahead, carrying a burlap sack.

"What's in the sack," I asked, after stopping.

He grinned sheepishly and pointed, "My cabin is over there in those trees, and I plant a garden each spring and have to have fertilizer."

He was picking up horse droppings from the four-horse teams that hauled wood into Fairbanks. I looked into his bag and verified this.

Next morning the story was about town that I had run my arm into the sack up to my elbow. By afternoon, it was no longer my elbow; it was my shoulder.

Nowitna River Patrol

*On a trapper's cabin sod roof were only slightly fewer
than one million field mice.* —SAM O. WHITE

IN FAIRBANKS, during the spring of 1937 high water covered all of
Wendell Avenue, the greater part of First Avenue, and extended
up Cushman Street to Sixth. It also came into my driveway at
Ninth and Kellum. Since I was equipped with an eighteen-foot
canoe and a twenty-foot shovel-nose poling boat, I had several
very busy days assisting flood victims, moving them to dry parts
of town, and retrieving trunks, suitcases and boxes of valuables
that floated about. Wooden sidewalks were floating around, as
well as dog houses and sections of picket fence.

The hardy people of Fairbanks took this in stride. At the time,
no one was there to tell us the flood was coming, and what to do
before it got there, and how to conduct our affairs, and how to
save our lives, and what to do afterward, and so forth.

Fairbanks was having a flood—and that was that. Everyone
pitched in and helped, and even the victims seemed to have the
attitude, "A flood—so what? In a few days it will be gone and
we'll clean up."

But that year it was quite a flood. One old-timer had a skookum
high fence around his lot on Wendell Avenue. Stovewood and
heater wood floated down the street past him. He opened his gate
and rigged a boom. Soon his lot was crowded with stove wood.
But that evening the water rose higher than his fence, and his new
collection of wood floated on down the Chena River.

That was the spring I planned a Game Commission patrol down
the Yukon and up tributary streams, and on May 23, 1937, Game

192

Warden Gren Collins and I left Fairbanks in the shovel-nose boat with a load of camp gear and plenty of groceries. We stopped at Nenana to take on extra gasoline and oil for our outboard motor, and found the folks there also cleaning up after the flood. At Tanana the Yukon River's banks were piled high with ice, and huge blocks of ice were scattered about the streets of the town.

We were anxious to get into the mouth of the Novi [Nowitna] River before the upriver trappers came out of the hills. From Tanana to the Novi, the Yukon River was walled in by ice towering high above the river level, and there was only one place where we could get ashore. As luck would have it, at that place lived an alien who had three big illegal bear traps, twenty-one firearms, and no license. We relieved him of this property; an alien in those days had to have a license to possess firearms. We sank the dangerous and illegal traps in the Yukon River.

We entered the mouth of the Novi early in the morning on May 28, and soon met the first boat with two trappers drifting down the river. An inspection turned up some contraband beaver fur [shot, not trapped], which we took over for the government. The trappers signed a release.

Upon determining they were out of practically all supplies and gasoline, we gave them coffee, sugar, a few beans, and a can of milk. We also gave them a gallon of mixed gasoline (two-cycle outboard mix of oil and gas) so they could be sure to reach Kokrines on the opposite bank of the Yukon where they could buy needed supplies. We then waved them on.

When they left, they appeared confused, as though they didn't know whether to be happy or sad. We had taken their contraband fur and the .22 caliber rifle with which they said they had shot the beaver. On the other hand, we had given them enough gas to cross the Yukon and food and coffee which they had been out of for several weeks.

We met more boats as we progressed up the Novi. Some had contraband and some didn't. We took the contraband fur and the guns with which they claimed to have shot the illegal fur. Then we gave those who were out of gas enough to put them across to Kokrines, and those who were out of food got some of the necessities, along with a little coffee or tea. Many of the trappers were traveling with their families, and each babe-in- arms got a can of milk.

In one boat we found a small roll of contraband, along with several beat-up .22 caliber rifles. Among the guns was a new .22 caliber repeater without a scratch or a speck of rust. When I asked the chap which gun he'd shot the contraband fur animal with, he pointed to the new shiny one. Taken somewhat aback by this honesty, I waited a minute or two and picked up one of the older guns.

"No, not that one," he said. "The new one."

I tried to give him one more out, and asked, "Are you sure?" He replied, "I should know which gun I used."

Of course I then had to confiscate the new one.

Nearing high ground forty miles upriver, we saw four-foot lengths of steamboat wood floating through the forest. It had washed up from the Yukon where it had been cut and piled on the banks for sale to steamboats. The wood-cutters took a terrific beating that year.

One day we saw a rabbit floating down the river on a log. He was doomed if he continued downstream. We pulled near and to our surprise he leaped into the boat. He cowered under a seat, but raised up and looked out on the river now and then. We were within a mile or two of high ground when he leaped out of the boat toward a nearby bunch of foam and floating brush. He didn't make it. In his weakened condition he struggled only a moment in the icy water and was gone.

We soon came to a trapper's cabin on the bank. Water lapped at its eaves. On its sod roof were only slightly fewer than one million field mice. Nevertheless, we tied the boat to the cabin and moved in amongst them. They were friendly little fellows, and as soon as we opened the grub box, they swarmed into it. We had to stand to eat, and cooking was impossible. Every time we opened the chuck box we found a couple of mice in it that had been shut in from the previous opening. They didn't seem to mind.

Then a strange thing happened. Promptly at seven o'clock that evening, every last mouse ran off the roof, leaped into the water, and swam into the woods. In one hour they all came swimming back and swarmed onto the roof again.

Then at seven o'clock next morning, they repeated their trek to the woods. We were packed and loaded when they returned, and as they again clambered onto the roof, we shoved off, leaving some cold hotcakes which we hope they enjoyed.

About noon we arrived at high ground on the Novi and went ashore and pitched camp. As we unloaded the boat we found about a dozen of our little friends from the cabin roof had come along too, and were doing quite well. Two more popped out when we opened the chuck box.

We camped at a bend where we could look both up and down the river, and divided the time into watches to catch up on sleep. According to our list, one trapper was left upriver and we figured he would show up soon.

After a time he drifted around the bend, and we hailed him ashore. In his boat, in a bed of grass, was a freshly-killed moose. His three dogs were eating off of one end, and he was eating off of the other. Flies were eating all over it. By the time he hit the bank he was explaining why he had killed the moose.

Except for the moose, he had been out of food for ten days and was hungry. He was tall, lean, John Lassion, a good-natured Scandinavian, probably in his late sixties. He kept apologizing for shooting the moose. He seemed to think I would see to it he was locked up forthwith with the key thrown into the Yukon.

I finally convinced him that the kill was legal under the circumstances. In Alaska, game can be killed for food when there is no other food available. We fed John three times in three hours before he left our camp, and each time he filled up on coffee, hotcakes, bacon and eggs. He was so hungry for such food that he was frantic. He ate like a pig, with the grease running down his chin.

Since we were not going any farther upstream, we gave him a good supply of food and plenty of gasoline. He had no contraband. He was very much respected along the river.

Back on the Yukon River, we stopped at Ruby, and went to Galena, Koyukuk and Nulato. All were hard hit by the flood. At Nulato, there was still water in Pop Russell's store, but we tied our boat to his door and moved in anyway.

Since there was nothing we could do because of the flood, we volunteered to help Pop clean up. That was a big order. Four shelves which stretched the length of the trading post had collapsed, dumping their contents into the water. They had held many cases of canned goods, and, of course, all the labels came off. No one could tell what was in the cans.

Gren suggested a "damaged goods sale," and Pop thought it a great idea. Since the trading post was still knee deep in mud, washtubs were lined up outside, filled by the unidentifiable cans. Pop established a substantial mark-down, and Gren started selling.

The Natives entered into the spirit of the occasion. Muskrat skins were legal tender, and Pop ended sans canned goods, but with a haystack of muskrat pelts. Everyone wanted canned peaches; many ended with sauerkraut.

About the only thing that really bothered Pop was the sad fact that his brand new Sears and Roebuck gasoline-motor-driven washing machine had been submerged in silty water for two days.

Gren and I spent a day taking it to pieces and cleaning every last part. Pop was very pleased. Some months later, when I was again in Nulato, he demonstrated to me how nicely it worked.

Arresting Aliens

Though it was 40 below outside, the front end of the tent was comfortable for us in light clothing. The back of the tent was tolerable.
—SAM O. WHITE

DURING A 1937 spring patrol to the Nowitna River, I seized guns and bear traps from an alien. He hadn't bothered to get the required license. At the time I warned him not to have guns again, or to trap or hunt, without an Alien Special License. At the time I suspected he didn't take the warning seriously. He had a poor attitude.

In February, 1938, I decided to check on him. I had sold my Swallow airplane, but I had a Stinson Junior under charter. A mechanic at Alaska Airmotive, went along for the experience.

At Fairbanks we fired up the Stinson, even though it was 35 degrees below. I flew down the Tanana River to Tanana, and down the Yukon beyond Birches, to where the alien operated. We had an 8×10 wall tent, a Yukon stove, and equipment necessary for a week-long wilderness cold-weather sojourn.

I spotted the alien trapper's trails and his occupied cabin as we flew over, and continued flying downstream as if we were a commercial flight. I made a wide turn and came drifting back to land on a bar behind a Yukon River island.

My thermometer read 40 below as we dragged our gear from the plane onto the island, which was heavily timbered, with a bountiful supply of dried spruce for firewood. My companion was apprehensive, thinking we'd freeze overnight, but I assured him the tent would be cozy once we had a fire in the Yukon stove.

We made good thick spruce-tip beds, covered the rest of the floor with spruce boughs, and had everything arranged for comfort as I fired up the stove.

Sam with fur seized from an alien trapper caught without a license. Airplane is a Stinson Junior. February, 1938. SAM O. WHITE, COURTESY DRAHS

I cooked dinner with plenty of tea for me and coffee for my companion, who soon peeled off his outer garments. Though it was 40 below outside, the front end of the tent was comfortable for us in light clothing. The back of the tent was tolerable, unless blocked by garments hanging from the ridgepole.

Both of us had good sleeping robes, and, about 9:30, after dinner when the chores were done, we turned in and slept well and warm.

At daylight, after a good breakfast, we took off on snowshoes for the south shore of the Yukon and soon hit one of the alien's traplines. We found several set traps on this line, and a dead lynx in a snare.

He was home, and was considerably surprised and upset to see me. I couldn't blame him. He was skinning a red fox, and two more foxes were hanging in the cabin thawing so he could skin them.

I searched his cache and cabin and found about $1,700 worth of fur—a lot of money in 1938.

Despite my warning of the previous summer, he had no license. He pleaded that he was going to buy a license before he sold his fur. I pointed out the pitfall to that kind of deal.

I followed one of his traplines, springing and hanging his traps, while he did the same on another. I figured he wouldn't be around for a spell to look after his traplines.

Since it was quite a piece to our tent, we all stayed in his cabin that night. He grumbled, but was hospitable enough under the strained circumstances. The mechanic was a good companion, and got a kick out of the proceedings.

Next morning I made the trapper hook up his dog team and haul all his fur, plus the two frozen foxes and the lynx, to our aircraft. It was then that it dawned on him that he was going to loose it all. He felt pretty bad about it.

With the camp equipment and fur I had to haul in the plane, I couldn't take him and his dogs, so I started him up the Yukon for Tanana, allowing him four days to make it. He was to meet me there.

The mechanic and I fire-potted the Stinson, got her running, and flew home. We had been gone from Fairbanks three days. A round trip to the same spot by dog team would have taken at least three weeks.

At Tanana, the case was terminated four days hence, favorable to the government.

Another alien who became my regular customer called himself Pete Smith, although his Russian name was Gregory something-or-other. I picked him up about once a year and relieved him of his guns. He took out a license in each name and said, "Now you can't touch me. I have two licenses."

I told him it wouldn't do any good, for he didn't have the required citizenship papers.

Deputy Marshall Enid Thompson was with me one day when we met Gregory on the highway. We turned and took after him. He sped up, but we drove him into a dead-end wood road, while Enid watched to see he didn't throw anything out.

"Ok Pete," I said. "Do you have any guns with you?"

"No. You know I wouldn't do that any more. I know better now," he said.

I made him get out of his car and searched it. I found a new shotgun, a new .30–06, and a new .22 rifle.

"Oh, Pete, you big liar!" I said, disgusted.

"Damn this country. It's no good. I'm going back to Russia," he complained.

I said, "You tried that once and they wouldn't have you."

He had tried to return to Russia and they had kicked him out.

For that bust it cost him $150 in addition to losing his three new guns.

He had no use for the U.S. government. He used to live where the runways are now at Fort Wainwright, a fine moose pasture then. I watched him closely because he was always poaching moose.

One day the local marshall went to his place and he pointed a .30–30 carbine at the marshall. A big mistake. Pete had several guns pointing at him before he could say "scat." He got a year and a day in jail for that little trick.

Kuskokwim and Stony River Patrols

. . . it was a beautiful sight, with the countryside sprawled out like a big map, with bright sunshine and sparkling snow. Next, the Alaska Range rose majestically ahead. The motor purred soothingly. —SAM O. WHITE

ON MARCH 1, 1938, I flew a ski-equipped, chartered Stinson from Fairbanks to Anchorage, where I was met by agent Jack O'Connor and a new Alaska Game Commission agent, Jack Benson. Benson was to be stationed at McGrath, a village on the upper Kuskokwim River. I was to assist him in the move to McGrath.

At O'Connor's Anchorage residence, Benson and I discussed the office equipment and household items I was to fly to McGrath.

"You'll have to take my dog. He's used to airplanes, and is friendly," Benson assured me.

To get acquainted with this reputedly friendly animal, I visited O'Connor's shed where it was tied. I had hauled many dogs in airplanes at various times, and wanted to know what I could expect.

As I stepped into the shed, a black, curly-haired specimen that looked like a cross between a spaniel and a wolverine, and seemingly with the wolverine's temperament, growled and rushed at me. It seemed he had taken an immediate dislike to me.

He was tied with a rope. I had no desire to fight a dog while piloting an aircraft through the Alaska Range, so I asked Benson and O'Connor to get a chain and a choke collar with which to more safely tie him in the airplane.

Thursday, March 3, was a beautiful day. Benson and O'Connor loaded the plane, while I made a walk-around pre-flight check. It was apparent there wouldn't be room for me to crawl in, once everything was loaded. With some of the freight still piled on the ground, I crawled into the "anxious seat" [pilot's seat] and never glanced at the dog. I heard threatening snarls as the loading was completed. I paid no attention, as I was busy planning the flight.

The dog was tied where he could lie down, but not stand or sit. He couldn't reach me.

I heard Benson and O'Connor close the door. They stepped out where I could see them, and gave me the highball. I fired up, checked everything that needed checking in those simple days of flying, and taxied onto the runway.

March 3, 1938. Leave Anchorage at 11:45 a.m. flying Stinson NC14168. Arrive McGrath at 2:45 p.m. 55 gallons gas.

I was soon airborne and headed west across Cook Inlet and towards some very interesting and beautiful country. The Little Susitna river passed underneath, and then the Big Susitna, and it was a beautiful sight, with the countryside sprawled out like a big map, with bright sunshine and sparkling snow. Next, the Alaska Range rose majestically ahead. The motor purred soothingly.

As I enjoyed the scenery, something cold and wet hit the back of my neck. Before I could analyze it, the wetness slapped me from ear to ear. Next a big shaggy black head laid itself peacefully on my shoulder. A lolling red tongue hung out as the dog panted happily. He had chewed through the rope, and was free in the cabin. No chain, no choke collar. I made a mental note to take O'Connor and Benson to task.

I could do nothing but keep going. He had command of the situation, and since he seemed to be in a jovial mood, it seemed wise to keep him that way. As we progressed through Rainy Pass, it seemed evident that the dog was also enjoying the ride and the scenery.

We arrived at the small Kuskokwim River village of McGrath [pop. 138 in 1940]. Einar Carlson, a trapper and a renowned hunting guide of the district, drove his dog team under the left wing of the Stinson and stopped his sled opposite the door to receive the freight. He had a well-trained and beautiful team of malemutes.

I opened my window and yelled to the crew that had arrived to unload the plane. "Don't open the door. There's a loose dog in here," I warned.

Too late. A bundle of black fury, growling fiercely, catapulted out the door and into the dog team. The team, of course, was not reluctant to fight a stranger with such bad manners. Somehow, though, they became diverted, and started to fight among themselves, while the rude stranger, with evident enjoyment, sat and watched.

That afternoon Jack Benson and his family arrived via commercial plane, and we all moved into the Alaska Game Commission house to set up the Alaska Game Commission office and the Benson household. In those days, such field offices were commonly combined.

Benson and I asked a few questions around town and poured over maps, and decided to make a patrol in the Tonzona country.

We equipped the plane with grub, wall tent, Yukon stove, and plenty of winter gear, and the next morning set out for the Tonzona Valley.

McGrath was then mostly on the west side of the Kuskokwim River at the confluence of the Takotna River and the Kuskokwim. There was no airport. The rivers were used as landing areas, and I had landed on the ice and snow at the mouth of the Takotna. A small landing strip lay just back of the old town of McGrath, but it had many shortcomings, being marshy, and only 1,000 to 1,200 feet long. It was responsible for several crackups.

There was also a good sandbar across the river on the Kuskokwim, which was much used as a wheel plane landing site during low water.

At low altitude we cruised about the Tonzona Valley and found fresh tracks in the snow where a trapper was apparently still trapping, although the season had been closed for two weeks. We selected a nearby lake, landed, pitched our wall tent and set up our Yukon stove.

Knowing trapping practices helps a warden on aerial patrol. A trapline along a timbered high ridge is for marten. A line along small streams is for mink and otter. A trapline trail that visits all the beaver ponds in the green vicinity suggests a beaver trapper. By flying low, a warden can tell about how many traps a mile are used, and how often the line is run.

In later years, when airplanes became common, law abiding trappers welcomed visits by flying wardens if only to break the monotony of the short arctic days. Besides, they liked assurance that if a flying agent notices that traplines have not been run recently, he will land to make sure the trapper is all right.

204 Sam O. White, Alaskan

March 7, 1938. Out on trail to Slow Fork. Jack goes west, I east, on Bob Dunn trapline. Find four marten traps set. Jack brings Dunn to Dunn's home cabin. I get back at 9 p.m. after 27 miles on snowshoes. All in. I sleep on floor with no bedding but canvas and parkas. Jack returns 3 miles to tent.

Dunn was an old-timer and was very cooperative. He told us where all his traps were set. Next morning I set out on one line, and Benson on another. I hadn't gone far when, in a stand of large, straight, spruce trees, I found a pole set, a trapping system used for marten [a pole leaning across a stump, with the trap set at the upper end]. A live marten in a trap hung from the end of the pole. He was a beautiful creature. As soon as he saw me he was full of fight, and used terrible language.

He did not appear to be badly injured, and I decided I could liberate him with little or no trouble. After all, a marten, basically a tree-minded weasel, only weighs two to three pounds. I was sure he would be eternally grateful.

I had a pair of heavy moosehide mitts with wool liners in my pack. I put these on and grabbed the marten. He was most uncooperative. He sank his teeth into my clothing every chance he got, but since it was loose, at first he didn't nail me.

I managed a strangle-hold on his neck with my right hand, with my thumb under his chin. He squirmed and shrieked, but I hung on. I got the single-bow trap in my left hand, and pressed on the spring. The trap fell from his foot.

He then came violently to life, and in my preoccupation with the trap, I relaxed my grip and he nailed me on the thumb that was supposed to be under his chin. Wow! It felt like a bunch of red hot needles. The moosehide mitt was as tissue paper in his jaws.

All my sense of loving kindness evaporated. I heaved him at the butt of a nearby spruce, but missed. He disappeared in the deep snow. He popped into sight about fifty feet away, and scurried up a big spruce. Instead of hiding and being thankful to be alive, he remained in sight and gave me a nasty cussing.

I finished that branch of Dunn's trapline and found no other victims. I sprung and hung up every trap, and made it back to Dunn's cabin that night. Benson showed up later, having completed the check of the line he had followed.

While we were running his traplines, our trapper friend wasn't idle. To our surprise and pleasure, he turned out to be a cook of considerable stature. He served us a moose stew and an exquisite pastry. The fine qualities of both were unexpected in that humble trapline cabin in the wilderness.

Thursday, March 10, 1938. Up early a.m. Squalls and snow. Warm engine [with firepot]. I attempt to take off. Lake too short, or sticky snow. Quit. Strong south wind came up. Ok for takeoff. Start up, and just at take-off-point the rocker arm assembly breaks. Take off cowling and repair. Ready for tomorrow. Weather not too good. No time on ship.

That rocker arm assembly repair was simple, and a lucky break for us. One of the little bolts on the rocker arm had broken. The push rod was jumping up and down with nothing to push against. The exhaust valve wasn't opening.

I found the four bolts that held the cowling on were the same size and length as the broken bolt. I put one of them in place, and our troubles were over. Three bolts held the cowling nicely, and one bolt held the rocker arm. We flew that airplane for a week after that, with no problems.

On March 12, I flew agent Benson toward the Alaska Range and landed him on a lake from where he was to patrol various traplines. He disappeared into the wilderness. I was to return and pick him up in a week.

I returned to Dunn's trapline and spent the next few days springing and retrieving his traps. By Friday, March 18, I had accumulated seventy-one #1 traps, fourteen #1 ½ traps, and one #3 trap from the Dunn trapline.

On March 19 I flew into McGrath to take Bob Dunn, our trapper friend, to pay his debt to society, and to get supplies. He pled guilty to violation of Alaska Game Law, and was fined $80. Being a reasonable man, he held no grudge against me. In fact, he was downright friendly, and blamed himself.

I then flew back to our tent camp with Dunn, including a good load of his supplies.

On Monday, March 20, I flew to the lake where I was to rendezvous with Jack Benson. He wasn't there. I flew to the Native village of Nikolai and tried to get someone with a dog team to search for him. The country is mostly timber and heavy brush, and seeing a person on the ground from the plane was difficult.

I cruised trails and circled cabins, but saw no sign of Benson. I returned to Nikolai and landed in a swamp, and had trouble getting off again. I ran into the brush seven times with no damage to the plane, and made it off on the eighth try.

I rented a cabin at Nikolai. Bob Dunn arrived and moved in with me. He was almost as concerned about Benson as I was. Next day I again flew over the area Benson planned to patrol but I could not find him.

I was raising the price of a dog team charter to where it was becoming very attractive to team owners, and was about to close a deal, when the cabin door burst open and, in a cloud of cold air, in staggered agent Benson. He was about done in. I breathed a sigh of relief, and Dunn immediately set a hot and scrumptious feed on the table for Jack.

Two Indian priests at Nikolai wore flowing black robes that would have been a bit more impressive but for the fact they were so dirty and smelly. While Dunn and I were in the village, they stuck around all day for fear of missing a meal. I think I detected disappointment on their faces when Benson arrived. Next morning we lost no time in leaving.

With Benson's arrival we had another problem. He had located another trapper whose traps were still set. This trapper had agreed to come to Nikolai with his dog team on a certain date. I was to fly him to McGrath and court.

He showed up on the date agreed, and I flew him to McGrath where his account with the Alaska Game Commission was squared.

IN EARLY APRIL, 1938, a few weeks after our adventure with Bob Dunn and others, I received an SOS from Benson, asking me to hustle to McGrath. He had learned of a trapper who, according to local information, had cut a wide swath around the game commission regulations.

I flew to McGrath, and Benson and I interviewed several locals. We poured over maps and decided the Hungry Lake country needed a visit. We didn't know the half of it.

We stocked the plane with plenty of good chuck and took to the air. We crossed the Swift and Stony Rivers and landed on a lake south of the Stony. Here we pitched camp and remained overnight.

Next morning we followed a few trails on snowshoes, and eventually walked into Hungry Village [now Lime Village. Pop.

38 in 1939] on the bank of the Stony River. It was exceedingly well named. Here we ran into a Native priest who at the time was riding high, but who was later dethroned when it was learned he was removing the innocence of various women in his flock. He reinforced the reports we had on the reported game violator.

We returned to our camp for the night. Next morning we took off to the north of the Stony where, from the air, we cruised some country that we decided had some things that needed looking into.

We landed on a lake and again pitched our tent. Next morning I took one trapline, while Benson took another. His, it turned out, was the longest. I wasn't to see him again for four days.

We found seventy-five traps set for marten and fox. It was well into April, long past trapping season. We sprung traps everywhere we went. At every turn we found moose killed for dog food and cached at intervals along the trails. I found a freshly-killed cow moose with an unborn calf, killed the previous day for dog food.

We found two trappers with poison. Don Block, the 14-year-old son of one of the trappers, also lived with them. They were driving twenty-two dogs, and all three were living on moose meat and beans.

We told them we were going to take them to court. They wanted to leave the boy to look after the dogs and the trapline.

"No. You won't leave the boy here. We'll take him in too," I said. I wasn't going to arrest him or charge him with anything, but I certainly wasn't going to leave a 14-year-old boy, no matter how competent, alone on this wilderness trapline.

They had to shoot the dogs. There was no way to take care of them. We gave them enough cartridges to do so. Benson stood in one place, and I stood in another, and we counted the shots as the two shot their dogs.

After the shooting, one of the trappers came into the cabin, red-faced and angry. Part of the cabin floor was dirt. He had a long barrelled .30–40 Winchester with which he had shot his dogs. Inside the cabin, he drove that gun into the ground clear up to the forearm. The gun was still there when we left.

We flew them into McGrath, and the Commissioner gave them each a year in jail. Don Block, the 14-year-old, stayed with Benson for six months, and he grew like a weed. He then stayed with me and my wife until his father got out of jail. While he lived with us

I told him he could eat whatever he wanted, and he was always going to the refrigerator.

On a balanced diet, that kid grew to be over six feet tall and weighed 200 pounds. He had the best temper and the best outlook possible. He went to school, and we had no problems with him. He got along well with the other kids. He was a very good boy.

He eventually became a licensed pilot, perhaps because of my influence. Last summer (1967) he was killed near Livengood when the plane he was in crashed.

[AUTHOR] In a November 3, 2005, letter to me, Roy Billberg, added details to the saga of trapper's son Don Block: "He became like a son to Sam and Mary, and was very close to them for the rest of his life," Roy wrote.

"He was riding as a copilot with Paul Hanson in Paul's B-25 Mitchell fire retardant bomber when the plane went in on a fire drop and crashed. They were both killed. I was there, flying with my father [Rudy Billberg] in his B-25. We were the next bomber to make a drop. When we landed in Fairbanks, we knew they were gone.

"Later, on the day of the tragedy, my father, mother, and I went to see Sam and Mary. They had already been notified. Mary talked to us immediately, but it took Sam about three minutes to come out of the bedroom. He came out wiping his eyes.

"I believe Don Block's death deeply hurt Sam and Mary. The reason I think so is their reaction to a gift later that fall. During hunting season I fired once to bring down a two-year-old bull moose that simply stood broadside, looking at me. I had the meat cut into steaks, roasts, and made some burger.

Dad and I agreed old-timers needed the meat much more than I did. I kept some, and gave two-thirds to Sam and Mary, and one third to Tillie Brockman.

"Tillie broke down in tears with the gift. Sam later told Dad that he and Mary had been so despondent they didn't know if life was worth while any more. He said they enjoyed the moose burger so much it gave them both the will to live. Dad and I decided that is why the moose stood there as if he wanted to be shot. It was for the old folks."

[SAM] The next several days were tough ones for both of us, as we got onto another poison-using, law-violating, trapper, but we stuck to it and ran out all the trails we could find, including several single-snowshoe tracks.

It was appalling to see the destruction of wildlife that had been dealt out by that irresponsible man in this wilderness where game was abundant.

We ended in a cabin on the Stony River, low on chuck. We were reduced to eating beans fortified by illegally killed moose meat we had seized.

Our last batch of beans turned sour and started pushing hunks of moose meat out of the kettle. We had things pretty well rounded up, with the violator in custody, and with him, we returned to our tent camp and our airplane.

The sun was out full blast and the trail was melting. We struggled on, tired and wet, and finally reached our tent. As we crawled into our sacks I observed, "It sure is getting dark early this evening."

"Take off your sun glasses, Sam," Benson told me.

We were both near exhaustion.

We flew to McGrath with the trapper and our evidence and readied for court. When he saw the evidence, the U.S. Commissioner was shocked, and in no mood to temporize. He delivered a scathing rebuke to the culprit and handed him a stiff sentence.

I steamed up, and the next day left McGrath for Fairbanks. Weather was threatening, with big thick wet snow squalls sweeping through the valley. It became increasingly difficult to fly around them, and I was caught in one and in a matter of minutes the airplane's wings picked up a heavy rime of slush. There it congealed. The ship staggered, and I had to do something, and quickly.

I knew where there was a triangular pattern of three round lakes. They weren't very big, but they were adequate for an emergency landing.

Despite the gloom and limited visibility, I found the first lake, but I had to land the ship hot, owing to the ice. As I touched down, the ice fell from the wings, and the ship took to the air again, being relieved of the load and the malformed air foil. A line of brush was approaching fast. Another lake was beyond it. I managed to boot her over the brush and land safely in the deep snow of the second lake.

Two hours later I took off, ducked more squalls and fog, and landed in mud at Fairbanks.

Jack Benson and I got together to figure the dollar cost of our joint field work. We were shocked at what we had spent.

Neither of us were fiscally-minded. We knew how to get the field work done, but keeping track of expenditures was something else.

Apprehensively, we made up the vouchers, got them signed, and bravely endorsed them.

We wrote the required reports, but avoided mention of costs. We may have exaggerated the hardships we had encountered, but our strategy was to drag a red herring away from the finances involved—at least until the brass in the head office had read the field reports, hoping to soften them up, so they would hesitate to get out the beheading tools.

We mailed the reports of accomplishments first. Somewhat later we mailed the bad news of our fiscal irresponsibility. In those days, mail often left Fairbanks days apart, so we knew we had a short respite.

We counted on the fact that the boss, Frank Dufresne, had been a field man for many years.

We sweated out the ominously long wait. When word finally arrived from Juneau, we were complimented on what we had accomplished, and mildly taken to task for our fiscal irresponsibility.

Our strategy had worked, but I imagine we were responsible for a few extra gray hairs in Juneau when they scratched around to find the money to pay our bills.

Medicine Lake and Mahoney

*Even on white water, Sam used a canoeing technique he learned from
Maine woodsmen. He stood as he paddled, using an extra long paddle.
He also stood while poling a canoe. In white water, the idea is to
see far enough ahead to be safe, he said.*
—LETTER TO AUTHOR FROM ROY BILLBERG, FEBRUARY, 2006.

ON VARIOUS TRIPS into the Circle country I learned that the
nearby Medicine Lake area was well stocked with game. I heard
this from old-timers and confirmed it on various trips I made
down nearby Birch Creek with dog team and canoe, as well as
flights over the area.

I became interested in investigating Medicine Lake itself. The
surrounding country is of an interesting and unusual nature.
Around the lake are big niggerhead swamps, with alternate patches
of timber, jack spruce, and potholes. Birch Creek runs nearby, and
is a beautiful stream.[1]

East of the Birch, beginning near the bar where a grizzly bear
once chased a big moose past my camp site, is referred to by Indians as "Mahoney Country."

The old-time local Indians kept clear of this spot. It seems
that many years ago a prospector and trapper named Mahoney
disappeared there, and when Indians traveled there afterwards
they heard unexplained screeches, which they attributed to the
lost Mahoney.

Circle Hot Springs, where springs flow a good volume of hot
water year-round, is about three miles from Medicine Lake.

---

1. Birch Creek is now a National Wild and Scenic river.

I kept a cache of aviation gas on Medicine Lake for a year or so, but had to remove it for safety reasons. Willie Moses and his wife Sarah had a cabin near the lake's outlet. They made a good living mostly from local fish and game, of which there was plenty.

One late winter day I landed on the frozen lake to gas up, but I couldn't find the three cans of gas I'd left there. As I searched, I heard a shout and saw Willie waving at me from his cabin. I snowshoed over to see what he wanted.

"We take care of your gas for you, Sam. We got it in the cabin," Willie said.

I went into the cabin and there, between the wood stove and the wall, were stacked my three full gas cans. I got it out of there in a hurry.

Of course Willie had a job with his dog team to haul the gas back to where he found it. He charged me seventy-five cents for hauling it to the cabin, and a like amount to return it.

I changed my gas cache to a swamp Willie was unlikely to find.

The outlet to Medicine Lake leaves the lake in the northern corner, and it is not easily found. I thought it would be interesting to take my eighteen-foot Old Town canoe, and not only give the lake a good look, but to follow the outlet down to Birch Creek.

One summer, during the slack field work season for a Wildlife Agent,[2] I ferried my canoe and light camp gear to as near Medicine Lake as I could get with my truck, and packed it the rest of the way into the lake. I spent a day canoeing around the mile-and-a-half wide by two-mile long lake, prying into corners, and watching six or eight nearby big moose feeding.

Next morning I went to the outlet, and soon came to where it spread into shallow clear pools. The water was from four to eight inches deep. It was quite warm, and, on the bottom was a white mineral deposit that appeared to be alkali. The water tasted bitter.

Large pike were lying in this shallow clear water. After a long tussle with my fly rod, I caught one of the big ones. He measured forty-eight inches long, and was eight-and-a-half inches deep, back to belly. I couldn't determine what these huge pike were doing there. They weren't feeding, and it hardly seemed a suitable place to spawn. Perhaps they were attracted by the warmth.

---

2. Sam's job title changed from game warden to wildlife agent in June, 1938. This trip took place sometime between 1938 and 1941.

Sam wearing his cumbersome winter flying coverall, with his Swallow biplane's engine running. Even wearing this clothing, he could fly no more than three hours in the open cockpit plane in below zero temperature. Sam O. White, courtesy Jim Branson

There were numerous bear tracks, and it was evident that bears were feeding on the pike, which were at a great disadvantage in those clear shallows. Many had backs protruding from the water.

I watched a black bear sow with two cubs lunge into one of these pools and come up with a wiggling, four-foot pike. With the pike extending on each side of her jaws, she ran across an opening of about fifty yards, heading for timber. The cubs, running on each side, ate off the pike as they ran. I figured the old girl would be lucky to have a mouthful for herself by the time she made timber.

I soon paddled clear of the shallow pools. The outlet creek entered some timber between fairly high, brushy, grass-grown banks. The creek was shallow and narrow, not more than three times the width of the canoe. Once I looked up and directly above me on the bank was a big black bear staring down into my face. He seemed to be mildly amused, and made no hostile demonstrations. He almost could have stretched a bit and given my ears a boxing had he felt like it.

Next, I began running into trees that had caved off the bank, and brush that interlocked over the channel. Mosquitoes were in vicious swarms. After I had used an axe to hack my way through a few such barriers, I caught a movement out of the corner of my eye. It was a wolverine, and he was patently watching me. I had heard that this bit of country was heavily populated with these animals. I ignored him and kept moving. Around the next bend I ran head-on into another log jam, across which I dragged the canoe. As I re-launched, I caught sight of the wolverine again. I should have settled his hash right there. I had had enough experience with these dudes to know he was up to no good.

Sam with two month-old wolf pups. In his day, wolves were looked upon as undesirable pests, with a bounty paid by the Territory. Today, the state of Alaska manages wolves as a valuable and desirable part of the environment.
SAM O. WHITE, COURTESY DRAHS

I passed a few more bends and came to some low banks, with a nice open spot where I decided to camp. I slid the canoe from the water and propped it upside down on a pole in case it showered. I built a fire for a cup of tea and hot food, and was settling down when I heard a scurrying behind me. I grabbed my carbine, swung about, and saw the wolverine again, dashing to get behind a tree. I swung, and from the hip, cut one loose.

The result was a diabolical, unearthly, scream, and the thought came that maybe such yowlings from wolverines had something to do with the Mahoney legend.

I was uncertain if I had killed, or merely wounded, Satan. I went to where he had disappeared and found and finished the brute. He had been a little too slow in getting his tail end behind the tree, and the bullet had just barked the tree and caught him in the after end.

I was hungry. After a quart of tea and some food, I crawled into my sleeping bag and slept like an innocent.

I was underway bright and early next morning. The push flies [mosquitoes] swarmed and bit; it was head net conditions with gloves. About noon, I was between high, narrow banks. As I paddled around a bend, I came upon a black bear. He was very close above me, standing on a partial tree trunk.

The tree had fallen. What was left of its trunk was a good eight feet above the water. It had broken half way across the creek, and the rooted half was still firmly anchored. The bear had walked out this half trunk with the evident intention of jumping from it to the far bank.

He became rattled when he saw me, and put too much steam into his jump. The rotten trunk broke, dumping him upside down into the creek, along with the end of the broken trunk. Both landed within a few feet of the canoe, splashing buckets of water into the canoe.

Much frenzied action suddenly took place in the canoe, as well as in the water. It was immediately evident that all the bear wanted was to get up the bank and away from me; fighting was the last thing on his mind.

Between my frantic efforts with the paddle, and the bear's attempts to lunge up the near-vertical, muddy bank, the water was pretty well torn up, and full of mud.

Finally, with the aid of the fiercest war whoop I could muster, he got a toe hold and scrambled up. His frantic scrambling rained goose grass, mud, and sticks on me and into the canoe. Another war whoop boosted him over the top. He disappeared into the forest.

When I recovered from the shock, I laughed until I was too weak to paddle. The canoe drifted and hung up on a snag.

It couldn't happen again in a thousand years; sadly, there was no one else around to enjoy it.

I paddled ashore, dumped water from the canoe, and continued to chuckle and shake my head in disbelief, while I cleaned out the mud, grass, and twigs. I could hardly believe what had happened.

Shortly afterward I was in beautiful Birch Creek, with its clear water and gravel bottom. I soon came to the Jump Off, where once a roadhouse stood, and Pete Bloom's cabin. Pete wasn't home, but I stacked my outfit in his yard, walked out to the road, caught a ride to Central, and later to Circle Hot Springs to pick up my truck.

The trip was over. I wouldn't recommend it to anyone. There is no scenery en route, there's a lot of shallow water, high banks, much mud, and wearisome obstructions across the channel.

However, I'd make the trip again if I figured I could see a bear perform another high dive. Seems unlikely.

Alaska-Yukon Boundary Patrol

*Sam is an expert woodsman, and it was a pleasure to be with him
on a trip of this kind. I don't know how anyone could have
done more than he did to make this patrol successful.*
—CLARENCE RHODE, WEEKLY ACTIVITY REPORTS MARCH 4, 1939 TO APRIL 8, 1939.

[AUTHOR] IN THE LATE 1930s, Canadian trappers were smuggling
wolf and coyote skins with attached leg bones into Alaska. With
these, they collected the bounty paid by Alaska for these animals.
Further, Alaska trappers were smuggling Alaska-caught marten
furs into Canada for sale (no open season in Alaska; open season
in Canada).

Both Canadian and Alaska trappers were known to be using
strychnine poison, available from druggists in Canada.

A cooperative boundary patrol to nail the lawbreakers was arranged between the Alaska Game Commission (Executive Officer
Frank Dufresne) and Major T. V. Sandys-Wunach, Superintendent of
the Yukon Subdivision of the Royal Canadian Mounted Police. Those
who made the patrol were Alaska Wildlife Agents Sam O. White of
Fairbanks, Clarence J. Rhode, of Cordova, and RCMP Constable W.
W. ("Baldy") Sutherland of Dawson City, Yukon Territory.

[SAM] For this patrol, Clarence and I chartered a six-place
Curtiss Thrush, a slow (94 mph cruise) plane. It had the reputation of being a great load carrier. It sold for $10,000 in 1930. Our
pilot was Leo Moore.

We left Anchorage March 9, 1939, fought bad weather, and had
to lay over at Nabesna Village (near Northway). There we found

The Curtiss Thrush while on the Alaska-Yukon Boundary patrol. "It was 34 below. We piled two Arctic sleeping robes on the engine and finally started it," Sam wrote. In this photo the engine is still being heated—the prop wouldn't clear the robes piled on the engine if the engine were started.
   Three snowshoes? What happened to the fourth?
   SAM O. WHITE, COURTESY JAMES KING

many of the Natives carrying Canadian money and learned the source of the money was Jack Dolan's Trading Post at Snag River in Yukon Territory.

The temperature remained low nearly all of March, often reaching 35 to 40 below, which made it necessary to fire-pot the ship for not less than an hour before each take off.

The slashed-out boundary provides an excellent landmark, and we had no difficulty in locating our destinations.

Clarence dropped me and some of the heavy camping gear off at the Walker's Fork Roadhouse (long gone), near Chicken, while Leo Moore flew Clarence on to Dawson City to pick up Constable Sutherland.

Sutherland and Rhode flew to the Snag Trading post. It was necessary to land some distance from the mouth of the Snag. This gave trader Jack Dolan time to cut off most of the leg bones from the furs of coyotes and wolves he had on hand. He had been saving them to smuggle across the boundary to collect the Alaska bounty [twenty dollars for wolves, ten for coyotes].

Clarence and Sutherland seized the keys to all of Dolan's buildings and found a generous portion of strychnine poison in his possession, as well as illegally purchased furs, which they seized. They finished cutting off leg bones of coyote and wolf pelts in

Clarence Rhode. Probably when with the U.S. Forest Service at Seward in the mid-1930s. Lois Irvin (Clarence Rhode's sister)

the post and took pictures of Dolan standing beside a box of eighty-four leg bones. Dolan was placed under arrest, and was flown to Dawson City.

Next day Clarence appeared as witness at the trial in which Dolan was found guilty on four separate counts involving poison and illegal trading.

On March 17, Clarence, Constable Sutherland and I were flown in the Thrush to the head of Sixty Mile River and cruised along the international boundary until we found the trapline of Louis Lyckens. We followed it from Lyckens' home cabin on the Canadian side, to thirty or forty miles inside Alaska. His line was about 125 miles long, with three trail cabins in Alaska. Eighty five miles of the line were within Alaska.

We found a meadow to sit down on near Lyckens' home cabin. Louis Lyckens had started for Dawson that morning with his entire catch of fur except for wolves with leg bones attached, which he had planned to take to the Alaska side.

We seized the wolves [skins with bones attached], searched the cabin carefully (even took out one stove and pulled up the floor) and found considerable portion of poison. We placed Louis' brother, Otto Lyckens, under arrest and obtained a statement from him that Louis had taken by use of poison twenty-seven marten, three foxes, and twelve wolves in Alaska during the closed season. He had no Alaska trapping license.

Clarence went up Miller Creek by snowshoe to the Glacier roadhouse and sent a wireless into Dawson to ask the police to pick up Louis Lyckens on his arrival.

March 20, 1939. It was 34 below, but the high wind of the previous day was dropping. We piled two Arctic sleeping robes on the engine and finally started it. Prisoner Otto Lyckens froze both ears. Clarence froze his nose for the second time on the trip. We loaded everything in the ship and decided to try to get off without double tripping.

The ship lifted half way down field but settled again, but it was too late to cut the power. Pilot Leo Moore dodged among the trees. The plane touched one but did no damage and he finally got her flying in the clear. A close call. We arrived at Dawson an hour later.

Lyckens was in bad shape so we broke into a shelter cabin (no shelters provided on Dawson field for public) and thawed him out. A police car arrived an hour later and we went to the RCMP barracks. We met with Louis Lyckens and obtained a release on his fur as well as a detailed statement of his illegal activities.

We attended the trial of the Lyckens brothers, who were found guilty. Louis Lyckens agreed to go to Fairbanks to stand trial, and his fur was left with Canadian police for safe-keeping.

At Dawson, from a drug store, with help from the RCMP, we obtained the names of trappers who had bought poison. These fellows would put out strychnine bait and contaminate a whole region rich in mammal and bird life. The birds fly off and die, and their bodies become new poison bait for mammals. One man spreading poison can kill animals across a huge area. He collects only a few pelts of the animals he destroys. Many crawl off and die in hiding, or the snow blows over their bodies.

Leo Moore flew me, Clarence, and Sutherland in the Thrush to Eagle, Alaska, where we spent the night. On March 24, we flew along the international boundary, dropping down to each river to examine it for sled trails crossing from country to country.

We were surprised to see mountain sheep adjacent to the boundary on the Alaska side, north of Eagle.

About forty miles out, we dropped over the high mountains and at the head of the Nation River, came to a country of low timber and rolling hills.

On the Nation we picked up a sled dog trail across the boundary, and flew east on it until we came to the home cabin of Oscar Erickson, whose name was on the list of buyers of strychnine.

We flew back down the Nation, mapping the trail cabins of Chris

Nelson, an Alaska trapper. We couldn't find a safe place to land on the Nation until we were within twelve miles of the Yukon.

Nelson was a trapper who was tripped up by pride of his killing ability. This guy kept his own score.

On the door of his twelve-foot-high cache we found written on the back of a label from a condensed milk can: "DU NOT OPEN THIS DOR A GUN IS SET TO KIL."

We opened the door with a long pole. There was no gun.

In the cabin was a stack of canned milk labels on which he kept a sort of diary. We kept them for Commissioner's court. They read:

Oct. 5. UP ETTRAIN CREEK. SHOT ONE MOOSE.

Oct. 6. ON ETTRAIN CREEK. SNOW STORM.

Oct. 10. BACK TO NATION RIVER. SHOT ONE MOOSE.

Oct. 14. UP NATION RIVER. SHOT TWO BULL MOOSE.

Oct. 15. SITTING TRAPS TODAY.

Oct. 16. SIT 10 LINK SNARES TODAY.

And so forth.

We took Nelson to Eagle where he was forced to settle his accounts with the law.

On the morning of March 31, Sutherland, Rhode, and I, on snowshoes and about one mile below the boundary on the Alaska side, met Erickson coming down the Nation River with his dogs and a big load of fur. He had a six-dog team, and was coming toward us fast. I stood in the trail and held up my hand, signaling for him to stop.

He realized who we were, and shouted at his dogs and cracked his whip to overrun us. Having two good capable men to back me up, I stood my ground. When it became apparent he didn't intend to stop, I swung my carbine on the dog team. I figured it wouldn't be murder to shoot a dog, if that was needed. He saw we meant business and put on the brakes.

Erickson had killed out the animals in the section, and was leaving with his pelts and what remained of his poison.

We frisked him and found his poison in a sock at the foot of his sleeping bag. His language was frightful, even with no ladies around to hear it. He saved his best broadsides for me, but he didn't neglect the constable or Clarence.

Then he turned to the Mountie and said, "For once you're powerless. You're in Alaska, and have nothing to say."

"We're going to your cabin across the line," I told him. "Turn your team around and hold it until I tell you to go."

I could see him figuring to make a break, or at least get to his cabin first. But I got onto a bulge of ice at one side with the carbine handy, and Constable Sutherland got onto the toboggan. That brought another verbal broadside from him, but to no avail. Sutherland went with him, and when Clarence and I arrived at the cabin, they were waiting for us.

Erickson said "You two s.o.b's are now in Canada, and are without authority." But Baldy Sutherland calmly turned to us and said, "I have a cache and cabin to search. Would you gentlemen care to assist?" We would and did, and found more poison.

We obtained a statement from him, admitting he had used eight bottles of strychnine each year for the previous three years. He was planning to move out of the country, since the fur was about gone.

We took the big bad boy to Dawson to face the King's court. He didn't like that. He would far rather have taken his chances in Commissioner's court at Eagle. But I heard later he was terrific with a bucksaw and that the King's woodpile really took a beating.

On April 4, 1939, Rhode and I cleaned up our remaining business with the Canadian police. Leo Moore then flew us to Fairbanks in the Thrush, where the plane was checked.

We had been lucky. The propeller hub was cracked on one blade. It likely wouldn't have lasted more than another hour of flight. Had it broken in the air it could have caused such a violent shaking (one blade of the prop gone) that the engine could have been torn out, with a certain tail-first crash.

By April 7 the plane was repaired and ready to fly, and we completed our journey in Anchorage, having flown about 3,500 miles in a month.

[AUTHOR] Clarence Rhode wrote the nine-page report on the boundary patrol, graciously crediting it, "By Wildlife Agents Sam O. White and Clarence J. Rhode."

A comment in it reads: "This trip has further proved that airplanes are the only possible means of properly patrolling our districts. Likewise, they offer the cheapest method. The inspection that can be given the ground from a low altitude is almost unbelievable. The tracks of nearly every type of game or fur can be readily distinguished and it is easily possible to note where [trapping] sets have been made along trails.

Clarence Rhode (l.) and Sam O. White, with a Gullwing Stinson, probably at Weeks Field, Fairbanks, in 1941, when Rhode was receiving flying instructions from Sam. Lois Irvin (Clarence Rhode's sister)

"All types of game can be observed from the air that would never be seen from the ground, and such things as hidden cabins or caches are easily discovered. With hundreds of miles of remote country in all of our interior districts, and the short periods when active patrol is essential for results, we can never fully police this country until we have our own planes to depend on."

The fine hand of one Sam O. White was probably involved in writing the report. The writing is characteristic of Clarence. It certainly wasn't written by Sam. It seems likely that Sam was peering over Clarence's shoulder as the report was written.

Clarence probably hadn't had that much flying experience in 1939 to easily recognize game tracks from the air. In 1941 Sam gave Clarence flying instructions, soloed him, and helped him get his pilot's license.

The boundary patrol report summarized: "Seven cases were handled on the Canadian side of the boundary, most of them involving the possession and use of poison, and involved in some way with the bounty frauds. Unquestionably, the Territory will save a considerable sum which would have gone toward illegal bounty claims."

The Hugo Stromberger Case

Wanton waste of wildlife always makes a game agent see red.
—SAM O. WHITE

THE WORST SUCH CASE of waste or misuse of game I encountered during my fourteen years of patrolling the Interior for the Alaska Game Commission was that of Hugo Stromberger, a ruthless killer of mountain sheep. A quarter of a century has passed and I still can't help but think of the beautiful valley where he lived as something of a morgue.

I met Stromberger on the Wood River dog team trail in 1924 when I worked for the U.S. Coast and Geodetic Survey. He was German-born, rather arrogant and aggressive, and he suffered from asthma. He had settled on Dry Creek in the Mount Hayes area, about eighty miles southeast of Fairbanks.

His main cabin was near a vein of lignite coal which he burned in his cook stove; another cabin was above timberline where he went in the summer to escape from pollen; a third cabin, on his trapline, was in the spruce forest, at a lower elevation.

He was alone for three to six months at a time, and saw his nearest neighbor, who was eighteen miles away, maybe once or twice during that time.

This chap had called a few times at my office in the Fairbanks Federal Building to get a trapping license. I had his place of operations on my list for several years as a must for a check-up, as I had seen a guide's report that the man was doing some free-wheeling with the game, especially mountain sheep.

Twice I had planned to go there, but each time I was diverted for duty elsewhere. Finally, in late November, 1939, I was set to go, and Wayne House, a capable wildlife agent from McGrath, agreed to go with me.

With my plane on skis, on November 30, 1939, I flew a tent and other equipment into a creek about eighteen miles beyond Stromberger's cabin. I returned about noon the following day with Wayne and the rest of our gear and supplies. We set up camp and crawled into bed early. Long before daylight on December 2, on snowshoes, we hit the trail for Dry Creek and Stromberger's main cabin.

It was slow going through deep snow, and we arrived at his cabin with little daylight left. His dogs barked when we were about fifty yards away, and the man came out. He was friendly, shook hands, and invited us into his cabin. Before we went in, I made our position clear.

"We are here on business and we mean business," I told him. "Right now I want to check that load on your sled."

His sled was in the yard with the dog harnesses still on the tow line. He walked over and stood beside it.

"This sled is mine," he said, "and you can't look at it."

I followed him and gave him the word. "We may be with you two or three days, and we are going to look you over real good," I said. "While we are here, we do not want any interference whatever from you. You will be treated with respect, and your rights will be observed."

At that, the man actually came to attention, saluted me, and said, "Yes, sir." He stood aside, and from that time to the end of the trip he was cooperative and gave us not the slightest trouble. Long after, I learned he had once been in the Prussian Army where he apparently developed a deep respect for authority.

We inspected the load on the sled and found the heads of two cow moose. We found six big fat rams on the ground, and nine more on the roof of the cabin under canvas and snow. There were traces of many more that he had fed to his dogs. He had very little moose meat left, and no caribou meat.

He had no food other than game meat and wild berries, but in the true spirit of the North, he offered to share what he had with us. We had brought three days' scant rations for ourselves, but we turned most of our grub over to him, as he was famished for beans and flour. We offered him a cigarette which he accepted eagerly. "I have had no tobacco for three months," he said, "and I'm a slave to tobacco."

With that, we took stock of our cigarette supply, figured a ration for the three of us on a three-day basis, and when we smoked, he smoked.[1]

At daylight we resumed our check of his cabin and grounds. The first thing we found was an 8mm Mauser carbine set over the door to shoot down in front when the door was opened. It, of course, was for bear, but since the roof had a six-foot overhang, a man was not likely to see it when opening the door. The gun went into the contraband pile.

We started digging through the snow in his yard and came up with the heads of a ewe and a lamb, in addition to the fresh meat that was lying all over the place. He also had sheeps' hams, sugar cured and smoked. They looked real good but we didn't try them.

Wayne called my attention to the fact that the man had not fed his dogs since our arrival. We couldn't stand by and see the dogs go hungry, so I told him to feed them on whatever he usually did, since so far as we were concerned it would make no difference in the charges. We watched him cut a big ram's carcass up and feed it to his dogs.

Next day we went to his cabin at the head of the creek. It was in a beautiful setting with a spring of clear cold water under a bank behind the cabin. The large volume spring didn't change temperature more than a degree or two from summer to winter. I forget the exact figure, but it was around forty degrees Fahrenheit.

Over this pool Stromberger had built an ingenious shack with racks where he said meat kept fresh for a month in summer without being bothered by flies. His cache here also contained four or five cured sheep's hams.

Digging in the snow around this place, we found two grizzly bear skulls, another ewe's head, and another lamb's head. When we totaled the score, it was two caribou, two moose, and fifty-one mountain sheep, which he admitted killing between July 1 and December 1 of that year.

He did a poor job of concealing the pride he had of his shooting prowess. He said, "I earn this by killing enough wolves to save more than double that game."

---

1. Apparently Sam took up cigarette smoking in the mid-30s; he wrote that he didn't smoke in the early 1930s. He smoked cigarettes for many years after retirement.

When I asked him if he collected the bounty on all the wolves he had killed, he replied, "Of course I do. I have to make a living." A later check of bounty records showed he had collected only five bounties on wolves in seven years.

Above the cabin, on a low ridge, was a mineral deposit where sheep had a lick. It was filled with small caves which generations of sheep had pawed or eaten out of the ground. Opposite this spot was a blind he had built. On the ground around the blind was probably a bushel of empty cartridge cases. It gave us the creeps to think of all that carnage.

We found two more set guns at the upper cabin, which we also confiscated. We spent the night there, and returned to the main cabin next day. It was a relief to get away from the upper cabin killing ground. It seemed to be marked with death. With fifty-one sheep we could prove, we could only wonder how many more were hidden in the deep snow. The thought that this had been going on since the man settled there in 1922, seventeen years earlier, was not comforting.

At the main cabin we selected our evidence for the court and sealed it into bags. We also took pictures. I was anxious to get Stromberger into the picture with the contraband, but I knew that the picture could not be used as evidence unless he was in them of his own free will.

Much to our surprise, as we arranged the contraband for the photo, he asked if he could get into the pictures. We told him yes, but that they might appear against him in court. He still wanted in, however, so we kindly permitted him to pose with his contraband.

The next day he willingly used his dog team to move a load of his contraband to our camp eighteen miles away. Then we allowed him to mush to Birch Lake where he could leave his dogs to be taken care of by friends.

Before we left our camp, we called on one of his neighbors. This man, too, treated us hospitably, but we found ewe sheep parts there, along with more than the legal limit of rams.

With the contraband at hand, the district attorney presented the Stromberger case before the U.S. Commissioner's court. There were some shocked people in the audience when the vast array of contraband materials was presented. When the set guns were laid out as evidence, there was a stunned silence. Stromberger pleaded guilty to five counts, and was sentenced to six months in jail and fined $150.

Stromberger had been furnishing meat to a ring of poachers, who peddled it mostly in Fairbanks. We found a postcard at his cabin from a tipster who lived on the Richardson Highway, telling Stromberger that "all was clear," meaning he could bring more meat to be sold.

His neighbor, the other defendant, however, elected to have a jury trial. When it came to explaining away the ewe sheep, the man put on a soul-wrenching performance. He was a dead shot, but he told the court, apparently with great effect, that he had aimed at a ram and hit the ewe.

When it came to explaining away the excess bag of rams, well, he was a prospector, and he was digging holes to bedrock to find gold which would be of great benefit to Alaska for sure, and he could not live out there and dig holes unless he could shoot all the meat he needed.

At the time in Alaska, all prospectors had little halos over their heads. The jury was composed of ex-prospectors and ex-market hunters. After hearing what the defense attorney said about me, I could almost see them thinking, "Just look at that well-fed wildlife agent. He never sank a hole to bedrock, and what's more, he never will."

The defendant was acquitted.

To a certain extent there were no hard feelings. The defense attorney was right on the bedrock deal. I haven't sunk a hole to bedrock yet, and the chance that I ever will are dim. However, it should be said that on many occasions I have been in prospectors' camps in very remote areas, and have dined with them on bacon and beans when moose and caribou were in plain sight, yet were perfectly safe.

"We couldn't begin to use a big animal like that," they'd say. "Nine tenths of it would rot. Too much waste,"

Instead of eating moose or caribou, they sometimes gave individual animals names, and if an animal failed to show up for a day or two, they'd be concerned. If it showed up again, they rejoiced.

FACING PAGE: *Illegally killed game seized at Dry Creek on Sam's biggest bust. With Wildlife Agent Wayne House, Sam seized two cow moose, two caribou, fifty-one mountain sheep, three set guns and arrested two market hunters. Major violator was Hugo Stromberger, on right. Sam is on the left. December, 1939.* SAM O. WHITE. COURTESY JAMES KING.

THE NATIVE PEOPLE of the Interior, too, were occasionally guilty of waste, but in a different manner. I am referring to their use of caribou and moose "fences" to snare animals—an efficient method used before they had access to firearms.

I first heard of these fences on a trip to the old Chandalar Native village (now Venetie). The fence there was twenty-five or thirty miles long. A smaller one was in the vicinity of Tetlin [near Tetlin Junction], and a much larger one on the Kechumstuk [in the Fortymile country] which was a good fifty miles long. In later years I flew over all of these fences.

The fences used natural obstructions where available, with long stretches built of poles, logs, brush, timber. Openings were left, usually near game trails, and snares set in them.

The snares were made of braided rawhide or rope, or old telegraph wire, if available. The waste came because the snares were not well attended. Often complete skeletons were found in them.

Where wire was used, it was sometimes broken and carried off entangled on the victim, leaving loose ends as a permanent threat of entanglement for other animals. Caribou antlers especially were vulnerable to tangling in wire.

The Kechumstuk fence made a sort of semi-circle around the head of Kechumstuk flats. It snared large numbers of caribou and quite frequently, moose. I once found a big bull caribou there in a wire snare and, although his carcass was somewhat loud, he had not been there long. He had uprooted the anchor, which was a dead stub about ten inches diameter and about fifteen feet long, and had bound himself with a loop of wire around his body that sank into the hide two or three inches. He had packed and dragged the anchor and wire about three hundred feet from the opening in the fence, and then had become entangled in brush and died.

As I came to these snares, I cut them into short pieces and packed the pieces away, discarding them in different places so they could not be used again. I chopped the rawhide and rope snares up with an axe.

The wire came from the telegraph line that connected Big Delta and Fairbanks with the U.S. Army post at Eagle. It had long since been abandoned, so I spent some time cutting this up, or if it was a long stretch, I dropped the wire to the ground from the tripods holding it.

I found many caribou skeletons with antlers entangled in this wire. Moose didn't seem to get caught as frequently, apparently because their antlers slant back. I did, however, find one moose carcass snared in the wire that was a real dilly.

The wire had been held off the ground with a tripod of spruce poles. The body and antlers of the moose were encircled with strand after strand of wire, so that a small jack spruce was bound to his antlers, and a dry pole was bound to his body.

He was a big bull, with antlers that spread just short of sixty-nine-inches. The wire bound the antlers so tightly that the ends flew apart two or three inches when I cut the wire. It was an awful mess, and a terrible death for the moose.

I think the Natives discontinued use of the Kechumstuk fence in the mid-1930s, as, at the time, there was a decline in the Indian population in the Fortymile area. By then, most of those who remained were armed with .30–30s, or even .30–06s, and they no longer needed to use snares to acquire moose and caribou.

Sam Resigns

Some local businessmen were more interested in the money the military brought to Alaska than in Sam's wildlife conservation efforts.

— AUTHOR

[AUTHOR] IN SEPTEMBER, 1941, Sam resigned his position as Wildlife Agent with the Alaska Game Commission.

It was wartime. General Simon Bolivar Buckner, Commanding Officer of the Alaska Defense Command, had been denied a resident hunting license. He went to court to challenge Alaska's hunting license laws.

The law specified, ". . . a citizen of the United States who has been domiciled in the Territory not less than one year for the purpose of making is permanent home therein . . . shall be considered a resident."

The sticker was the phrase, "for the purpose of making a permanent home." A citizen, although a resident for a year, needed to prove he or she planned to remain in Alaska permanently before he could be issued a resident license.

A nonresident license cost fifty dollars, about twice the monthly pay of an army private. With war looming, soldiers were pouring into the Territory. Many wanted to hunt.

Buckner's challenge was a much-discussed subject. Sam White talked about it with Lt. Colonel L. V. Gaffney, Commanding Officer of the new Ladd Army Air Forces field at Fairbanks.

Disturbed by Gaffney's comments, Sam reported the conversation to Frank Dufresne, his boss, and the Commission's Executive Officer, saying, "I was plainly informed that this is only an opening wedge, and that they fully expect to gain sweeping concessions

233 Book Two: Game Warden/Wildlife Agent

before this thing is settled. Gaffney also remarked that they would 'blow the Game Commission wide open.'"

Dufresne repeated this to General Buckner.

Sam soon learned of Dufresne's indiscretion.

In a January 27, 1970 letter to James G. (Jim) King, Sam wrote, "I received one more vicious stab in the back when the Executive Officer (Dufresne) returned a whole envelope full of confidential reports back to the commanding officer (Gaffney) at Ladd Field. I was then rendered helpless and useless to the old Alaska Game Commission."

It was then that Sam resigned. "Twice I was offered every inducement to return to the Commission, but I was through," he wrote King.

He added, "Game Commissioner John Hajdukovich took one look at the wreckage and he quit too. It was the most astounding thing one could imagine."

He was offered $800 more a year to return to his old job. His reaction? "If I was worth that much more to them, I should have had it before I left."

Buckner believed Gaffney's claim that White had fabricated the story he had told Dufresne. Gaffney wrote a long letter, of which Dufresne later said, "...fifteen paragraphs were devoted to attacking Sam, and one paragraph to an explanation of the incident."

Buckner passed on to Dufresne Gaffney's thinly-disguised suggestion that both Fairbanks wardens (Sam White and Clarence Rhode) be fired.

Dufresne believed Sam, and had no intention of firing his Fairbanks agents, but the damage had been done, thanks to his indiscretions.

Another factor influenced Sam. An increasing number of his cases against game-law-violating GIs had been dismissed by the courts. He was pressured by some local businessmen in Fairbanks to "go easy" on the military.

For fourteen years Sam had worked endlessly to bring respect for the Game Commission's regulations. He had enforced the laws regardless of whom was involved. Now some business men and the military wanted special concessions, and, in Sam's view, the top officers were the worst.

Was the clock being turned back to the old wide-open days? To honest Sam O. White, it appeared to be a battle he couldn't win.

Book Three

BUSH PILOT

Sam O. White, Bush Pilot

Sam, you land like moose ptarmigan [big bird].
I think you come dead quick! —WILLIE MOSES

IN THE FALL OF 1942, within a few weeks of resigning my job as Wildlife Agent I became Chief Pilot for Wien Airlines. I flew mail, passengers, and freight from Fairbanks to bush villages. My annual salary jumped from $3200 to $7200. The switch seemed a natural one. It was Noel Wien, CEO of the airline, who had sparked my dream of getting into the air in 1924, and he and his brother Ralph had taught me how to fly.

I had held a commercial pilot's license for more than a year. I knew the airline routes well, as well as the country between the routes.

I enjoyed making mail runs. I bumped into old friends everywhere I went, and I liked visiting with them as well as providing them with a needed service. I spent my days flying, and my evenings shopping for everything from pins and diapers to light plants, axes, and saws for the people in the sticks. And woe to the pilot who forgot the nipples for the baby's bottle. Villagers had two weeks between scheduled flights to write their orders, but they never got around to it. They were always caught by surprise when the mail plane arrived, resulting in a half a dozen folk at a time shouting verbal orders, and thrusting loose money at me. I had to have a portable accounting outfit in my pocket and "make book" even at forty-five degrees below.

Rural Alaska was changing fast. A few prospectors were still scattered about, and many trappers, but they soon began to leave the hills for construction jobs. Along with World War II's drain on manpower, the building boom was just getting started, and before long I was hauling passengers out of the river villages and packing very few of them back.

The woodcutters at Fairbanks stopped cutting wood in favor of the higher construction wages, and Fairbanks became an oil-burning town. It was the beginning of the end of the old Alaska.

Some old-timers stayed put in the bush, and made the transition to catering for airplanes instead of dog teams. One of these was Joe Anicich who owned and operated the Tower House, the saloon and roadhouse at Tanana. In its day it had prospered, but as Tanana faded, so did his business. Joe was proud and independent. No welfare or relief money for him. He allowed as how he'd stay there and make his own way, and he did.

Joe hauled loads of gasoline to the airport with his elderly white horse. One morning he found the horse had died during the night. For a time he was inconsolable, for he loved that animal and had lavished great care and affection on it. But he bowed to changing times, and bought a small Caterpillar tractor to continue the hauling.

And, of course, I spent far more time in the air, and that had innumerable possibilities for fear and excitement. Fire in the air is terrifying. That happened to me once when, appropriately, I had as a passenger Maurice Smith, a Bureau of Land Management fire control man. He later became editor of the *Jesson's Weekly* Fairbanks newspaper.

I had run into the willows at Holy Cross and dinged a wing tip. After making temporary repairs, I took off with Maury for McGrath. As the engine warmed and settled to cruising, we smelled smoke. Later, to our discomfort, we thought we could see an occasional curl of smoke. We were over Reindeer Flats on the Innoko River. There was no place to land until we got to Flat.

The smoke quit over Flat, and we had tentatively identified the smell as burned willow leaves scooped into the engine cowling on take off. Nearly all bush fields in those days had four-foot-high, pencil-thin, willows growing on them. So, we pushed on to McGrath where Charlie Koenig, another old-timer who had gone modern, was gas-up man, field manager, and all-around helper for pilots.

On landing, I told Charlie about the smoke smell, and the wing tip, and asked him for some dope and a brush. "Go eat your lunch," he said. "I'll fix your wing tip for you."

He did, and it was an excellent job. He also scooped about a bushel of dry, scorched willow leaves out of the cowling.

Although I ran errands for the people scattered around the bush, I was more than repaid in most cases by their generosity and hospitality. For example, W. R. "Blank" Blankenship, who owned the trading post at Kiana, always furnished me with meals and lodging. He refused to take my money, and I was always treated as a member of the family. Even when Blank was very low on gasoline, he could always dip up enough to get me to Kotzebue.

Blank was with the U.S. Geological Survey on the Arctic Coast in the early days of surveying. One of the earliest maps was a topographical survey strip about four miles wide along the principal rivers, with no connecting links in between. Blank told me about packing supplies from the Noatak River into the head of the Colville River for the short summer's work.

He waded in ice cold water up to his hips and fought swarms of murderous mosquitoes. He told of having to kill his faithful lead dog, Prince, because the mosquitoes were eating his eyes shut. He buried the dog on the bank of a creek about two or three miles above Umiat, and named it Prince Creek.[1]

In those days, as today, pilots often had to deal with emergency cases of sickness or injury. These were the stickiest deals, as most emergencies seemed to occur in the worst weather, often after dark, and in next to impossible places to land and take off.

One trip I remember vividly involved a woman school teacher who was desperately ill at a river village. The only float ship available at the time belonged to a friend of mine who was recuperating from an injury. I took it and flew to the village, arriving just as darkness was closing in.

We loaded the poor woman, who was suffering terribly. Out on the river, driftwood was running, and the fading light made it hard to see. I got the plane into the air without hitting any driftwood, but at about fifteen feet, the motor quit. I managed to land again in the swift water and a boat caught me and pulled the plane ashore.

The carburetor had nearly fallen off. Two studs were gone, and none were available in that village. I tied up and sent a radio message. Help.

---

1. Prince Creek remains on maps today.

Next morning early both Wien and the Army arrived. We got the sick woman into town and she survived. But during that night I suffered the agonies of hell right along with her.

I also had a few races with the stork. Won every one of them, but some of the margins were close.

On one such trip I was flying a Travel Air 6000B. There was lots of room in it, but it was a slow flyer, not an airplane with which to race the stork. My expectant mother was a very fine lady but she had waited too long to head for town and medical assistance.

My only other passenger was an elderly trapper who had never married, and knew nothing about the business of having babies. We were hanging over the wilderness with about a hundred miles to go to Fairbanks when the trapper tapped my back.

"Sam," he says, "this woman is having pains. We got to do something."

"Ole," I said, "I'm busy flying this airplane. Everything that has to be done, you have to do. Spread some mail sacks and lay her flat on the floor."

This was done, and then commenced one of the longest hours I have ever put in while flying. I should have logged a hundred hours for it. Fortunately the radio was working, and when I parked the ship at Fairbanks I hit the ground running and let the taxi man who was waiting, the trapper, and the ground crew take care of things.

Another emergency which, despite its seriousness, hit me on the funny bone. I was on a mail run one summer day when I picked up what sounded like an emergency message, but I couldn't make it out because of poor radio reception. The radio operator at Wien's nearest station was exceedingly good at picking such messages out of the air, and when I arrived there, she had put it together.

"Man half drowned needs medical aid . . . crackle crackle . . . Send Sam . . . blurp blurp . . . etc.

After refueling I was on my way and landed about an hour later to find everyone in the village out to meet me. They had a young man on a stretcher in the dirtiest sleeping bag I have ever seen. It was covered with candle grease, moose tallow, and lots more that couldn't be identified. A good bit of tension was floating about, and no one was saying much.

"Vertical or horizontal?" I asked. No one got it at once, but finally one villager said, "Lay him down."

I told another villager, "You jump in here and take care of this guy until we get to the hospital."

In due time we arrived at the airport where a doctor and nurse were waiting, having been alerted by the Wien radio system.

"Can he walk to the ambulance?" the doctor asked. I didn't know, so I looked at his companion.

"No," said the other Indian.

"Why not?" the doctor wanted to know.

"He's got no pants," the Indian said.

So they got him on a stretcher and put him in the ambulance. The doctor asked me to stick around while they X-rayed him on the chance he might be able to return with me. I went to the Wien terminal for a cup of coffee, and to visit friends.

The station agent took the telephone call from the doctor. He became agitated. "Gunshot wound!" I heard him say in a loud voice. Then it was my turn to become agitated.

"Tell Sam to go back to his mail runs," the doctor said. "I have to keep this man here. There's a bullet wound in his ass."

VISITING WITH OLD-TIME Alaskans was a privilege and a pleasure. One winter when I flew for Wien out of Fort Yukon I often spent evenings in town visiting four old chaps in the white man's ward at the Hudson Stuck Memorial Hospital. I had known them all for years. They were well worn from hardship and age, but each had made his mark in Alaska, and was honored and respected. They included Charlie DeBieu, Mr. McDaniels, and Tony Rose, all longtime prospectors. The fourth was J. L. Thomas, known as Tommy the Mate because of his long experience on Yukon River steamboats.

One night Tommy the Mate asked if I would get him a liverwurst sausage the next time I was in town. I brought him one that was three feet long and three inches in diameter. I recall him sitting up in bed and slicing off chunks, which he ate with great relish. He kept the sausage hidden under blankets, but eventually a nurse found what was left.

It didn't take an intellectual giant to figure out the source, and I was in the doghouse with the nurse.

During one summer I flew a Coast and Geodetic crew out of the village of Stony River on the Kuskokwim River. One day while I was at the village word came that an injured man was at the headwaters. To rescue him I would have to land on a beaver pond.

I immediately took off for the headwaters of the Stony River [village and river with same name] and soon arrived over the L-shaped beaver pond. I spotted three or four men at the upper end. I could land on it all right, and I decided it was long enough for a take off by using both length's of the L.

At the bend of the L was a large beaver house. It was high enough so that when I went around the curve I would have to have enough speed to lift a wing over the house.

I landed, and as I taxied to the men, I planned my take off. The beaver dam was at least twelve feet high, and between high banks. It was anchored to the banks as well as to a large rock near the middle of the dam. The river banks closed in below the dam, so I was going to be in a groove for fifty yards after clearing the dam. This was a bad feature, since I would have to hang on the prop to gain altitude until I cleared the trees.

The injured man was in misery. He had jumped off a bank onto a log. The bark slipped, and he landed astraddle. Ouch.

We got him into the ship and I taxied to the end of the pond where the men pulled the ship back as far as they could into the brush. Meantime, three men went down to the dam in case we didn't make it and needed help. One man remained to signal me when the men had arrived at the dam.

He soon gave me the highball, and I laid the whip to my old L-5G Stinson N40013. We made the mud and water fly. Luck was with us. The take off progressed from point to point as planned, and when we reached the beaver house at the corner of the L, I had speed enough to lift the right wing over it.

The next hurdle was the dam, where the water was just a few inches from the top. I think I cleared the dam by about four inches, then I had a few bad seconds hanging on the prop before I began to pick up speed.

I flew to Bethel, and a truck came down to the riverbank to pick up the patient. The driver told the suffering Indian, "You'll be the first patient for our new woman doctor." [AUTHOR: Probably Dr. Harriet Shirmer.]

At that, the poor man begged, "Sam, take me back to the beaver pond."

Many things can put a plane down—swallowed valves, broken wristpins, water in gas, ski harness failure, ice or frost on wings—and they have all happened to me. So, with the odds of flying bush around the North, the day came, of course, when I was the object of an emergency mission. It happened at Circle City in the winter of 1942, and was by far my worst wreck.

It was war-time, and many aircraft parts and supplies were either hard or impossible to get. I worried about the ski harness on a Gullwing Stinson, and talked it over with Noel Wien, who agreed it should be changed. But, we had no new shock cord with which to replace it. I didn't fly this ship much, and was concerned lest one of the younger, less experienced pilots, was caught in the air with a ski harness failure.

It was me who got caught.

I was flying into the Yukon Valley with twenty-two five-gallon cans of gas aboard, tied down in a cargo net. I had crossed the head of the Salcha River at 4,000 feet and was letting down, and had the lake in sight where I was to deliver the gas. It was a beautiful day with no wind, but at 2,000 feet I hit turbulence and CRASH—a ski harness broke, and one ski suddenly pointed straight down. This threw the plane into a graveyard spiral. My use of controls didn't stop the spiraling as the plane swiftly headed down. Then CRASH, the other ski harness broke. Both skis were now jammed in vertical position.

This stopped the spiral I was in, and I regained control. I had but 900 feet altitude. I not only couldn't climb, I couldn't hold what altitude I had. My air speed was eighty-five miles an hour, and I was gradually losing altitude.

I got on the radio and advised everybody who was listening that I was in a jam and was going to try to make Circle for a crash landing. There was no place else to go. Eagle was about the same distance, but higher, so that was out.

Following the Yukon River, I looked for a stretch of glare ice but found none. I thought of two lakes I knew which the wind swept clear of snow every winter, but one was too high, and the other too far away.

About that time, I reached a point where the Yukon turned north, and I had a tough decision to make. At the rate I was losing altitude, I knew if I followed the river I would coincide with the surface before I reached Circle. So I took the all or nothing alternative, left the river, and made a beeline for Circle. The tree tops kept getting closer, as, with the motor wide open, I gradually lost altitude.

I called Fairbanks and reported I was getting ready to land at Circle. I didn't have altitude enough to circle the field, so, hoping no other aircraft was in the way, I flew straight to the field, and was lucky to make it. Two feet of hard-packed snow lay on the field. The skis and landing gear plowed a furrow down to and through the grass roots. I went from eighty-five miles an hour to zero in fifty feet. The landing gear came off in pieces. The left wing took a beating. The plane didn't overturn.

Four cans of gas split at the seams and gas gurgled everywhere. When workers cleaned up, the motor was disconnected from the plane and rolled away after a few wires were snipped.

I shoved my right knee into the instrument panel during the landing, and it cracked my right hip. When the plane stopped, I was still in the seat with the belt in place, in snow nearly up to my waist. I was rumdum.

Strong hands yanked me out. Ed Moore, a Wien pilot and longtime friend, was a small man, but he dragged me out of there like a sack of oats. He leaned me against the fuselage and braced me there while my head cleared.

A line of about thirty Indian men, women, and children stood by the runway fence looking frightened. They kept their distance. Finally one, Willie Moses, got brave and came to me. He shook my hand, and said, "Sam, you land like moose ptarmigan [big bird]. I think you come dead quick!"

Then all the men came over and shook hands. The women shook hands. The kids lined up and shook hands too.

This activity shook some of the cobwebs, and Ed steadied me over to the Northern Commercial Company store. An old friend, a good reliable Scotsman named Macgregor, ran the place. They eased me onto a couch in a sitting position. Then Mac did the most wonderful thing. He placed a fifth of Johnny Walker Black Label in front of me. The pain and terror vanished. The old head cleared up.

About two hours later, Noel Wien flew in with the Travel Air to pick me up on what was likely his one-hundred-thousandth rescue trip. Seven weeks later I was flying again, none the worse for wear.

Koyukuk Mail Runs

Flying passengers is a tremendous responsibility. Passengers are
dependent entirely on you. In a forced landing it is your responsibility
to keep them alive in cold weather, and in summer to protect them
from hordes of insects. It can be a tremendous job to protect passengers
who are inadequately dressed. They will travel in winter in oxford
shoes, cotton socks, and business suits (men), dresses and high-heeled
slippers (women). It seems they place a higher premium on appearances
than they do on life and comfort, and they seem not to mind
giving their pilot plenty to worry about.
—SAM O. WHITE, FROM AN AUGUST 6, 1966 INTERVIEW.

WHEN I STARTED FLYING for Wien Airlines in 1941, their routes were
all known to me, but the demands on me other than flying, were new.
To keep track of the many requests for needles and pins and boat
engines and bales of dog fish, I used up many a notebook. At first I
ran all the errands, but I had to sleep sometime, so I gradually turned
the shopping requests over to the Wien office force.

A typical early 1940s winter mail run into the Koyukuk country included the flight from Fairbanks to Alatna, two hours ten
minutes. Alatna to Bettles forty-five minutes. My load included
mail, supplies, and a deputy U.S. Marshal on some kind of a
"mum's the word" investigation.

From Bettles I flew the deputy and a helper to Hackett Creek,
above Bettles, and landed them on a river bar. The snow was arm-
pit-deep and fluffy. I waved goodbye and took off in a cloud of
snow and flew back to Bettles for the rest of my load for Wiseman.
A pile of freight at Bettles had arrived by riverboat the previous
summer. It needed to be flown to Wiseman.

I remained overnight at Bettles, and the next day flew a few loads of freight to Wiseman, and checked on the Marshal. They were ready to come out. Snow was so deep on the bar that I had to split the load and make two trips to Bettles with them. Again, I remained at Bettles overnight. Weather was making up and I was concerned.

Next morning, with the deputy and helper aboard, I took off for downriver in air that was full of holes, with violent gusts. We got to Hughes and the wind was sure whooping it up. Since it was starting to snow, I decided to hole up there. It was clear that whatever kind of a storm was coming was a good one.

On my final approach to land on the Koyukuk River at Hughes, turbulence was so violent that the fire extinguisher came out of its bracket on the floor, and started to float around the cabin. It slammed into the skylight, then caromed off, and just missed the deputy's left ear. He grabbed it with both hands and hung on for dear life.

I made sure not to botch the approach and landing, as the thought of having to go around for another try was too much to contemplate. I made it on the first attempt, but I couldn't relax until Les James and his well-trained crew had seized the plane, held it down, and had it tied solidly to the river ice.

At the James' Trading Post, Mrs. James had one of her famous lunches ready. The deputy had a weakness for King Oscar brand sardines. He wanted to buy a case from Les James to take home to Fairbanks. In wartime, some items could be bought in outlying areas that were unavailable in Fairbanks. I told him we were overloaded as it was, that we couldn't take on any more weight, period.

Later, at Fairbanks, I received an invitation to have lunch with him at his home. Among other things, he served me King Oscar brand sardines. Of course I smelled a rat and asked him where he had found the King Oscar brand in Fairbanks.

"I didn't. I slipped them into my baggage at Hughes by doing a little careful rearranging," he told me, gleefully.

We had the usual laugh over this, but it wasn't a new gag. Many bush pilots have had this one pulled on them where there were no facilities for weighing baggage.

At Hughes while we watched the weather, Les suggested to me that it was time to turn his thirty or so butter kegs over so the brine would cover the upper now-presumably-dry ends. We repaired to the basement, and while helping to turn kegs I discovered a wine keg with a spigot and suggested we sample the vintage. We did, and it was excellent.

We were stuck at Hughes for two very pleasant days while the wind blew a northeaster with snow a-plenty. During that time the butter kegs were turned over with great regularity.

The third day dawned clear and cold and I fired-potted the engine for a couple of hours and took off with the intention of returning to Fairbanks via Stevens Village.

At the usual place on the Yukon, above Tanana, we ran into the famous Yukon ice fog, with about a 300-foot ragged ceiling, and two miles visibility. As we flew toward Fairbanks, this deteriorated to close to nil nil, and at last, as I glanced down to the ice below, I saw black spots. They were ravens, walking.

I turned while a turn could be made, got out of there fast, and flew back to Tanana, which was open and clear.

We arrived back in Fairbanks in due time.

On my next flight to the Koyukuk with the mail, I flew Fairchild 71 NC10623, a tough old monster powered by a 420 hp Wasp B. It was good for freighting and general knocking about.

During wartime, even though Wien Airlines had a good priority rating, there were many parts we couldn't get for aircraft maintenance. Wien mechanics were capable and resourceful, and usually could come up with something to keep us in the air. CAA (Civil Aeronautics Administration)inspectors were aware of this, and not only did they pass some things that weren't in the book, at times they assisted in finding a solution to the difficulties.

On this particular trip, in the dead of winter, in addition to mail, I had a load of three or four hundred pounds of perishables. The intake pipes on the Wasp engine were aluminum; steel intake pipes couldn't be had.

As I flew over the Melozitna River, two of these aluminum intake pipes took a notion to break. The engine bucked and snorted. I very much disliked having to set that load of perishables down on the Melozi and freezing them, so I started experimenting with mixture and throttle.

I had a hill to climb over and a ridge between the Melozi and Indian River which would put me into the flats just below Hughes. Somehow I coaxed her over the ridge, and got onto the Indian River. If another intake pipe had cracked there would have been head lettuce for the moose on the Melozi that day.

I made it to Hughes, somewhat shook up. Les James and I pawed through his pile of pipe, nuts, bolts, hose connections, and what have you, and came up with an astonishing array of odds and ends. From that I got the intake pipes more or less repaired. This allowed me to head for Alatna and Bettles.

En route to Alatna, I made radio contact with Wien radioman Doug Matthew at Fairbanks, and wept on his shoulder with my troubles. He wrote down the things that would make me happy and assured me they would be en route next day.

At Alatna I stopped for a cup of tea with the veteran missionary ladies—they had held down that post for many years, and were enormously capable. One was a school teacher, the other a nurse.

At Bettles, where I landed on the Koyukuk River, (the runway built upstream at Bettles Field was not yet there). I received instructions from Wien to haul what freight there was for Wiseman. Five tons had arrived there by riverboat the previous summer. I called Doug at Fairbanks and told him I was at Bettles and about to take off with the first load for Wiseman.

He came back with the information that my buddy, Bill Hautala, was en route with the intake pipes I needed, and should be about there. I looked out the window, and Bill was overhead. His plane was on wheels, and couldn't land. I ran out in front of the Fairchild and Bill dropped me the life-saving package.

I made the first trip to Wiseman with the "make do" repair I had made at Hughes, and I probably could have finished the job with it. But, at 40 below I could imagine what it would be like spending a night or two on the ground between Bettles and Wiseman. That night I mounted the two new intake pipes, but saved the two old ones just in case. My fingers were numb by the time I finished.

Next morning dawned cold and clear. I fire-potted the old Wasp until it was good and warm, and she fired up immediately. Dave Tobuk, who lived at Bettles, hustled to bring the freight down to the river where I was parked, and helped me load it.

At Wiseman, Bill English Sr. had arranged to have me unloaded. The round trip was not much more than a hundred miles, so I carried minimum gas and big loads. Since it was winter, and very cold, with short daylight hours, it took two days to move the freight, but it was accomplished at last, and the old Wasp was still full of vitamins, and with the new intake pipes was honestly and reliably putting out its rated horsepower.

On my last trips, my passenger was a youngish itinerant preacher. The freighting trip fell right in with his plans. One night he preached at Wiseman to a full audience, lacking one. The next night he preached at Bettles with a good turn out. I spread myself out on the floor beside him and promptly fell asleep. He preached a long and windy sermon accompanied by my snorts and snores. When I awoke everyone was laughing to split their sides.

Ernie Johnson, who probably set foot on more of the Koyukuk country than any other man, was almost in hysterics. He told the story many times afterwards, and it always brought the house down. With his Scandinavian accent and use of words, he would again go into hysterics, and so would everyone around him, including me.

The preacher had a brass trumpet that looked as if in expert hands good music could come from it. Sadly, dismal and harsh notes emanated from it when blown by the preacher; it sounded like a bunch of ravens on a garbage dump.

"Why the trumpet?" I asked.

"I'm handicapped in that I can't sing," he explained.

It was his practice when he had made a point during his sermon to let go with a few toots on the trumpet, much to everyone's amusement. Since he had many points, there was much tooting.

I became quite fond of him. Every time he rode with me and I was taxiing in the snow I had him back on the tail, in the prop blast, steering me around, where he performed like a veteran. It's very helpful to have such help when flying an airplane on skis. I complimented him on how quickly he had caught on.

At last, since we had become well acquainted, he confided to me. I had sort of figured it out, but I didn't let on. He was looking for a prosperous Indian village where there were no missionaries.

I guess I about broke his heart when I told him that such a combination had never existed in Alaska.

With the freighting from Bettles to Wiseman completed, I flew back to Hughes, accompanied by the preacher. We spent the night there, and he preached to the good people of Hughes, accompanied by my snores and his tooting trumpet. The people got a big bang out of this, and they have a story of their own on how I livened his sermon.

The next day we arrived at Fairbanks, and I haven't seen or heard of that young chap since. I hope he is alive and well. Many of the young men of that era were lost in World War II. I worry that could have been his fate.

During that same winter, on another trip to the Koyukuk with Fairchild 71 NC10623, weather was lousing up badly as I slid over the Oldman and Ray River summit, but I made it into Alatna and Bettles, and then to Wiseman. The weather was getting worse, and the air was full of holes, with wind in big gusts.

At Wiseman I took aboard an Eskimo mother and three children that ranged from three to six, and an old Eskimo, reputed to be in his nineties. He had never ridden in a plane.

Since these were war years we did many things that weren't by the book. For instance, Old Grandpa Peejoiack, the 90-year old, sat on a box. Since there was no safety belt for him, I tied a rope around his middle. He was as safe with the rope as he would have been with a belt.

The gusty crosswind during our takeoff at Wiseman kept me busy on the rudder, but we made it and I climbed for what little altitude was left by the low ceiling.

If the air was full of holes when I landed at Wiseman, it was now one big hole. Violent and conflicting air currents heaved us this way and that. When I settled to cruising speed, I chanced a look back at Grandpa Peejoiack. He was in the very back of the cabin, looking out the windows, and hanging on for dear life. Far from being air sick, he had a big smile. Since this was his first flight, for all he knew, all airplane rides were like this. I could see that his attitude was, "I'll never get another ride, so I'm going to enjoy this one."

The poor Eskimo mother wasn't having any such fun. She was desperately holding two children on the floor of the plane with her feet. She was just plucking the third child off the ceiling like a ripe berry. By the time she got that one anchored, one of the other kids had come loose and was floating around in mid air. And so it went.

If things had been normal, I would have landed at Bettles and tied the airplane down where it belonged until this thrice accursed storm had passed. But, alas, there was no chance of relief at Bettles or at Alatna. In both places, whooping cough was making the rounds, and these kiddies had never had this malady.

Therefore, with the screeches of three children in distress

competing with the roar of the old Wasp, sometimes seeming to drown out the sound of the faithful engine, we struggled on. Our only salvation was at Hughes. It would have been impossible to get to the mountains that were between us and the Yukon, much less get over them.

Hughes lies on the bank of the Koyukuk River in a valley, and under the foothills of Indian Mountain. We were in a northeaster, and around Hughes and Indian Mountain, northeasters kick up one heck of a fuss.

It was not reassuring to sit there trying to stabilize a bucking airplane while trying to fly a fairly straight course with a load of passengers who were totally dependent on me for their lives.

The Fairchild was mounted with a pair of large Wien Alaska Airlines Skis, the best Alaska ski then made. They were big, and the air was so violent that the pressure drove them up against the oleo [shock absorbers] and spring, and then sucked them down with a bang, first the right one, then the left. I was thankful that safety cables had been put on the oleos, otherwise they wouldn't have held up under such abuse.

Another glance back told me that Grandpa was still smiling, and still desperately hanging on. The poor mother was still pinning two kids to the floor with her feet, and hanging onto the other for dear life. The children seemed to have weakened, for I could no longer hear them above the sound of the old Wasp.

In this manner we caromed down the valley under the lee of Indian Mountain, and we at last came to Hughes. There were some surprised residents at Hughes when we roared over town. I hadn't been able to touch my radio, so busy had I been at the controls.

I made a slow drag below town, managed a long and careful turn to return into the wind to land. It had to be a sure shot deal, because in that terrific turbulence it would have been about impossible to keep away from the hill on a go-around.

As we came drifting and bouncing in, I saw Les James and his crew out in the ice in two groups. I sat down a little short, and drifted between them. They threw themselves on the struts and led me to the tiedowns. It was sure a comforting feeling to know we were down, no one was hurt, and the plane was undamaged.

That storm howled for three days. On the fourth day a big snow storm arrived, so we had to wait four days before we could finally fly on to Fairbanks.

All mail runs to the Koyukuk weren't such hair-raising experiences. Many trips went off like clockwork, leaving them so routine there would have been nothing to write about. But there were some hair-raising trips that I'll never forget.

That was one of them. ·

Geodetics in Winter

Perhaps no man knew more about arctic survival in all seasons than Sam White. I listened carefully whenever he spoke of this subject, or of northern flying.
—RUDY BILLBERG, LONG-TIME ALASKA BUSH PILOT.

DURING THE WINTER of 1942–43, while flying for Wien Airlines, Steve Miskoff and I were under charter to the Air Force for a geodetic control group.

Japan seized the Aleutian Islands of Attu and Kiska in June, 1942. There was fear that Japan might invade mainland Alaska. Air Force airplane numbers were building in Alaska, but maps were inaccurate, and their pilots often got lost in the vastness of the Territory. The Air Force decided to re-map the Interior.

In December, 1942, a geodetic control group arrived at Fairbanks from Headquarters, First Mapping Group, Bolling Field, Washington, D. C. A lieutenant Meyers was the officer in charge. His assistant was Sergeant Emory. Their assignment was to obtain astronomical observations to establish precise latitude and longitude of designated ground control points in interior Alaska.

These points were prominent natural features and small settlements. The points were to be used with charts of aerial photography which the Army Air Force had taken from 20,000 feet in the summer of 1941. These aerial photos were so secret they weren't named; each was numbered. The Air Force refused to allow the numbers, with locations identified, to leave Washington D. C. The

253

*Sam sits on the wing of the Wien Airlines Travel Air 6000B and pours gas
in, five gallons at a time, while Corporal Benecki passes him the cans. "It
was cold." Air Force charter, 1942.* Sam O. White. Courtesy DRAHS.

only way one could determine the location of a photo was to have
seen and recognized the area.

I had memorized much of the area that was involved. Early on,
I had many arguments with the crew about where the photos were
taken. I looked at a picture and told them that lake, or that bend
in the river, or that island, is at such and such a place. For some
time they wouldn't buy it. After many trips to the wrong areas
they let me decide where the photos were taken and allowed me
to fly them there to establish an exact control location.

The primary instrument used by the team held a pool of mercury. Known stars reflected from the mercury pool, while a radio tuned to the BBC (British Broadcasting Corporation)in London provided exact time. Mathematics gave the exact longitude and latitude. Meyers needed a clear night with visible stars, a close approximation of where we were located, and the exact time.

Stars aren't visible in Alaska in summer because of the long daylight hours, hence the work had to be done during winter.

In our two ships we carried equipment for arctic living, as well as more than usual rations.

At first there were two parties. I flew for one, and Miskoff for the other. When beset by fog, bitter cold and snowstorms, for safety, we flew together.

When they arrived in Alaska the Air Force crew thought there were towns and hotels everywhere. On maps they had seen place names like Chandalar, Caro, and others, and figured that each was a town with a hotel. Any number of named places on Alaska's maps were [and still are] nothing but abandoned mines, or even trappers' cabins.

When they learned we were going to have to use a tent, they figured they'd rather go to war in the Pacific. I managed to convince them we could live comfortably in a tent with a Yukon stove, and that's the way we did it.

We'd take a tent, a Yukon stove, and three or four weeks of grub and disappear into the wilderness. The use of radios was forbidden, except for an emergency, a wartime ban. Everyone was busy; no one was going to hunt for us if we were lost. It was up to us to be very careful.

On one trip, we had a Texan. He was just as afraid of cold weather as he was of a grizzly bear. One cold day when we were camped out he insisted, "We're getting out of here." So we steamed up and flew out of there. He went back to Texas and they sent another officer.

The area we worked in the winter of 1942–43 was north of Fort Yukon. We based at the Alaska Game Commission cabin at Fort Yukon. For the most part, Steve took the western area of our plot, and I worked toward the Canadian border.

December 8, 1942, was cold, and indications were that it would grow colder. On that day I flew a Gullwing Stinson, with Steve in a Cessna Airmaster on my wing, as we headed north from Fort

Yukon. We picked up the Coleen River and followed it to several miles above Ed Owen's cabin. We were headed for where the Old Crow River crosses the border and flows into Canada, near the head of the Old Crow Flats. That is somewhat north of sixty-eight degrees north latitude and well above the Arctic Circle. The boundary between Canada and Alaska, which follows the 141st Meridian at that point, is marked by a series of six-inch diameter, four-foot high, iron posts set in a concrete base. Lieutenant Meyers wanted to locate a station as close as possible to one of these posts—boundary monument thirty-three. He doubted we could find it.

"We can land on a lake about three hundred yards from that monument," I promised.

From the Coleen we flew over a hill to Bilwaddy Creek, a tributary to the Old Crow. It was nearly noon, and light from the low-hanging winter sun was at its best. As we approached the snow-covered lake, I saw monument thirty-three sticking out of the snow like a cut thumb. There was no underbrush, and it really loomed.

I circled to pick a spot on the lake to land, and pointed, "There's your monument," I told Meyers.

Both of us landed. The temperature was 32 degrees below zero, with clear skies. Meyers put on snowshoes and walked the 200 yards to the monument. He returned beaming. From that day he had more faith in my simple and basic method of navigation.

We pitched camp, cut spruce boughs for the floor of the tent, and sawed plenty of firewood. We slid poles under the skis of the aircraft to keep them from freezing down, put down anchors for tie-down ropes from the wing lift-struts and tail, drained oil from the tanks, and put on wing covers to keep frost off.

The temperature hit 45 degrees below that night, which meant no work could be done because the mercury in the instruments froze. Mercury freezes at 38 degrees below.

Next day we marked out a runway for a safe take off and cut more dry wood for the Yukon stove. That night the stars arrived dutifully in the level pool of mercury, the BBC time signals came in on the radio, and the mercury didn't freeze. Thus, the location was nailed down with the proper latitude and longitude.

The next morning dawned much colder, and ice fog appeared here and there. It was necessary on these shortest and coldest days of winter to have a very accurate timetable to depart camp. Steve and I started the gasoline-burning fire-pots inside the canvas shrouds to heat the engine oil and engines when it was still dark, for it would take at least an hour before the engines would start.

One can take off and cruise with poor and deceptive lighting, but at arrival at the next landing site, we wanted to have the best light available to pick a spot where no landing had previously been made.

At that time of year, light is best for about fifteen minutes at noon, and we tried to be at our next landing spot at that time. Light deteriorates rapidly after that, and becomes treacherous. One can land after this condition sets in, but it takes more room. One must guess from prevailing winds where snow drifts are, and how severe they may be. At this time of year some snow drifts might as well be concrete blocks.

We flew to Husky Lake, landed, and made camp. It was 50 below that night, so no work was done, but the next night was favorable and the station completed.

Next stop was a big lake east of Arctic Village. On our flight over it was bitterly cold. The air was clear but our visibility was restricted by what looked like a blue steel wall. It looked as cold as it was.

It remained in about the same place in relation to our progress. It was never any nearer, or any farther. In landing in this kind of light one has to "feel" his way down, expecting to hit a big drift any second.

I had seen this cold blue wall before and I had a hunch we were in for something out of the ordinary.

If a landing is made in the most favorable fifteen minutes, one can dimly see snow drifts, and other ground features. At about twenty feet above the ground, there is a moment when one can, when looking at a certain angle, see the ground with fair clarity. As the angle of descent changes, and the plane's nose rises, everything blots out and only a flat white surface can be seen.

In that moment of clarity you have to see everything you need to see for a safe landing, and you can then ease the airplane onto the surface.

When over the lake, despite the war ban on radio use, I talked to Steve and asked him to land near the best patch of timber, so we would have shelter and plenty of wood close. Steve picked an area, landed and parked.

On my landing approach I saw Steve's taxi tracks clearly until I was about thirty feet above the ground. Then my angle of sight changed and I could see nothing. I had experienced this before and was prepared for it. I used very little power, let the plane settle slowly and had no difficulty. It was 55 degrees below, and Steve and I knew it was going to get colder.

Our ships were in a little cove. We made camp, pitching our eight-by-ten wall tent down low with a good part of its five-foot walls folded under and weighed down. We tromped the snow down inside the tent, and spread a generous depth of spruce tips. We hewed two birch logs flat and placed the stove on them.

The snow melted around the logs. The log ends froze in as solidly as if they had been laid in concrete. Snow melted clear to the ground directly under the stove, leaving what we called the "sump hole." Coffee grounds and dishwater could be poured in the hole without danger of pollution, as the waste solidified at once. All available space inside the tent was piled with stove wood, so we wouldn't have to open the flap any more than necessary. We did everything we could to assure survival.

The temperature dropped, and kept dropping. We felt it and heard it. Trees popped, and at times it sounded like a barrage of small arms fire. We kept a good fire in the stove, and I crawled outside to evaluate the sparks and went back to adjust dampers for good draft and a minimum of sparks. I cautioned all hands to leave the damper alone and keep their eyes on the inside of the tent top, watching for signs of sparks.

The temperature reached 65 degrees below, and remained there for several days. We assigned two-hour watches and kept the fire going, cutting enormous quantities of wood which we tiered up all around the tent. An inch or more of frost repeatedly collected on the inside of tent, and twice each day we covered everything and knocked it off. We were comfortable enough, but we were hanging by a thread, so to speak, and any little mishap could have spelled disaster.

The tent was our only salvation. Should it burn, we would be doomed. It was too cold to fly, and overnight survival at 65 below with no shelter or heat would be unlikely. We had to wait for the cold spell to break before we could work, or even fly out of there. As it was, with the stove functioning well, we were fairly comfortable.

There was no chance of taking off with a plane at such low temperature. The friction on the dry loose snow wouldn't allow the skis to get up enough speed for lift off. Even had we been able to get into the air, there was great danger a motor would swallow a big chunk of cold air it couldn't digest.

On the first night there, the Wien Gullwing Stinson I was flying narrowly escaped destruction; only luck saved it. I had chopped holes in the ice, set in stakes, and filled the holes with water. I looped ropes around the lift struts and left them hanging loose while the stakes were freezing in.

Since it was only about 100 feet from the tent to the plane, I didn't tie the ropes that night. There was little likelihood of wind. Should wind come, up I could leave the tent and tie the ropes.

A resounding boom came in the wee hours of night, accompanied by a distinct jar we all felt. Next came a long rumbling that sounded like distant big guns. It was the ice expanding by the then-45-below temperature.

In the morning my ship was at least two feet higher than when I parked it. A new, half-mile-long, pressure ridge ran directly under it. The tie-down stakes had not risen, but the ship had ridden up on the pressure ridge. Had the wings been firmly tied down, as was my custom, they would most assuredly have been pulled down and broken.

We cooked and ate and drank coffee, although I drink mostly tea. Hot coffee taken hot right out of the pot on the stove was cool enough to drink easily when poured into a cup. There was no game or life visible or moving. We occasionally heard wolves howling on the nearby hills where they were probably looking for luckless caribou.

We had to stay there several days to get the point nailed down, for Hitler was jamming the BBC time signals, and the mercury pool froze into a tight black ball.

After three days it began to warm, and, finally, the Air Force boys got their work done and we took off. It was quite an experience for the boys from Texas, Georgia, and the Carolinas.

On the next trip, we split up again, Steve headed for the Chandalar with his crew, while I took mine to Howling Dog on the Porcupine River. We landed on a small marsh lake and made camp.

We had landed amidst a rabbit [snowshoe hare] pasture. The animals were at a population peak. At dusk they swarmed out of the thickets and began to eat our tent ropes. We foiled them by covering the ropes with grease heavily fortified with pepper. Snowshoes and other potential edibles were hung out of reach. At night I could stand in one spot with a flashlight and easily count fifty rabbits.

We endured cold weather and ice fog, and after a few days some of the boys became restless and edgy. Unhappy men who are closely confined can be explosive.

It was time to create a diversion and liven things up, so I spun yarns about bears that didn't den up, mean wolves, wild wolverines, and crazy lynxes.

Their eyes were wide by the time I finished setting the stage. When the boys got to arguing among themselves about how much was true and how much wasn't, I left the tent with a flashlight. I caught a rabbit in the beam, sneaked and grabbed. I missed the first two, but I caught the third one, and tossed it into the tent.

There was a loud grunt, followed by as near pandemonium. There were shouts and curses and pots and pans clattered. The stovepipe came down and the tent bulged and writhed, and finally spewed forth three men and a rabbit.

By then I was doubled up and incoherent, and while they all smelled a rat, they weren't sure what had hit them. The rabbit was all over the tent so fast they didn't see it before it—and they—knocked over all the candles and put them out. One of the boys got kicked in the chest and said it really hurt.

"I don't know what kicked me!" he said.

We rescued the tent from possible fire, re-pitched it and put up the stovepipe. When I confessed what had happened, the boys were so relieved it wasn't something worse, which might repeat the performance, that I was forgiven. It furnished merriment and met my goal of blowing away the blues that had started to permeate camp.

From there we flew to another location between the Porcupine and Black Rivers where there were two hills, a saddle between them, and a lake in the saddle. From the standpoint of landing, the lake was crosswise in the saddle, not lengthwise as they usually are. This put a steep hill at each end of the lake. I had to figure out how to get the plane down safely.

It was cold and calm as I slipped the airplane sideways down one of the hills, then straightened to touch down.

Said Sergeant Emory, USAF, "Sam, you aren't so damned smart. I *prayed* you down."

I said, "Keep praying; we have yet to get out of here."

Getting out wasn't as difficult as it looked. In a few days we were at another lake, finished our work there, and late one afternoon took off for Fort Yukon. We had a passenger, a Native trapper named Tim Wallace who had come over to our camp from his trapline and wanted to go to town.

It was ok with me and ok with the Air Force boys, so we took him along. We ran into a blinding snowstorm near dark and it was evident we wouldn't make Fort Yukon that day. I managed to land on a lake I knew. By then it was so dark I couldn't see where the drifts were, and by that time of year, they are hard as concrete. I picked a spot sheltered by spruce trees and we made a very short landing run. Fortunately, the snow was deep and soft.

While I was taking care of the ship the others dragged the tent out and Tim Wallace had it up so fast and so neatly that it impressed me as much as it did the Air Force boys. We were boiling coffee and heating the beans when across the lake through falling snow we saw a light bobbing among the trees. It neared, and soon a voice hailed, "Is it Sam? Are you all right?"

"Is there any place in Alaska where they don't know you?" Lieutenant Hank Kragiel, who hailed from Connecticut, wanted to know.

"Not around here," I said. "No one else with a plane would likely be out here this time of year on a night like this."

By then the light had reached camp. It was carried by Philip Peter, another Native trapper whose cabin was three miles away. He had heard us circling, thought we might be in trouble, and had come to see whether he could help. That was the spirit of the North, and it made an impression on the Air Force guys.

Philip had dinner with us and when he returned to his cabin he carried with him some real luxuries for a bush trapper.

Next morning we got away and made Fort Yukon to refit for another trip.

We had proved that geodetic work can be done, but not easily, in the deep cold.

We bided our time, working elsewhere on the Koyukuk, Kobuk, and Kuskokwim Rivers, and when the time was right, we returned to the head of the Koyukuk River and the Husky Lake region. The Arctic Village area was taken care of in two nights, and could have been done in one but for Adolph jamming BBC the first night.

I made an extra trip from Bettles to a lake just above Caro, the old abandoned mining camp on the north bank of the Chandalar River, and established a cache of gasoline, extra provisions, and equipment. We then flew to Bearpaw Lake in the heart of the valley of the Middle Fork of the Chandalar River, where we made our tent camp.

Snow was deep and we tromped it down good. We were there nine days. In the evening of good days, arctic fog seeped through the pass just above our camp and prevented our seeing the stars. Once we had a clear night, but Adolf jammed the time signals so we had to wait another few days for a clear night. It was around 30 below.

In the meantime, temperatures dropped to 55 below. Our camp was an 8×10 wall tent as usual, but this time we had an Airtight wood stove instead of a smaller Yukon stove. Although the Airtight wasn't so good to cook on, it was better for heating the tent, since the fire could be more easily controlled. It also took bigger chunks of wood that lasted longer.

Based on the number of bear-clawed trees, the valley was a rendezvous for grizzly bears. What they lacked in size they seemed to make up in numbers. Marten were numerous. They came to our camp, and had little fear. Caribou were about, and often came to the lake. Mountain sheep could be seen on nearby hills. Wolves arrived on the lake nearly every night.

We didn't molest any of the game, for we had boneless beef obtained from the post exchange at Ladd Field, Fairbanks, and it was plenty good.

Water in the lake was so mineralized we couldn't use it even for washing dishes, or any other camp function. Lake ice, when melted, proved just as slick and resistant to soap. For water, we resorted to melted snow, of which commodity there was plenty.

Finally, the good night arrived with 25 below, no arctic fog filtering through the pass, and Hitler must have been asleep, for the BBC time signals were not jammed. Stars dutifully came into the mercury pool, and we nailed the point down for keeps.

The next day we flew to our cache near Caro, gassed the plane, cooked a big feed, and remained overnight. Then it started to snow. That snowstorm was a humdinger, and we could not move at all the next day. It snowed about twenty inches.

The sky cleared on the third day, and we flew to Bettles where we prepared for another Geodetic expedition.

More Winter Geodetics

Inside, the igloo, made of woven willows, and covered with sod, was the shape of an inverted bowl. At the back was a two-feet-square window—a six-inch thick piece of ice, which let in a spooky sort of light. —SAM O. WHITE

FROM BETTLES, I continued the winter 1942–43 Air Force Geodetics charter with Lieutenant Meyers and his assistant. After a few days rest and restocking of equipment, from Bettles I flew equipment to five-mile-long Chandler Lake, which lies in a pass at the summit of the Brooks Range. Included was a drum of stove oil in five-gallon cans, and an oil stove. There are no trees and no real firewood at Chandler Lake. Next day I flew in Lieutenant Meyers and his assistant and camp gear.

We pitched a new 8×10 tent, with extra rope and canvas for a tent door windbreak. We anchored all on a sandy point with piles of boulders, and spread caribou robes for wall-to-wall carpet. With the wind howling, we could walk on it in comfort with bare feet. There was no snow, except for occasional drifts; the wind had carried it out of the pass.

Ice on Chandler Lake was six feet thick, and solid blue from top to bottom, as Bert Stewart at Fort Yukon had told me in 1927. With an ice chisel, I cut a hole and measured its depth. The geodetic crew fished through the hole, but never got a nibble.

Eskimo Simon Paneak[1] and his nomadic clan were camped in snow banks several miles below the lake, and they had a fish cache

---

1. Formally, Dr. Simon Paneak, who held that honorary degree from the University of Alaska Fairbanks. He received it for his work with Brooks Range biological researcher Dr. Lawrence Irving.

Winter, 1942–43, Sam and the Air Force Geophysical party was camped high in the arctic Brooks Range at Chandler Lake. Tent ropes are secured with rocks. Six feet of blue ice lay on the lake. There is no firewood around the lake; the tent was heated with an oil stove.
SAM O. WHITE. COURTESY DRAHS.

on Chandler Lake. It was made of ice slabs cut when the ice was six inches thick. Trout were tiered inside this cache like cordwood.

On arrival at Chandler Lake, with the plane I circled their camp on the Chandler River, but could see nothing but a sled or two, and a few sled dogs. Their living quarters were in the snowbanks.

We had no sooner pitched our tent when two big dog teams came tearing into camp, driven by Simon Paneak and Elijah Kakinya, both of whom I had known since 1927–28 when they crossed from the Arctic Slope and came down the Sheenjek River into Fort Yukon.

The dogs Simon and Elijah drove that day were big and savage, and would as soon eat a white man as a caribou. But the Eskimos and their smallest kids were safe around them, and they were well-trained to the Eskimo commands. They were also well fed and fat, since there were many caribou in the country.

We made a big pot of coffee, for these men were coffee hungry. They were living on caribou, mountain sheep, fish, and had had no white man's grub for some time. I cooked each a big beef steak, which they didn't like as well as caribou.

We visited as wind shrieked and our tent ballooned.

On our second night the wind died, the stars came out bright, and Adolf wasn't jamming BBC's time signal. We should have ended our sojourn at Chandler Lake then, but it was not to be.

At Bettles, Meyers and his assistant had made up a star list, using the Chandler Lake position on an old map. I told them of the discrepancies, suggesting they might use an assumed position I could give them. They ruled against me. So, on that perfect night when the stars were brightly shining, and the lack of wind made the work easy, not one star showed up on the mercury pool.

They then accepted my assumed position, and made up a new star list. Then came a blizzard, and we sat interminably in the tent. When the wind let up occasionally, we sortied around the lake for exercise.

One day, with the temperature at a mild zero, as we sat in the tent, came an ominous rumble. It was so loud we could hardly hear one another speak. It was a caribou herd on the move.

We stepped out and gasped at the sight. The close-packed mass of animals averaged about 300 feet wide, and the nearest animals passed within twenty or thirty feet of our tent. That herd streamed by us for a full half hour. Stragglers of ones and threes followed.

It was a stupendous sight. The geodetic boys were awe-struck. They didn't make a move to shoot any, not even a straggler.

We continued to sit out storms. We cooked and ate. We waited for clear and calm for fourteen long days. Our Eskimo friends visited several times. At the request of the geodetic crew, they brought some furs, mostly red and cross fox, and a few wolverine.

I was appointed referee, and selected the best skins. The geodetic crew realized they were privileged to select the best from such an unusually large assortment, and they were willing to pay premium prices. Fur from the Arctic doesn't singe as soon as Interior furs, nor do they get rubbed as much, probably from lack of brush and trees in the environment.

Simon Paneak was just learning the value of money, and he accepted cash. To others of his nomadic group, money had no meaning; it was so much paper. If they had taken any it might have ended as a fire starter, with a little punk, and under flint and steel.

I had a broken tailpost on the Stinson, and flew to Fairbanks

Sam O. White with Simon Paneak, leader of the Anuktuvuk Pass
Eskimos, near Chandler Lake, 1954. SAM O. WHITE. COURTESY DRAHS.

to have it repaired. I shoved off early one morning with close to
$700 worth of Paneak's fur. I was to exchange it for as much white
man's grub as I could obtain.

The fur brought nearly $1,000 at the Fairbanks Northern Com-
mercial Company. After I had purchased mostly coffee, tea, ammunition, sugar, flour, and a few other items, there was money left.

"Should I credit it to the Anaktuvuk people, or return the cash
with you, Sam?" the N.C. man asked.

I reasoned it would be better to credit them, knowing they had
no easy access to a trading post.

When the agent entered the credit on the books, he discovered
Simon and other Anaktuvuk people already had a comfortable
credit for furs that Sig Wien had flown in several years earlier.

At Chandler Lake I explained to Simon and others who had
sent their furs that they could have another plane load of grub,
with no more fur needed.

I don't think he understood. He simplified the transaction in
his mind; "We sent a load of fur, and got back a load of supplies."
That put a period on it as far as he was concerned.

I tried to explain, but in the end he still looked confused.

I was thankful the deal was with a reputable company, for I knew
the Anaktuvuk folk would eventually receive their full value.

The perfect night finally arrived. Stars rolled into the reflecting pool of mercury on the minute. Adolph was asleep, for there was no radio jamming of the BBC time pulse. The difference between the assumed and the map position was thirty-five miles east and west, and fifteen miles north and south.

Next day I fired up the Gullwing to leave. There was a twenty-mile-per-hour breeze. Blowing snow had polished the lake ice to a mirror surface. I couldn't maneuver for a take off without help from ropes tied to the skis, and with the crew hanging onto the tail to help steer.

We jockeyed for twenty minutes, going round and round. Cutting power to idle still allowed the ship to creep and get out of control. The crew had no traction. They could push me, but their feet slid out from under them. We finally got off, but it had been a struggle.

It was a pleasure to return to Bettles. Roadhouse operators Ike and Mabel put on good feeds which were especially appreciated after my indifferent camp cooking.

At Bettles then lived 80-year-old Fritz Werther, who, in his youth, had been in the German Army. He was much impressed with brass, and Lieutenant Meyers, of course, was "brass."

I had known old Fritz for years. Whenever I landed at Bettles, he showed up. If I remained overnight, he came to the roadhouse at 7 a.m. He wore an old stocking hat that was so dirty it stood stiff and straight atop his head. He entered and assumed an attitude of attention, bowed at the waist, lifted the cap, and loudly said, "Good morning, chentlemen."

He then turned to me and in the same voice said, "You too, Sam."

This always brought roars of laughter, which didn't seem to bother the kindly old-timer one bit.

Another old-timer of Koyukuk fame was Ernie Johnson,[1] who had a cabin at Bettles, but often kept the fires burning at the roadhouse for Ike. Ike was inclined to be economical on wood, and usually had one skinny stick in the 100-gallon-size drum made into a stove. This about kept the drum warm, but didn't do anything to increase temperature in the room.

---

1. Famed as one of the old-timers who guided author Robert M. Marshall in the Brooks Range around 1930. "Ernie is an exception, competent above all men in the North country," Marshall wrote in his classic book *Arctic Village*.

268 Sam O. White, Alaskan

Commonly, Ernie stoked the stove and left. Ike would come from the kitchen and extract two or three sticks from the drum before they had caught fire and remark, "Guess he wants to burn the joint down."

Ernie would soon return, stuff the stove again, and get a good fire blazing. "No shortage of wood around here," he would remark.

NEXT TRIP FOR THE Air Force geodetics crew took me to the Arctic Coast in March. I landed at Barrow and had to climb out of the window of the Travel Air I was flying because it was completely filled with camp gear. As I awkwardly worked my way through the tiny window, some school children were lined up nearby. "There is Sam!" they shouted. "Hello Sam."

An attractive school teacher tried to shush them, telling them, "You must not call him Sam. Call him Mr. White."

It didn't work. To them I was always "Sam."

From Barrow we flew toward the Colville River, carrying an extra drum of gas. Since there is little firewood on the Arctic Slope, we carried stove oil to burn in a converted Yukon stove. We worked out a radio schedule with Stanley Morgan at the U.S. Signal Corps station at Barrow. We were to call every night at eight o'clock, with no other calls except in an emergency.

The generator in our plane quit, the battery went flat, and we missed all of the schedules. We also had to hand-prop to start the engine.

Barrow was nearly out of reindeer meat, but with the aid of the Reverend Klerkoper I was able to get some. That same night a polar bear was killed in Barrow. I told my Air Force crew that I had been unable to get any reindeer, but I had managed to get some nice fresh polar bear meat.

The first night in camp I made a stew, but the boys wouldn't eat it even though I dug in and pronounced it good. "No bear for us," they said.

Before the second meal I told them the truth, that the meat, in fact, was reindeer, but they wouldn't believe me and still were having none. Next day I abjectly apologized for my deceit, but they still wouldn't touch the meat. I was reduced to begging them to partake, and they did so on the fourth day, but only, I think, because by then they were so meat hungry they would have tackled a skunk.

The Wien Travel Air 6000B often flown by Sam, here under charter in 1943 by a geodetic crew of the Air Force. The airplane was about ten years old at the time. Sam is in the light-colored coat behind the plane's lift struts. Sam O. White. Courtesy DRAHS

I was caught in a whiteout, with the Geodetics crew aboard. We were in the hills, and it looked as if there was going to be a crash for sure. I couldn't see a thing—it was as if I were flying in milk. I saw a blur ahead, which turned out to be a band of caribou. I immediately landed among them. They scattered before the plane, with caribou leaping from under both wings. I expected to hit one, but the situation was so serious I didn't care. It would wreck the plane, but it wouldn't hurt us.

If we hadn't found those caribou I don't think we'd have made it. They chopped up hard snowdrifts where I landed that would probably have busted the gear on my plane that day. It was a good lesson.

The work was finally done, but our gas supply was very low. We had enough to reach Barrow in a straight shot if we didn't have a headwind.

We took off in brilliant sunshine. As soon as we got over the hills we ran into fog banks and whiteouts. At the head of the Topagoruk River, about 110 miles from Barrow, we caught it good and heavy. The hills began to blot out, but fortunately I had spotted a possible landing place a few minutes earlier.

I swung back to it and put down in a narrow river with ten-foot banks. Unfortunately, the straight stretch of the river was short, and at each end was a perpendicular ledge and a right angle turn. To stop I had to kick the plane into a snowbank where it went in deep.

We dragged out the tent, pitched it, and built a snow wall around it. We were low on stove oil, and I told the boys we would run the stove one hour in the forenoon, and one hour in the afternoon to cook, dry clothes, and get warm. There wasn't much enthusiasm for this, but they accepted it.

Our first problem was to get the ship turned around. We shoveled deep into the snow and found a few wrist-thick willows, each the length of a broom handle. We froze these into the ice as deadmen, fastened ropes to them in the form of a Spanish windlass, and used another willow as a twister. We could move the ship but a few inches at a time; it required three days of painstaking work to back it out of the snowbank and turn it around.

Our troubles were not over. On take off, the plane simply would not clear either of the two ledges in the creek bottom.

Dissension broke out in camp on the day we got the ship out of the snowbank. The boys demanded we keep the oil fire burning until the oil was gone so they could "...be good and warm for a few hours before we freeze to death."

I told them our only chance for surviving was to continue rationing our oil. I made them a proposition. We would hold a shooting match to decide whether we did it my way, or their way. They agreed.

We had a .30 automatic M-1 carbine, and I suggested they draw lots for one man to shoot against me. We would each fire three shots at a good target. They accepted.

As I had hoped, the man who won the draw was the least experienced. I shot first and made three hits dead center on the target. My opponent was a little shaken by my "luck", and after two good shots, his third went wild.

Groans and cheering intermingled, with me doing the cheering. All of this served to some degree to take their minds off our troubles. We dug in the snow for an hour or so and got enough willow sticks to make a fire and boil a pot of coffee, which helped to restore morale.

Since we couldn't take off from the river, I located a suitable bench on the mountainside a quarter of a mile away. It was smooth enough and, I hoped, long enough for us to get into the air. It would give me about 800 feet for the initial stage, after which there was a six-foot drop-off, then another 350 feet of smooth going. I figured the ship would be "almost" flying at the end of the 800 feet and it would settle gently on the second smooth stretch, then start flying.

We broke camp in early morning, and moved all the gear up to the bench. We manhandled the plane there, with the boys pulling on ropes to help the engine. We jettisoned about twenty-five pounds of cargo, which served two purposes; it lightened the load and gave us a better chance of getting airborne; and it provided markers for the runway. We scattered it along the sides of the bench so I would have something in the pervading whiteness on which I could keep aligned. Finally, where I figured the skis would touch down after the drop-off, we beat the soot out of several lengths of stovepipe, making a black spot on the snow.

After we loaded the ship carefully for the best possible performance, we climbed aboard, cinched our belts, and I poured on the coal. It went about as I had hoped, although the boys claimed the touchdown was three feet short of the soot patch.

Our luck hadn't really changed. We ran into a whiteout just as we reached the big bend of the Meade River. We landed and sat for an hour. I was about to give the word to make camp when the snow lifted as suddenly as it had come, and we took off. Gone by then was any chance of making Barrow on the gas we had. All we could do was fly as far as possible and hope for the best.

It was late in the day and visibility was poor when the gas gauge hit the peg at zero. Just then I saw a telephone pole loom out of the murk. That couldn't be right, so I shook my head, and it turned into a lead pencil sticking out of the snow. That didn't make any more sense than the first impression, and I concentrated and made it look like what it actually was, a single joint of stovepipe protruding from the snow.

A stovepipe meant an igloo,[2] and an igloo meant shelter, at least, and possibly, supplies too. The old Wright engine was running beautifully, mostly on its reputation I guess, but that igloo was too good to miss and I put her down. While I tied the ship down and drained the oil, one of the boys went to look at the igloo. He was soon back. "We can't stay in there," he said, crestfallen, 'It stinks.'"

---

2. "Igloo" means "house," or a shelter.

I went to check out the "stinking igloo."

The entrance was divided on each side into three chambers of blocks of six-inch-thick ice, about four feet square, set on edge. One chamber held whale meat, another had seal meat and a seal poke. Another held four or five bushels of a delicious arctic fish something like a herring.

On the other side, one chamber held a few waterfowl, and others were filled with nets and other fishing gear. The odors were a little overpowering at first, but they were good clean smells which we could quickly get used to.

Another door, at the far end of the entrance tunnel, opened into the igloo itself, which was made of woven willows and covered with two or three feet of sod. The inside was the shape of an inverted bowl, and at the back was a window about two feet square, the pane of which was a six-inch-thick piece of ice. It let in a spooky sort of light.

We moved in and hooked our Yukon stove to the stovepipe I had seen. We still had five gallons of stove oil, although the boys did not know this. I had kept it hidden in a snow bank at our previous camp, and sneaked it back into the ship when we left.

The stove burned very little oil at the lowest carburetor setting, and at that setting provided enough heat to cook a stew and make coffee. An igloo is a good deal warmer than a tent, and the one we were in remained comfortably warm for five or six hours after the fire was turned off.

We carried the battery from the aircraft inside and warmed it. We were only thirty-five miles from Barrow, and I figured they should be able to hear us even with a weak battery.

The battery was hot when we rushed it back to the ship and hooked it up. Barrow responded instantly to my call. I heard Stanley Morgan, "Where are you, Sam? We've been worried."

I told him we were at Meade River in a very comfortable underground apartment, that we were out of gas, with the tanks so dry they would probably crack open if we didn't get some liquid into them soon.

"Sig Wien is here. He'll bring you gas tomorrow morning," Stan said. We heard one of his dogs, Penny, barking, and a deep growl from Chief, a big Newfoundland. Mrs. Morgan was a wonderful cook and we thought we could hear the sounds of cooking, and even fancied we could smell it.

Morning seemed an awful long time coming. No one was hungry for breakfast. We gulped coffee. There was scarcely a sound. I glanced at the ice window now and then, but it didn't seem to be getting lighter. Finally, I could stand it no longer and went out for a look.

I heard a slight sound in the passageway, like a faint breeze, but when I released the outside door, it was torn from my hand and I was smothered with snow. The grandfather of all howling blizzards was under way.

I secured the door only after wrestling with it and the wind, and broke the sad news to the boys. They sort of collapsed and we settled down to ride it out.

The storm lasted four days. I was thankful we were in a igloo. I doubt we could have held a tent down against such winds. On the fifth day it cleared and we were happy to see that the plane's tie-down lines had held; the Travel Air was still fastened to the ice.

Sig Wien, Stanley Morgan, and Ned Nusunginya showed up before long with three cases of gas. Two hours later we were in Barrow. We had been gone fourteen days on a trip that we had expected to last three days.

When the boys started to unload the plane they came across my cache of stove oil. There was still a quart or two in the can and a roar went up. "Rationing us on heat when he had all this left! Pour it down his neck!"

But to do that they had to catch me, for at the first roar I was on my way, leaving Ned Nusunginya to put the faithful Travel Air to bed and to groom it for another day.

Close Calls While Flying

I hate to fly off a tower-controlled airport.
I like to make my own decisions. The lakes and rivers make
a better airport for me, for then I am on my own.
—Sam O. White. Letter to Richard Wien, January 16, 1956.

DURING THE THIRTY-EIGHT years I flew various airplanes, I had a few close calls that I remember vividly. One of the first was with my Swallow biplane NC422N in late November, 1931. It likely wouldn't have happened if I'd had more flying experience.

I was on a wildlife enforcement patrol in the Lake Minchumina country where I had arranged for a river freighter to leave a gasoline cache of six cases with trader/roadhouse operator Reginald White. I wanted to do quite a bit of patrolling in the area, so I was counting heavily on this gasoline.

At Lake Minchumina I flew to the roadhouse for my gasoline. There I learned another pilot had taken it all during the summer, agreeing he would replace it immediately. He had not replaced it. He was new in Alaska, and had not learned the rigid but unwritten code among Alaska's pilots about cached gas.

I stayed at the roadhouse overnight, and next day flew around the lake trying, unsuccessfully, to find at least five gallons of gas.

There was nothing I could do but return to Nenana to pick up a load of gasoline and fly it back to Minchumina for my operations there.

Next morning a wind blew a gale, from the wrong direction, of course. I fired up anyway and figured I'd have a small gas reserve when I reached Nenana. I flew just above the tree tops, where I could see the trees twisting and writhing in the strong wind. Not a comforting sight.

At Nenana, the wind was still strong and gusty. I didn't have enough experience to set her down there. The old Swallow wasn't a good plane to handle such winds. I took one look and continued flying toward Fairbanks, hoping I could make it, but knowing quite well I couldn't.

I kept drilling away, and just beyond Nenana ran out of the wind, which was a great help. The gas gauge was low, and I switched to the reserve. I had fifteen minutes left in the air.

I cut across the big bend of the Tanana River between Nenana and Fairbanks, hoping the gas would last until I was over the river again.

It didn't.

I was in the worst possible place when the motor quit. With a silent engine, and wing-wires whistling, I headed for the river. I had to make a sharp right turn. I didn't know much then about banking and maintaining altitude. The river was bordered by tall trees and it appeared as if I would have to be plenty lucky to get over them.

I barely squeezed over their tops. In so doing I lost much speed, so much that I plunked down hard in deep loose snow. I'd have broken my landing gear had that snow not been such a good cushion. At least, I didn't break anything.

The temperature was 30 below. I made camp, cut firewood, and had a good fire. I guzzled plenty of hot tea and a sliver of moose roast and some rolled oats. They tasted pretty good.

Next morning, Joe Barrows, flying a Bellanca CH-300 with a load of passengers from Fairbanks to Nenana, spotted me. Since snow was deep and he was heavily loaded, he didn't land, but circled and waggled his wings to let me know I was marked down and could expect help.

An hour later Lon [Alonzo] Cope arrived in a Fairchild 54, picked me up, and flew me to Nenana where I bought two cases of gasoline. He flew me back to my airplane and left.

When we arrived, Percy Hubbard, flying an Eagle Rock biplane, was there from Fairbanks with a case of gas. Percy remained until I was gassed up, fired up my plumber's pot, warmed the engine, and got it started.

He was parked on the river in line with my takeoff route, but there was room for me to get off and climb a couple of hundred feet before I reached his Eagle Rock. Accordingly, I booted the gun and away I went. I had just started moving good when I ran into an overflow. This slowed me. I was locked onto the take off and I wasn't going to cut power there. I slowly rebuilt speed, and finally horsed the old girl out of the snow. Percy saw me coming and became certain I was going to crash into him.

He started to climb out of the cockpit. It was too late. I leap-frogged over the Eagle Rock with what I would almost swear was less than half an inch to spare. Percy had draped himself over the edge of his cockpit like a wet dish rag. I kept going. Soon we were both in Fairbanks.

Percy repeatedly told me how close I came to him. He didn't have to tell me, I knew it all too well. I still had a lot to learn about flying.

We laughed about it as though it were a good joke. It wasn't really funny.

In another event with the Swallow, I was at Ruby when a local character, an Indian, came out on the river ice and wanted a dollar and a half to help me gas up.

"No," I said. "I do my own gassing up. Please stay away from the plane," I said.

I was pouring gas from a can when I felt the airplane trembling and heard a crash. This guy had walked on the lower wing and had put both feet through the fabric. He was all tangled up.

I jumped down and pulled him out. He still wanted a dollar and a half. I booted him off the river. I had to cover that wing with canvas. I drew it around as tight as I could, and sewed it on, but after I took off and headed for Tanana, it came loose. I saw little pieces of fabric vibrate, then pop out from under the canvas and go floating off. There was a big hole in the wing when I got to Tanana. I had to stay there all night and patch it again. I froze that patch on with water.

Next day, the ice holding the patch lasted until I got to Minto Flats on my way to Fairbanks. Soon I was again losing fabric. There wasn't much left of the patch when I got to Fairbanks.

I wouldn't dare try that now.

In still another Swallow contretemps, I once started from Fairbanks to Tanana when something went wrong with the motor. I returned to Fairbanks and found that a primer line had broken. We fixed it, and I flew off and got just over the hills, when something else went haywire. I returned and called the mechanic, and he fixed that.

Again, I flew over the hills, and suddenly the control stick came out of its socket; and I was sitting there with a loose stick in my hand. I looked down and saw that the socket was made of two pieces with a thin bolt holding the pieces together. The bolt had broken.

A tiny stub was sticking up. I ducked down and flew with the stub. I was steaming, and too mad to turn back.

I somehow managed a landing on the Tanana field with the stub. I don't know how I did it because when I had a firm grip on the stub, my head was down inside the cockpit, and I couldn't see ahead.

At Tanana I made the holes on the two pieces bigger, and slipped an ordinary stove bolt through them. That bolt stayed there for years—I don't think I ever changed it.

In those years you had to be able to do everything yourself. If you didn't, you could easily get stuck somewhere for a long time.

Ten years after my forced landing of the Swallow with empty gas tanks, strangely, I had another close call within three miles of the same place. By this time I knew what I was doing with an airplane. In April, 1942, I was flying four U.S. Air Force Geodetics on a charter with Wien Airlines Travel Air 6000B NC9844.

We left Flat that warm, windy morning and gassed up at McGrath. I planned to land at Nenana to get more gas, as the Travel Air, although a first class aircraft, was slow, and had a short range.

I bucked wind from McGrath. We landed at Minchumina and got a little gasoline, but not enough. Duplicating my experience of ten years earlier, I figured to land at Nenana for more gas. Head winds held us back. I finally flew down near the treetops and made a serious business of bucking the breeze. As in 1931, I saw the trees just below the plane twist and writhe in the wind.

And, as happened ten years earlier, the wind was howling down over the Nenana hill, even more so than it had been on the previous occasion. Landing was out of the question.

I tried to use my radio, but the battery was dead. I computed my time in the air against the gas I had left, and I figured I could make it to Weeks Field in Fairbanks if I flew absolutely straight.

Another factor entered the equation; it was growing dark. The clincher came when we ran into a heavy snowstorm. I bucked it for a ways, but soon realized we had to spend the night on the river.

This time I didn't wait for the gas to give out. Since it was dark, and snowing hard, it wasn't the best time to pick a strange landing spot.

I reduced altitude enough to get a better look at the Tanana River below, and selected a spot in a slough between two islands. I figured it would be less likely to have rough ice, with a minimum of stumps and logs. Also, I thought there was enough snow to cover any log that might be lying there. Another hazard I figured would be minimized by the narrow channel, was big snow drifts.

Before touching down I made a last desperate call to Fairbanks to tell the company [Wien] where we were and what we were doing. I mentioned the blinding snowstorm and named the islands we were landing between. If the message got through, I knew Noel Wien would know exactly where we were.

I was not surprised when there was no response, although Fairbanks was just twenty-five miles away.

I went drifting in for a landing on what appeared to be a flat white surface bordered by trees and brush, as if everything was nice and rosy. I set the old Travel Air down gently. There was no jar at touchdown. Snow flew as we sped up the channel on the landing run. I half-expected any minute to feel a jolt from a stump or drift pile. No such thing happened. We simply came to a stop as in any normal landing.

It felt wonderful.

We got out and didn't even look around. We dragged our tent and stove out and went to the nearby bar, pitched it, and got out the chuck. Lt. Robert Atwood, one of the Air Force Geodetic crew, cooked. We ate and felt better. Snow continued to fall so heavily that we could see only a dim outline of the Travel Air.

We awoke to brilliant sunshine. My heart skipped a few beats when I looked at our landing tracks. We had skimmed over a big log the snow had not covered. A big stump had passed under one wing. At another place we slipped between two stumps that both wings had cleared by inches. A few feet in front of the plane was a big drift pile of dryki, and logs with gilpokes pointing in our direction.

If the visibility had been good, I never would have made it; hell, I never would have tried it.

About 8:30 that morning Noel Wien showed up in a Cessna Airmaster with two cases of gasoline. By a freak atmospheric condition, my radio message was not heard at Fairbanks, but Dishoo

Ulen, at Wiseman, 200 miles to the north, had picked up every word and had relayed it back to Fairbanks.

Noel and I were talking and looking with amazement at the junk the Travel Air had missed, when we heard another airplane motor and Fred Gentry showed up with two cases of gas.

A few minutes later in came another airplane. It was Ken Swift with two cases of gas.

It was becoming a problem where to park all the airplanes. All three had landed on a bar 100 yards away, which I did not dare tackle in the dark. None landed in my area because the Travel Air was in the way.

We gassed up and loaded the faithful Travel Air with our camp gear and passengers. Soon we were all in Fairbanks, ready for further adventures.

Once when I was flying for the Coast and Geodetic Survey, with the Wien Fairchild 71, I had just delivered a load at a wilderness lake in the Kyyu Flats and was taking off. As I cleared trees at the end of the lake, a terrific racket broke loose up front. Manifold pressure and rpms dropped.

To compensate for the loss of power, I laid on full bore and tried to get around. It sounded like the Maxim machine guns I heard so often during World War. I staggered around and lined up with the lake and, though clipping saplings, went in and sat down.

The engine had blown a spark plug, seat and all.

We moored her to the shore and I went to the tent where the boys were camped and relaxed. I couldn't raise anyone on the radio, but I knew there would be relief as soon as I was an hour or so overdue.

My confidence was not misplaced. At about 11 p.m, a Cessna Airmaster on floats, another Wien ship chartered by the Survey, buzzed camp and landed. Pilot Steve Miskoff was at the controls, and Commander A.N. Stewart was with him.

I had a list all made up and was building a platform around the engine from which a mechanic could work. I knew it would take a new jug [cylinder] for the Wasp radial engine to fit her for the air again. Steve checked my list for needed parts, and they left. I remained with the ship.

Late that day Herman Smith, a Wien mechanic, arrived and worked that night in a veritable cloud of push flies. Mosquito repellent consisted of an inflammable liquid sprayed that was about as hard on the victims as on the assailants.

Smitty got the job done. We gave her a two-hour run-in, and I was back in business.

In 1952, while flying for the U.S. Geological Survey in the Kobuk River valley, geologist Don Nichols climbed into my Stinson L5-G with me and I made a normal take off from the Kobuk River. I had reached about 800 feet when the motor quit cold. The plane was over timber, and our backs were to the river. There wasn't a whisper left in that poor motor.

I whipped the plane around right quick and headed for the river. The river bank was lined with high spruce trees. I aimed right at them, and kept air speed up as well as I could without power. Just before we got to the trees I popped the flaps, and the aircraft ballooned and floated over the trees. I then stuck the nose down at the water, flared, and sat down. We then floated merrily down to camp.

Don got out on a float with the paddle, and urged the plane toward shore. Just below camp, Bob Sigafoos met us with a rope, and we led the critter to camp and tied her up.

Within a few days, Kotzebue pilot John Cross picked me up with a float ship and I went into Fairbanks, where I collected my spare engine and a mechanic. Back at Kavet Creek we pulled the

Sam and his beloved L5-G Stinson. 1940s. Noel Wien, courtesy DRAHS

dead engine and installed the spare. After a week-long delay, we were on our way again.

The dead engine had a burned valve from taxiing downwind. It broke off and the engine swallowed it through the piston head.

The airplane engines we used in the 20s and early 30s weren't as reliable as modern engines, but they weren't as complicated, either. Nevertheless they gave us quite a bit of trouble.

An aircraft engine is made up of a number of alloys, and each has a different expansion coefficient. One alloy expands more than another, consequently when an engine is put together, a little tolerance must be allowed here and there. When you start an engine it runs rough, but as it reaches operating temperature, the various alloys have expanded to fit, and the engine then runs smoothly.

Early engines were run up to 1750 rpms. We thought that was fast. A little later, engines turned up to 1850 rpms, and even later it was 2200, and then 2650. We just couldn't believe in such high speeds. I was scared of running an engine so fast, and often felt like pulling way back on the throttle.

However, we found that if a modern engine is run at the manufacturer's recommended speed, with the right manifold pressure, it lasts just fine, actually much longer than did the early, slower-speed engines.

Archie Ferguson

Tell Maurice King I'm where we had the trouble with the parrot.
—Archie Ferguson

I FIRST MET ARCHIE FERGUSON at Tanana one cold winter day in 1931. The village had no airport. In winter, those of us with aircraft landed on the ice of the Yukon River. Few planes landed at Tanana then, and when one did, villagers flocked around it. To pilots, that meant plenty of free help.

That day about half of the town folk were with me and my airplane, even though it was bitterly cold. I was preparing to fly west and north.

We heard a roar from downriver; an airplane coming from the west, therefore it must be Archie, who lived at Kotzebue.

The rumble of the motor seemed too great for a mere ninety horsepower; as it neared, it sounded as if several hundred horses were yanking that airplane along.

The biplane came into sight, and sure enough, it was Archie's Great Lakes Trainer. The British engine had short exhaust stacks and no muffler. The cylinders exhausted directly into the air with a deafening blast.

As the plane neared, the other half of the townspeople flowed out of their cabins and onto the river ice. The landing strip was soon crowded with people in colorful winter garb. Two airplanes in Tanana in one day—both at the same time—was too much to miss.

Archie circled and made a nice landing, stopping near my Swallow. He climbed out, a bit stiffly, for he was cold despite his warm clothing; riding in an open cockpit in winter is cold no matter how one dresses. He was a short, square man with a big smile and twinkling eyes.

Archie Ferguson.

As the crowd gathered around, Archie and I met, shook hands, and talked. Soon, it seemed as if we had always been acquainted. One of his first remarks, "Christ, I like to fly, Sam. Don't you?" sticks in my mind.

I admitted that I too loved to fly.

"How do I get to Fairbanks without following the river?" he asked.

"Easy," I told him. I gave him my map with the route marked. "Follow the route I've marked and it's shorter."

"Good enough. I'll just follow the dotted line," he said.

Everyone turned to and filled Archie's tanks with gas, and he flew off to Fairbanks. The biplanes we flew in those days were slow, and they didn't hold much gas. When we left one place for another we filled the tanks.

When I returned to Fairbanks, Archie was still there. We got together in Archie's hotel room, and he told me stories. After telling a tale, Archie always produced his high, rasping, laugh, and I joined in.

After that, I met Archie on the Koyukuk River, on the Yukon, on the Kuskokwim, and, of course, on his home ground of Kotzebue. He was always full of life and enthusiasm, and he was always in a hurry. If there was an opportunity to make a few dollars, Archie would spot it, and when he spotted it he acted.

For instance, I was at Kotzebue flying for the Coast Survey, when two Air Force fighter planes strayed and ran out of gas. They belly-landed beside the northwest shore of nearby Selawick Lake.

The planes had little damage and there were no injuries. Archie immediately fired a telegraph to the Air Force, offering to put their planes on the Kotzebue field with no further damage, and in a specified length of time, for a price I believe was $1500.

The answer came back. No.

Summer went by and nothing was done about the two planes. At freeze-up, an Air Force plane arrived with an officer and an enlisted man. They were to remove a few instruments, and destroy the two planes. They were authorized to pay $75 to charter Archie's boat. Archie laughed. "For $75 I wouldn't even start the engine." He quoted a much higher price. After wires zinged back and forth, the higher price was authorized, and the expedition got under way. The planes, a model about to become obsolete, were destroyed. Archie made the profit he had sensed could be made.

I put in a season flying with the U.S. Coast Survey from Kotzebue, Archie's base. He was contemplating building a long warehouse. Based on Archie's specifications, I drew the plans,[1] making an error of a few inches. The Eskimo boss carpenter overcame it in a most ingenious and effective way. However, he wanted me to know I had made a mistake. He brought the plans to me and with great severity pointed out where I had fouled up. Archie got a kick out of that.

He got his huge warehouse, and after it was completed and filled, he told me, "Sam, I like to build things. But after I get them done I don't give a damn for them."

He built a restaurant. It was a substantial building, with 2×6 studding. Archie had planned to insulate it with hay, but the hay didn't arrive, and the building was ready to insulate.

Archie was never stuck. He could always come up with something that would do. He insulated his restaurant with beach gravel. I have often been there during storms, summer and winter, and I could never hear a sound from outside the building.

It was a good business, with an ice cream machine popular with the local Eskimos. He had two or three Eskimo girls running the place and waiting on the customers.

Over his restaurant door Archie hung a big sign, "America's Farthest North Restaurant."

At the time it was. But shortly, a prominent Kotzebue lady built another restaurant four measured feet farther north, and across a narrow street. The two buildings, side-by-side, claimed the same distinction.

The lady restaurateur sent a snoop to Archie's place to order hotcakes. He measured them to establish average size. Archie's

---

1. A set of mechanical drawing tools that belonged to Sam is included in the Sam O. White display at the Dead River and Area Museum in Stratton, Maine.

lady competitor then ordered her cook to make her hotcakes a quarter-inch larger than Archie's.

While flying from Kotzebue, I slept in a room above Archie's restaurant. Wien Air brought in flocks of tourists, and they ate in shifts at Archie's. One evening I returned from a heavy day of flying and was stopped by Archie.

"Sam, two young sweet things are sleeping in your bed upstairs, and every bed and room in the house is full. But that's all right. You can sleep on that couch in the restaurant by the window," he said.

That was ok by me, and that's where I turned in. Next morning as I opened one eye I was conscious of a buzz of voices. On opening the other eye I saw that the restaurant was full of Wien tourists. One shift was eating at the counter, and there was standing room only where two other shifts, waiting their turn, filled the restaurant.

What was I to do?

I decided on a bold move. I slowly got out of bed in my shorts and a T shirt, gathered my clothes, and started for the kitchen. I didn't have much trouble getting there. The tourist ladies took one look and scuttled out of my way. As I progressed through the mob, now and then I heard a stifled squeal, but I made no contact with anyone and reached the sanctuary of the kitchen.

At another time I was sitting in the restaurant when it was filled with Wien Air tourists. Archie came tearing in, five minutes late for his radio schedule, as usual. The radio room was in the rear of the restaurant. Archie barged into the jam of tourists. A little old lady spotted him and squealed, "You are Archie Ferguson, aren't you?"

Archie, who was quick on the quip, roared, "No. That's Archie Ferguson over there," pointing at me.

He then tore himself away from the lady, who hung on valiantly, but to no avail. I heard Archie mumble, "God damn the tourists anyway. Why in hell don't they all go to Mexico and not come here to bother me."

In another episode in which tourists figured, one calm sunshiny day I landed a float Bellanca in front of town, and taxied to the front of Archie's restaurant. The place was swarming with tourists. When they saw me they rushed to the beach, urged on by the tourist guide.

"There. See him. He's one of the best known and most famous of Alaska's bush pilots," he roared.

About then Archie ran to the beach. He yelled, "Sam, what in hell are you doing in there. Get out quick, and park over there," pointing to another spot. "A Jap submarine sank there during the war, and they haven't taken the torpedoes out yet."

I feigned great fright and moved my plane to where Archie had pointed. The tourists got a big charge out of that. I think some believed Archie's claim.

Tommy Thompson was flying on the same job I was that summer, and our ships were of identical speed. Tommy was newly returned from flying P-47 Thunderbolt fighter planes in Europe in World War II. He was a precise pilot and loved to fly in formation.

We flew up and down the coast many times every day. When we were both flying back to Kotzebue he liked to tuck himself under my wing and fly in formation. When that happened, I just looked and flew straight ahead, and let Tommy do all the flying. We arrived wing-to-wing many times. At Kotzebue he peeled to the right, I peeled to the left.

Archie finally accosted me and asked, "Sam, what in hell are you and Tommy doing up there with your wings overlapping?"

"That isn't my doing, Archie. Tommy thinks he's still flying Thunderbolts over Germany, and he sneaks up behind me and tucks his wing under mine."

Archie said, "Tell him to get to hell away from you. You know damned well you and I do everything backwards. No good will come of his monkeyshines."

Archie had a military surplus tanker barge the Navy had used to haul crude oil. It had never been properly cleaned of the crude. He filled it with aviation gasoline and anchored it in front of Kotzebue, where waves rocked it. Tommy and I burned gasoline from it all summer, and our Lycoming engines never faltered. The gas from this barge, instead of being the normal blue, was a dirty brown, and produced an exhaust with plenty of smoke.

When I arrived at Fairbanks that fall, Jim Hutchinson, my mechanic, had me look inside the engine. It was filled with soot.

"How the hell did that engine run long enough to get you home?" he asked.

Hutch was absolutely the top aircraft mechanic at Fairbanks. One day in the 1940s when he was working on my aircraft I pawed through his tool box. To my great surprise I came up with two special wrenches with my initials on them. I had them made in 1929 by Charlie Peterson's machine shop. They fit the engine of my 1929 Golden Eagle.

"What are you pawing around in my tool box for?" Hutch asked.

I held the wrenches up and said, "To get back my lawful property you have feloniously had all these years."

Hutch put his tools down and walked to my tool box, pawed a bit, and came up with three wrenches with his initials plainly on them.

"You were one wrench ahead of me," he grunted.

W. R Blankenship, a trader at the village of Kiana, was once riding from Kotzebue to Kiana with Archie. Blank, as he was called, knew nothing of airplanes. While flying over Hotham Inlet, Archie showed him the instruments one-by-one, and explained their functions.

Archie somehow missed the oil pressure gauge, and after a lengthy lecture on the others, Blank put a stubby finger on it and asked, "What's the matter with this one, Archie. It seems to be dead?"

Archie was shocked. "Oh, good lord, that's my oil pressure." He did an abrupt turn and just made the Kotzebue airport as his engine began to freeze up.

I had heard how Archie, while flying, jumped around and kept touching the controls, but I had never been up with him. One day he flew to Kiana and I went along for the ride. He did hunch around in his seat, and he kept putting his hands on various controls, although he didn't move them.

He was a capable bush pilot, no doubt about that. In those days the field at Kotzebue was short, and the only obstructions were man-made. The U.S. Signal Corp wireless station sat squarely on the northwest corner. For some reason the Signal Corp boys decided they needed a high antenna, so, to install a forty-foot-high pole, they dug a hole at the middle of, and on the end of, the runway.

It was easy to see that if a plane came to the short runway at the height of the pole, it would surely over-run the other end. Archie and I talked forcefully with the Signal Corp boys, but they had their minds made up, and went ahead with the installation.

I left that day for Kivalina and when I returned to Kotzebue, flying a missionary lady who had been around for many years, the pole was up. The wind was such that I had to land from that end of the field. I flew around a little, and the lady became nervous. I finally got it figured out and came in beside the pole, then slipped the airplane sideways behind it and landed.

A few minutes later Archie flew in. When he saw the pole he came down to its level, then climbed out again, and cut all kinds of maneuvers, as he stared down at the pole. When he got tired of that, he did just what I did—he came down and slipped sideways behind the pole and landed. Neither of us had any leeway. When we stopped we were very close to the end of the runway.

We had another little talk with the irresponsible guy in charge of the station, but he wouldn't budge.

"Help me gas up, Sam. I'm going to Nome," Archie requested. I helped, and he took off.

About two and a half hours later a message came to the Signal Station from their commanding officer in Nome. One of the Signal Corp men showed it to me. "Take that pole down and report when down."

Problem solved.

Archie was a good businessman. Beside his Ferguson Airways of two or three planes, he had trading posts at Kotzebue and elsewhere. He was involved in mining. There being no docks at Kotzebue because of shallow water, steamers had to anchor a mile or so offshore. Goods and passengers were lightered ashore, and he owned a lighterage service.

Archie also had ocean-going boats and barges, one of which, with an Eskimo crew, towed barges that often went as far as the Aleutians.

That Eskimo captain had his own method of navigation. It was accurate and effective. It may be he used a method similar to that used by the arctic coast Eskimos on tundra that I once observed with considerable wonderment.

I was camped at Peard Bay in a small shelter hut with some U.S. Air Force Geodetics. I had my Bellanca aircraft tied down about 300 feet away, but because of dense fog, had not seen it for two or three days. One day the fog was so dense you couldn't have seen an egg on your nose. Nevertheless, that day two Eskimo families with teams of twenty dogs each, drove directly to our cabin. Since the cabin was occupied, they built two big snow igloos nearby and happily moved in. We invited them into the shelter cabin, which was small; they filled every available space.

We treated them to doughnuts and coffee, for which they were grateful. In turn they gave us some fish we were pleased to receive, which were delicious.

I still don't know how they found the cabin in that fog. Perhaps the lead dogs knew the way, or, perhaps the Eskimos had a system of navigation I never learned.

Archie had a few close ones with his airplanes. He told me about once taking off from a small damp field. His radio produced a lot of static, he said. He had just cleared the end of the field and was up about a hundred feet when suddenly the aircraft controls felt sloppy, and he realized the only thing he was hearing was static. There was no sound from the motor; it had quit cold.

He calmly put the airplane down in low willows as if he were landing on blacktop.

His most violent crash was in 1941, when he was flying a four-place Stinson 180 miles from Kotzebue over the Zane Hills in the Koyukuk watershed. I heard him tell the story several times.

His plane was forced down by a load of ice, a wing sheared when it hit a tree, the engine tore out, and Archie was knocked unconscious. His passengers were a doctor and a restaurateur. Archie received a broken arm, and was generally banged up. The passengers were ok.

Search planes had few clues where to look. Archie found the plane's apparently dead battery in a snowdrift, heated it, connected it to the plane's radio, and reached Fairbanks. The battery faded before he could give his position.

On the fifth day he again heated the battery with a fire, made contact, and yelled, "Tell Maurice King I'm where we had the trouble with the parrot."

Two years earlier, Archie was flying with King, one of his pilots. With Archie was a parrot he had ordered from Outside. They ran into extreme turbulence. Archie was busy controlling the parrot, while King was busy controlling the plane.

King remembered where they had been, and Archie and his passengers were duly found and rescued.

Archie decided to salvage the wrecked plane. He hired a group of Kotzebue Eskimos and their dog teams to retrieve it.[2] They dug the plane out of deep snow, hooked sixty dogs to it, and with it

---

2. AUTHOR: U.S. Fish and Wildlife Service Predator Control Agent Frank Glaser was in Kotzebue when the plane arrived. He described it for me: "The team of nearly seventy dogs was stretched far ahead of the airplane, moving it swiftly over the snow. Seven or eight dog sleds, carrying tents, tools, food, bedding and extra clothing, were strung out behind the airplane. Eskimos sat inside the airplane, while others skied alongside and at the head of the dog team. It was a spectacular and triumphant arrival."

on its skis, pulled it back to Kotzebue. The plane was rebuilt in Archie's shop by an Eskimo crew supervised by an A & E mechanic. He flew that airplane for many years afterward.

Excitement seemed to be a full time companion of Archie Ferguson. I watched one unforgettable incident. He had parked one of his Cessna airplanes on the beach, facing the ocean. A storm drifted snow up to its wings. With a crew of Eskimos, he shoveled it out, fire-potted the motor and started her up.

After a suitable warm up, he poured the coal to it, but the ship refused to move. Eskimos on the tail and wing tips pushed and rocked. Still it wouldn't move. Next a swarm of Eskimos rocked and pushed, but it still wouldn't budge. Archie got out of the plane to help. He put Lazarus, an old, crippled Eskimo, in the pilot's seat with instructions to push on the throttle and ride the plane out of the hole. Once out, he was to shut it down by pulling the throttle closed.

Lazarus performed properly, and Archie's added push moved the aircraft out of the hole. But when the machine went forward, Lazarus froze with the throttle half closed.

On half throttle, the ship headed across the ice of the Arctic Ocean. It almost flew. The skis left the snow momentarily, then the plane settled, only to dance along the snow and again settle. It bounced from crest to crest of snowdrifts for about three miles where it stopped when the snow surface changed and the skis would no longer slide.

Meanwhile, Archie had two big dog teams chasing the airplane. He rode in one of the sleds, yelling at the top of his voice.

When the airplane stopped, Lazarus fell out headfirst. By then the motor had stopped, having emptied the fuel tank it had been running on.

Lazarus came hobbling back to meet the dog teams, wailing, "Oh dear! Pretty near I fly!"

No one could ever get him in an airplane after that; he forever after regarded airplanes with great suspicion.

Then there was Archie's polar bear with which, to my sorrow, I became involved. He was flying in the Selawick valley with one of his Eskimo helpers when, about forty miles inland, they spotted, a polar bear sow with a cub.

Archie landed and dropped the Eskimo off with a rifle. When he tried to shoot the sow, the gun's action was frozen. Condensation in it had turned to ice. The bear charged the Eskimo, who ran behind the airplane. Archie gunned the engine so his airplane wouldn't fall victim to the bear. The bear followed the plane, and they went around and around on the tundra. Finally, when Archie had outdistanced the bear, he went back to his Eskimo hunter, who piled in.

Archie took off. They thawed the rifle's action with the heater in the plane. Archie re-located the bear and landed. The Eskimo shot the bear, and they caught the small cub.

I was Kotzebue at the time, en route to Fairbanks. Archie put a collar and a chain on the cub and had him tied. Though he was cute, the little tyke was mean.

I was warming the Bellanca I then flew, and Archie came to me all smiles and good will. "Sam, I want you to take that polar bear cub to Fairbanks for me. When you get there, all you have to do is call Pan American Airways. They have the papers and a crate ready to ship him to the Baltimore Zoo."

I sez, "Ok Archie. But for heaven's sake put him in a crate. He doesn't like me one bit."

"Oh sure. We have him in a good crate," he assured me.

I climbed into the plane and was checking instruments as the plane warmed. Archie and a couple of Eskimos came back with a dog team and something in the sled covered with a blanket. I paid little attention while they loaded the crate.

Tex Swanson, my mechanic, a hard-bitten guy, crawled in beside me and we were soon off, headed for Fairbanks. It was a beautiful sunny day.

When we were over the head of the Kobuk River, I saw Tex turn his head kind of quick-like, and peer into the back of the plane. Next thing I knew he had, like a coiled spring, vaulted over the back of his seat. Half way down the plane he collided with the bear, which had broken out of the cage. There was much bumping, many snarls, and an abundance of explosive language. It seemed to me that Tex was out-doing the bear by a slight margin.

Then Tex had a bright idea. He grabbed a down sleeping bag and engulfed the bear with it. Immediately, the sun disappeared, and I couldn't see the sky any more. It was blotto blotto. The bad weather was all inside the plane—the obscurement was the cloud of down floating inside the plane.

Tex wrestled the bear down and trussed him with remnants of the sleeping bag and some rope, then anchored him to a seat where he could do no harm.

Tex crawled back into the seat beside me, panting like a dog. His clothes were in shreds.

At Fairbanks, I called Pan American to come get their bear. They knew nothing of a live polar bear. They had not built a crate for one.

I wired the Baltimore zoo. Yes, they wanted a polar bear, but they knew nothing of the one I had.

I staked the bear in my back yard for three weeks while we made out papers and built a crate.

That bear had an appetite for raw eggs and hamburger, and demanded both in great quantities. However, his first morning exercise was to lunge for me when I showed up with his breakfast. His intent was to disembowel me. He did succeed in nearly disrobing me a couple of times.

We had a blizzard. Some kind soul brought a box in which the bear could shelter. When he set it down, the bear leaped at him, and nearly tore his pants off. The bear then demolished the box. The kind soul went home feeling less than kindly toward that "cute little bear cub" in Sam's back yard. The bear seemed to enjoy the blizzard more than he did good weather.

A chap who lived several blocks from me had six huge sled dogs. They were not pets. He used to let one at a time loose, and I often thought it a blessing he didn't let them all go at once.

One morning while I was feeding the bear one of those big dogs charged, with a bead on the bear. I leaped out of the way and the dog hit the bear, or the bear hit the dog—I could never decide which. It was all a blur. There was a great thump and suddenly the dog was fifty feet away in the shape of a very active upside-down capital U, running hippity-clinch for home. I never saw him again.

Eventually the wheels turned and meshed. The bear was shipped to the Baltimore Zoo. I have no doubt he wrecked the joint when he got there.

Often, when Archie was flying from Fairbanks to Kotzebue, and he didn't have a full load (a full load for a Cessna with Archie was all he could crowd in and stomp down) he would call at local airlines and finish his load from their Kotzebue bins. When he arrived at Kotzebue he would message them and thank them for the material that topped off his load.

Once he went Outside and bought two Cessna Air Masters, an economical and efficient plane. He engaged a pilot who had

293 BOOK THREE: BUSH PILOT

been to Alaska who said he had once flown from Fairbanks to Kotzebue. They arrived in Fairbanks with the two ships, and had them checked and serviced for the flight to Kotzebue.

I thought the chap flying with Archie could use a little help, and offered to give him a map and explain some of the landmarks on the route to Kotzebue.

"I flew the route once, and I guess I can again," he said, spurning my offer.

Before take off, Archie told him while in the air to stay where he could keep an eye on him.

They took off and the pilot followed Archie for a time, but he eventually wandered off. Archie tried to round him up, but couldn't find him. Archie then concentrated on getting himself to Kotzebue.

The pilot didn't arrive at Kotzebue that day, nor the next. The search was on. With the amount of gas in his ship he had enough to fly to Kotzebue and 100 miles more.

On the sixth day of the search, the plane and pilot were found on a Yukon River sandbar below Stevens Village, ninety miles northwest of Fairbanks.

The plane was on its back. The weather was warm, and mosquitoes murderous. In the load carried by the lost pilot's plane was a $700 fur coat belonging to Bess Magids Cross, plus cucumbers, lettuce, and tomatoes for Archie's store.

The pilot wore the fur coat to ward off mosquitoes. He was tired of tomatoes, cucumbers, lettuce, and celery.

Archie immediately named him "Wrong Way Corrigan," after the famed pilot who started out for California from New York in a Curtiss Robin, but landed in Ireland.

When he was flown back to Fairbanks I saw him at the Wien hangar, but he saw me and ducked. I never saw him again.

The plane wasn't badly damaged. Its gas had mostly been used, so it was fairly certain he had been in the air nearly six hours. Where he had been during those hours is anyone's guess.

He was probably a competent pilot Outside, but there were almost no radio aids here, and he didn't have his watersheds figured out.

I had many a feed with Archie in his restaurant at Kotzebue. When I was stuck there in bad weather, and Wien had a lot of tourists in town, occasionally some of the workers didn't show up at the restaurant. On such occasions, I sometimes jumped behind the counter and waited on customers.

The first time I opened the cash register I found no pennies, nickels, or dimes. There were two-bit pieces, and four-bit pieces and silver dollars all mixed up in several compartments. Bills of all denominations were also mixed. There were many checks.

Atop the register was a two-quart pitcher full of silver dollars. A coffee can next to it was also full of silver dollars.

I straightened the register. I put the silver from the coffee can and the pitcher in a bag and gave it to Archie, leaving the pitcher and can in place, having a presentment they would be used again. When I finished, the cash register was as neat as a pin.

The checks, however, were a problem. Most had been to the bank two or three times, and, each time had been marked NSF. Some were two and three years old. I bundled them and gave them to Archie.

Two or three days later, when I again found myself behind the counter, I found the register again messed up. The bundle of NSF checks was back in the drawer, taking up room, needed for real money.

I never tried to straighten it again. Archie was the businessman, not me. He knew better than me the best way to do business north of the Arctic Circle.

Once, in Kotzebue, I installed a new variable pitch propeller on my plane. To get the ship licensed after this installation I had to have a cooling kit installed over the engine. The kit was an expensive affair, with two sheets of aluminum that fit over the barrels of the flat-bed engine. It was a nuisance, since with the kit in place it was not possible to get at the spark plugs, plus, the engine ran ten degrees warmer with the kit.

Archie wanted to go to Cape Espenberg, a flight part way across the open sea, and he needed a float ship to land there, so he asked me to take him. I had not thoroughly checked the engine with the kit in place, but we took off for Espenberg anyway. The ocean was really rolling, and the engine became warmer and warmer. I didn't know at what level it would end.

Finally, it stabilized at ten degrees over normal. We landed at Espenberg amidst floating ice, and Archie went ashore in an Eskimo boat to transact his business, then returned to the plane.

As we flew back to Kotzebue, both of us wondered which way we would attempt a landing if the engine quit. Waves were about six feet high, and it was very cold. Again the engine stabilized at ten degrees above normal.

We made Kotzebue ok. Archie said, "Now what are you going to do about your hundred dollar kit?"

"Take it off and throw it into the Arctic Ocean," I told him, and that is exactly what I did.

After that flight, Archie and I sat down to coffee and lunch. While we ate, Archie recounted the whole trip to listeners in his restaurant, not neglecting to castigate the man who made the kit.

Archie was truly a pioneer flyer. His exploits were many. He seemed to have no fear of airplanes. He flew bad and good weather. He was aloft on days when it would have been more judicious to stay on the ground. I guess money was incidental to our flying. What was more important to us was to fly behind the mountains to see if anyone there needed a load of supplies, or medical care.

Those big river valleys sure looked great from the air, and we learned to read all kinds of signs from the air. It was inspiring to see moose going about their daily lives summer and winter, to see great bands of caribou, and white mountain sheep on high.

Archie led a most interesting life, and there was never a dull moment when he was around. Alaska will never be quite the same without him. He died February 4, 1967, at age 72, and is buried at Kotzebue.

Flying the Bush from Ruby

The old crate rattles, shakes, and shivers just like it always did, and
reminds me of the old Buckeye mowing machine on our Maine homestead
—SAM O. WHITE, REFERRING TO HIS BELOVED STINSON L5-G.
LETTER TO RICHARD WIEN, JUNE 19, 1961.

IMMEDIATELY AFTER World War II, I wanted a four-place airplane.
At the time, they were about as numerous as hen's teeth. Every
airplane manufacturer in the United States had been building war
planes. Few were satisfactory for bush flying.

I sized up the surplus market of WWII military aircraft. Two
looked promising—the Stinson L-1, and the Stinson L-5G. I
contacted surplus dealers, many of whom had L-5s, but they
were vague about the model. It took a month for me to find the
G models in Detroit. I bought two of them still in their crates.

Steve Miskoff and I went to Michigan to fly them back to
Fairbanks. They were fine flying ships, but they needed a lot of
changes to suit my needs. We attacked the one I flew with a ham-
mer, cold chisel, and hacksaw, and took out the useless junk.

The oil cooler was way down front, with three-foot-long
outside oil lines. Aircraft mechanic Fred Seltenreich put the oil
cooler on top and on the right side of the engine. There it was
turned upside down to allow oil to drain back into the engine.
This prevented the oil from freezing in the cooler after the engine
stopped. This position reduced the length of outside oil lines from
three feet to six inches.

When I finished modifying N40013 no one would have recognized it for an L-5G. It had a flat safety-glass windshield like a

Sam (in plane) with his L-5G Stinson on the Togiak River while on charter work for the U.S. Coast and Geodetic Survey.
Sam O. White, courtesy DRAHS

Norseman[1]; the air intake was rearranged; the dual controls were removed; a straight push-pull rod in micartee guides ran back to the flippers; the trim tab control to the flippers was re-routed with the control crank overhead in the roof, and the housing for the flexible cable was straightened by adding a geared drive so there were no loops in the housing; the rear seat was removed and a hammock seat installed; an aluminum roof and belly were applied.

Seltenreich engineered an eight-gallon center section fuel tank that was installed overhead, one of the finest pieces of work I have ever seen. The tank was triangular, and there had to be notches and grooves in it here and there. When it was done, it went into place with a perfect fit. It was light and strong.

I also had a left-side beaching door, so when on floats the pilot could get out either side. The ship was lined and floored with plywood. The long, curved control stick was shortened, and the curve taken out.

---

1. In 1953 Sam told me the windshield cost $1200. Author

A lot of testing went on to prove everything. It all worked perfectly.

I used this ship mostly on floats and skis, very little on wheels. It was not a high performer on floats, but was a good performer on skis and wheels, and did reasonably well on floats.

Most of my float work was government contracts at sea level and with cool air. For twenty-one years I flew this ship all over Alaska, summer and winter, and it was never cracked up.

What put this ship over was its capability for the kind of work I demanded. In it or on it were hauled some unusual loads. I carried an eighteen-foot canoe tied to the floats, and a fourteen-foot flat-bottom john boat that was forty-eight inches wide. It also hauled dog sleds, beams, 2x4s, 1x4s, shiplap, plywood, sheet iron, roofing, and anything else that could be jammed into it.

I hauled a couple of full seal pokes in it on a hot day during the second year I had this plane. The smell remained as a permanent attachment.

Hauling patients on a stretcher was easy, since the entire right side opened with two big doors. A badly injured person could be loaded without further injury, an important medical consideration.

With this airplane I made open ocean landings, landings on mountains, ridges, in saddles between mountains, rivers, lakes, lagoons, once in blueberry bushes, and several times in mud. It would take off in wet mud on floats, as it had a surplus of power and a variable pitch prop.

I sold N40013 in 1967 after twenty-one years of faithful service. Shortly afterward, it caught fire and was destroyed.

I think it died of a broken heart.

[AUTHOR] Sam flew for Wien Airlines as a bush pilot from 1941 through 1944. He then left employment with Wien Airlines, bought a Bellanca airplane, which he named *Yukon Bush,* and branched out on his own, calling his business Yukon Bush Air Charter. In 1945 he won a contract to fly mail from the Yukon River village of Ruby.

He found it too expensive to own the Bellanca as well as his beloved Stinson L5-G, and shortly sold the Bellanca. His Stinson L5-G was the only plane he owned for the remainder of his flying days.

Much of the following is based on his years at Ruby.

[SAM] In 1947, I flew from the village of Ruby, on the Yukon River, with a contract to fly the mail twice a month to Cutoff Village on the Koyukuk River. The village was on low ground, subject to flooding and ice damage from the Koyukuk River. The villagers had no two-way radio until the late 1940s when I arranged for the Territorial Department of Communications to install one. It came just in time. In May, 1950, an emergency radio call came from Cutoff. A disaster was in the making. There was not enough water in the Koyukuk River breakup to float the ice away. It had jammed just below Cutoff, backing the river up, and the water was rapidly rising.

In a matter of a few hours, high water and blocks of ice on the rampage would have wiped out the village.

The Air Force at Ladd Field, Fairbanks was asked to help. They contacted me, because Cutoff was not on any map. Three officers hurried to my home and I spotted Cutoff on the map for them.

They flew over Cutoff most of a night, dropping about thirty bombs on the ice jam. The jam was broken, and Cutoff was saved.

About 1950, Cutoff residents decided to move downstream to a site on higher ground, which they accomplished over several years. New log houses were built. A well inside each gave every family an endless supply of pure water. Proper outhouses were built. The new village was named Huslia, after a nearby tributary to the Koyukuk River. In the mid-1960s, about 180 Koyukon Indians lived there.

Before Cutoff moved, I usually left Ruby early mornings to fly there. I often had several flights to make from Cutoff before I returned to Ruby.

On one such trip, one of the Native residents wanted me to fly to a lake near the headwaters of the Huslia River to fly his wife out, as she was expecting to go to the hospital soon. It was winter, and my plane was on skis.

I arrived at the lake all right, and since I expected only a woman and two minor children as passengers, I was surprised to find the man's brother there also. He also wanted to be flown out.

Overflow water lay atop the ice, and the footing wasn't very good. I told them it would require another trip to bring everyone out. I was flying my L5-G Model Stinson with a 190 hp engine with a constant speed prop. It had lots of room. These folks had no conception of the proper loading of an airplane.

I learned in my early days of flying Alaska's bush that if I wanted to use all available space in my aircraft, I could stand aside and allow the Natives to load it. All their lives they pile bulky loads into pint-sized canoes made of canvas and little else, or dog sleds, where room is also at a premium.

These folks went ahead and loaded. The man made space for himself and in went a radio, a sleeping bag, a duffel bag. Then came a front shoulder of frozen bear meat with the claws still attached; the claws ended just inches from the back of my neck. Next came a couple of two-pound lard pails of rendered bear fat. Finally came the mother and her two children and all her paraphernalia, which rivalled that of the man.

They then announced they were ready to take off. They did kindly leave room for me to work at my job in the front end.

I thought the best way to show them I couldn't make it with such a load was to make a run down the lake, and return to unload the excess.

I poured the coal to the plane and horsed it around a bit, and suddenly the darned critter took to the air. Furthermore, it flew ok, with plenty of control and everyone, including me, was happy.

About then it started snowing, but I flew low over the Huslia River and followed it down, and we arrived at Cutoff safely. I was clearly overloaded. Why that airplane behaved as it did that day I have no idea.

On my next trip, Peter Mark, of Huslia, wanted me to fly a load of supplies to a pothole lake between the Huslia and Dagitli Rivers. "A runway has been marked on the lake," he assured me, and added that I need have no worry about the ice—it was safe.

I took a good load of his supplies and arrived at the lake. He had a runway marked all right, but the area was full of blackfish holes [openings in ice created by a school of milling blackfish], and the only way I could get down on the lake from that direction would have been with a helicopter.

I buzzed around and looked it over and decided I could land across the lake and skim the edges of the blackfish holes. But there was another problem. There was every indication of overflow under the snow. It had been very cold, and I figured there might be some decent ice on top of the overflow, as commonly happens.

I went for it. Everything worked fine until the ship came to a stop. It then broke through the overflow ice and sank to the main ice, which, luckily, was only a foot down. So there I sat in a foot of water.

Peter Mark arrived with his dog team and we unloaded the ship, cut some spruce poles, and tromped down the snow. I fired up and pulled the ship up onto the top ice, with poles beneath the skis to hold her up. I left her idling and climbed out to check things out, and decided I could make it.

I laid the whip to old N40013, she took the bit in her teeth and scooted across the blackfish holes, and I was in the air.

On another trip from Huslia, Peter Mark's wife Laura was at a distant lake with a three-month-old baby. She was a powerful woman and could trap and do camp work as well as any man. Peter had a load for me fly to Laura. I was to land in a swamp about half a mile from her cabin.

I buzzed the cabin and landed on the swamp. It was 50 below, and the snow was three feet deep. Laura showed up with a sizable dog team as I was putting the motor cover on to hold heat in the engine. She parked the sled about thirty feet from the ship.

Included in the load was a frozen hind quarter of moose that weighed about 250 pounds. There was the usual canvas and fur robe on Laura's sled. The appropriate place for the frozen quarter was in the rear of the sled, near the handlebars.

I managed to get the quarter in my arms and flounder to the side of the sled with it. I stumbled in the deep snow with the heavy, awkward thing. I was losing my grip as I neared the sled. I was ready to cast it onto the pile of fur and canvas when a faint squeak emanated from the bundle of fur. My God! Laura's three-month-old baby! I couldn't recover my grip on the quarter, so I put all my strength into diverting its course. I managed to heave it nicely beyond the sled into the deep snow, but to do so sapped every ounce of my strength. The near escape also scared the living daylights out of me.

Laura saw me slump onto the sled. Despite the fifty below temperature, I mopped my brow, and was so weak I could hardly stand.

She arrived, took in the situation at a glance, but said nothing. She lifted the baby, fur and all out of the sled, and placed it on a mound of snow. Then she started loading the sled herself. I let her. My strength was temporarily gone.

The Koyukon Indians can sure hold a poker face under stressful conditions. Seemingly she didn't react to that close call. For me, it was too darned close to "scratch one baby."

Another flight I made from Huslia was for Jimmy Huntington, who wanted me to fly a load to a lake near the head waters of the Huslia River. The lake had a high bank around one side and one end. It was windy, and the air was full of holes [turbulence]. We arrived over the lake, and the situation didn't look good. The wind was wrong, but I decided I could come in crosswind and over a line of brush, and set her down ok. It was important to Jimmy that he get there with the supplies, and I didn't relish hauling them back to Huslia.

I flew off some distance and made a very careful approach to the lake. I was dragging her over the edge of willows under power when suddenly the bottom fell out. We had hit a sinker. We hit the ice with a resounding whack that jarred our spines.

I gave her a burst of power, then cut it. We had broken through six inches of overflow ice. The Wien Alaska Bush skis saved the day. Instead of hooking under the shell ice, they rode out onto unbroken ice. We came to a stop, unloaded, and gave the ship a good once-over.

Nothing was damaged. We camped there that night. I chose not to fool around with that wind again.

There were, of course, innumerable trips that went off like clockwork. It is the trips where you meet resistance that you remember.

It was often my lot to haul big sled dogs, and it was amusing to notice the reactions of individual dogs. It was similar to the response of people. Some got air sick. Some cowered and refused to look out. Others peered out the windows and tried to see everything they could while panting excitedly.

At Ruby, Alfred Gurtler had a team that flew so much that whenever the doors of an airplane opened, they rushed to it and started to climb in, sled and all. Whenever a plane came near his team, Alfred had to anchor the sled to keep them from trying to get into the plane.

Some pilots not familiar with the country and its needs, have refused to haul dogs in their nice clean planes. But in bush Alaska, dog teams were among the items that had to be hauled if a pilot was to provide service and stay in business. My airplane was the working equipment of the people, and it had to move all sorts of things.

Of course it wasn't always pleasant to load a bunch of smelly dogs, or for that matter, a full load of dog fish [smoked and/or dried salmon] but it kept me eating, and that was important.

There were times when I had in the same load a well-dressed and very proper Public Health Nurse, a few sled dogs, and a bale or two of fish. From the nurses' point of view, this was probably far from ideal, but in my day, bush villages had rather primitive accommodations. The plumbing was often in the open spaces, with the only running water found in the nearby river. The nurses I knew adjusted to these circumstances quickly, with rare exceptions. In some of these places they were ready to ride anything just to get somewhere else that would be different, if not better.

One reverend I flew from one village to another sat on a bale of fish. On another trip he sat on a bag of onions. On both flights he had a legal safety belt. He vowed that his seat was very comfortable. In fact, he got a big charge out of it.

Some men of the cloth I have known became well indoctrinated in the ways of the land. One Yukon River village I often visited had a very narrow landing strip on the river ice that fronted the village. One winter day I flew to this village, determined wind direction, and as I was about to land, I recognized Father Plomondon in the middle of the runway. He was working like a beaver. I circled for about fifteen minutes while the good Father continued to labor frantically.

He finally straightened, shouldered shovel and axe, and gave me the highball to come in. A Native woman, desiring ice for water, had chopped a hole six to eight feet long, three feet deep, and three feet wide smack in the middle of the runway blue ice. There was an overcast, and enough snow so that I wouldn't have seen it. Father Plomondon happened by and saw it. There was no time to get help, so he got busy on his own and did a first class job of runway repair under pressure.

In some villages, ice is the source of household water; the Natives chop it out of a river in chunks and haul it home with their dog team and pile it on racks. When they need water, they chip chunks into a container and take it inside to melt. Fortunately, most do not chop the ice out of aircraft runways, which, during my time, were on rivers adjacent to the villages. Few villages then had land runways.

At one village it was sometimes convenient for irresponsible parties to dispose of their dead dogs on river ice used for the aircraft runway. Hitting a frozen dog is akin to hitting a rock. Pilots had to learn to locate the dogs from the air, and corkscrew around them on landing.

Across much of Alaska is another menace to pilots, and most folks would never guess its identity. It is the horse fly, or moose fly, whichever you prefer to call it. This thrice accursed creature becomes abundant around July 1. You park your plane and close all doors. You think you're safe, but when you return, they are inside, seemingly by the hundreds.

They are an inch long, fly like a bullet, and bite like a bulldog. You can swat them, and they bounce off and come back for more. The only effective cure is a bug bomb. You open the door a crack and give the plane a good dousing of DDT.[2] They all disappear, but they are still in the plane. They are devilishly foxy. They hide behind the instrument panel.

For fifteen minutes after dosing them with a bug bomb you walk around while the push flies [mosquitoes] chew you. You go back to the plane and the moose flies are all gone—so you think.

You climb in with passengers, fire up, nothing happens, you check and run the engine up, all is ok. You lay the whip to her for the takeoff. Just as you get to where you can't change your mind, something goes by your ear like a bullet. As you take to the air and start to relax, you discover your passengers are fighting a lone moose fly, batting it about like a pingpong ball. The fly seems to enjoy the game.

You look cautiously at the instrument panel, and you see, crawling out of nooks and crannies, more moose flies. The onslaught is about to start. You open two windows, and give the DDT a squirt behind the instrument panel. Out they come in swarms and the suction from the windows drag them out into the prop wash along with a hat or two, or maybe a pair of gloves and miscellaneous comfort bags.

Only after the passengers have attended to the last obstinate fly can you relax and look for river bars or other possible landing sites should you suddenly need it.

You reach your destination and land in the midst of more swarms of push flies and moose flies. You are right in their dining room.

I sometimes wonder why I ever decided to fly the bush.

---

2. This helps to date Sam's writing; DDT, of course, is no longer used in the U.S.

Life Along the Yukon

The old days of bush flying disappeared in the 1950s.
—SAM O. WHITE

MODERN CONVENIENCES were mostly lacking in villages along the Yukon during the years I spent there. As often as not, situations were controlled by make-do and makeshift. Humor played an important part of life, and I tried to add a little of it whenever I could.

At Ruby, a village on the Yukon River, come Thanksgiving nearly all members of the "high society" there were invited to the U.S. Commissioner's house for dinner. By Ruby's standards, it was a gathering of notables. Included were a trader, the postmaster, the local bush pilot (me), and others. I was honored to be included. The commissioner was a lady, and she was competent both as an official, and as a holiday cook. Dinner was announced. The table was heaped with a big turkey and all the trimmings, except for the gravy. Madam Commissioner couldn't get it to thicken. We were all hungry and dinner was cooling while her futile attempts continued. Something had to be done.

Finally, I said, "Mrs. Commissioner, did you by any chance use snow water to mix your gravy?"

"Why, yes, I did, Sam," she responded. "Is that what is wrong?"

I assured her it was, and that there was no use to struggle with it. We could eat it thin and like it. This brought a few feminine comments from around the table, such as, "Well I never knew that."

I knew that the big drum near the kitchen stove was full of snow water, used for all kitchen needs. Further, I knew that my "snow water" statement was nonsense.

A few days later I met one of the ladies on the street. She gave me a withering look and tartly scolded, "Confound your hide Sam, I've been making gravy out of snow water for fifteen years. You know perfectly well what you told Mrs. Commissioner was nonsense."

She gave me another withering look, and moved on.

I should have reminded her that we had eaten a hot meal, thanks to my remark.

A NUMBER OF LADY U.S. Commissioners served in the various river villages. One I knew inherited the office from an elderly chap who had gone to Fairbanks and died. She assumed the post stone cold, and her first task was to gather and straighten the records. Her predecessor had used a big stack of old *Saturday Evening Post*s as a filing cabinet. However good the *Post* might be as a magazine, it is wanting in a number of respects as a filing cabinet. About all you could say for it was that it kept everything flat.

There was no record in which issue and which page to turn to to learn about "Number one discovery on Trail Creek." Or, for that matter, for anything else.

In addition, every magazine was not used to its full capacity, nor in any special order. She found that a written request from Midnight Creek with notice of assessment work done, had been presented for recording, complete with recording fee, but the recording was not done. This assessment notice of work done bore a date three years old.

Further rooting turned up several like instances from other creeks. In about the eighth or tenth issue was a pioneer's pension check for a man who had been dead for several years. A few pages over was another check for the same man. The pension checks were still arriving.

Since a considerable stack of the *Post*s were used in this manner, it was necessary to go through the entire stack, page by page.

She found many twenty dollar bills, and all were accompanied by a notice of assessment work accomplished, bearing dates three years past or more.

There was no evidence of malfeasance. The pension checks were there to return to the Territorial government, and the records, so far as they were carried out, were as straight as a string and checked out.

The new Commissioner lost no time in entering the various assessment notices on the books, and returning to the Territorial government the unused pension checks, accompanied by a report on the demise of the recipient.

AT RUBY, A SOURDOUGH named Jack patronized a correspondence Lonely Hearts Club. About every second year he managed to save enough money to send for a bride. The brides arrived first class, all expenses paid by the sourdough.

Invariably these ladies could not stand the solitude and rough living of the Yukon, and invariably in one to two months, headed back Stateside. On their departure, Jack escorted them to their means of conveyance—a bush plane or steamboat—and paid all the bills back to their starting point, with a little extra.

He would then cinch his belt and start saving for the next try two years hence.

The last bride I saw arrived on the riverfront of Ruby in April. Water lay on the ice for 100 feet out on the river. She was helped out of the bush plane by the pilot. She wore high-heeled slippers, a pretty dress, and a fancy hat with flowers, an incongruous sight in that time and place.

When she saw the log cabins perched on the riverbank, and a dog team or two tied nearby, she looked very uncomfortable.

She stayed a month or maybe two, and we saw little of her around town. One day I saw her in town and she confided, "Mr. White, I'm leaving next week. This town is not too bad, and Jack is a fine man and I like him, but, oh my God, that house!"

True to his customary procedure, Jack did the right thing by paying her return fare. He was a remarkable man.

DANCES WERE A MAJOR form of entertainment in the Yukon River villages, and too often much liquor flowed. One Christmas, at a Koyukuk River village to which I flew the mail, [Author: probably Cutoff] I managed flights to get all the Christmas mail to the village, as well as the turkeys that had been ordered.

I left the liquor orders out.

I then spent Christmas eve there, expecting it to be a peaceful and quiet stay.

I'd been invited to Christmas dinner at the trading post. On Christmas eve, at around two p.m. as darkness neared, a local

Sam with his Stinson L-5G frozen in ice, September 11, 1959.
SAM O. WHITE, COURTESY DRAHS

preacher and I watched an airplane land on the snow-covered river ice and park under the riverbank. There the pilot peddled booze. The preacher and I slipped up close and listened.

The fifths that went for $7.50 on the Yukon, had somehow become more valuable en route and were going for $18 on the Koyukuk. The selling was rapidly accomplished, and the pilot took off into the night.

I had tried.

HOSPITALITY IN THE villages is tops in this uneasy world, as well as in the adjacent bush where I sometimes had to spend a night or two in an Indian's trapping cabin. Such Indians may not have much, but what he has you are welcome to. You may sleep on the ground, as most of these cabins have no floors except for mother earth. There you roll out your sleeping bag, and you will most likely be furnished with a dried moose or caribou hide for a mattress. This, with moose meat and beans, and a few frozen wild berries, is far superior to a shakedown under a tree at far below zero temperatures.

To illustrate this point, consider the following: After a mail run on a cold winter day, I flew back to Ruby late one evening to find pilot Steve Miskoff two days overdue.

Next day, to search for Miskoff, with Johnny May as observer, I flew to the Novi River [Nowitna], and cruised toward its headwaters. There we hit the jackpot.

Near the Novi we spotted Steve's aircraft sitting on a frozen lake. We swung over to the Novi, less than a quarter mile away, and at a cabin was the missing pilot, waving frantically.

We landed on the river, and parked the ship on a river bar.

Steve's plane had blown two jugs (cylinders) at the same time, the only incident I've ever heard of when two went at once.

He had calmly set his plane down on the lake.

Next step, of course, was for me to fly out and bring him repair parts.

Wearing snowshoes, we stomped down a runway for take off of my plane. When it was ready, we went to the cabin which belonged to William Bergman. He was already boiling a kettle of moose meat, knowing we would soon arrive. The cabin had no floor but mother earth. We feasted and drank quarts of black tea and slept well and warm in the sleeping bags we always carried, and on caribou hides our host spread for us. Compared to siwashing under a tree, basic as the accommodations were, we were in the lap of luxury, thanks to our hospitable Indian host who offered his all for our comfort and use.

Next morning the snowshoed area had frozen solid, but the world was full of dense fog. Nevertheless, we fire-potted my engine and I started her up. I took off from the now-firm runway and flew up through a hole. It was hopeless. Fog was everywhere. I spiraled back down through the hole, landed, and parked the plane and got it ready for the next day, hoping the fog would dissipate. It did, and everything was roses.

Joe Barstow, a blacksmith, was an old-timer at Circle City. In the late 1920s, Joe, like everyone else, was waiting for the road (Steese Highway) to come through from Fairbanks. He knew he had a few years to wait, but he was getting ready. He acquired a Model T Ford, which he rebuilt into what he called a "general utility vehicle." He replaced the rear wheels with sprockets. Then he extended the frame, and on this extension he mounted bull wheels about the height of the old wheels, only these were made of laminated lumber and were a foot or so wide. On these wheels he bolted lugs for improved traction. When connected with the forward sprockets, it provided a much reduced gear ratio.

Joe mounted a saw frame and a circular saw on the front of the contraption. Behind, he attached a couple of old buggies, like those drawn by horses in which stricken swains took girls for rides in the 1890s. He rigged bows over these and stretched canvas tightly over all so that he had a couple of covered wagons for living quarters and storage.

It was his plan, when the road arrived, to travel in a leisurely manner and to make expenses by filing saws, sharpening and repairing scissors and knives, and sawing wood.

Joe measured out a circular course in town, and drove around this many times with the covered wagons in tow, checking his gas consumption and miles per hour. I rode around with him once, and the thing worked after a fashion, with much smoke, harsh grindings and shaking. It was a picturesque outfit.

You might ask what a Model T Ford was doing in Circle before the road got there. Many years earlier, a road of sorts had been hacked out from Circle to Central (30 miles), and Circle Hot Springs (40 miles). At first the road was for horse-drawn rigs only. Later it was improved enough so a Model T could get through when the ground was frozen, or real dry, and a couple of Model Ts were shipped in by steamboat.

Joe's planned destination was Valdez. He figured two or three years would do it. But alas, it was not to be.

Tired of waiting for the road, he took off for Eagle Creek and crossed Eagle Summit. He stopped near where Leo Moore and his wife lived near the road, took sick, and died.

Joe's Model T and covered wagons sat there long after that, and might still be there today. He was a good, kind-hearted man, and actually realized part of his dream, since he traveled nearly a hundred miles and crossed Eagle Summit, which was doing pretty well, considering.

IT HAS BEEN MANY YEARS since stern-wheeler steamboats plied the Yukon. I remember three of the biggest; *Susie*, *Hannah*, and *Sarah*. Each was 1211 gross tons. A somewhat smaller *Isham* had the most powerful engine. I heard that the firemen did not like to handle the extra four-foot lengths of wood it took to feed the *Isham*'s engine.

Wood cutters along the banks of the Yukon sawed huge piles of wood to feed the fireboxes of these big steamboats; it was an important business in those days. All the firewood was cut by hand; chainsaws hadn't been invented.

These riverboats hauled passengers, and some freight. The bulk of the freight was loaded on barges that they pushed up the river (they didn't tow), or sometimes tied alongside.

By this method, great tonnage could be moved in one trip. I've seen five barges, loaded to the hilt, pushed upriver by one steamboat.

Crews of these riverboats had to be skilled in reading the water to determine safe depth. It wouldn't do for a boat thus loaded to pile up on a gravel bar. The channels and river bars change annually. At breakup, huge chunks of ice gouge new channels, and move sand and gravel bars.

Ice jams occur every spring on the Yukon, one reason being that the Yukon rises south and flows north and west. It first breaks up at the headwaters and middle, where spring arrives earliest. Downstream-flowing ice piles up on the still-solid lower river ice. Sometimes it raises complete Ned.

During summers after spring floods have left the Yukon I have seen where ice had jammed and dammed the river, forcing ice over the banks; then the power of rising water shoved ice over the banks. House-size chunks of ice were pushed across country, leveling trees up to a quarter mile from the river. The trees are still in frozen ground, so they are sheared off close to the ground. Downed trees are ground into match sticks and toothpicks, then deposited in piles in depressions here and there.

Ice breakup on the Yukon is a good demonstration of the ultimate power of nature.

Local industry in the river villages was generally confined to trapping in the fall and winter, and fishing during the summer. The fishing depended mostly on fish wheels, comprised of a wheel mounted between two floating logs, with baskets on the ends of usually two spokes of the wheel. Turned by the current, the baskets scoop salmon out of the water and dump them onto a chute that feeds them into a holding box.

These fishwheels cannot be used in clear water because the

fish can see and dodge around them. But they are very effective in the silty Yukon.

Once in a while, if a village has a little surge of prosperity, a sawmill springs up. Lumber can then be shipped up and down the river to other villages via barge and river boat. Such was the case at Ruby where a friend of mine repaired an old sawmill, and went into business, using logs he cut upriver and in the spring floated them down the Yukon to Ruby.

I asked him to build me a one-room cabin at Ruby as a base for my flight operations. We didn't agree on a price, but he furnished the lumber and built the cabin. There have been few deals in my life when I have given a man a blank check for a job, as I did in this case. I like to remember it because when he gave me the bill, it was remarkably reasonable.

On my frequent flights up the Yukon I often flew over the winter camp where this honest man cut his logs and hauled them to the river bank. If I saw a pile of boughs on the snow-covered sandbar, I landed.

On one occasion, he had broken down and hadn't turned a wheel in five days. I flew to Fairbanks, where I was headed anyway, and got the parts he needed and delivered them to him next morning. Shortly he was logging again.

I often stopped for a pot of coffee and lunch, which was always a pleasure. His capable and attractive wife did the cooking. She had been brought up by her parents to know how to cook.

Late one April I had orders to pick up this fellow and his helper and fly them to Ruby. Snow was deep and soft, but he had wallowed out a runway long enough for me to get in and out.

To return to his logging camp, we were all set to leave Ruby about four o'clock next morning while his runway was still frozen. His helper asked if I thought I could get our load into that small runway "without any trouble."

My friend answered for me. "That is for Sam to worry about."

It was a compliment in my book.

[AUTHOR] Sam didn't mention the sawmill man's name on his typed copy of this essay, but at the end, in Sam's handwriting, were the words "Steamshovel John." Was that the name of the owner of the sawmill?

Jack Sackett

Jack swung around and shot a big grizzly almost within arm's length. It had just reared up to attack. He said it was his closest call with a bear.
—SAM O. WHITE

OUTSTANDING AMONG the rugged individualists in the trading business along the Koyukuk River was Jack Sackett. He was a clear thinking man of great principles and unswerving honesty. His presence in a community was a stabilizing factor. He had been a police officer before he came to Alaska, and for a time, during its goldrush heyday, he was Nome's Police Chief.

I believe he came to Alaska in 1898. He loved the Noatak, Kobuk, and Koyukuk country, and prospected all of these rivers for many years. One had to be hardy and self sufficient to survive as a prospector in northern Alaska in those days. Because there was a limited variety of supplies available, he and his partner lived largely on meat.

There were vast herds of caribou, and mountain sheep were available, as was an occasional moose. Jack told me how he and his partner once ventured a short way from camp to kill a caribou. They shot two of the animals in a ravine, and were about to dress them, when Jack spotted a grizzly bear galloping toward them. When the bear neared, with his .30–30 Winchester he tumbled it, for he was a crack shot. His partner, a short distance away, shouted, "Bear behind you."

Jack swung around and shot a big grizzly almost within arm's length. It had just reared up to attack. He said it was his closest call with a bear.

One winter he and his partner wintered on the north end of fifteen-mile-long Walker Lake at the head of the Kobuk River.

"It was very cold and forbidding country, and there was a sinister aspect to the lake as it banged, moaned, and groaned all winter, with ice expanding, contracting, and forming pressure ridges," Jack said. He was glad when spring arrived, and the ice went out.

When the lake was clear of ice, he and his partner built a log raft, put their belongings on it, and started down the lake with a favorable wind propelling them. A few miles beyond the half way point, the wind changed and blew them back to where they had started. They were becalmed for some time. A favorable wind again blew them part way to the south end. It switched again, and blew them back north. He said it took two weeks to get to the south end of the lake with their raft.

Jack told me of a lone spruce tree far up the Noatak River and on a bench, away from the river. He said Eskimos never molested the tree, nor did prospectors.

I was in the Noatak country around 1936 and flew up the river to see if there really was a lone spruce far up the river. It was there all right, miles from any other tree. When I next saw Jack I told him that I had seen his tree. He was greatly pleased; it brought a shine to his eyes.

After many years of prospecting the Noatak and Kobuk Rivers, he moved to the Koyukuk, where he prospected for a time. Later, he ran a trading post for Billy English at Wiseman. After that he ran the trading post at the original Bettles, which is eight miles below the present Bettles. My first visit to old Bettles was in 1925 as a passenger flying with Noel Wien. He landed on a bar above the roadhouse, and for many years at Old Bettles we landed our planes on the river in the winter, and on the bar in summer, provided the river was sufficiently low.

From Old Bettles, Jack prospected his way down the Koyukuk. Eventually he arrived at the picturesque village of Cutoff (also called Cutoff Trading Post and Old Cutoff). It was so-called because it is at the lower end of Treat Island. The river splits around this large island, and many miles of river travel can be cut off by following the east channel at the right stage of water.

Cutoff was an isolated Native village. Its only connections were with two other villages on the river. There was very little travel between these villages. Here Jack, who was getting on in years, settled down and built one of the most picturesque trading posts in Alaska.

This was excellent fur country, especially for mink. It was little exploited by outside trappers. Jack prospered, and so did the Natives who came under his influence.

In those days the entire season's trading goods arrived in summer on one river boat. There was no way to restock until the next year. That meant that with the arrival of that boat, goods for more than 150 people had to be on it. Normally, when the boat arrived, shelves in the trading post were bare, and the Natives' caches were empty. At such times, everyone lived on game meat, fish, and wild vegetation, although a few provident folk might have a few beans left.

When Jack first established his trading post at Cutoff, only a generation or two separated the Koyukon Indians from first contact with whites—the early Russians. An occasional Indian still carried on forbidden pre-white practices.

He once told me a story to illustrate this. The annual boat had arrived, and he had a mountain of stuff on the riverbank that had to be stored in caches and stocked on the bare shelves of the trading post. He had hired local men to do this work, and was busy supervising. There was much confusion.

In the midst of this activity, a well-known Indian of the old school arrived and sat in the trading post for some time without saying anything. Jack, being busy, didn't pay much attention to him.

Finally, Jack asked him, "What's the matter, Toby? You want to talk?"

"Yes, Jack. Maybe I want to talk," he responded.

"Go ahead and talk, Toby," Jack urged.

Toby's problem was an unpopular white man on the Yukon River. No one had any use for him. Indians and whites alike kept clear of him. Toby was old, had been brought up by the old rules, and still lived by them. He was known to have killed several Indians in the distant past.

Now, it seemed, he wanted to kill this much-disliked white man, but he realized he had better have some white man advice on the subject before acting. He had traveled to Cutoff, a long way from the Yukon, to talk to Jack about his plan.

Jack, busy stocking shelves and getting his year's supplies into storage didn't take Toby seriously, so he said, "Go ahead and kill the old s.o.b. Someone should have killed him long ago," and continued working.

After a while it dawned on him just what old Toby was alluding to, and that the old Indian was serious.

Jack ran out of the trading post, hollering for Edwin Simon, who had the fastest boat in the village. "Hurry, Edwin, get that boat of yours going. We've got to catch old Toby," he urged.

They headed downriver full speed and managed to catch old Toby two thirds of the way to the Yukon. There Jack laid the law down in no uncertain terms, that Toby had better lay off killing any white man, as well as Indians, as the times had changed, and the great White Father in Washington did not look with favor on killing.

After he had told me the story he said, "Now wouldn't I have been in a pretty fix. That Indian would have told a court that I had told him it was all right to go ahead and kill the man. I'd have had to get on the witness stand and admit that I told him to go ahead and kill him. That would have been a sad day for this old police officer."

The village of Cutoff had problems. It always had a spring flood, and some floods were nearly disastrous. The village was on a low bank on the outside of a sharp bend. At breakup, ice floating downriver set toward this bank. Several cabins were close to the bank.

Nearly every spring the residents either took to the hills during breakup, or they took to a boat and tied to a tree in back of the village. Jack told me that one spring they were in a boat twenty-eight days before they could get their feet on solid ground.

During many breakups, ice rushed downriver in big pans that slid up over the bank and at times actually overhung the cabins as they were pushed by the current. It seems they always broke off and fell on the bank with a terrific crash just after they had passed the last cabin. If they broke off while overhanging one or more cabins, the many tons of pan ice could obliterate any cabin on which it fell.

I always enjoyed Jack's stories. He was first class company, and I often stopped at Cutoff just to visit. In addition, of course, for years I delivered mail there.

Life was rather primitive in this village, but I liked the people much. They got along well, and paid their bills. Moose and caribou were always plentiful—the caribou used to come as far as the Zane Hills and the Dakli River, both only a few miles north of the village.

In 1931 or 1932 I was flying my Swallow biplane down the Koyukuk River, when I saw a lot of Natives on a bar, with many individual fires. I had big doughnut tires, so I landed. The people were roasting wild geese entrails. They had cut the entrails into two-inch strips and had threaded them on willow sticks. They roasted the front strip, and while eating it, they roasted the next one on the stick, and so on, until the stick was empty. Nothing was lost but the honk.

Jack was an expert at grading furs. I've watched him work, and he was very fast and accurate. Unlike most traders, he paid for his yearly supply of goods with cash. This was an outlay of many thousands of dollars. He didn't like to owe anyone.

Once, while settling up with him for some flying, I saw him reach under his bed and haul out a battered suitcase. I was shocked to see a pile of large denomination bills, and even more of smaller denominations. Also in the suitcase was a revolver that would have made a good museum piece.

I said, "Jack, you shouldn't keep all that money here. There are people of doubtful character running up and down this river with outboard motor boats. Some day I'll come in here and find you and Lucy (Jack's lovely Native wife) knocked in the head."

He made no answer, and knowing Jack as I did, I said no more. That fall I noticed he had a checking account in a Fairbanks bank.

I kept two air mattresses at Cutoff for the convenience of my passengers when it was necessary to overnight there. They didn't last long. The kids used them as toboggans on the rough board floor. When I pulled the slivers out of them they resembled sieves.

Jack's son John, who we called Barney, when he was three and four years old used to like to pummel me. He is now known as John, and is making a good and honorable mark for himself. I once grabbed several cans of milk from a case in the store and shoved them under my shirt. While Barney was retrieving them, I'd grab another one or two and stick them in my shirt. Barney then called, "Mama, Sam is stealing milk."

Sometimes when I came into Cutoff after a hard cold day and he got too pestiferous I stuffed him in a mail sack and hung him on a spike in the gable end of the trading post. Sometimes he'd go to sleep there, with his head just above the edge of the sack.

This displeased Lucy; she got a little vexed at me, so I quit hanging him up. One night after he had pummelled me unmercifully and pulled my hair and in other ways had beat me up, I ignored him. He said, "Sam, why don't you hang me up in the mail sack?" The small children of Cutoff could stand on the riverbank and talk like wild geese; they often called geese down to shotgun range of the hunters in the village. They could effectively imitate moose, caribou, and bears. They had an uncanny way of looking at an aircraft in flight and telling you who flew it.

On the evening of January 12th, 1957, a message came to me at Hughes for me to go to Huslia next morning to fly my old friend Jack Sackett to the hospital.

I arrived at Huslia before daylight on a bitterly cold day. But things had changed. Jack knew it was the end, and he decided he wanted to die among old friends and relatives. I visited with him for an hour. That night he was gone.

The Koyukuk lost a good and honest citizen who had done much good for the community. Few men attain the status among fellow citizens as did Jack Sackett.

[AUTHOR] In 1953, I was a full Professor, and Head of the Department of Wildlife Management at the University of Alaska (now UAF). Graduate student Wilbur "Burt" Libby, who was studying beaver, and I, were flown by U.S. Fish and Wildlife Service agent Ray Woolford, to the upper Huslia River. The local Koyukon Indians had urged the Alaska Game Commission to increase the trapping limit for beaver, saying they were plentiful along the Huslia River and adjacent drainages. Libby and I were to assess beaver numbers and report to the Game Commission.

For a week or so, we drifted in our canoe down the winding Huslia, diverting frequently to check tributary streams and nearby beaver ponds.

When we reached the broad Koyukuk River, we paddled ashore for a tea break. As we were boiling a kettle, Edwin Simon, an elder Koyukon from Huslia, passing by in his boat, came ashore and joined us, and we had a nice visit. He told us it was only a short distance downstream to Huslia.

That day we drifted to the village and went ashore. Jack Sackett and the villagers welcomed us. Jack had received a radio message from Ray Woolford that he wouldn't be able to pick us up. We were to return to Fairbanks via Wien Airlines.

We had a several day wait for Wien pilot James "Andy" Anderson to arrive on his scheduled flight from Bettles. We could

Edwin Simon, a respected Koyukon Native elder, of Huslia, in August, 1953. He stands next to the wall of the just-built school house at Huslia. Note the sphagnum moss chinking of logs.

Graduate student Burt Libby and the author lived in this new school building for several days.
AUTHOR

fly with him to Bettles, where we could catch a scheduled DC3 flight to Fairbanks.

The residents of Huslia had just completed building a new log school building. School hadn't started, and we were invited to stay in the school while waiting for Andy.

Late that day Burt and I were contemplating some way to make a meal from what little food we had left, when Johnny Sackett, then around 10 years old, arrived and told us we were invited to dinner by his parents, Jack and Lucy.

The invitation was repeated every evening for the three or four days we waited for Andy's arrival. Lucy Sackett was a great cook, and we very much enjoyed the food she served. We enjoyed even more the stories that Jack told us after dinner. He was a great raconteur, and he modestly recounted adventures of his half century of experiences in northwest Alaska. Bush hospitality was at its best with trader Jack Sackett and his wife Lucy. They had never heard of either Burt or me.

A day before Andy was scheduled to arrive, a float plane circled the village, landed on the river, and taxied to the bank. The familiar figure who climbed out of the plane was Sam O. White. He had dropped in to visit Jack Sackett and other village friends. Sam White sure travelled widely in bush Alaska.

We had our usual pleasant visit—visits with Sam were always pleasant. He liked people. Sam wasn't heading for Fairbanks, so he couldn't help us.

The local Koyukon Indians were right, beaver were abundant, and partly based on Burt and my recommendations to the Alaska Game Commission, the annual limit for that section of the Koyukuk was increased.

In 1953, if anyone had told me I would one day write a book about Sam O. White—and that I would also write a book with Wien pilot James L. Anderson—I wouldn't have believed them. Nor would I have taken seriously a prediction that young Johnny Sackett, growing up in Huslia, would one day become a power in Alaska's legislature. Yet, all of these events did happen.

Flying for a Coastal Survey

Operation limitations for [Sam White's] Stinson L5-G, Serial 4609, type certificate 764: Climb or level flight 140 mph. Glide or dive 169 mph. Flaps extended 90 mph. Ailerons drooped 81 mph. Take off weight land 2250. Take off weight sea 2250.

IN THE LATE 1940s, I won a government contract to fly my Stinson L5-G airplane on floats during a summer season for a Coastal Survey party. Work started in Bristol Bay on the Bering Sea. Violent weather and big tides made the flying difficult and hazardous. I had previously flown mostly in the Interior, from freshwater lakes and rivers. Now, for the first time I had to get a tide book to learn the times and sizes of low and high tides.

I flew from Fairbanks to Anchorage and picked up Commander Newton A. Stewart and flew to Naknek through Lake Clark Pass, a route through the mountains on the southwestern side of Cook Inlet. We crossed Lake Clark, and eighty-mile-long Iliamna Lake, and arrived at the Naknek Air Force base.

From there I flew supplies and equipment across Nushagak Bay to Pike Lake where we set up a camp. One day I flew to the village of Dillingham. I had heard tales of airplane float landings there, and had talked about it with local pilots.

At low tide there is several hundred feet of mud from the water's edge to the gravel beach. Tidal variations are commonly around eighteen feet. I was warned to be careful in taxiing through mud to the beach; anchors lost in the mud are a hazard to the fragile floats of an airplane.

The tide was low when I arrived. I slowly taxied through the mud, peering on both sides for anchors. I had nearly reached the gravel without seeing or hitting an anchor, but the nervous strain was too much. I stopped. Wearing hip boots, I got out and prodded around the floats. As I stirred the gooey mud, a horrible stench arose. Gurry (fish parts waste) from local salmon canneries was mixed with the mud.

I disturbed the carcass of a hairless dog. It popped out of the mud and looked me right in the eye. The pilots I had talked with hadn't mentioned dogs as local hazards.

We turned the ship around and loaded it, preferring to pack the cargo a short distance through mud than to do more taxiing in this loblolly.

I was to haul more gas from Dillingham to the Pike Lake camp, so my assistant remained at Dillingham for the day. I taxied through the mud into the water and delivered my load.

When I returned to Dillingham my assistant had my next load ready. He had also removed and piled on the beach several menacing and wicked-looking anchors.

After the third load that day, it was late, and a storm was threatening. I parked the aircraft high on the beach, and tied it to a log. We went to a hotel and turned in.

About one a.m. a knock came. It was a truck driver, and a Good Samaritan if there ever was one. "Your plane is in a tough spot. You'd better come with me and I'll help you," he said.

We jumped into his truck and he rushed us to the beach. Green spruce trees had been uprooted up the bay by the storm, and had floated en masse to drift into the beach near the plane.

One tree was in front of the plane. Two others were close. Outside of the ship was a bunch of trees with a root mass hung up on the beach. They threatened the ship with every wave surge.

Across the root mass was balanced a big green spruce tree that swung back and forth like a gate with every wave. About fifteen feet of the treetop hung four or five feet directly above the plane.

The tide was rising, and something was going to bust loose in a few minutes, and my method and means of making a living was going to disappear unless quick action took place.

The truck driver remained cool and all business. "We'd better move this one first," he said, hooking onto the big spruce root and dragging it onto the beach with the truck. One-by-one he dragged them away while I acted as chain man for him. He cleared the area without putting a scratch on my aircraft. Then he helped us re-park and secure it for the remainder of the night. He drove us to the hotel. I tried to pay him for his kindness, but he would accept no payment.

"I didn't want to rob you. I just wanted to help you," he said.

When I completed the flying from Dillingham, I landed on a freshwater lake and sloshed buckets of water inside and outside the old L5-G to clean the mud. Clothes had to be washed. The smell of that mud clung to everything.

The Bering Sea coast weather was vicious and so changeable that I never knew when I left a place whether I could land at my destination—or if I could get back to my origin.

In time we moved camp to Osviak Lagoon north and west of Hagemeister Island. The move was a bit on the hair-raising side. After takeoff from Pike Lake I had to fly over the ocean where waves constantly beat the rocky shore. For some distance there would have been little chance for survival if an engine quit.

While at the lagoon camp, a powerful storm arrived. It ripped several well-pitched tents. I watched Alfred Gallucchi, one of the engineers, throw himself onto a tent that had been flattened. Wind picked the tent up with him on it and waved him around in the air several feet, and dropped him with a thump.

Al was made of stern stuff, and he rode her through by hanging on for dear life. I think that wind would have blown the tent and Al clean out of the country had not one of the main guy ropes been tied to a firm stake.

From this camp, I flew crews to several lakes, and put a couple of men on Hagemeister Island. I'd take people out in the morning, and hope I could pick them up late in the day to return them to camp. Weather was so unpredictable I often wondered if I'd ever see them again.

After a week or so, I was assigned to haul gasoline and supplies from the twenty-mile distant village of Platinum. We had run our supply so low that I had only enough to make Platinum; not enough to return.

At take off, visibility was perfect, with sunshine, an unusual treat. At Platinum there was a northeast gale, and Goodnews Bay was upside down with whitecaps.

I had to get the plane into a pool a local mining company had dredged into the shore. Their shop was adjacent to the pool, which had a few barges in it. The tide had to be high for me to taxi into the pool.

I searched my tide book to find the time for high tide at Platinum. "Same as Lima, Peru," it read. I then searched for the Lima entry; the answer turned out to be reasonably correct.

I sure as Ned couldn't land in Goodnews Bay, as rough as it was, and I couldn't return to the lagoon camp or anywhere else on the piddling amount of gas I had. With no choice, I landed on the ocean on the lee side of a sand spit. I then taxied through the thoroughfare into Goodnews Bay. In Goodnews Bay, one minute I saw blue sky through the windshield, and the next I peered into green water. Occasionally a big wave broke over the engine and windshield. This was new to me, and I wondered if I was going to survive, and have an aircraft left. My engine stopped three times when huge waves rolled over it. I taxied into the bay, and shut off the engine to allow the plane to drift back toward the pool.

On the fourth tack I figured I would just about make it into the narrow entrance of the pool. As I was about to shut the engine off to drift back, a big wave sloshed over the engine again and up on the windshield—which suddenly became a "watershield."

The engine stopped, and I started drifting back. I tried to start the engine in case I needed it, but it wouldn't start. I was out of gas.

I stood on a float, intending to fend the plane off the rocks when we got there—and the darned plane drifted right through the middle of the entrance and into the calm pool, as if it had eyes of its own.

When I was safely tied, I relaxed on a barge for a few minutes. I then went into the mining company's shop, where they poured me a cup of coffee. I had been through a wringer.

The wind blew for three days, and Goodnews Bay stood on its ear. I was anxious to get back to camp. They couldn't fly until I returned.

At the end of the third day, the wind died enough so that I could haul three loads of gas into camp. I returned to Platinum to stay overnight. Next day I hauled gasoline like mad and got a good supply into camp. The following day I hauled even more gas.

A few days later I was tagged to fly with charts to a Coast Survey ship in Kvichak Bay, and to return with other charts.

I landed beside the ship and started to drift toward the open sea. They put an outboard-powered boat over, which soon overhauled me. The crew and I exchanged greetings and packages, and the boat headed back.

I felt very lonesome, being such a tiny speck on so much water, with a very distant shoreline. While I had no doubts about it, I was relieved when the engine started and I was able to take off and fly back to our Osviak Lagoon camp.

I HAD A CONTRACT to fly for the Coastal Survey again the following season. I was to start from Platinum.

I left Fairbanks about May first. Breakup was occurring on the big interior rivers. The Kuskokwim River was in flood. It's about 600 miles Fairbanks to Platinum on the route I followed. I hauled a load of cased gasoline with me.

Since the Kuskokwim was in flood, and ice was running, I couldn't land anywhere along the river to buy gas. With all the flat land under water, and much floating ice, it promised to be a hairy ride.

The weather, however, was on my side, and I had good visibility. Downstream, I saw half-mile-long ice floes, the width of the Kuskokwim, with dog team trails plain on them. These trails had been made many miles upriver.

A black bear prowled restlessly on one floe, apparently not liking it one bit. He was a mile and a half from shore in one direction, and a good half mile in the other. His chance to get ashore didn't look good, for the pan he was riding was breaking up.

Below McGrath, I landed on a lake where wind had pushed ice cakes to the far shore, and refueled from my cargo. I was half a mile from the nearest shoreline. I had seen no one for many miles, and I felt sort of lonely. In the air again, it looked like the whole country was under water.

Before I left the Kuskokwim valley, I saw another big ice pan of many acres. It had drifted at least fifty miles downriver. Near its middle, two dog team trails joined, forming a Y. A fox was on this pan, and he, like the bear I had seen, was in a tough situation.

I landed at Platinum late that evening. We soon established a camp at Carter Lake, north of Platinum, and operated from there for nearly a month.

We then moved south to Port Heiden, on the north side of the Alaska Peninsula. Clouds were about, and it was wet and cold but flyable on the day we left—standard for the Alaska Peninsula.

I flew to Naknek to pick up some things needed at Port Heiden. I had a big load, and had to take off of long and narrow Northwest Lake, which is practically in the village of Naknek. A bank rises all the way around this lake.

The previous year when I flew from this lake I looked for a takeoff to the south, but when I lined up for it, I saw the skeletons of three aircraft on the bank—aircraft that didn't make it. One was a Sikorsky. Therefore I turned and went to the other end to line up. Then, when I looked down the lake, I saw two more airplane skeletons bleaching there. They didn't make it either.

This time I had a bigger load, and the wind wasn't very favorable. I screwed up my courage and took off anyway.

As I flew down the peninsula, weather became steadily worse. There were lakes, and I could have landed if necessary. But from Cinder River there was a dry stretch, with no lakes. I was beneath a ceiling of 200 feet, with short visibility. Pools of fog started making up on the ground, and connecting streamers came down from the ceiling. I was just abreast of it, and was happy to get to Port Heiden safely.

I had a cache of 700 gallons of gasoline on a lake there, and Ken had a like amount on another lake farther down the Peninsula. We made a deal. Whenever we used out of each other's caches, we would settle up over a big dinner at the end of the season.

We soon noticed that our gas caches were getting low faster than they should have. There were a few bootleggers with airplanes on the peninsula who sold booze to cannery crews on pay day. These crews were mostly Natives, some of whom would go on big drunks. The result? Loads of salmon arrived at local canneries, with no one to work them.

These gentry were refused food and shelter at the canneries, nor could they buy gasoline from them. When any of our survey group arrived at the canneries, we were treated royally. Food and shelter was available to us.

It soon became obvious that bootleggers were stealing our gasoline. A tent was pitched on the lake where Ken had a gasoline cache, with sleeping bags, rations, and dishes. I landed there one day to occupy the tent and found two bootleggers in the sleeping bags. They had eaten nearly all the rations, and the place was a mess. They also had some of our cased gas in their airplane.

I removed this, roared and threatened, telling them they must replace what they had stolen or I would call in the U.S. Marshal. They took off. I never saw the pair again. They didn't replace any of Ken's gas.

While working out of Port Heiden we saw from three to fifteen big bears every day. They never bothered us around camp. I had to chase some of them off beaches by buzzing them with the airplane so we could discharge loads. They usually went a hundred or two yards and sat and watched us.

One evening two of the light keepers on that job climbed a mountain to their light. They wore coveralls, raincoats, and rubber boots. When they arrived, a big bear came upon them. When the bear neared, they ran. The bear followed. Half way down the mountain one of the men petered out. He stopped and kicked off his rubber boots.

The bear sat and watched.

Hip boots off, he again ran. The bear followed. The two reached the lake where their tent was pitched. Instead of diving into the tent, they ran into the water up to their waists.

The bear sat on the beach, watching them.

The cold water soon paralyzed one of the men; his legs would no longer support him. The other fellow had to hold him up. About then, one of our planes came along and chased the bear away.

Bear encounter rule number one: never run from a bear. That only tempts the bear into chasing—and the bear can run faster and farther than you can.

From a camp we established on Black Lake, Commander Stewart and I flew to a very small, crescent-shaped lake. It was ok for takeoff with the wind blowing, but marginal when the wind died.

Stewart completed his work just as the wind stopped. A thin mist arose from the water, enough to distort vision and destroy depth perception.

I didn't think we would make it off on the first try, and we didn't. But we felt it out, and I cut the gun. We taxied back and tried it again, and again failed. We squared away for the third time, and this time it looked like we were making it. I lifted one float out of the water, and suddenly we were in the grass.

I cut the power and pulled the mixture. We bumped through the blueberry bushes and across a three-foot wide, marshy creek, and into more blueberry bushes before stopping, 400 feet from the lake.

With a little more beef, which I figured we would have as soon as the boys in camp missed us, I thought we could turn the plane around.

"I think you and I can turn it around ourselves," Stewart said.

I sez, "Ok with me."

Stewart was also a pilot, so I told him to get into the front office and give me full power in thirty second bursts, and to idle the engine for sixty seconds to cool her off.

I got onto the tail and nudged it as a signal to Stewart. He poured the coal, I heaved and we made a little headway. He cut for a cooling-off period, and we went at it again. After about a dozen tries the plane was halfway turned around. I was panting like a dog and was about pooched out.

We switched places. Stewart didn't have the weight I have, but he heaved best as he could, and we gained a bit more ground. When I felt no more heaving with full throttle, I knew he too was pooched out.

We switched places again, and this time I tied a rope to the tail. When he blasted the power I threw myself into the rope, only to have it break. I landed fifteen feet away on my back in a puddle of icy water. This should have killed me, as I was hot and steaming. Instead, it brought out my reserve energy, and the next time we got her turned around and astraddle a little creek.

About nine o'clock that evening the other ship from camp flew over, looking for us. They looked in the lake, but not in the blueberry bushes, and flew back toward camp.

"They'll be back," we said, in unison. We knew those boys.

Sure enough, an hour later, they returned. This time they saw us and landed.

With cushions we sat on the lakeshore waiting wind. Without it, neither plane could get out with passengers. We boiled a pot of tea, and told yarns.

Finally, wind came. Banks of the creek, which the plane straddled, were soft and marshy. With the extra help nudging it for a start, I walked her right down the creek and into the lake as easy as could be. By then the wind was making waves, and both of us climbed our aircraft out of there like scared cats.

I was at main camp one day, with three working parties out, when I saw a storm coming. I suggested to the boss I had better retrieve my men. He agreed, and I hustled them back to camp as fast as I could. By then the wind was blowing fifty miles an hour.

Another plane that worked from our camp was still out. Gene Effler, the pilot, had taken a work party to a distant lake with his Stinson Jr. Soon the Port Heiden radio reported wind blowing fifty-five miles an hour with gusts to sixty-five. It was dark, and raining hard.

Worried about the other plane, I told the boss I'd go look for it. I didn't know if I could bring the crew back, but I would try.

Light was sufficient for me to follow the shoreline; I could see the water surface, and wet mud. From the shoreline I had to fly eight miles across the tundra to the lake. I set a compass course and came out at the lake. I couldn't see much during those eight miles. I circled the lake but didn't see anything.

On my next circle, I spotted the floats of their airplane on the surface, in mid-lake. The airplane was submerged, upside down. On a third circle I saw flashes on the beach from a flashlight that had gotten wet, but still worked a bit. All three men were there, and looked ok.

The waves were very high, and I didn't know what was going to happen when I landed. After a few hard thumps by the waves on my floats, I was down. I faced the wind and eased the plane back to the beach where I picked up two of the men. The third fellow was Jack Chamberlain, a six-foot 200-pounder who had been a B-29 bomber pilot during World War II. He didn't have a very good opinion of bush pilots.

Chamberlain was amazed that I had arrived to pick them up. I said, "You stay right here. Don't leave this beach. I'll be right back for you."

"No you won't. You won't get back here tonight. I don't see how you managed to find us this time," he declared.

I repeated, "I'm coming back tonight to pick you up. Don't you leave this beach."

Everyone at the main camp was out to help with my plane when I landed, and with that wind, I needed all the help I could get.

I flew back, mostly in the dark, through a heavy rain and wind, picked Chamberlain up, and got him safely back to camp. It was so dark by then, I landed almost by feel.

Next morning Chamberlain shook my hand and said, "Thanks a lot. I've sure revised my opinion of bush pilots." I told him that was nice, that his opinion needed a little revising.

Talk about wind. That Alaska Peninsula country has it. September, with the fall winds, arrived, and a few of the parked aircraft of our operation were damaged. I filled the large float compartments on my plane with water to make it too heavy for the wind to lift. Nevertheless, winds backed the plane onto the tundra, sometimes as much as three plane lengths, but it was never damaged. The drawback, of course, was all the pumping I had to do to get rid of the water before I could fly anywhere.

So ended that season on the Alaska Peninsula. I regretted having to leave the big bears. I got well acquainted with a few of them—I knew where they hung out, what they looked like from the air, and enjoyed seeing them.

I flew back to Fairbanks via the beautiful Tikchik and Wood River Lakes, stopping at Stony River and McGrath to visit friends.

It was a good season.

Alaska Peninsula Bear Encounters

*Merely seeing them close, with their great bodies and their huge
imperturbability as they went about making a living, was
nothing if not pleasurable.* —SAM O. WHITE

THE LATE 1940s found me on the Alaska Peninsula, with my L5-G
Stinson under charter by the U.S. Coast and Geodetic Survey.

The work involved surveying and mapping that great wilderness, using the latest system of the time, setting up stations and
using lights to be instrument-read at night and deciphered by a
mathematical formula.

I had nothing to do with that highly technical operation. My
job, and it was full time and sometimes a touch more, involved flying the personnel where they needed to go, weather permitting.

The weather on the Alaska Peninsula is, putting it mildly,
capricious. Our work was centered at Port Heiden, a beautiful
spot when the sun shone.

This was the home of the great brown bears. I commonly saw three
to fifteen of these huge carnivores in a day's flying. Their deep-worn
trails ambled in every direction. It was their country and well they
knew it. We were the intruders and they furnished us plenty of work-
connected thrills. Merely seeing them close, with their great bodies
and their huge imperturbability as they went about making a living,
was nothing if not pleasurable. They were the grizzlies of Wyoming,
Montana and California, but darker colored and larger from a mil-
lennia of abundant living under more favorable conditions.

At Heiden, our center of flight operations, was a secluded lake,
big enough to allow heavily loaded take offs, and so located that
no matter from what quarter the wind, lift-off was no problem.

Our headquarters camp had been occupied by some branch of the military During World War II, possible a weather detachment. A warehouse had been built and left. We found it unoccupied and resoundingly empty.

We appropriated it for the storage of supplies and material. Our tents were pitched in the yard nearby, utilizing some of the wooden platforms left by former occupants.

Our dining room was a 10×12 waterproofed canvas tent. A second one allowed Louis Johnston, our culinary artist, to carry on his specialty without interference or discomfort. Louie was the man of the hour, being an unpretentious sourdough cook of broad mining/logging/construction camp experience. He had been to the top of a good many mountains and was unafraid of hoot owls and wolves, and asked nothing more than to be away from bright lights, skid row and the huddled masses. He was thoughtful, neighborly, and kind. He always managed to have a little booze stash to keep his liver functional, his gizzard active and his rheumatism in partial check. He was not slow to furnish a fellow sufferer a share of his precious and costly remedy should it be required.

At one of our spike camps at Black Lake, a shoulder of meat from a caribou I had knocked over for camp use soured during a spell of muggy weather, and was disposed of by being placed in a burlap sack and buried on the beach below camp. Foxes dug it up. The meat had merely ripened to their undiscriminating taste, and they ate it appreciatively. As evidence of gratitude and good faith, they left the sack lying limp but intact on the beach.

I reburied the sack, a little skeptical about what might ensue. Nor was I long in doubt. Next day the sack had been exhumed and left on top of the ground in its former position. I took a shovel to the site and re-buried it. While digging, I saw a mischievous cross fox grinning from nearby coarse marsh grass and sedges. I made out only his sharp features and laughing eyes, and I suspected additional mischief was even then in his planning stages.

I used an old Indian trick, and pretended not to see him, re-buried the sack as formerly, and, for his private pleasure, casually dropped a few scraps I had filched from the dining tent.

The sack was dug up again, and I was quick to note that the furry excavator draped it precisely over a certain bush each time. Our little game continued all the time we were at the lake camp. I developed a cross fox friend out of the incident. I would bury the gunny sack and put out a few fox tidbits where he could not fail to find them. To show his trust and gratitude, he repeatedly pawed up the sack, and left it at the same place every time.

There were foxes and mice, ducks, geese, swans, shorebirds, gulls, raucous loons and dabchicks, but the antics most impressive were furnished by the big brown bears engrossed in their day to day living. The dish-faced, hump-shouldered brutes were often seen near camp. We could hear their deep roars as they challenged, or simply bespoke, each other.

One big bruiser I especially remember was very dark. He sat himself comfortably on a little 300-foot distant knoll, and gave the camp a long, unhurried, survey. He eventually ambled on, having posed satisfactorily for the camera-armed personnel. Like any good neighbor, he proceeded about his business without making any trouble or disturbance.

Another bear mired down in the mud shoreline of the nearby bay at a minus tide. As the tide flooded, it raised his vast bulk by flotation, and he swam ashore. Only his great dignity had suffered.

Under normal conditions, at low tide the bay shore was exposed for a distance of several miles, and from one half to one mile wide. The receding salt-chuck exposed acres of shellfish, and tons of similar food common to the local ecosystem. Several bears commonly fed in tide pools for an hour or two, or until the tide turned.

During low tide, after the sea water had drained away, several gullies ten to twenty feet wide, and of variable depths came briefly to light. Here, apparently, was the tastiest concentration of hors d'oeuvres, where the bears did their happiest feeding.

I generally overflew these hodge-podges of bear activity at 300 feet or less, traveling to and from some light station my work required. Thus I had a grandstand seat for observing those great animals so happily engaged in surely their favorite pastime. It occurred to me, however, that the gullies might be a source of danger, should their unstable walls suddenly collapse and bury any unfortunate bear under tons of gooey mud. Could there be occasional casualties?

The answer almost banged me in the eye. Targeted in on the lake for a landing, I was paralleling one of those deep washes where a huge old boar, a regular feeder in the bay, was in the bottom, enjoying his evening meal.

Suddenly, both banks caved, almost simultaneously, and he was engulfed. I was not about to miss this conveniently arranged free lesson in natural history, so I circled and kept an eye on the cave-in. I circled once, twice, thrice, just above stalling speed, and if there was any sign of a mud-engulfed bear I failed to see it.

Just about the time I was about to congratulate myself on being a witness to a big brown bear having been done in by drowning, impact, and suffocation, a violent commotion erupted and a powerful set of huge, mucky shoulders emerged, dripping, into the daylight, treated themselves to a shake or two, clambered to a little firmer footing where the natural food arrangement had been untouched by the cave-in, and resumed feeding as though nothing had occurred to disturb the order of his day.

This graphic illustration made it clear that the bear loss by mudfall, submergence, and drowning was, in a word, negligible.

To enjoy another bearish episode, one must be aware of, and sympathize with the little known, lonely, profession of light keeping. In a surveying sense it requires being present at a certain predetermined spot, and making sure that a special light is shown at a certain time. Thus the surveyor working in connection, can sight his sensitive instrument on the exact spot and plot it suitably on paper. The end result is an accurate map.

Alaska Peninsula weather is notorious. Many were the days and working nights spent in the sack for the simple reason that it was impossible for the men to carry on with the work in a continual downpour. When a good night, weather-wise, came along, the poor, self-sacrificing light keeper was up on his mountainside, no matter how much of a struggle was required to get there, his lonely lighted beam aimed bravely toward the observing party sometimes miles away.

In many instances, it meant several lights beamed from several different locations in order to obtain optimum results. Other than rain, there was fog and miasmas to consider. After one good night of creditable accomplishment, the surveying personnel could look forward to several days of inactivity and boredom while the rain poured. All they had to do was eat, smoke, read, play cards, argue women, politics and jurisprudence and try to offset total time loss by doing sack time. Under these circumstances it was not surprising that these men developed a tendency for profound sleep.

In our party were two light-keepers who had to be hauled near their station by tracked land vehicle. I was told to check on them every flyable day. This was an easy task, as I had work parties beyond where they were located. I overflew their tent sometimes twice a day.

One morning, the weather being favorable, I was over their tent about 7:00 a.m. To no great surprise, time and location being what they were, I saw a very large mahogany-colored bear sniffing around the tent. It was startling to see how well he matched the height of the 9x9 tent, as he stood on widespread hind legs, front legs dangling.

No human activity was visible, so it became my duty to rid the place of the bear. I gave the monster a buzz as close as I dared, wringing every possible decibel of sound out of my revved up motor and flattened-pitch propeller.

The first overpass merely alerted the intruder to the fact he was no longer unobserved.

My second overpass was just above his bushel-sized head, and only inches beyond his considerable reach on tiptoe. The third buzz, which made the tent walls billow from the prop blast, was successful. Finally, the idea that not all people liked him must have penetrated, and he decided to seek the elsewhere I had desired.

I gave his belated decision a boost, harassing him until he was well over the hill and running, and even then I hung around to make sure a reverse decision did not send him back to the tent.

I then resumed my merry way, slightly annoyed at the time and aviation gas expended. What the dumb beast did not grasp was that his very bulk made him a sacred cow. No matter the strike or bite capability of the flying machine, even the merest contact with him would have resulted in a broken neck for the witless driver, and the plane metamorphosed into a strew of wreckage.

When the two light-keepers returned to main camp, I queried them about the early morning visitation of the big bear with seemingly a peeping-tom syndrome, and my concommitment buzz job.

Their mouths dropped open. "What bear? What buzz job?" they asked.

Oh well.

One of the young pilots on this job, call him a "Johnny Nitwit," was returning to camp at day's end after driving his highly maneuverable Piper PA18 on a re-supply mission. His competence in the air was commendable, but he was unable to distinguish the acceptable from the unacceptable in human-to-human conduct. The outcome was ludicrous, but only in a wry, grim way. It could as well have been the opposite.

As Nitwit neared camp, a big brown bear wandered into his view. He was ambling along, head swaying lazily, big feet in-turned, nothing on his mind but what a delectable supper he would wrest out on the tide flat. It isn't likely that the nearby tents or the human occupants concerned him.

For Johnny Nitwit, the twin-headed demon of Opportunity and Temptation climbed into his cockpit. Without even trying not to succumb, tickety-boo, he was off and running. With the discordant roar of his 150-hp Lycoming, he repeatedly dived at the wandering bear, working that great mass of fat and fur toward camp.

That bear was afraid of nothing on the tundra, but the airplane, full of sound and fury, was beyond his experience. He was quick to discover that if he maintained a bee-line toward the peaceful tent camp, he was harassed less than when he tried to deviate.

In the manner of a giant rabbit, his great clawed rear feet, overlapped his great clawed fore feet as he reached for distance. He ran full tilt, fleeing the noisy Piper. Soon his tongue was hanging out. He was putting his all into running, and trying to do more.

Those of us in the survey camp, aroused by the peculiar antics of the distant plane, admired the skill of the driver. However, soon, the purpose of his wild maneuvering was properly interpreted by even the least of the nimble-minded. The crew took action without the need of orders. The Commanding Officer was Newton A. Stewart, a captain in the Naval Reserve.

At the unexpected nearing of the lone, hairy, disheveled and angrified brown bear, the crew exploded with a sudden burst of activity. Adequate or not, a battle plan instantly developed. With .30-30 Winchesters in hand, men scurried up the warehouse fire ladders. One badly flustered crew member, never having previously been bear-menaced, dropped his weapon as he climbed. He didn't descend to retrieve it.

Meanwhile, having instigated this unseemly hullabaloo, Nitwit, no doubt laughing uproariously, veered off and sought his lakeside mooring location.

As the bear neared, Louie, our beloved culinary artist, decided suddenly to move from the cook tent, with its inadequate, thin walls, to the dormitory tent, with its identical thin, cloth walls, the protection of one as questionable as that of the other. Why he chose to switch is not for me to say. However, when he had previously left tent number two, as a matter of habit, he had tied the flaps securely against the constant wind. In his rush to get inside, he tried to wedge himself between the flaps without undoing ties. An impossibility. So, there was Louie, generous of girth and beam, stuck half way in, immobilized in the tent flaps, and vulnerable to the bear's ravages, should he decide to unleash them.

The bear arrived in camp. Captain Stewart and I stood frozen; we didn't dare move.

Realizing that the .30–30s were inadequate to deal with that angry mountain of flesh, and having sympathy for the poor bewildered creature so unceremoniously driven among us, Captain Stewart brought the scene under voice control. "Don't shoot," he ordered. So that there could be no mistake, he repeated it several times.

The bear passed within twenty feet of us, and being all steamed up, he smelled pretty strong.

Realizing he was no longer menaced by the big noisy bird, the bear took a few moments to recover his breath and his emotions, popped his teeth a few times to demonstrate what a big bad creature he could be, and sauntered off onto the tundra. He had paid Stewart and me no attention.

Had the bear's monstrous head sifted the facts and connected the humans on the ground with the lame-brained idiot in the flying machine, he might have declared instant and total war, and might even have gained the victory.

Within minutes, Captain Stewart was in radio contact with the Coast and Geodetic Survey headquarters. He must have spoken earnestly and very positively into the cold ear of the transmitter. When he came out of the radio shack he said confidentially to me, "There'll be no more of that damned foolishness. Sam, was that silly fool trying to get some of us killed?"

By the studiously quiet way he spoke, I knew he was still boiling inside, as was I.

From that day forward Johnny Nitwit was conspicuously absent. No one mourned the loss. I happily picked up the flying slack with my Stinson L5-G.

Flying to Utopia

Hughes, 9/1/62. Weather blotto blotto. Mail and two passengers for Utopia still undelivered.

—SAM O. WHITE. MEMO TO CHIEF BUSH PILOT RICHARD WIEN

[AUTHOR] AFTER BEING AN independent bush pilot from 1944, when he left Wien Airlines, Sam was rehired by the airline in 1955 and stationed at Hughes, where he distributed mail, freight, and passengers along the Koyukuk River with a Cessna 180. Scheduled flights of Wien mainliners (DC3s and F-27 Fairchilds) connected Hughes with Fairbanks in most of those years.

Utopia, known as Indian Mountain airfield on flight charts, was a trapping and mining area about thirty miles east of the Koyukuk River village of Hughes. A Cold War radar site was built there in the 1950s, and operated by the Air Force.

The FAA *Airport/Facility Directory* warns, "West end of runway at base of a cliff. Approach from east only. Successful go-around improbable. Winds in excess of 20 knots may produce severe turbulence."

The 4,100-foot airfield, lies at the steepest angle (to 12%) of any airport in Alaska.

[SAM] For seven years [1955–1962] I flew the U.S. mail, passengers, and freight to and from Utopia, a U.S. Air Force base in the Koyukuk Valley. The name wasn't appropriate from a small plane pilot's viewpoint. It had a one-way air strip that had been built years earlier by Mac McGee, who had a placer gold mining operation on nearby Indian River.

In the early days, because of the then ten to twelve percent slope, you parked your ship sideways at Utopia to prevent it from running downhill and into the Indian River. Later, a level parking area was constructed.

During the seven years, 1955-62, when Sam flew as a bush pilot from Hughes for Wien Airlines, the main airplane he used with a Cessna 180, shown here with Sam standing near.
SAM O. WHITE, COURTESY DRAHS

There was a surprisingly long list of hazards to overcome in landing at Utopia. The list seemed to grow with my every trip.

The strip could be approached from one direction only. A 4,000-foot mountain rose on the west end. It was bordered by ridges on both sides. On approach, an airplane was in a slot. There was a point of no return—you had no choice. Beyond that you *had* to put the airplane down.

Wind came from all points of the compass and buffeted an airplane as it flew into the slot, and continued to buffet all the way to ground contact. The field ran about east and west, and strangely, a south wind was the best. Since the field ran east and west a south wind logically should have been a crosswind. But it wasn't. By some freak of the perversity associated with this field, as a south wind crossed the south ridge bordering the field, it turned and swept right down the runway. I could handle this wind up to and including twenty-five knots. God be praised. Unfortunately, a south wind was the least common.

The northeast wind was the worst of the lot. It quartered on your left tail as you landed. I learned to handle this up to seventeen knots, and beyond that I did not experiment. I flew a Cessna 180 mostly, and in this wind I barreled in with half throttle, gradually reducing power to one fourth throttle to touch down. I touched down on the inside wheel, and held her there—and you better not bounce, not even a little. You held her down on the one wheel with the inside wing low to keep from drifting, and you gradually brought the other wheel into contact. At this juncture came the ticklish point of transferring control from air to ground. If you accomplished this without a disaster, you had it made.

There was also a northwest wind that posed its own hazards, but I soon learned how to handle it from various angles and at various velocities.

The black bear hazard at Utopia was at times nerve-wracking, though sometimes good for a belated laugh, while the frayed ends of my nerves quit vibrating. At times they were all over the runway. Sometimes the Air Force boys tried to drive them off, but bears don't drive any better than pigs; pigs have to be pulled against the desired direction of progress.

Some bigger bears stood their ground and popped their teeth. That discouraged trying to drive them off the runway.

One day I flew over the field and, as usual, checked it for bears, wind, and other hazards. I saw bears around the borders of the field, but there were none on the strip itself. I watched a six-by-six stake-body truck leave the buildings and head for the runway parking lot. It was loaded with about twenty GIs.

I made my approach and reached the point of no return, only to discover about all of the bears on Indian Mountain had converged on the strip and were scattered all over it. I was committed and had to continue. Somehow I had to get that airplane on the ground among the bears.

I saw a couple of sows with cubs. I envisioned hitting a cub and having an enraged mother digging into the wreckage of my plane to get at me.

I continued drifting in, hoping for an opening. But the opening didn't materialize. I touched the wheels just short of one big old sow, and bounced over her. I touched down again and bounced over a cub. When my bouncing was all done, a big old black-as-night boar ran in front of the airplane from my right. My brakes squealed and the bear disappeared behind the motor, and I braced for the shock, visualizing rending claws, torn metal, and popping teeth.

From the corner of my left eye I saw him exit from under the left wing. He was sure making time. How he ever got through the propeller and past the landing gear I will never know.

I glanced to the right and saw just opposite me the six-by-six truck. I taxied to the parking area and climbed out. The truck barged up and the GIs all whooped their excitement. Several had cameras, and wanted me to go back and bounce over some bears again.

The black bears at Utopia were brazen. I was once invited to a barbecue by the Air Force boys. The boxed spare ribs came to the barbecue pit in a pickup truck. When a GI jumped into the truck to hand the ribs to the cook, the box was empty.

About then one of the boys yelled, "Look," and pointed across the runway where four black bears were hightailing it for the brush. Each bear was carrying ribs it had filched while en route from storage to the barbecue pit. They had to have been in the bed of the truck when the driver left. He hadn't noticed them.

There was one other hazard on that strip that I didn't know about until it hit me between the horns. I was drifting down the slot for a touchdown, feeling safe. The day was hot and the sun was beating down like fury, and, I thought, not a breath of air was stirring.

All three wind socks (standard on this field, and which, because of the frequency of high winds, had to be replaced monthly) drooped limply.

As I got about 200 feet from touchdown, and fortunately through habit I was planning a wheel landing (instead of a three-point), I noticed a commotion in grass bordering the runway. Rocks and coarse gravel lay outside of the grass line. I had not seen this commotion sooner. It was a violent dust devil, and it was tying knots in the tall grass.

My passenger was an Air Force chaplain Lieutenant who had previously ridden with me.

The wind devil moved at right angles across the runway, and we were going to coincide with it. I aimed the plane's nose to hit it dead center, and lifted the tail a little higher. There was nothing else I could do.

When the whirling wind got under the airplane it boosted us straight up. I had just enough speed for rudder control, and a light amount of aileron control. The thing wanted to twist us around and head us into one of the ridges that paralleled the runway. When a wing wanted to drop I used full ailerons. I walked the rudder busily to keep lined up with the runway.

As we gained altitude, I firewalled the throttle and stuck the nose down. The prop was in low pitch and we started down nose-first. Half way to the ground I cut the throttle, and had just enough control to flare and make a good landing. I had barely enough room to stop while still on the parking area.

My passenger, as calmly as could be, said, "Well now, I'll be writing home about that one for the next two months."

Maybe he didn't know just how close that one was. I swear I distinctly saw a big black X when I looked through the windshield at the spot where we were going to hit. In all my years of flying that had never happened to me before, and it never did again. I had to handle it without experience.

Things worked my way that day.

The Early Bush Planes

Few, other than Sam, ever flew his Stinson L-5, as it was his pride and joy. If by chance you were invited to fly it, you could consider yourself as one of few—you had to be a special friend for that privilege.
—James L. (Andy) Anderson, bush pilot at Bettles Field, in letter to author, February, 2006.

To those of us who flew them, the early bush planes assumed the status of old friends, each with its own individuality. For all-around bush work I rated the Bellanca Ch-300[1] and Ch-400 as number one. Number two was the Travel Air[2] 6000B. Number three was the Fairchild 71.[3] Another pilot might rate them differently, but most experienced bush fliers of the time would probably rate all three of the above as among the tops.

Close runner-ups were the Stinson SM8A and the 1933 Stinson Junior. I never flew the SM8A, but other pilots praised it. The 1933 Stinson Junior had good performance and was an excellent four-place ship. After that model, Stinson built their planes a bit heavier, and added flaps. This resulted in a decrease in performance; nevertheless, they were still good bush airplanes.

Next came the Gullwing Stinson, a great favorite with passengers for it had comfortable seats, and was very stable. It was a good, rugged ship, but heavy. Very nice to fly, but a bit too low

---

1. The Bellanca six-passenger CH-300 or Pacemaker, appeared in 1929. Most had Wright J-6 engines of 300 h.p. The Senior Pacemaker, CH-400, had a Pratt & Whitney 420 h.p. Wasp.
2. The Travel Air 6000B cruised, with six passengers, at 110 mph, carried a payload of about 1,000 pounds.
3. First produced in late 1928, the Fairchild 71 had folding wings, cruised at 110 mph, and had a payload of 1400 pounds. Used a 400 to 450 h.p. Pratt & Whitney Wasp engine.

343

The year was 1966. Wien Airlines had a three-day job of hauling ten tons of freight from Alphabet Lake, forty miles to Ruby. Jim Dodson flew the Bellanca (aloft), Noel Wien flew the Wasp-powered Fairchild 71. Some tractor parts, disassembled, weighed 800 pounds or more. What appears to be tractor treads can be seen in the door of the Fairchild. Photo is signed, "Best to Sam White. Noel Wien."
NOEL WIEN, COURTESY DRAHS

on performance on bush fields. It had vacuum-actuated flaps, and once a pilot got used to them, performance improved; on takeoff, roll the wheels down to the last inch of the field and pop the flaps. This boosted the old girl off the ground almost straight up for fifty feet. But that was as high as you went until you had bled off a few angles on the flaps. And don't make the mistake of dumping the flaps, or you speedily found yourself back on the ground.

The Bellancas were all airfoil. The fuselage was an airfoil and lifted its own weight and the weight of the engine. The lift struts carried their weight, and likely a bit extra. Bellanca wings were long and wide, with a high-lift airfoil. There were no flaps; none needed.

Bellancas were rugged, with the finest of workmanship—thoroughbreds from tailpost to engine mount. In competent hands this ship with a Pratt Whitney Wasp Junior engine hanging on the nose was the ultimate in safety. It would pack a terrific load, and fly just right with it.

Sam White's favorite bush plane, a Bellanca CH400, with mechanics.
SAM O. WHITE, COURTESY DRAHS

If the motor quit at a couple thousand feet, you could glide around a bit and take a little time to select a landing place. If you kept water out of the carburetor, with a Wasp Junior there was little chance the motor would quit.

Pilots new to a Bellanca had a tendency to overshoot landings. Those planes would float, even with a big load. Once a pilot was accustomed to this, he did his floating on the approach, and when passing over the last stump, he pulled the nose up and it would sit down gracefully.

The Travel Air had a long fuselage with lots of room; so much room in fact that it was easy to load too heavily toward the tail. It was a good performer, and handled well in deep snow on skis. Also, like the Bellancas, it was a good float plane.

Travel Air 6000B NC9844 had the typical instrument and controls of the planes of those days. Included on the panel were oil temperature and pressure gauges, head temperature, compass, altimeter, air speed, and bank and turn. And, of course the throttle, mixture, and carburetor heat controls. Gasoline gauges were in the wing butts. Master fuse and battery were under the pilot's seat. Gas tank selector valves were to the left of the pilot's seat on the wall.

The Lear T30 radio seldom worked because the generator usually quit working soon after leaving town, and the battery went to hell fast, which resulted in radio silence and hand-propping the engine.

The steel or fuselage frames of all of these old ships were magnetized, and compasses didn't work. It was no use to demagnetize them; the first solid bump the plane received afterward caused the magnetism to return. There was no de-magnetizing equipment in Alaska.

The only compass we could make work was a remote control unit with the elements in the wingtip, and this was beyond our patience to install in those days.

The Fairchild 71 had a little heavier wing loading and a narrower chord. But they were built for work. They flew easily and precisely, and were the work horses of the North Country. They took off with a rush and landed about the same. Even so, they were good performers for tight places, and were excellent on floats.

These were some of the tools the old bush pilots worked with, and those with which I was familiar. They were first class tools,

Sam O. White (left) and Noel Wien with a Fairchild 71 at Weeks Field, probably in the early 1940s. Airplane in background is a Stinson. The photo is signed "To a real pioneer, my best wishes, to Sam White. Noel Wien." Noel Wien, courtesy DRAHS

too. We were faced with a lot of short, rough runways, and often, too heavy loads. We *had* to know how our aircraft performed under a wide variety of circumstances.

I remember seeing a few take offs by other pilots that seemed to me the ultimate in skill. Once, in the dead of winter, I saw Noel Wien take off at the Crows Nest on the Chandalar River in a very narrow and short lagoon. Flying a Bellanca Ch-400, he had to cope with shoulder-deep snow that was as light as feathers.

The ship wallowed down to the take off point like a thing alive, turned, and climbed gracefully to the top of the snow, and soon took to the air. It was the most beautiful take off I have ever witnessed. No other Alaska pilot I have known could have exceeded the skill needed for that performance.

Another take off that impressed me was made by Johnny Lynn at Fort Yukon one summer. The old field there had a lagoon at one end, and a slough at the other, with high timber just across the narrow slough. Johnny was flying a Cessna Airmaster. I watched him segregate his load for proper weight and balance. He had two passengers. He put the heaviest in front, the lightest in the rear.

He used every inch of the runway, didn't pull the ship off abruptly, but skimmed over the water to pick up speed, and climbed gently over the trees—an impressive display of skill.

I don't suppose Noel or Johnny would remember these instances. In both take offs, these men knew as soon as they started precisely where they would lift off, and at what angle they would climb out.

Winter flying in the early years was complicated by the need for heating an aircraft's motor for an hour or more before it could be started. We had a canvas cover tailored to fit an airplane to direct heat to the engine from an old-fashioned gasoline-burning plumber's pot that we sat beneath the engine. While the heater was burning, one had to remain close to prevent wind from blowing the canvas, catching fire, and spreading the fire to the plane. With short daylight hours, if you planned to fly, it was common to heat your engine in the dark, hoping to be ready to take off by daylight.

One winter day at Fairbanks when it was 40 below, I planned to fly down the Yukon River. I was at Weeks Field for an early start. So was one of our better and famous pilots, who flew a Bach, a cumbersome-looking airplane.

I was parked with a Stinson Junior in a corner of the field, directly behind the Bach. Both of our planes were on skis. The

*Sam's L-5G with an aluminum boat he flew from the Koyukuk River
into his "moose pasture" lake.* Sam O. White, courtesy DRAHS

Bach's owner warmed his engine with a plumber's pot as I draped
the Stinson's engine with canvas plus a sleeping bag, fired up my
plumber's pot, and stood by for an hour or so waiting for the heat
to liquefy the engine oil in my Stinson.

His engine warm, the owner fired up his Bach and blasted away
with power, but his skis were frozen down. He couldn't move. In
a matter of minutes I could have chinned myself on my prop; the
blast from the Bach blew right onto my motor, chilling it back
down to the air temperature. Even the canvas cover couldn't keep
the icy blast out.

While a crew jacked up the Bach's skis one at a time to clean the
bottoms, I reheated my motor, and re-covered it to hold the heat.

Again, the Bach blasted away and refused to move. The icy blast
immediately cooled my engine, and, again, I could have done gym-
nastics on my prop without it budging. That's no exaggeration.

I gave up any thought of going anywhere that day, and helped
get the Bach into the air. We ended using a tractor to drag the big
awkward thing to the end of the runway.

That didn't do it either, so we jacked the skis up again, cleaned
them good, and at last the Bach took to the air and was gone.

The next day was good enough for me anyway. We did have fun pampering the old Bach.

Before the advent of the Bellancas, Fairchilds, Stinsons, and other cabin planes, there were the open cockpit models. The most prominent were Jennies, Standards, Swallows and Wacos—airplanes on which Alaska pilots cut their teeth. Pilots flew them summer and winter with passengers and light freight. In winter, pilots and passengers were, of course, swathed in clothing.

One would think that passenger fares of that day would have been prohibitive. Such was not the case. It was actually the cheapest way to go.

Travel by dog team, the only winter alternative, was just as expensive. One had to add roadhouse costs for perhaps two or three weeks. Also riding a dog sled in the numbing cold wasn't much different from the discomfort of an open cockpit. Generally, the cockpit wasn't as bumpy.

In summer, travelers could go by boat, but the cost in time—commonly weeks compared to hours in an airplane—for miners, at least, cut into an already short working season. Air travel helped to extend the working season for miners, and offered greater convenience to trappers in remote areas. To go by air was the ticket, and Alaskans grasped it immediately. Air fare was insignificant when compared with other transportation methods which knocked big hunks from a productive season.

I owned two of the old open-cockpit airplanes. The first, a Bone Golden Eagle, was so inadequate that I hardly had time to get frozen in it before I got rid of it, and bought a PT Swallow biplane (Curtiss Primary Trainer Swallow).

[AUTHOR'S NOTE: In 1931 when Sam bought his PT Swallow, built at Wichita, Kansas, its welded steel tubing covered with fabric was considered the latest and best airplane construction.]

At 35 degrees below zero, three hours was just about all I could take in it, regardless how many clothes I wore. The Swallow's fuel tank, an extension of the front cockpit, was directly over the passenger's feet and shins.

Some of the other early biplanes had the same feature. I once overheard a pilot complain that the tank was leaking gas on his shins and it made them cold. Next, I saw a mechanic on his back in the cockpit, feet hanging over the edge, with a cloud of vapor sizzling up from the tank. He successfully soldered the leak, and

Early bush pilots at Fairbanks included (left to right) Noel Wien, Sig Wien, Herman Lerdahl, Noris Johnson, Herman Joslyn.
NOEL WIEN, COURTESY DRAHS

no one at that stage of aviation thought anything of it. [AUTHOR: Today the tank would be removed, drained, filled with non-explosive gas, and only then repaired.]

Another not-so-unusual instance in those years was a runaway plane. Early planes didn't have self-starters; they were started by someone (often the pilot) swinging the prop. I recall seeing at Fairbanks a pilot prop his plane, and having it start with a roar because the throttle had been set too fast. It jumped the chocks and started to wander around the field. Several men chased it. Pilot Harold Gillam, passing by, caught and bulldogged it down. Had he not, there soon would have been parts strewn about from parked airplanes.

One of the first flying suits I wore while flying the Swallow in winter was a one-piece cover-all made of caribou skin tanned hair on. Caribou hair is brittle, and the suit constantly shed. That suit caused two forced landings; the first time a wad of hair was caught in an oil line; the second time a wad of hair was in the gas line.

I didn't wait for the third time.

I gave the suit to a smaller man for a sleeping bag. I bought six Italian-surplus sheepskin overcoats that had been made for the military Alpini of World War I. I had one good suit made from them. It was easer to get into and out of than the caribou skins, but the old limitation still held; three hours at 35 below was all I could take.

There were, of course, other makes of aircraft used in Interior Alaska in the early years, both open cockpit, and closed cabin types.[4] The Stearman open cockpit plane was a hot little number. The Curtiss Robin and Thrush were good cabin planes.

Stepping up to larger and heavier work planes, the American Pilgrim, and the Noorduyn Norseman were both good. I flew a Pilgrim with a Pratt-Whitney Hornet engine. Either the engine, or the prop, was so rough that the airplane vibrated the end of my nose and made me sneeze, a poor situation while landing. I solved the problem by putting a strip of tape from cheek to cheek across my nose.

WHEN CARS WERE BECOMING more common in the early days of Weeks Field, it was a convenient place for old-timers who had never driven to learn the intricacies of shifting gears, steering, and all of that. It was common to see some old-timer slowly driving around and around the field. Some couldn't coordinate shifting, and drove in low gear, or second, or got stuck in high gear. Automatic transmissions were yet to appear.

When a plane arrived to land, the pilot buzzed the field, sometimes two or three times, before the old-timer in the car or cars would give way.

In 1925 an airplane, with a pilot and a lady passenger, fell into some cottonwood saplings near Weeks Field, breaking the airplane.

Jake Marks, a local tailor, known by his newspaper ads as "Two Pants Jake," explained the crash, saying, "He shifted gears too quick."

Perhaps Jake was one of those learning to drive on Weeks Field.

---

4. When early pilots switched from open cockpits to cabin planes, they at first complained, "I can't see out." It didn't take long for them to adjust.

Les and Pat James, Hughes Traders

*I think Sam did most of his writing during the seven years he was
stationed at Hughes for Wien Airlines. He was sometimes grounded for
days due to weather, and had very little to do. I stayed there several
times during those years. After supper, Sam disappeared upstairs and
we heard his old typewriter clicking away.*
—JIM KING, IN A NOTE TO THE AUTHOR, MAY, 2006.

FOR SEVEN YEARS (1955-62) I was stationed at Hughes, a village
on the Koyukuk River, flying for Wien Airlines, distributing mail,
freight, and passengers to surrounding villages.

I first saw Hughes in February, 1932, while bundled up trying
to stay warm in the cockpit of my Swallow biplane, and flying
down the frozen, winding Koyukuk River. A blizzard was in
progress, visibility was limited, and growing worse. I stayed low
to keep the river in sight.

Hughes was a cluster of fifteen to twenty cabins on the left
riverbank. Smoke came from only one cabin, and the village had
a deserted look. I circled, preparing to land, but couldn't see the
river's snowy surface. A man, wearing a distinctive red checked
shirt, left the cabin with the smoking stove pipe and walked to
the river's edge.

I set up for a landing, using the checked shirt for a reference.
I made a gentle touch-down and taxied near the man and shut
her down.

Half frozen, I awkwardly climbed out of the rear cockpit. The
checked shirt was worn by Gus Wagner, who I had known for years.
All the Natives were away on their traplines, and he was the only
man there. Gus was acting as caretaker for trader George Light, who

was in Anchorage on business. No locks and keys were needed on the Koyukuk in those days, and well-stocked warehouses and stores were left open. Gus kept a few items from freezing, and saw to it that weather didn't damage anything at the trading post.

Gus had been a cook for the popular Model Cafe in Fairbanks. Anyone who cooked for the Model was a good cook.

The blizzard raged for several days, holding me in Hughes. That gave Gus an excuse to cook. He baked pies, cakes, dough-nuts, and moose roasts. During that blizzard I must have put on several pounds.

The following winter, around Christmas, I again landed at Hughes, and found trader George Light there. He was in bad health. I tried to talk him into flying to Tanana with me to see a doctor. He refused because he was waiting for the local Indian trappers to bring in the Christmas holiday fur. I stayed overnight, and aided him as much as I could.

After that, I often landed at Hughes and became acquainted with its Native population. In the summer I landed on a nearby river bar, as at the time there was no runway at Hughes. Later, when I flew float planes, I landed on the river.

The next trader to arrive was Les F. James and his wife Esther, commonly called Pat. They bought out trader George Light in December, 1938. In 1939, with Native help, Les built, with logs, a picturesque new trading post and roadhouse. Huge overhead log beams spanned the building from wall to wall.

Leslie F. James was born in Ellsburg, Missouri in 1883. He and Pat came to Alaska in 1935, and Les first worked as a drag-line operator for mine owner Dave Strandberg at Folger, Alaska. One winter he worked repairing aircraft in the old Star Airlines hangar at Anchorage.

The James' trading post was heated by a large drum heater, which took four-foot lengths of firewood. The building was wired for electricity. At first there was a gasoline generator; later, as the place prospered, two Witte diesel generators were added. These served for several years, but then Les, ever progressive, began to distribute electricity in the village. With just about the entire vil-lage electrified, a power house was built that contained two Hill diesels and a Caterpillar light plant.

A schoolhouse was built, and eventually, as the village grew, Hughes became a regular stop on the Wien Airline main line route, plus a distributing point for the surrounding bush. The James'-built runway was then big enough to handle small airliners.

Hughes was [and probably still is] one of the neatest villages in Interior Alaska. The local residents' log cabins were in precise rows, and kept in good shape. The villagers were proud of themselves and their surroundings.

The trading post/roadhouse included accommodations for travelers. I found it a great place to weather storms. If I was flying a mail run from Fairbanks, or elsewhere, and got sealed into the Koyukuk Valley, I headed for Hughes to sweat out weather there. I was assured of good food, a warm dry place to sleep, plus loads of fun.

In 1942 Les acquired a riverboat, and for the next three years he hauled freight from the Yukon River, up the Koyukuk River, to Hughes for both the trading post and village. During this period the James' bought a D-4 Caterpillar tractor with a blade, and started to build an airport runway at Hughes. The first step was to move all the Natives' log cabins back away from the river. Next, they sacrificed their garden patch, which became part of the runway. A stand of large, tall, cottonwoods was also removed.

At first the runway was a thousand feet long, with cottonwood trees on both sides. It was like landing in a huge shed with both ends knocked out, for the trees nearly met overhead.

They acquired a Stinson Station Wagon, with which their son Johnny James, a proficient pilot, flew goods to the trading post. In the meantime, bit by bit, year by year, they extended the length of their airport.

It was a comfort for bush pilots when the James' installed a radio. We could then get the weather (most important), and pilots could tell Mrs. James how to cut the pie, depending upon the number of passengers we had. Four pieces was the acknowledged minimum. More passengers called for another pie.

Steve Miskoff, one of the Wien pilots, made tickets that read, "Ticket good for one piece of pie at the Hughes Trading post."

Esther "Pat" James was long a regular radio operator for Wien Airlines, and a very efficient one. Her musical voice carried exceedingly well over the air, and she was always on hand for emergencies. She was an expert at deciphering garbled messages. This saved the day for many an accident victim, or those stricken with illness in some remote place.

A night spent at the James' was always enjoyable. Mice were abundant at Hughes, which called for a number of cats at the trading post. They had free roaming privileges. I sometimes spent evenings making houses out of Hills Bros coffee cartons for the cats to play in. The kittens loved them. They sped through the many openings I had cut, while others lay in wait and pounced on the runners. Sometimes they moved so fast it was hard to tell if they had gone through a box, or around it.

Among the cats was Scooter, a big black and white tom. I've watched him lay in wait on one of the local caches, and with a terrific yowl drop on the head of an unsuspecting dog, dig in his claws, and hang on.

The dog would take off with a dismal howl, with Scooter riding. That cat knew how far to push this dangerous pastime, for most of the dogs in Hughes were big sled dogs. Old Scooter would drop off the fleeing dog, and before the dog could gather his wits, the wily cat would climb another cache and be out of reach.

Scooter lived to the ripe old age of twenty-two. I think I saw the last bird he ever caught; he was so proud of it that he brought it to my room. I rubbed behind his ears, scratched his belly. He then sat and ate the bird.

I spent many evenings watching Les grade furs, giving every owner a square deal. I also watched him put up orders for families who were on traplines. He always threw in an extra free treat for the children.

Early on, Les installed a sawmill capable of producing planks, squared timbers and, of course, boards. He also had a planer with which to finish the lumber. A power take-off on the D4 Caterpillar ran the mill.

Window sashes in the upstairs rooms were hand-made by Les. They were professional quality, and as good as any that could be purchased at a lumber yard.

Few men have the skills of a Les James. He was an operator of heavy duty machinery, adept with bulldozers and draglines. He "walked" [drove] a dragline from Hughes, across Indian Mountain to the head of Indian River, a distance of about twenty miles. In so doing he traversed cliffs, sidehills, climbed steep hills, and finally took the machine over the crest of Indian mountain. I often flew over the trail he followed and, looking down on it, wondered how he had accomplished such a stupendous task.

Les was generous, and loved Alaska, especially the Koyukuk country. He once chartered a Wien Airlines Fairchild F-27 propjet airliner in winter to give the University of North Dakota basketball team (his home state was North Dakota) who were playing in Fairbanks, some perspective on Alaska. The plane flew from Fairbanks, over Hughes, and along the Koyukuk River. "Those kids cannot get any idea of Alaska by visiting Fairbanks," he said.

Les also loved Alaska's wildlife—the moose, caribou, and other critters. He was greatly disturbed during one winter when wolves were so abundant they killed about eighty-five percent of the moose along the Koyukuk.

Les often asked me what I was seeing in the way of wildlife on my various flights. He was an ardent fisherman and loved to angle for the big shee fish that run up the Koyukuk to Hughes and points north.

In November, 1966, fire destroyed the living quarters, the trading post, the power house, and all but two warehouses of the trading post.

All were rebuilt on the old site, bigger and better.

Les James passed away in the spring of 1968 at the age of 84. It was a great loss to the Koyukuk country and Alaska. He was a leading citizen, and a great builder.

Sam and the Wien Family

Dear Richard:
You and I are kindred spirits. We like the wide open spaces. I
wouldn't swap places with the automatons on the Outside for all the
coffee in Brazil. In my visits Outside I have been asked, "How can
you spend your life in such a desolate country?"
To my notion there is no such thing as desolate country in Alaska.
The forests are full of beauty, the tundra has its majestic beauty, the
lakes, the rivers, and the mountains and valleys all have beauty be-
stowed on them by God.
They are all peopled by wild animals who are self sufficient in
their own right. When man comes along with his "improvements" and
makes trails, rustic bridges over trickles of water, benches for people to
rest on, his chest expands and his head gets bigger and he fancies that
he has made a great improvement on the original. Phooie says I. I like
it the way it was in the beginning.
—SAM O. WHITE. LETTER TO RICHARD WIEN, JANUARY 16, 1956.

[AUTHOR] IN AUGUST, 1924, pioneer pilot Noel Wien attempted
to fly a mining engineer named Ingram and his woman secretary,
Billie Hart, from Fairbanks to the Kantishna country. Bad weather
forced him back to Nenana, where the party spent the night.

Sam was also in Nenana at the time. It was the first meeting of
Sam O. White and Noel Wien.

Forty years later Sam remembered that meeting, and even the
names of Noel's passengers. The efficiency of air travel, plus the pilot's
relaxed and friendly demeanor, planted a seed in his mind.

In 1925 Sam flew as a passenger with Noel Wien to Bettles,
and perhaps elsewhere. Fairbanks was a small town where almost
everyone was acquainted. Sam and Noel became firm friends, a

relationship that continued as long as Sam lived, and eventually extended to the entire Wien family.

When Sam left his Wildlife Agent job in 1941, Noel hired him as Wien Airline's Chief Pilot almost before Sam's resignation signature had dried. In 1955, when jobs for Sam as an independent bush pilot had partially dried up, Noel found the perfect niche for him as a Wien Airline pilot stationed at Hughes. There he remained for seven years.

Sam and Mary had lived at 902 Kellum Street for several years when Noel Wien built a new home directly across the street, also on Kellum. In May, 2006, Richard Wien talked to me about Sam.

"It wasn't long before the three of us Wien kids [Richard,

Richard Wien at Bettles, September, 1955. He was learning the ropes of bush flying with help from pilot James L. "Andy" Anderson who pioneered the scheduled routes from Bettles for Wien Airlines. AUTHOR

born July, 1935; Merrill, born April, 1930; and Jean, born Jan. 1933] were at Sam's house much of the time. He was like an uncle and part of the family. In a way, he became kind of a second father," Richard remembered.

"I remember riding on his back on his lawn, and sitting on him as he played with us. He was so generous. He always gave us ginger ale, which he loved, and always had on hand. An indelible memory is Sam's booming voice. We loved Sam. Couldn't help it.

"As a little kid I once arrived at Sam's before breakfast. He cooked bacon and eggs for me. My mother became upset when I arrived home and she had my breakfast ready. I think Sam liked to tease my Mom. Of course she dearly loved Sam like everybody did, but sometimes she became upset at the things he did.

"Sam was principled in so many ways. Right was right and wrong was wrong, and when you knew him, this became very clear. He was a great role model, not only to us Wien kids, but to numerous other young people. In recent years I've encountered a number of Fairbanks men, who, as youngsters, regularly visited and were influenced by him. Several have commented to the effect, 'Sam White, beside my dad, was probably the most influential person in my life.'

"Of course he was an accomplished woodsman and pilot, and a great story teller.

"Even today, thirty years after his death, when faced with a moral problem, I find myself thinking, "What would Sam think about this?

"Sam's philosophy that things are not as important as people, and his scrupulous honesty, made him a wonderful role model.

"Mary, Sam's wife, was always pleasant and, like Sam, very generous. She always greeted us, and then she might wander off into her own room, or she might sit and knit or crochet and listen as Sam told his stories.

"Sam had two major accidents that resulted in serious injury. The first was when his airplane's skis both broke loose while in flight. They pointed straight down, making a safe landing just about impossible.

"He crashed on the Circle City airport with his plane's throttle wide open," Richard remembered. "It was an astonishing feat for him to survive. I was there when my Dad arrived back in Fairbanks with him in the Travel Air. I was still pretty young, but I remember him lying on his cot in his living room as his broken bones healed. During those weeks I often went to see how he was doing."

"I remember Sam's other major accident even more vividly," Richard told me. "I was nearly 15, and old enough to know how serious it was.

"It happened in the winter of 1950 at his cabin at Ruby. The temperature was forty below. Sam filled his Coleman pressure lantern with fuel that was stored outside. He pumped the lantern up, and hung it overhead in the warm cabin. As the cold fuel warmed it expanded. The lantern couldn't handle the pressure and it exploded. Sam was sprayed with burning gasoline.

"He wore long underwear, which probably saved his life. He sustained severe burns on his hands, and head from the neck up. His only memory of the incident was scrambling on hands and knees from the cabin.

"An emergency radio message reached Fairbanks. Sam

wanted Noel to pick him up. He didn't want anyone else (he had also asked for Noel when he crashed at Circle City). With a Cessna 170, Noel flew to Ruby, despite the forty below zero temperature, confirming the bush pilot's adage that emergency flights (the newspapers call 'em mercy flights) always seem to come during tough weather.

"Merrill and I were at Weeks Field when our Dad landed with Sam. His burns were horrific, and I can hardly stand to think about it even today. We were absolutely crushed.

"We visited him in the hospital. Both Merrill and I thought we could deal with it, but we couldn't. Sam's hands looked as if he was wearing two big gloves."[1]

Sam went to a burn center near Seattle for skin grafts. On his return he spent about a month in the Fairbanks hospital. Without use of his hands he could do nothing to help himself. His wife, Mary, did much of the required nursing for him.

"The burns changed Sam. He never fully recovered. His face healed well, but he never again had a strong grip," Richard said. "I went to see him almost every day during his recovery at home. He squeezed rubber balls to regain hand strength, but it took months before his hands were strong enough even to hold the control stick of an airplane," Richard remembered.

Richard and Merrill both became professional pilots like their father. Merrill, five years Richard's senior, became Chief Pilot for Wien Airlines. Richard became Chief Bush Pilot for the airline. While Sam was stationed at the Koyukuk River village of Hughes for the airline, he was under Richard's authority.

Richard, as well as other interior pilots, was much influenced by Sam's insistence on flying with adequate emergency gear to be safe, and even comfortable, if forced down.

"If Sam goes down he wasn't going to just survive—he planned to enjoy life," bush pilot Rudy Billberg once said.

Richard remembered, "Sam drilled into us to carry a tent and wood-burning stove in our airplanes. He made many stoves out of five-gallon kerosene cans (which had heavier gauge metal than five-gallon gas cans) and gave them to Merrill and me, and to other pilots who were his friends. He had tents made that were about six by six

---

1. Sam's hands were still bandaged and recovering from the burns when I first met him in July, 1950. AUTHOR

A gasoline-burning plumber's pot used to heat aircraft engines during winter sits atop a wood-burning stove made for Richard Wien by Sam O. White. Inside bottom of stove is lined with asbestos. A telescoping stovepipe is used, and a 6×6-foot emergency tent folds to fit inside the stove. Stove and tent provide emergency shelter and heat, and are carried in an airplane in the event of a forced landing in a remote area. Author

feet. They folded to fit inside the stoves. The stoves had telescoping stove pipes.

"Sam could probably set up one of those tents and stoves in his sleep. He once made us watch how he did it. It was and is a slick, simple, and important survival tool.

"When Sam flew, if anything prevented him from reaching where he was bound, he commonly landed, pitched a tent for the night, and, in winter, firepotted his plane when ready to leave. He was at home in the bush, and it didn't matter to him where he was. Few pilots then, and fewer today, are so well prepared or as capable.

"To this day, I feel pretty naked flying in winter without a stove and a tent, and I have influenced other pilots on this. Thus, Sam's influence is still felt today in Interior Alaska's flying circles," Richard commented.

Sam was so close to the Noel Wiens that he regarded them almost as his family. He would have done anything in his power to help them.

In August, 2006, Merrill remembered, "I ferried Sam's L-5 back and forth from Hughes several times. Once I was putting the battery in his airplane at the float pond in Fairbanks with the help of Doug Millard, and I did what you are not supposed to do—I connected the negative terminal to the battery before the positive terminal.

"When I hooked up the positive terminal, I touched the fuel line from the overhead fuel tank with the end of a wrench and it melted a hole through the copper line and created a flaming stream of fuel on to the fabric belly.

"We thought we were going to lose the airplane until Dave

Yackle, nearby, who saw what was happening, got a big rag from his pickup, dowsed it in the water and threw it to me. 'Wrap it around the fuel line,' he called.

"Every time I had tried to stop the fuel, of course I had been burned. That wet rag solved the problem and we saved the airplane.

"When Sam found out about it he was very upset that I was burned, even a little, and said he wished I had just let it burn. That airplane represented most of his net worth. After he sold the airplane, the new owner duplicated my action with the battery, and he wasn't able to save the airplane."

> *Fairbanks, 6-5-67*
> *Dear Richard and Merrill: Well, N40013 burned to the ground yesterday. Sure feel sorry for the guys that bought it. Same deal as you had Merrill. Tool handle from battery to gas line. I never thought it would happen again.*
> *Sincerely,*
> *Sam*

Merrill also remembered, "Sam let me use his only car to go to Ladd Air Force base [near Fairbanks] after I was drafted, and he walked where he had to go. All through my military experience, he wrote me letters of encouragement and advice on how to deal with the stress of military life, and how proud he was of me."

Merrill added, "Mary White helped me with my homework many a night after school. And I often remember Sam's baked bean roasts he did every year where it was cooked in a hole in his back yard and he invited all his friends. They tasted so good. And all the genuine pure maple syrup he had shipped from Maine to give to friends."

Once, when Richard was struggling financially, Sam learned about it:

> *Hughes, July 7, 1961.*
> *Richard: This is between you and me. I got a couple of thousand in the bank that ain't working and is immediately available. If you need it to hang on with until some fires start, let me know. No interest and no sweat. Your Pal, Sam.*

Richard and Merrill formed Merric, Inc., a helicopter and air taxi service at Fairbanks. The nineteen-foot-long tail boom on one of their helicopters was damaged while on contract with the Bear Creek Mining Company near the village of Kobuk. To replace it, they pulled the boom from a helicopter at Fairbanks and flew it in a C-46 to Hughes. Sam agreed to fly it with his L5-G Stinson the 100 miles or so from Hughes to Kobuk.

"Sam was getting up in years, and his old Stinson didn't have a lot of power compared to modern planes. We had to strap the boom on the floats with the blunt nose forward. It was a real wind catcher," Richard remembered.

"This was a big deal for Sam—very iffy. But he was willing to give it his best. He requested, 'You fly with me, and stay close.' This I promised to do.

"After a long take off run, Sam lifted off the river at Hughes and staggered over the trees toward Kobuk. I flew beside him with a Beechcraft Bonanza. It's a fast airplane, and the struggling L-5 was barely doing eighty mph. I zigzagged, and flew just above stalling speed to stay close, where Sam could see me.

"Near Kobuk, I flew ahead to land so I could run down to the river to help him. Sam didn't appreciate that. He gave me the worst chewing out I ever had from him. 'You went off and left me, and I told you to stay with me," he roared.

"Sam saved us. We had a contract to fill, and getting that boom to Kobuk was the only way we could do so. It was a real adventure for us, and, of course, for Sam too. He was proud of the way his old airplane handled that awkward load," Richard remembered.

Sam found a small lake, big enough for landing his float L-5 Near the Yukon River, south of Indian Mountain. He flew lumber there and built a shack. Until he quit hunting in his old age, that's where he annually killed a bull moose, his and Mary's winter meat. He referred to the place as his "Moose Pasture," or "Mud Hole." Others called it "Sam's Lake."

Richard remembered, "He always wanted Noel, Merrill and me to go hunting with him there. Once we were all there, sitting around a campfire yarning, when we heard a loud splashing in the lake.

"There's a moose," Sam said.

"I jumped up to go look. I tripped and fell over some wire and several empty five-gallon cans. It made a terrible racket," Richard remembered.

"Oh man, I really did it," I thought.

"Sam just laughed, but he never let me forget. After that he occasionally referred to the "Haywire Moose Camp.""

Hughes, 6-20-60
Dear Noel: What I saw at the Mud Hole would do your heart good. Two moose were in the west meadow feeding happily. Three huge old behemoths were in the east meadow by camp. They moved over and gave me room to beach, and went on feeding.

Later, others came in, fed, and left. I sat on a gas box in the meadow in plain sight surrounded by hordes of vicious push flies, and just enjoyed the whole show.

See you all this fall, Sam

According to Richard, "The camaraderie between Noel and Sam was special. You didn't say anything against Noel Wien around Sam White. If you did, you might get yourself decked. Likewise, my dad loved Sam, and would do anything for him."

In the spring of 1938, Noel landed his Ford Tri-Motor (the largest airplane then in Interior Alaska) on wheels on the ice of Harding Lake, about forty miles southeast of Fairbanks. He replaced the wheels with skis, loaded twelve passengers and freight, and started to taxi across the lake.

The ice was three feet thick, but during winter an earthquake had created a crack. In and near it ice was weakened and soft from recent sunny days. Fresh snow concealed the crack. Noel taxied into it, and the Tri-Motor dropped into it.

The wings and tail rested on firm ice, preventing it from sinking in forty feet of water. The passengers stepped out onto the ice without anyone getting wet. Noel and his copilot escaped through an overhead door in the pilot's compartment.

"My mother (Ada) called Sam White and other friends, asking for help," Richard told me. "To rescue the plane, fourteen men worked five days and nights next to that hole in the ice, using tripods, cables, winches, and heavy timbers. My mother credited Sam for doing much of the organizing and the work," Richard recounted.

Sam's position for Wien Airlines at Hughes ended after seven years. "Sam earned his way for Wien at Hughes," Richard said. "It was the perfect set up for him at first. He had an intimate knowledge of the Koyukuk region from his Wildlife Agent days, and his earlier time with Wien Airlines. He liked and respected

Noel Wien's Tri-motor Ford partially submerged through ice on Harding Lake. Spring, 1938. NOEL WIEN, COURTESY RICHARD WIEN

The recovered Tri-motor Ford, with tripods, and cables used to extricate it. Sam O. White in foreground. NOEL WIEN, COURTESY RICHARD WIEN

the Koyukon people who lived along the Koyukuk River. Many were his close friends. In turn, they liked and respected Sam. That was perfect from a business standpoint.

"The position didn't require long hours of flying—after all, Sam was 64 in 1955 when he assumed the Hughes job. The position did, however, require an experienced, skilled, pilot, especially to

Ralph and his wife Julia Wien, and their children Bobbie and Jimmie (far left and far right). Noel Wien and his wife Ada are in center. Behind them is the Wien-owned Hamilton all-metal airplane with which Noel made the first flight ever from Alaska to Siberia.
NOEL WIEN, COURTESY DRAHS

fly in and out of the Air Force station at Utopia, and to the narrow strip at Hog River.

"The situation changed in the 1960s. Wien Airlines started phasing out older model bush planes like the Cessna 180 Sam flew at Hughes. Federal Aviation Administration's rules were also changing. Our pilots were now required to have an instrument rating, which Sam lacked. Sam hadn't practiced some of the required check flight maneuvers the FAA insisted on. To make it easier for him, I went to Hughes to give him check rides, which was difficult for me; Sam was a competent pilot before I was born.

"Sam was always a very proficient pilot—no passenger was ever hurt while flying with him—and he got the work done.

"It was time for Sam to retire. He was 71, and, among other reasons, Wien Airlines was no longer going to base an airplane at Hughes. I simply couldn't tell him he was through, that we were closing Hughes as one of our bush stations. We wanted him to go out on a good note. I didn't see how he could, for Sam loved to fly, and he loved the bush.

"Sam was ahead of us. My father received a letter from Sam, who had heard of his pending retirement from other sources. In the end my father was the one who confirmed to Sam that the Hughes station was closing. I'm glad I didn't have to do it."

Hughes, 10/6/62
Noel: I hear at Utopia and other places that I am to be retired soon. Of course I expect it, and I raise no objections. Damn wonder I been kept on this long, although I feel that I am still capable and competent. So no sweat. See you, Sam.

[AUTHOR] When Sam White learned to fly, Ralph Wien, Noel's older brother, was his primary flight instructor, although early-on, Noel gave him some dual time.

The relationship between a student pilot and his instructor can become very close. This was true of Sam and Ralph Wien.

A student's first attempts to make coordinated turns, to land a plane without bouncing, to take off without swerving, and other learned skills, make flying seem complicated and an impossibility.

After time, and much coaching, the skill comes. With Sam, it came slowly. He was 38 years old. He needed sixteen hours of dual instruction before Ralph felt he was safe to solo, which he did in his first airplane, the Golden Eagle, on August 5, 1930.

"Tuesday, August 5, 1930. Soloed in my own ship today," Sam triumphantly wrote in his federal daily diary.

Nine weeks later, on October 12, 1930, Ralph Wien was killed while piloting an airplane at Kotzebue. Sam recorded the tragic event in his federal daily diary:

October 13, 1930. About town and up to [landing] *field. Ed Young* [a prominent local pilot] *breaks news to us of Ralph's death, and asked us* [meaning Sam] *to break news to Julia, the widow. Entire day spent in providing comfort and attending affairs for Mrs. Wien. For my own part, I will never get over sorrowing for my friend and instructor Ralph Wien. He was a brave man and a firm and true friend.*

Noel and his wife Ada were in Minnesota. Sam sent them a telegram, RALPH KILLED KOTZEBUE CRASH LETTER FOL-LOWS GOD BLESS YOU.

Ralph was killed while piloting a Packard diesel-engine-powered Bellanca. The plane banked about thirty degrees to make a land-ing approach when suddenly it nosed 400 feet straight into the

ground. Father W. F. Walsh, head of the Kotzebue mission, and
Father Philip Delon, his passengers, were also killed.

The airplane had dual controls. Noel believed that a passenger
became frightened when Ralph banked, grabbed the dual controls,
and froze.

Sam White's letter to Noel about Ralph's death (here slightly
condensed by author) provides some insight into his sensitivity,
and the depth of his feelings:

Dear Noel:

*Reports have been very conflicting but the latest and final report taken from an interview with an eye witness, Brother Feltes
[a licensed pilot] differs from the other versions. Brother Feltes
says there is not much to tell. The motor was throttled down and
the plane banked at an angle of about thirty degrees for a landing,
when suddenly it nosed down and headed straight for the earth
and did not swerve from a straight course to the ground.*

Ed Young and S. E. Robbins [Alaskan Airways' pilots] *and
others say that they know that the controls were jammed.*

*It is my firm and positive conviction that the controls were
jammed by something falling on them when the ship was banked.
I will never believe anything else. Ralph's death has left a vacancy
in Fairbanks that will never be filled.*

*I have a wonderful memory of him, big, kind, clean, deep-thinking, honest, and tolerant. You cannot realize how we loved
him. He soloed me in the only way I could ever have soloed. We
made three hops together on that evening. I had taxied to the end
of the field and placed the ship in position for take off. I throttled
down the motor to receive my instructions. Ralph said, "If that
landing had been good I was going to solo you this time, I have a
good notion to anyway."*

I said, "Hop to it."

*Ralph jumped out of the cockpit and came back to me and said,
"Be careful on the take off and when you land," then he gripped
my hand and said, "Do just as you would do if you wanted to
please me." He stepped aside and I soloed. The whole town was
at the field and no one knew I was soloing until they saw Ralph
emerge from the dust.*

*I made two hops and S. E. Robbins, a crack pilot, congratulated
Ralph warmly on the way he soloed me. Several days after, when I*

had about six hours, Ralph said to me, "I am certainly pleased the way you are getting along. Just be careful and you should make a good pilot."

I felt very deeply his interest in me and his efforts to help me along, and I told him with much feeling that I owed him something more than money. Every day I felt as if I must make good if for no other reason than to please Ralph, and now that feeling is magnified a thousand times.

He died a man's death, at the stick, and I can envision him to the last instant, cool and calm, struggling for control of the ship. The memory of Ralph I shall always maintain, it will help to make me a better man. I can see him as vividly today as I could before he left Fairbanks, and I always will. When such good men have gone ahead it makes it easier for us to follow. God help me to die as nobly as he did.

There is one comfort. It is only for a short time and we will see him again. He is there to meet us when we take our first faltering steps into the great unknown. We shall love him there as we loved him here. [signed] *Sam*

[AUTHOR] RALPH WIEN was buried at Cook, Minnesota. The Ralph Wien Memorial Airport was dedicated at Kotzebue in 1951 by Alaska's Governor Ernest Gruening.

Ralph Wien left wife Julia and two sons. One of the sons, Bob, became a Wien Air Alaska captain in the 1970s.

After the death of Ralph, Noel completed Sam's flight instructions.

Sam White's Legacies to Alaska's Wildlife

When I left the Game Commission, I was confident that Clarence Rhode would see to it that Wildlife Agents would take to the air.
—SAM O. WHITE

[AUTHOR] IN 1927 Sam O. White was the ideal man to pioneer the concept of wildlife conservation in the quarter of a million square miles of northern Alaska where he became the first game warden. When asked why he became an Alaska game warden, he said, "Because I wanted to stop the killin' and the burnin'."

He broke new ground, and he made a difference. Only a man of his stature, his depth, his integrity, his ability, and his likable personality, could have accomplished all he did.

This former Army Sergeant, a survivor of the frontline hell of World War I, was a powerful six-foot-two, and 200 pounds. Deep-voiced, and self-assured, he easily dominated lawbreakers when he collared them.

Once a violator refused to come in when ordered by Sam. "He was a little bitty guy who told me, 'If you want me, you'll have to take me,'" Sam said.

"I picked him up by the scruff of the neck and threw him into my pickup. He didn't let out a peep on the drive to town," Sam remembered.

He was a master woodsman at home in the wilds. He was an accomplished rifleman. Few Alaskans could match this former lumberjack's skill with an axe. He could set up a summer or winter camp quickly, and he knew how to live comfortably anywhere in the bush. He was an expert canoeman. He had been a trapper, and knew the tricks of trappers to hide their sins. He was a skilled tracker. In

Clarence Rhode and the Twin Beachcraft airplane he used for annual caribou surveys. April, 1958.
J. Malcolm Greany, U.S. Fish and Wildlife Service

addition, he became a superlative airplane pilot, knowledgeable of Alaska's conditions.

His challenge was to convince Alaska's Indians and Eskimos who lived from the land, and whose hunting had never been restricted, that his cause was to their benefit.

Others to be convinced were the undisciplined leftovers of the hordes attracted North by turn-of-the-century gold rushes. Many of these continued at small mining operations, or prospected for minerals. During winter, many became trappers.

Sam had to convince everyone that the big free and easy was over, that a new age was upon them. One way to do it was to carefully enforce the new regulations.

That he did.

All residents of sparsely settled Alaska depended upon game meat for food. They didn't kill for sport or trophies. Most were unaware of, or ignored, the Alaska Game Law of 1902, which had set seasons and bag limits, and protected females and young of big game, but had never been enforced. Everyone killed moose, caribou, deer, Dall sheep, and goats, including the young and females, throughout the year, without regard to limits. Most of these folk knew wildlife numbers were declining.

Sam was strict in enforcing game laws, but he used common sense. He didn't arrest Natives who hunted for their subsistence in ways that did not seem wasteful, even if it violated the law. In this, he was more of a referee or perhaps coach, than a cop. He did enforce the regulations against market hunting by Natives for money to buy whiskey.

As for the "burnin'", miners set fires to expose mineralized areas. Trappers burned to clear brush and make travel easier, as did some Natives. One of Sam's duties was to post notices everywhere he went in a program hopefully designed to stop the deliberate setting of fires.

Outlaw trappers used strychnine poison to kill wolves, foxes, marten, and other furbearers. In so doing they also killed other meat eaters that picked up their lethal baits, including birds and bears. Use of poison, of course, was illegal. Legitimate trappers despised the poisoners.

In his early years as a warden Sam snowshoed hundreds, perhaps thousands, of miles of traplines, sifting snow through his snowshoes at trappers' bait stations as he searched for poison. At the same time he made sure no traps were set during closed season.

In a typical Sam O. White encounter, while on a trapline patrol, he came upon a dog team-driving trapper he suspected of using poison. Searching the man's sled, Sam found bait presumably used where traps were set. "Is this stuff poisoned?" he asked.

"Nope," was the answer.

"Then you won't mind if I feed some of it to your dogs," Sam suggested.

"Go ahead," the trapper agreed, which Sam did, proving that at least those baits weren't poisoned.

In the early 1950s, James G. (Jim) King, now retired from the U.S. Fish and Wildlife Service (FWS), studied wildlife management at the University of Alaska (now UAF) when I (author) taught that subject there. After graduation, he worked for the FWS in wildlife enforcement, and became a qualified pilot and then Flyway Biologist for Alaska. He and Sam were friends. In an August 21, 2005, letter to me King wrote:

"Sam's legacy in introducing flying to wildlife management has been reported, but his role in ending the use of poison, market hunting, killing game to feed dogs, shooting of beaver, calf and cow moose, and other destructive activities, has not. Most bush residents, Native and white alike, deplored the destruction.

"The honesty and fairness with which Sam administered the new conservation laws carried on to the time of Clarence Rhode, then Ray Woolford (1950s Wildlife Agent at Fairbanks), and to those of us who came after. The old-timers were well aware that these rules had restored a lot of depleted species, and often reported violations, sometimes by letter from remote villages. It was a wonderful thing to be a part of."

ANOTHER LETTER, dated Oct. 10, 2005, came to me from Sidney Huntington, who has lived all his life in and near the Koyukuk River valley. In 1993, with Sidney, I wrote about his life in the book *Shadows on the Koyukuk; A Native's Life along the River.*

Sidney wrote, "We of those days all remember Sam O. White. He knew everyone, and we all knew him personally. He had very good relations with all people. Furthermore, he was not hated by anyone that I know of.

"He was the first game warden to use an airplane in enforcing the laws and regulations. He was always fair and helpful. About the time Sam arrived, the law on beaver was changed; suddenly we could only trap them, not shoot them, as we had always done. The difficulty was, no one knew how to trap beaver through the ice, when their fur was prime, and the season was open.

"Sam taught people in villages along the Koyukuk and elsewhere how to trap beaver under the ice during the winter season. His beaver set was called the "Sam White beaver set," and it worked pretty fair, too. Some of us developed modifications of his system, but he got us started on the right track.

"The snare came into play later [also for beaver under the ice]. There was a 'Sam White snare set' that didn't work too bad. We experimented and improved that set too.

"Sam greatly respected the elderly Natives of the Interior. The moose bag limit was one. He knew that Indians used moose hides from pregnant cows killed during late March because they make the best skins for clothing. Such skins, stretched from a cow carrying her calf, are more uniform in thickness than other moose hides. He was aware that some individuals used more than one moose a season. He never asked questions of them.

"He was strict in his enforcement of closed trapping seasons for mink, marten, fox, lynx, beaver, wolverine. Thoughtful trappers realized that trapping seasons were established by the Game Commission for the time fur was prime, thus more valuable. Sam regularly seized unprime furs on the theory they were taken when the season was closed. He was also strict in enforcing the catch limits for beaver because they had been shot out in some areas, and needed a chance to rebuild.

"He was real hard on those who used moose meat for dog food. They could get the limit penalty—up to a year in jail.

"The elder Indians living on the Koyukuk, including John Oldman, Chief Henry and his wife Bessie, Edwin Simon, and Chief Olin of Huslia, gave Sam White all the credit for restoring moose along the Koyukuk River. At a memorial potlatch for her husband, Bessie Henry spoke. She said that ". . . if it wasn't for Sam White we would still have very few moose."

"Before Sam arrived and enforced the laws, the Koyukon Natives killed moose year-round, including cows and calves.

"He knew how to apply the law. People really liked him. They knew his word was good, and that he would not be unfair.

"Sometimes people worried about people in a remote area and who hadn't been heard from, perhaps through the fall and winter. They asked Sam if he flew that way to check on them. Sam never failed—he did the checking, and always reported his findings to the concerned person.

"Sam really understood the needs of people in the bush. They were his friends. He became even more popular after he started flying for Wien Airlines hauling mail and passengers.

"I first met Sam at Nulato, in July, 1932, when I was 17. A bunch of us kids were playing ball. Sam's Swallow biplane flew over us twice. The second time he was low enough so that we could see him in the rear cockpit as he motioned that he wanted to land on the ball field.

"We cleared the field and Sam landed. The mission grounds were fenced. Sam's plane had no brakes, and he ran into the fence, bending one blade of his propeller.

"We helped him as he straightened it. He drove a stake into the ground for a gauge, and turned the good blade of the prop to touch the gauge, then he brought the bent side over. It missed the gauge by one-half to five-eighths of an inch. He worked at straightening it all afternoon, and finally got it pretty close.

"To check it, Sam revved up the engine while all of us kids held the plane in place. The propeller seemed to do fine. For his take off, he lightened the plane by unloading his extras, including a length of aircraft cable, which he gave to me.

"I later used that cable to snare a grizzly bear at our Hog

River trapping cabin. [That story appears in Sidney's book.]
"Sam was a good man, a real Alaskan," Sidney's letter concluded.

AS A GAME WARDEN, Sam had to overcome much opposition. In a 1968 interview, he remembered, "I was talking with a federal judge in Fairbanks, standing on a corner next to the bank, when the judge said, "I don't approve of you arresting old-timers for shooting a moose in the summer. The game was here for the people when the country was opened up. The country is still developing, and you should let them have it any time they want it."

Sam asked him, "What are future generations going to do?"
The judge replied, "They won't need game."

SAM'S LEGACY is not limited to his success in preaching a conservation ethic for wildlife. He pioneered the use of the airplane in wildlife law enforcement and management. So far as he knew, and as far as long-time wildlife professionals in Alaska know, he was the world's first flying game warden/wildlife agent.

In 1930–31 it took great self-confidence to climb into an airplane and head across the Territory of Alaska. There were no radios, poor at best weather forecasts and reports, no aviation charts, no accurate maps. Runways were commonly river gravel bars summers, and river and lake ice winters. Even Weeks Field at Fairbanks was an unpaved former ball park.

Sam had hardly acquired a pilot's license when he boldly started making long flights. His surveying experience with the Coast and Geodetic Survey no doubt helped with his navigating. In event of a forced landing, not unusual in those years, he had the ability to survive with the equipment he carried.

Echoes of his impact as a flying game warden still reverberate. Recently (2006), a man who, in 1941, was trapping in the Kantishna country, told me an airplane had flown over him when he had traps illegally set.

"I scurried to pick up those traps," he said. "Sam White's reputation was well known to all the trappers in that country."

In this instance, to have the law observed, all Sam had to do was to fly over the man's trapline.

At first, for Sam, flying was a new enforcement tool, plus a leap into efficient transportation for doing his job (for sealing beaver). At about the same time, he broke new ground by making aerial counts of moose. He was likely the first wildlife official anywhere to officially make a herd count from an airplane.

Today, of course, managing Alaska's wildlife depends heavily upon the use of airplanes and helicopters. In addition to law enforcement, planes make possible accurate big game and waterfowl counts. Airplanes can be used to control predators, keep track of wildlife movements, make reproduction studies (calf counts), support research, perform rescues, search for lost individuals. With a plane, wildlife administrators can get to areas of interest quickly, without spending days or weeks of travel time.

SAM WAS STUBBORN, otherwise he'd have never flown as a game warden. His use of an airplane instead of dog team and boat was strongly opposed by his bosses. But "the aviation" as it was referred to in *The Fairbanks News-Miner*, was plainly the way to go, and he knew it. He continued despite being in hot water for flying his plane during working hours, for using government time and equipment to service his plane, and even for using gas in his patrolling plane paid for from his office budget.

After reporting his first aerial moose count on the Tanana Flats near Fairbanks, he was told, ". . . take annual leave for that day, and get out with your dog team and do a proper survey."

The Juneau brass didn't have a clue that their widely respected and capable Fairbanks warden was revolutionizing wildlife enforcement and management.

It took a while, but eventually the hard facts emerged that airplanes were here to stay, that they were eminently useful for Game Commission work. The fourteenth Annual Report of the Alaska Game commission (1937–38) included the following:

> Airplane travel is becoming more and more important and necessary in enforcement of the game laws in Alaska. This type of travel was utilized during the past year by engaging passage whenever practicable on regularly scheduled flights, by chartering one plane which was flown by an Alaskan Wildlife Agent [Sam O. White] who is a licensed pilot. The last method proved to be by far the most economical and effective.

That report also said for that year there was 25,000 miles of patrol by air, and only 1,161 by dog team.

By 1940–41 the Alaska Game Commission owned three airplanes (a Monocoupe, and two Fairchild 24s), flown by three pilot agents. Sam O. White was not among them—he had resigned his position as a Wildlife Agent.

A few years after Sam resigned, the Game Commission jumped headlong into a full-blown aviation program. "That led me to believe they were just waiting for me to get out of the way," he said, adding, "I didn't reap much of the fruit for my victory."

The dynamo who mostly built on Sam's flying-for-wildlife legacy was Clarence Rhode.

Rhode was a tall, slim 21-year-old when, in 1934, he arrived from Washington state and went to work for the U.S. Forest Service at Seward for sixty dollars a month.

Rhode came by his interest in wildlife honestly. His father was a fish-culturist and game warden in Washington state, and Clarence had absorbed the idea of conservation of wildlife at an early age. By the time he was 15, he was a deputy warden in Washington, and had decided he would spend his life working with fish and game.

Clarence went to work for the Alaska Game Commission in 1935. By 1936 he was Acting Assistant to the Executive Officer of the Commission (then Frank Dufresne).

As a Wildlife Agent enforcing game laws, he was stationed at Cordova, Fairbanks, Juneau, and Anchorage. He worked with Sam White on a number of occasions. The best known was their joint Alaska-Canada boundary patrol with the RCMP in 1939.

Sam gave Clarence flying instructions, soloed him, and arranged for his private pilot's license. Clarence went on to get commercial and instrument ratings.

During World War II Clarence was on furlough from the Game Commission, and flew commercially in Alaska, waived from the draft because of the critical need for bush pilots in the Territory.

After the war he became supervisor of the newly created FWS Aircraft Division and helped develop the aircraft facility at Lake Hood, Anchorage. It was then that he started acquiring military surplus planes. These were modified at the Lake Hood shop to accommodate needs of wildlife pilots operating in the bush. A number of innovations designed for the wildlife planes were later certified by the FAA (Federal Aviation Administration) and remain in general use today.

Clarence rescued military radios scheduled for destruction at a depot in San Francisco. "You can have whatever you want," he was told, "but you'd better hurry." Radios were on a conveyer belt, headed for a press that cubed them into masses of glass and metal. He rushed to the moving belt and worked up a sweat whisking radios off. He loaded the stuff into a surplus Grumman Goose airplane and flew it back to Alaska. In the early 1950s the FWS Alaska radio network rivaled that of the FAA and the military.

In March, 1953, I [AUTHOR] flew over the Brooks Range as a passenger with Clarence Rhode in the FWS Twin Beechcraft N788 (this plane is now in the Alaska Aviation Heritage Museum in Anchorage). On that flight he talked easily by radio with his Fairbanks office. On another occasion I was a passenger with Fairbanks FWS Agent Ray Woolford in a Gullwing Stinson flying over the Fortymile country, when Ray used his plane's radio to talk with FWS offices in Anchorage, Fairbanks, and Juneau. The signals came in loud and clear.

Clarence Rhode's initial enthusiasm for and understanding of the value of aircraft in wildlife work came from Sam. He built a fleet of airplanes, and started a pool of highly qualified pilots and mechanics who carried on the conservation work of the FWS in Alaska until the state took over management of fish and game in January, 1960 (statehood arrived in 1959), and after, for migratory bird and refuge responsibilities.

In 1948, Clarence became the Executive Officer of the Alaska Game Commission and Regional Director of the FWS.

Clarence Rhode was killed in 1959 in a crash of a FWS Grumman Goose in Alaska's Brooks Range.

THUS, SAM O. WHITE, a far-sighted one-time Maine lumberjack with a seventh-grade education, who persisted in his devotion to the use of airplanes, proved their worth as a tool in wildlife management. Clarence Rhode picked up the torch and completed the modernizing of wildlife management in Alaska with airplanes.

Sam left a double legacy for Alaska's wildlife; he broke trail working to convince Alaskans that wildlife conservation pays, and, despite personal sacrifice and formidable opposition, he demonstrated that airplanes were practical for enforcing regulations, and for managing, Alaska's wildlife.

Sam

Since I quit flying I have only seen a doctor at a distance and want to keep it that way. It is my belief that when you are past 70 if you can walk and breathe there is nothing they can do for you anyway.
—SAM O. WHITE

[AUTHOR] THE SMALL FRAME HOUSE at 902 Kellum Street in Fairbanks (now gone), where the Sam O. Whites lived, had green siding, old-style rectangular windows, and somewhat rusted metal roofing. A scrawled sign on the door frame instructed, "ring the bell."

Entering, you passed a couple of large tool boxes in the entry way, and found yourself in the living room. The small kitchen was in the rear. A hole in the top of the simple kitchen table always provoked a visitor's question; Sam designed it to hold an upside-down ketchup bottle. A wood cook stove dominated for years, and was replaced by an oil burning kitchen stove, one of the first in the neighborhood.

The living room was austere but had a few very comfortable chairs, one of which was braced with wire. To the left was a well-worn couch. For a time the living room floor was partially covered with Sears Roebuck linoleum; at another time it was covered with thick, brown rattan.

Sam explained the rattan: "Men like to wear boots, Mary pestered me so much when I walked in with a little mud or snow on my boots that I couldn't stand it. She wanted me to take my boots off every time I came in, so I ordered this floor covering.

"Dirt or snow from my boots goes through the mesh and can't be seen. Once a year I pull it up and shake it while Mary cleans the floor. I replace the mat, and that's that."

"If I had my way, I'd live in a cabin in the woods where none of that sort of thing matters. But Mary has to have her comforts."

Several dozen pictures decorated a wall, including one of the World War I era in France, Sam's mother, his beloved L5-G Stinson, a signed photo of former bush pilot and airline owner Bob Reeve.

There was a large writing desk, usually covered with letters and magazines. Next to it was an old aircraft propeller made into an ash tray.

Sam and Mary had two cats. One or the other seemed always to be meowing to go out or come in. Having to get up and open the door repeatedly got on Sam's nerves. He built what he called a "cat escape hatch," by sawing a hole in the front door where he inserted a wood box. On the ends of the box were two flaps hinged to swing both ways, one inside, and the other outside, with springs to close them.

Sam named the cat that first figured how to use the escape hatch "Wisenheimer," and the other, which took a couple of days longer, he named "Dumbkoff." (Letter to author from Roy Billberg, 11/05.)

"Well, I am retired from the flying game. Put in thirty-five years at it. Was straight bush flying, all by the seat of the pants and no fog [instrument] license. Open cockpits, OX5s and all single engine Stinsons, Fairchilds, Swallows, Winkle Bird, Wacos, Bellancas, Robins and Thrushes, Standards, Pilgrims, and others. All to the tune of about 14,000 hours." (Letter from Sam to Bob Schipper, 8/7/68.)

Frank Glaser, *Alaska's Wolf Man* (book by author), left his trapline at Savage River to become a predatory animal control for the Alaska Game Commission in the spring of 1937. Sam taught Glaser how to drive, and helped him cope with government forms. The two worked together until 1941 when Sam resigned from his Game Commission position. Before that, Sam had given Glaser the examination for becoming a registered big game guide, which he handily passed.

"Little Miss Sam White was in to see me this fall. She is 10 years old, typical full-blood Indian. I flew her mother to the hospital to have this child in about as bad weather as I could well handle.

"The way I tell the story, I came to a low ridge I had to cross. On this ridge two bull moose were fighting. They heard me coming and jumped apart and I went through between them. I cannot say what they did after that. Some even believe that part of my story. Anyway the mother was so grateful that she named the child Sam White before she was born." Sam. (Letter to Bob Schipper, 12/24/70.)

Sam became a member of the Dorman H. Baker post of the American Legion in 1926, and remained a member. He wrote snippets about his military service in World War I, but nothing detailed. A note in his federal diary leaves one wondering . . . "November 11, 1933. Fifteen years ago overlooking German line, at Pandieres, Paguy, Villers, etc. . . ."

Sam's wife, Mary, once told an interviewer that Sam was "painfully popular." It wasn't painful to Sam; he thoroughly enjoyed people, and loved to visit. Jerome Lardy, who over many years worked at various FAA stations in Alaska, frequently took the elderly Sam O. White shopping in Fairbanks. He commented that ". . . it took hours."

People recognized and stopped Sam, and he often launched into some long wilderness story. "Drove me crazy," Lardy complained.

No matter how annoyed he became, he never stopped taking Sam to Safeway. (Michael Carey, "Gentle Bachelor made Alaska Better, Friends Proud," *Anchorage Daily News*, Oct. 5, 2003.)

"Heap fun. In my next life I want to steer a steam log hauler again." Sam. (Letter to Evelyn Stevens. 6/30/68.)

Inside a cabin, a trapper once pointed a .30–06 rifle at Sam, who, as usual, was unarmed. Sam quietly stared at him. The man, shaking, held for a time, then put the rifle down. Sam checked it, and found a cartridge in the chamber.

"Bob, I am swamped. Do you know of a red-headed secretary who wants a job to sort Xmas cards for an 82-year-old sourdough? I love 'em all, but this Xmas card bizness is getting out of hand. Twenty-five to thirty-five cards a day, and it started two weeks ago." Sam. (Letter to Bob Schipper, 12/17/73.)

Sam was celebrated in Fairbanks for his bean hole beans, which he learned to make in Maine logging camps. He dug a hole in his back yard on Kellum Street, laid a layer of rocks in the bottom, inserted a fifty-five gallon oil drum, and lined the outside of it with rocks.

For a time, when the fire in his bean hole was blazing high, Sam might get a call from the fire chief who lived near.

"Do you have a fire in your back yard, Sam?"

"I do."

"Do you have a permit?"

"No, I don't have a permit."

"That will cost you one gallon of beans."

In later years, he bowed to the city's ban on open fires, and oven-baked his beans.

SAM'S BEAN HOLE BEANS

Sam whumped up no less than four and a half gallons of beans at a time. "I baked those big batches so long I don't know how to make a small one," he claimed.

This meant starting with twelve pounds of white navy beans and two pounds of salt port. Pick the rocks out of the beans and soak overnight in cold water.

Early in the morning, parboil the beans to the point that when you blow on them, the skin cracks.

Rinse and drain. Layer the beans in a large kettle, cast iron preferably, beans first, with diced salt port. Midway add one chopped onion. Finish with more beans and pork

Weigh the onions down with beans, or they'll float to the top and burn.

Pour in four cups of molasses, two tablespoons of dry mustard, a big handful of salt, and four cups of warm water. Then fill the kettle with enough water to cover the beans.

Earlier, you have built a fire of birch wood (birch is best; other long-lasting coal-holding wood like cottonwood may work) in the bean hole. When coals are formed, build the fire up again to be sure to have enough coals. Once the hole is full of coals, half of them must be shoveled out.

At this point, coals from the birch fire in the bottom of the bean hole should be red hot. Drop the kettle in. Cover kettle with more hot coals (those you shoveled out), and seal over with dirt. The rocks on the sides of the hole are hot, of course, and they and the coals keep the temperature of the beans about 500 degrees.

When he had to forsake his bean hole, Sam baked his beans in an oven at 400 degrees for five or six hours. In the oven the pot must be checked so it doesn't run out of water. An hour before he expected the beans to be done, Sam let them go partially dry in order to brown them, adding water when they had reached the proper color.

Now he's ready to invite thirty-five people to dinner. "I've baked those big batches so long, I don't know how to make a small one," Sam said. He and Mary couldn't eat four and one-half gallons at a time. (Jo Anne Wold, "Bean Hole Beans," *Fairbanks Daily News-Miner*, Oct. 8, 1976.)

Sam built a small cabin at his "moose pasture" on the Yukon flats, where, for many years, he annually bagged a moose he and Mary ate through the winter and shared with friends. Nailed to the cabin, was a sign: "SAM WHITE'S CACHE. CHUCK, COVER, HEAT. FILL YOUR BELLY, BUT NOT YOUR POCKETS. LAY OFF GAS."

The sign reflected Sam's sourdough background. The cabin was shelter with food and heat for anyone who needed it.

"My head is in the clouds and my heart is with our beleaguered wild animals who are taking a frightful beating from rich hunters and dumb biologists. The balance of nature was nulled and voided with the invention of gunpowder and again with repeating firearms." Sam. (Letter to Bob Schipper 7/30/71.)

"Speaking of the old federal Alaska Game Commission, they did one hell of a good job. We may not have been loved, but by thunder, we were respected." Sam. (Letter to Ray Woolford, former Wildlife Agent. January 11, 1968.)

"The Territory had a few game wardens, but they were so busy poaching that they didn't have time to help the wildlife. I was just the first one who took it seriously." Sam, referring to the 1920s. (Letter to Evelyn Stevens, April 12, 1969.)

A friend once asked Sam about a rumor that Sam didn't charge the sick or injured he flew from the bush to a hospital. "True sometimes," Sam revealed. "I figured they had enough problems without my adding the cost of airplane charter."

"We are snowed under in Fairbanks. It has snowed over 100 inches and is now packed down to plus forty inches. The wind is blowing a right smart clip. First we have a cold spell, and then a copious snowstorm, and this repeats itself every four or five days with intermittent winds. Just as you begin to think, "Well, it can't snow any more," it cuts loose and exceeds the bounds of probabilities, and I might add, reason.

"Two-thirds of Fairbanks' roads are paralyzed. All the fire hydrants are buried deep, and roofs are collapsing. One new expensive building collapsed like a pricked balloon.

"There are many collisions; at intersections one can hardly see an approaching car. The berm on each street is chin high to a tall moose. There are injuries, too. There are many cheechakos [newcomers] who don't know how to drive on snow and ice. And there are some who do not know any better than to bring a white car into snow country; one or two local nitwits have snow white cars.

"Speaking of moose (which I wasn't), the moose are moving into town to escape the wolves. They are also moving onto plowed highways for the same purpose. Now and then a car and a moose clobber each other.

"Recently, a friend of mine came driving around a bend and here was a big bull in the middle of the road. My friend was driving carefully, but he couldn't stop, so he scooped up the bull, who sat on the front of the hood and ran like hell with his front feet until the car stopped.

"The bull was very indignant and threatened to toss the whole works off into the woods. Then he seemed to forget the whole thing and stalked away in great dignity, browsing as he went." Sam. (Letter to Bob Schipper, 12/25/70.)

"A guy was going to take over and land my plane for me coming into Eagle during a very windy day. He was under arrest for illegal trapping. I shoved the cold end of a .22 automatic under his jaw and he found out right quick how mistaken he had been, and I went ahead and landed." Sam.

"Damn good thing I got old when I did. I can't take this modern stuff. The merest scent of hippies gives me indigestion and pains in the neck." Sam. (Letter to Bob Schipper 7/30/71.)

Scientists have long been divided between those who believe reports that the Northern Lights can be heard, and those who say it is impossible. Sam O. White said he had heard them. "They have to show up on a night that is fairly cold, and when there is a good display. They kind of crackle and swish. The sound dies into kind of a hum after the flickering or dancing slows down," he explained. "After the Dancin' Slows Down." (*Alaska Today*, Vol. 7, May 1979–April 1980.)

"Sam White was unique. Where else could I as a young man hear firsthand stories of World War I, and stories of the Civil War from a man who knew men who had fought in it? Where else could I hear stories of Old Alaska from a man who was a part of it, and who had such a vivid memory of people, places, events?

"Sam had several uncles who were Civil War veterans. Although they lived normal lives, they had been changed by that war. He told me, 'One time when I was a boy, a local man threatened members of my family. My uncles paid him a visit. He departed for parts unknown, and never returned. You see, Roy, each of my uncles had killed so many men during the Civil War that to kill one more would have meant nothing to them. No one trifled with my uncles, even when they were old men. They had a side that was as cold as ice.'

"Sam was a civil war buff, and I remember him telling endless stories of campaigns, battles, and generals. He knew details of uniforms, and even what some generals had for breakfast before battles." Roy Billberg. (Letter to author, November, 2005.)

"Sam loved moose, and he loved protecting them. One day he was canoeing on the Yukon Flats when a cow and calf swam across the river ahead. They struggled across the river only to be faced by a cut bank about five feet high. The cow easily leaped to the top, then turned with her nose down, waiting for the calf. The calf jumped and jumped and tried, but it couldn't make it.

"Sam said, 'I knew it was dangerous, but I had to help that calf. I nosed the canoe to shore beside the calf and went to give the little guy a hand up. The calf, probably because it was exhausted, allowed me to pick it up. And, you know, the mother moose stood looking down at me quietly while I lifted the calf straight up to the edge where it got its footing. The mother nuzzled him and they walked away.

"'There is no animal more dangerous in the bush than a mother moose with a young calf. But, she knew I was helping them.'" Roy Billberg. (Letter to author, February, 2006.)

"Sam hated wolves for years, mostly because they preyed on moose. He occasionally spent an hour or so regaling me with stories of wolves, how vicious they are, and how they are dangerous to people, and how they often kill moose for fun and allow the carcass to waste without eating from it.

"In the year he died, he started talking wolves during one of my visits. He suddenly stopped, his face softened, and he smiled, 'Yeah, Roy, but I guess like everything else in the woods, wolves have their place in nature too, and they have a right to be there.

"He never mentioned wolves to me again." Roy Billberg. (Letter to author, November, 2005.)

"I am so sympathetic to wild animals now that I do not want to inconvenience them at all. I'm just plain sissy with age." Sam. (Letter to the Reverend Patterson Keller, March 16, 1966.)

"One spring when we had a premature warm spell on the Koyukuk, a flock of about fifty geese arrived. There was no open water. Temperatures went to 20 and 30 below for two weeks.

"The geese had all parked on a bar. I landed nearby on the ice of the river. I walked among them. A few would get out of my way, but some were so far gone they could not stand up.

"Foxes were hanging around and nipping off a few.

"I collected all the bread and crackers available locally and offered it to them. There was no grain. They ate a little, but most wouldn't.

"They all perished. It was sad." Sam. (Letter to Evelyn Brown, April 12, 1969.)

Rudy Billberg arrived in Nome in 1941 to fly for Wien Airlines, and continued to fly Alaska's bush for forty years. Noel

Wien introduced him to Sam White, and they became friends and remained so until Sam's death. In his book *In the Shadow of Eagles*, he described White:

"Sam was huge, powerfully built, and he had a booming voice. Despite his size and sometimes bluster, I soon learned that underneath he was kind, just, and generous.

"Sam's generosity and concern for others was legendary. One cold winter day in the early 1950s I received an urgent call. My friend Bob Buzby had left Anchorage in his Piper Tri-Pacer to take his family to their trapping cabin in the Alaska Range. He was to have returned for more people and cargo, but was two days overdue. The caller asked if I could get a plane and search for him.

"I had no airplane of my own at the time, so I went to Sam. He immediately loaned me his beloved L-5 Stinson. "Use it as long as you need it," he said. He went to the airport with me and helped me preheat and start the engine. Then he loaded aboard his more-than-adequate emergency equipment.

"Bob's Tri-Pacer had run off the end of his runway and tipped over, with no injuries. I flew most of the family back to Fairbanks in Sam's airplane.

"Finished, I tied Sam's L-5 to its moorings, unloaded the emergency gear, drained the oil, and drove to his house. After telling Sam of the rescue, he sat down, much relieved.

"By the way," I said. "Bob wants to know what he owes you for the use of your plane."

"At the time, Sam made his entire living with that plane.

"He jumped to his feet. 'He owes me nothing,' he roared. 'Maybe you can do me a favor some time. If you can't, do it for somebody else.'"

"That was typical of Sam White."

On Saturday, November 25, 1961, more than one hundred friends gathered in Fairbanks at the Club 11 to honor Sam O. White on his 70th birthday. The party was organized by Noel Wien and other of Sam's friends. Congratulatory telegrams and letters that poured in from throughout Alaska and the South 48 were read.

Alaska's Governor Bill Egan perhaps best expressed the sentiment of the crowd in a letter (here slightly condensed by author).

Dear Sam:

The occasion is a fitting tribute to a man whose life has been dedicated to those things which mean so much to betterment of the standards of living for all citizens. I recall numerous mercy flights of yours which resulted in saving lives of your fellow men.

It has been a privilege for me to consider myself one of your personal friends for more than three decades. Through the years, expression of top respect and admiration for Sam White has always been the rule whenever groups who know you have gotten together, from one end of Alaska to the other.

This is a sincere expression of gratitude from Bill Egan for all that you have done for our Great Land—Alaska.

[SIGNED] Bill (William A. Egan, Governor)

From a former associate of Sam's in the Coast and Geodetic Survey: "Sam is truly an outstanding character, one of the finest men I have ever known. One never needed a signed contract with Sam—his word was the best guarantee one could want. Without Sam and his trusty canoe, we could not have finished the levels in the [Grand] Canyon in 1921. Sam was equally trustworthy on the triangulation party in Alaska in 1922, and later. I can understand why he has so many friends in Alaska." (Floyd W. Hough, former U.S. Coast and Geodetic Survey Chief.)

Another tribute came from Hank Kragiel, member of a WWII-time winter geodetics party flown by White:

"Sam is one of Alaska's great pioneers, a tremendous personality with a heart as big as he is. So honest it hurts—a true Samaritan.

"I have lived and worked with Sam out there in the frozen wilderness. If it hadn't been for Sam, I'd probably be buried out there now.

"One winter afternoon, after a forced landing, a Native Indian snowshoed into our humble camp and offered his services to Sam. He had heard the disabled plane from a distance and instinctively knew it was Sam White. He came willingly and anxiously to offer his services to Sam. I saw similar instances of such devoted loyalty repeated. Why? Because Sam went out of his way to befriend these people.

"Sam is as much a part of Alaska as the eternal snow in her majestic mountains and the Northern Lights. Alaska is fortunate to have him. Speaking for myself, I am a better man for having known him. Sincerely, Hank."

Flight Plan Closed

"Alaska is a great land. One feels its greatness. I cannot imagine living anywhere else. It is here I hope to end my days."
—SAM OTHO WHITE.

SAM FULFILLED THAT wish December 14, 1976. He was 85.

In 1961, for his 70th birthday party, Wien aircraft mechanics Jennings Johnson and C. Ernie Hubbard wrote and performed the following ode to Sam:

Once there was a flying man who came from the state of Maine
Yet he deserves a front row seat in Alaska's Hall of Fame
He forgot more about this frozen land than we will ever know
He speaks the language of the moose, the wolf, and caribou
    Let's drink to old Sam White
    Yes, lift your glasses high
    As long as there's Alaska
    Don't let his memory die
    That he was making history
    Never once occurred to him
    For I doubt if we'd have been here
    If it weren't for men like Sam
He flew an old Bellanca plane—with prayers and lots of luck
From Hughes and Allakaket to the frozen Ikpikpuk
The *Yukon Bush* he called his plane, the Natives knew it well
How many ways he served this land would be awful hard to tell
    Let's drink to old Sam White
    Yes, lift your glasses high
    As long as there's Alaska
    Don't let his memory die
    That he was making history

Never once occurred to him
For I doubt if we'd have been here
If it weren't for men like Sam
There's poems and there's legends that tell of others' fame
And yet compared to Old Sam White, they are civilized and tame.
A modest man, not one to gripe, he's going strong today
When many a man at half his age are dropped along the way.
Let's drink to old Sam White
Yes, lift your glasses high
As long as there's Alaska
Don't let his memory die
That he was making history
Never once occurred to him
For I doubt if we'd have been here
If it weren't for men like Sam

LIFE WASN'T EASY for Sam in his old age. His income declined precipitously after 1962 when he retired from flying for Wien Airlines. Once, after Sam's retirement, on a cold winter day, his bush pilot friend Rudy Billberg suggested that he and Sam walk to town for a cup of coffee. Sam's warmest coat for the outing was light wool—inadequate for Fairbanks winter. Rudy marched him to town and bought him a good down coat. The act brought Sam to tears.

"You once told me to do a favor for someone in exchange for the use of your L-5," Rudy reminded him.

Mary, Sam's wife of forty-six years died in October, 1974, after which he lived alone at their Kellum Street home. He suffered from arthritis, and needed help to shop for groceries. The fast-paced life of modern Fairbanks with growing crime, multiple modern gadgets, confusing traffic, and crowds of people, was a horrific change from the calm, easy-going life of his early years. He railed against the problems of an overgrown, modern, Fairbanks, in half-serious, half humorous letters to friends.

Even so, in his declining years, he said, "If Alaska is good enough to live in, it's good enough to die in."

SAM WAS A LIFE member of the OX5 Aviation Pioneers (membership is limited to those who flew with an OX5 engine). In 1926

Sam O. White as portrayed by Alaskan artist Harvey Goodale.
COURTESY BOB REEVE FAMILY

Sam O. White, in his eighties. COURTESY STAN PATTY

he joined the Dorman H. Baker Post of the American Legion and remained a member. Other memberships included the Tanana-Yukon Historical Society; the Eagle Historical Society; the Veterans of World War I, and a lifetime membership of the Pioneers of Alaska, Igloo No. 4.

Survivors included sons Burnham W. White, Jesse N.White, Harland O. White and his wife Julia Janet, as well as a sister, Diette Therrien, all of Maine. As this is written (2006) only Harland and Julia White survive.

Sam was stricken by a sudden paralytical stroke October 16, 1976, and ten days later, on December 14, he died in the Intensive Care Unit of the Fairbanks Memorial Hospital. He was a guest at the Fairbanks Pioneers home before being hospitalized.

Memorial services for Sam were held December 17, 1976, at Chapel of Chimes [Fairbanks] under the auspices of Pioneers of Alaska, Igloo No. 4.

Following is the December 15, 1976, editorial that appeared in the *Fairbanks Daily News-Miner*:

SAM WHITE

We noted not long ago that in this year when we are looking back on the history of our country and our state, we in Alaska have lost several of our closest friends who've provided the very personal links we have with our history. Tuesday Sam White joined their number, taking a place not so much as a character of history, but as a symbol of the Alaska in which he lived.

There are a lot of impressions we get from the names "bush pilot" or "sourdough," but Sam White was one of the best examples of the traditional picture of that even more elusive name, "Alaskan."

He was the type of person many of us envisioned before we came to Alaska. For many, he was the type of person who made the greatest impression on us when we were getting to know Alaska as newcomers or children—and for many he was the type of person who led us to choose to live here the rest of our lives.

Sam White not only experienced Alaska to the greatest degree, he gave much of himself to making it a better place to live and to its earliest movements in managing our resources.

He combined what were then two fledgling professions, flying and game management, and is equally famous in both. As a pilot he is remembered as one of the last remaining contemporaries of those who made "bush pilot" the magic name it is in Alaska. As a game warden, he set a legendary standard as a just and reasonable public official, combining a dedication to duty with a lot of good common sense.

Sam White's passing comes at a time when many of us feel we've lost part of the Alaskan life style which he symbolized. The fact that he is remembered so well, and will be missed so much, gives us hope that this is not happening yet.

Richard Wien was executor of Sam's will. Sam requested his ashes be scattered, ". . . into the most inaccessible part of the Yukon Flats, far from any habitation, into a patch of timber or brush or into a marsh as the case may be, by Richard and Merrill Wien together, or by either one separately."

As he requested, Sam's ashes were scattered from the air over his favorite Yukon Flats moose pasture by Richard and Merrill Wien, and his son Harland.

Harland was with Sam when he died.

The old pilot's last words? "I guess I'll turn the motor off now."

References

CHAPTER 1
White, Sam O., "Eustis Ridge," Sam O. White collection. Stories file, archives, University of Alaska Fairbanks. 1969. 3pp.
White, Sam O., "Sam White, Alaskan. I Go Surveying." Part I, *Alaska Sportsman*, December, 1964. p. 8.

CHAPTER 2
A Letter From France. Sam White exhibit, Dead River Area Historical Society Museum, Stratton, Maine.
Billberg, Roy Douglas. Letters to author, 2005 and 2006.
Early Alaska Bush Pilot Interviews. Interview of Sam O. White on December 2, 1961, by Sandy Jenson. Box 6, Folder. Sam O. White collection, archives, University of Alaska Fairbanks.
Maine Adjutant General's Book (for military career).
Mayse, Charley, "Church Army Gets Praise," *Fairbanks Daily News-Miner,* May 27, 1967.
Phillips, Maine, *Maine Woods,* December 29, 1910 (description of Sam O. White's bear kills).
Schipper, Robert. Interview by author at Stratton, Maine, October 14, 2005.
White, Julia. Interview by author at White home in southern Maine, October 16, 2005.
White, Sam O., "Aircraft History and Other Experiences," an interview by U.S. Fish and Wildlife Service employee Evelyn (Brown) Stevens at the White's Kellum street home in Fairbanks, June 20, 1968. 18 pp., single-spaced. Copy of transcript in author's files.
White, Sam O., Letters to Bob Schipper. Various dates. Sam White exhibit, Dead River Area Historical Society Museum, Stratton, Maine.

CHAPTER 3
White, Sam O., Chapter One, "Sam White, Alaskan. I Go Surveying." *Alaska Sportsman.* December, 1964, p. 8.

CHAPTER 4
White, Sam O., "My First Two Winters in Alaska," Stories file, Sam O. White collection, archives, University of Alaska Fairbanks. 6 pp.

CHAPTER 5
White, Sam O., "The Good Life in Fairbanks, Alaska in the early 1920s."
Stories file, Sam O. White collection, archives, University of Alaska
Fairbanks. 10 pp.
White, Sam O., Tape recorded interview by Neville Jacobs, University
of Alaska Fairbanks Oral History Program. June 21, 1974. H76-
38-01.

CHAPTER 6
White, Sam O., "Wood River Sheep Hunt, 1924." Stories file, Sam O.
White collection, archives, University of Alaska Fairbanks. 7 pp.
White, Sam O., Letter to Reverend Patterson Keller, Sundance, Wyoming,
March 16, 1966. Sam O. White collection, archives, University of Alaska
Fairbanks.

CHAPTER 7
White, Sam O., "A Canoe Trip on the Salcha." Stories file, Sam O. White
collection, archives, University of Alaska Fairbanks. 7 pp.
White, Sam O., Letter to author, July 8, 1975.

CHAPTER 8
White, Sam O. Aircraft History and Other Experiences. Transcribed
from three cassette tapes recorded on June 20, 1968, at the Fairbanks
home of 77-year-old Sam O. White, by U.S. Fish and Wildlife Service
employee Evelyn (Brown) Stevens. Copy in author's files.
White, Sam O., "Dan Mckenzie." Sam White collection, University of
Alaska Fairbanks archives. 8 pp. A detailed report by Sam O. White
to the U.S. Coast and Geodetic Survey, probably completed by White
in Washington D. C. in early 1926. Signed "Sam O. White, Signalman,
U.S. Coast and Geodetic Survey." Copy in author's files.
White, Sam O.,"Sam White, Alaskan. Part II More Surveying," *Alaska
Sportsman*, January, 1965. p. 44.
White, Sam O., Log Book Nos. 1 and 2, Fairbanks to Eagle. Sam O.
White collection, Box 5. No Folder. Diaries. Archives, University
of Alaska Fairbanks. These two hand-written (by Sam) log books
provide a detailed look into the daily work of White and Mckenzie
on the Shaw Creek to Eagle reconnaissance.
White, Sam O., with Neville Jacobs. Interview of White by Jacobs,
June 21, 1974. University of Alaska Oral History Program. H76-
38-03. White recounted from memory his 1925 Shaw Creek to
Eagle reconnaissance.

Chapter 9

White, Sam O., Tape-recorded interview of Sam O. White by Neville Jacobs, June 21, 1974. UAF Oral History Program H76-38-01. Transcribed by author. 28 pp., double-spaced.

White, Sam O., "The Lost Mine," Stories file, Sam O. White collection, archives, University of Alaska Fairbanks, 2 pp.

White, Sam O., "Old Times Along the Yukon," Stories file, Sam O. White collection, archives, University of Alaska Fairbanks. 10 pp.

Chapter 10

Billberg, Roy. Letter to author, November, 2005.

White, Julia, Tape-recorded interview with author at Harland White home in southern Maine. October 15, 2005. 5 pp.

White, Sam O., "Aircraft History & Other Experiences," an interview with Sam O. White at his home in Fairbanks on June 20, 1968 by U.S. Fish and Wildlife Service employee Evelyn (Brown) Stevens. 18 pp, single-spaced. Copy in author's files.

White, Sam O. "Early Alaska Bush Pilot Interview," With Sandy Jenson, December 2, 1961. Sam O. White Collection, Box 6, Folder. 38 pp. Archives, University of Alaska Fairbanks.

Chapter 11

Early Alaska Bush Pilot Interviews. Interview of Sam O. White on December 2, 1961, by Sandy Jenson. Box 6, Folder. In Sam O. White collection, archives, University of Alaska Fairbanks.

King, James G., Notes provided author on early history of Alaska Game Commission, May, 2006.

Field Diary and Travel Record, 1927–28 U.S. Department of Agriculture, Sam O. White. Sam O. White collection, archives, University of Alaska Fairbanks.

Sherwood, Morgan, *Big Game in Alaska; A History of Wildlife and People.* Yale University Press. 1981.

White, Sam O., "Old-Timers of the Yukon-Fort Yukon and Vicinity," Stories file, Sam O. White collection, archives, University of Alaska Fairbanks. 18 pp.

White, Sam O., "Aircraft History and Other Experiences." A tape-recorded interview by U.S. Fish and Wildlife Service employee Evelyn (Brown) Stevens, June 20, 1968, at the Sam White Residence in Fairbanks. Copy of transcription in author's files.

White, Sam O., "Sam White, Alaskan. Part III, Northern Game Warden," *Alaska Sportsman*, February, 1965. P. 47.

CHAPTER 12
Billberg, Roy, Letter to author, February, 2006.
White, Sam O., "Aircraft History and Other Experiences." A tape-recorded interview by U.S. Fish and Wildlife Service employee Evelyn (Brown) Stevens, June 20, 1968, at the Sam White residence in Fairbanks. Copy of transcription in author's files. 27 pp, single spaced.
White, Sam O., "Old Timers of the Yukon-Fort Yukon, and Vicinity." Sam O. White collection. Stories file, archives, University of Alaska Fairbanks. May, 1966. 18 pp.

CHAPTER 13
White, Julia, tape-recorded interview with author in southern Maine, October, 2005.
White, Mary Burgess. Interviewed by woman journalist Mike Dalton and Doris Southall (the latter a nurse) at Fairbanks, July 22, 1973. University of Alaska Oral History Program. H78-01-01 and H78-01-02.

CHAPTER 14
Field Diary and Travel Record, 1932 U.S. Department of Agriculture, Sam O. White. In Sam O. White collection, archives, University of Alaska Fairbanks.
King, James G. "Pre-Statehood Alaska," *Flyways, Pioneering Waterfowl Management in North America.* U.S. Dept. of the Interior, Fish and Wildlife Service, 1984.
Sherwood, Morgan, *Big Game in Alaska; A History of Wildlife and People.* Yale University Press. 1981.
White, Sam O., "Aircraft History and Other Experiences." A tape-recorded interview by U.S. Fish and Wildlife Service employee Evelyn (Brown) Stevens, June 20, 1968, at the Sam White Residence in Fairbanks. Copy of transcription in author's files.
White, Sam O., "Navigation, Bush-type, and Working on the Map of Alaska." Stories file, Sam O. White collection, archives, University of Alaska Fairbanks. 12 pp.
White, Sam O., "Sam White, Alaskan, Part IV-Learning to Fly." *Alaska Sportsman*, March, 1965. p. 48.

CHAPTER 15
Sherwood, Morgan, *Big Game in Alaska; A History of Wildlife and People.* Yale University Press. 1981.
White, Sam O., "Aircraft History and Other Experiences." A tape-recorded interview by U.S. Fish and Wildlife Service employee Evelyn (Brown) Stevens, June 20, 1968, at the Sam White Residence in Fairbanks. Copy of transcription in author's files.

White, Sam, O. Diary entries Jan. 25, 1930–March 17,1930. U.S. Dept. of Agriculture, Field Diary and Travel Record, Sam O. White collection, archives, University of Alaska Fairbanks.

White, Sam O., "Dogteam Toklat-Kantishna Patrol with Jack O'Connor." Stories file, Sam O. White collection, archives, University of Alaska Fairbanks. 7 pp.

CHAPTER 16

White, Sam O., "Aircraft History and Other Experiences." A tape-recorded interview by U.S. Fish and Wildlife Service employee Evelyn (Brown) Stevens, June 20, 1968, at the Sam White residence in Fairbanks. Copy of transcription in author's files. 27 pp, single spaced.

White, Sam O., "Dog Team Toklat-Kantishna Patrol with Jack O'Connor." Stories file, Sam O. White collection, archives, University of Alaska Fairbanks. 7 pp. No date.

CHAPTER 17

White, Sam O., "Beaver Sealing, Yukon-Kuskokwim, Innoko-Koyukuk via Aircraft." 5 pp. Sam O. White collection, Stories file, archives, University of Alaska Fairbanks.

CHAPTER 18

White, Sam O., "Yukon Traders." Stories file, Sam O. White collection, archives, University of Alaska Fairbanks. 10 pp. February, 1966.

CHAPTER 19

White, Sam O., "Wild Man of Nation River." Stories file, Sam O. White collection, archives, University of Alaska Fairbanks.

CHAPTER 20

White, Sam O., "Sam White, Alaskan. Part V, More Game Patrols." *Alaska Sportsman*, April, 1965, p. 56.

Field Diary and Travel Record, 1937, U.S. Department of Agriculture, Sam O. White. In Sam O. White collection, archives, University of Alaska Fairbanks.

CHAPTER 21

White, Sam O., "Sam White, Alaskan. Part V, More Game Patrols." *Alaska Sportsman*, April, 1965, p. 56.

Field Diary and Travel Record, 1937, U.S. Department of Agriculture, Sam O. White. In Sam O. White collection, archives, University of Alaska Fairbanks.

CHAPTER 22
White, Sam O., "Aircraft History & Other Experiences," interview of Sam by Evelyn Stevens, June 20, 1968.
White, Sam O., "Yukon Patrol," Stories file, Sam O. White collection, archives, University of Alaska Fairbanks. 2pp.

CHAPTER 23
Billberg, Roy. Letter to author dated Nov. 3, 2005.
White, Sam O., "Aircraft History and Other Experiences." A tape-recorded interview by U.S. Fish and Wildlife Service employee Evelyn (Brown) Stevens, June 20, 1968, at the Sam White Residence in Fairbanks. Copy of transcription in author's files. 27 pp., single-space.
White, Sam O., Field Diary and Travel Record, U.S. Department of Agriculture, 1938. In Sam O. White collection, archives, University of Alaska Fairbanks.
White, Sam O., "Kuskokwim & Story—Patrol." Stories file, Sam O. White collection, archives, University of Alaska Fairbanks. 7 pp.

CHAPTER 24
Billberg, Roy, Letter to author, February, 2006.
White, Sam O., "Medicine Lake and Mahoney," Stories file, Sam O. White collection, archives, University of Alaska Fairbanks.

CHAPTER 25
Alaska Game Commission, Final Report, July 1, 1958 through December 31, 1959.
Rhode, Clarence J., U.S. Dept. of Agriculture, Bureau of Biological Survey, Weekly Itinerary and Report of Activities, January 3, 1937 through June 30, 1942. Copy in author's files and a second copy at The National Conservation Training Center, Shepherdstown, West Virginia 25443. A CD was to be made of this copy.
Shamburger, Page. *Classic Monoplanes,* Modern Aircraft Series, New York. A Division of Sports Car Press. 1966.
White, Sam O., "Aircraft History and Other Experiences." A tape-recorded interview by U.S. Fish and Wildlife Service employee Evelyn (Brown) Stevens, June 20, 1968, at the Sam White Residence in Fairbanks. Copy of transcription in author's files.
White, Sam O., "Sam White, Alaskan. Part VI, Chasing Violators," *Alaska Sportsman,* May, 1965. p.65.
White, Sam O., and Clarence J. Rhode. "Report on Alaska-Yukon Boundary Patrol, March 9-April 7, 1939. A copy of the 9-page report is in the author's files.

CHAPTER 26
White, Sam O., "Sam White, Alaskan, Chasing Violators," Part VI, *Alaska Sportsman*, May, 1965, p. 54.

CHAPTER 27
Sherwood, Morgan, *Big Game in Alaska; A History of Wildlife and People.* Yale University Press. 1981.
White, Sam O., Letter to James G. (Jim) King, Jan. 27, 1970. Copy in author's files.

CHAPTER 28
White, Sam O., "Sam White, Alaskan—Commercial Pilot." Part VII, *Alaska Sportsman*, June, 1965, p. 56.
White, Sam O., "Emergency Flight," *Trim Tab*, January 10, 1972.

CHAPTER 29
White, Sam O., "The Bush Mail on the Koyukuk; in Early Days of Flying," Stories file, Sam O. White collection, archives, University of Alaska Fairbanks.
White, Sam O., Interview by Mrs. Elaine Williams, at Fairbanks, August 6, 1966. Sam O. White collection, archives, University of Alaska Fairbanks.

CHAPTER 30
Billberg, Rudy, as told to Jim Rearden. *In the Shadow of Eagles.* Alaska Northwest Books, 1992.
White, Sam O., "Chandler Lake, Bear Paw Lake, and You Too Sam." Stories, Sam White collection, archives, University of Alaska Fairbanks. 10 pp.
White, Sam O., "Sam White, Alaskan, Part VIII—Air Force Charter Trips." *Alaska Sportsman*, July, 1965. P. 34.

CHAPTER 31
Marshall, Robert, *Arctic Village*, The Literary Guild, New York, 1933.
White, Sam O., "Aircraft History and Other Experiences." A tape-recorded interview by U.S. Fish and Wildlife Service employee Evelyn (Brown) Stevens, June 20, 1968, at the Sam White Residence in Fairbanks. Copy of transcription in author's files.
White, Sam O., "Chandler Lake, Bear Paw Lake, and You too Sam." Stories in the Sam White collection, archives, University of Alaska Fairbanks.
White, Sam O., "Sam White, Alaskan, Part VIII—Air Force Charter Trips." *Alaska Sportsman*, July, 1965. P. 34.

CHAPTER 32
White, Sam O., "Aircraft History and Other Experiences." A tape-recorded interview by U.S. Fish and Wildlife Service employee Evelyn (Brown) Stevens, June 20, 1968, at the Sam White Residence in Fairbanks. Copy of transcription in author's files. 27 pp. single-spaced.
White, Sam O. "Navigation, Bush-type, and Working on the Map of Alaska." Stories file, Sam O. White collection, archives, University of Alaska Fairbanks. 12pp.

CHAPTER 33
Rearden, Jim, *Alaska's Wolf Man*, Pictorial Histories Publishing Company, Missoula, Montana, 1998.
White, Sam O., "Archie Ferguson as I Knew Him," Stories file, Sam O. White collection, archives, University of Alaska Fairbanks. 12 pp.
White, Sam O., "Flying the Coast and Geodetic Survey out of Kotzebue." Stories file, Sam O. White collection, archives, University of Alaska Fairbanks. 5 pp.

CHAPTER 34
White, Sam O., "Bush Flies—Moose Flies." Stories file, Sam O. White collection, archives, University of Alaska Fairbanks. 5 pp.
Cline, M.S., "Huslia—A Village on the Move," *Alaska Sportsman*, June, 1967. p. 25.

CHAPTER 35
White, Sam O., "Sam White, Alaskan; Life in the River Villages," Part XI. *Alaska Sportsman*, October, 1965. P. 53.
White, Sam O., "Snow Water and Gravy—A Touch of Yukon Society." Stories file, Sam O. White collection, archives, University of Alaska Fairbanks. 7 pp.

CHAPTER 36
White, Sam O., "Jack Sackett, Prospector & Trader of Alaska." Stories file, Sam O. White collection, archives, University of Alaska Fairbanks. 4 pp.

CHAPTER 37
White, Sam O., "Flying the Surveys in Bristol Bay." Stories file, Sam O. White collection, archives, University of Alaska Fairbanks. 13 pp.
White, Sam O., "Aircraft History and Other Experiences." A tape-recorded interview by U.S. Fish and Wildlife Service employee Evelyn (Brown) Stevens, June 20, 1968, at the Sam White Residence in Fairbanks. Copy of transcription in author's files. 27 pp, single spaced.

CHAPTER 38

White, Sam O., "Flying the Surveys in Bristol Bay," Stories file, Sam O. White collection, archives, University of Alaska Fairbanks. 13 pp.

White, Sam O., as told to Charley Mayse, "Bear Encounters, A Fact of Life in the Alaskan Bush," *Great Lander Shopping News,* March 21, 1984.

CHAPTER 39

White, Sam O., "Utopia." Stories file, Sam O. White collection, archives, University of Alaska Fairbanks.

CHAPTER 40

White, Sam O., "Airplanes of the Early Days, and Two Pants Jake." Stories file, Sam O. White collection, archives, University of Alaska Fairbanks. 5 pp.

White, Sam O., Letter to Professor Thomas M. Griffiths, University of Denver, Colorado. One page. Dec. 5, 1966. (Describes instruments and pilot controls in Travel Air NC9844.) Sam O. White collection, Museum, Dead River Area Historical Society, Stratton, Maine.

Shamburger, Page. "Classic Monoplanes," Modern Aircraft Series, Sports Car Press, Crown Publishers, 1966.

CHAPTER 41

White, Sam O., "The Story of Mr. & Mrs. L. F. James and the Hughes Trading Post," Stories file, Sam O. White collection, archives, University of Alaska Fairbanks. 7 pp.

CHAPTER 42

Billberg, Rudy, as told to Jim Rearden, *In the Shadow of Eagles; From Barnstormer to Alaska Bush Pilot, a Flyer's Story.* Alaska Northwest books, 1992.

Harkey, Ira, *Pioneer Bush Pilot; The Story of Noel Wien.* University of Washington Press, 1974.

White, Sam O., Letter to Noel Wien re death of Ralph Wien. 2 pp. Not dated. Sam O. White collection, Museum, Dead River Area Historical Society, Stratton, Maine.

White, Sam O., Letter to Richard Wien, July 7, 1961. Copy provided author by Richard Wien.

White, Sam O., Letter to Noel Wien, October 6, 1962. Copy provided author by Richard Wien.

White, Sam O., Letter to Richard Wien, June 5, 1967. Copy provided author by Richard Wien.

Wien, Richard and Merrill, E-mail to author, August 8, 2006.

CHAPTER 43

14th Annual Report, Alaska Game Commission, July 1, 1952–June 30, 1953.

Huntington, Sidney. Letter to author, Oct. 10, 2005.

King, James G., "Pre-Statehood Alaska," *Flyways, Pioneering Waterfowl Management in North America.* U.S. Dept. of the Interior, Fish and Wildlife Service, 1984.

King, James G. (Jim), Letter to author dated Aug. 21, 2005.

Rhode, Clarence. Regional Director's Report for 1954. U.S. Fish and Wildlife Service, Juneau. 9 pp. Jan. 17, 1955

Rearden, Jim, "Clarence Rhode," *Alaska Magazine*, January, 1980.

Sherwood, Morgan, *Big Game in Alaska; A History of Wildlife and People.* Yale University Press. 1981.

White, Sam O., "Aircraft History and Other Experiences." A tape-recorded interview by U.S. Fish and Wildlife Service employee Evelyn (Brown) Stevens, June 20, 1968, at the Sam White Residence in Fairbanks. Copy of transcription in author's files.

Index

About the Author

JIM REARDEN has written twenty-two books on Alaskan subjects, and more than 500 magazine features. He has received many awards for his writing, including "Historian of the Year," from the Alaska Historical Society for his book *Alaska's Wolf Man.*

He is a Navy veteran of World War II and served aboard a destroyer escort in the Central Pacific war zone.

Rearden studied fish and game management at Oregon State College and the University of Maine, receiving degrees from both. For four years he was head of the Department of Wildlife Management at the University of Alaska Fairbanks, and for eleven years he was Area Biologist for the Cook Inlet commercial fishery for the Alaska Department of Fish and Game.

He served twelve years as a member of the Alaska Board of Fish and Game, and the Board of Game. In 1976 President Gerald Ford appointed him to the National Advisory Committee on Oceans and Atmosphere, where he served for a year and a half.

He was Outdoors Editor for *Alaska Magazine* for twenty years; simultaneously he was a Field Editor for *Outdoor Life.*

In 2005, the University of Alaska Fairbanks awarded Rearden an honorary doctor of science degree for his teaching, conservation work, and writings. He holds a private pilot's license.

He lives at Homer, Alaska, with his wife, Audrey, in a log house he built himself.